The **Rough Guide** to

WITHDRAWN

Yosemite, Sequoia and Kings Canyon

written and researched by

Paul Whitfield

Jef

ROUGH GUIDES

www.roughguides.com

Contents

Active Yosemite
colour section
following p.144

Wild Sierra
colour section
following p.240

◄◄ Hang-gliding in Yosemite ◄ Scrambling on Matthes Crest, Yosemite

Introduction to

Yosemite, Sequoia and Kings Canyon

Yosemite National Park and the conjoined Sequoia and Kings Canyon national parks are the gleaming granite jewels in California's Sierra Nevada mountains, thick with lush meadows and dense forests of pine, fir and cedar. They're all within half a day's drive of Los Angeles and San Francisco, so visitors are plentiful – yet the parks are diverse and massive enough to soak up the crowds, allowing you to appreciate their immense beauty and find solitude if you look for it.

More gushing adjectives have been thrown at **Yosemite National Park** than at any other part of California – but however excessive the hyperbole may seem, once you enter Yosemite Valley you realize it's actually an understatement. Simply put, **Yosemite Valley** – only a small part of the park but the one at which most of the verbiage is aimed – is one of the most dramatic pieces of geology to be found anywhere. From massive, 3000ft cliffs streaked by cascading waterfalls to the subtle colourings of wildflowers, the variations within it can be both enormous and discreet.

Through it all runs the **Merced River**, meandering among wildflower meadows where mule deer graze, while black bears secretively forage the surrounding woods. It's a place that can be experienced on a variety of levels: many people just spend a day in Yosemite, doing a quick, thrilling whip around the top attractions; others return frequently to photograph, hike, explore, observe the wildlife or just soak up the atmosphere.

Many of the same qualities are equally abundant in **Sequoia and Kings Canyon** national parks, a hundred miles southeast of Yosemite. Glaciated granite peaks and domes rise above coniferous forests, whose groves are presided over by the giantest of the **giant sequoias**. Elsewhere, rivers have cut deep into the rock, nowhere more so than in **Kings Canyon** itself, reputedly the deepest valley in the US. **Hiking** is the main attraction in these parts, either gently strolling around the meadows among huge trees, or heading off for days into the vast backcountry.

Fact file

• Roughly fifty miles by forty miles, Yosemite National Park covers **1169 square miles**, about the size of Rhode Island. Over 94 percent is designated **wilderness**. Sequoia and Kings Canyon parks are larger, jointly covering **1355 square miles**; 87 percent is designated wilderness.

• Sequoia National Park was America's second national park (after Yellowstone) and was created on September 25, 1890. Yosemite National Park followed just a week later on October 1. Yosemite was declared a United Nations **World Heritage Site** on October 31, 1984.

• Yosemite receives 3.9 million **visitors** a year (down from 4.2 million in 1996), while Sequoia and Kings Canyon jointly get around 1 million.

• Yosemite varies in **altitude** from 2000ft in the west to the 13,114ft summit of Mount Lyell on the park's eastern boundary. Sequoia and Kings Canyon have a similar range, topping out at the summit of Mount Whitney (14,497ft), the highest point in the Lower 48 states.

▶ Taft Point, Yosemite

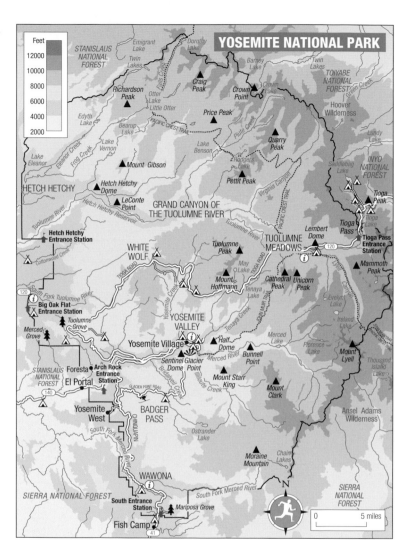

Feet	
12000	
10000	
8000	
6000	
4000	
2000	

YOSEMITE NATIONAL PARK

What to see

Seven miles long and just one mile across, **Yosemite Valley** is where you'll find some of the world's most famous granite architecture – including **Half Dome** and rock climbing's holy grail, **El Capitan** – as well as many of America's tallest waterfalls, with **Yosemite Falls** topping the lot. This is the geographic, spiritual and business heart of Yosemite National Park, with most of the accommodation, over half of the

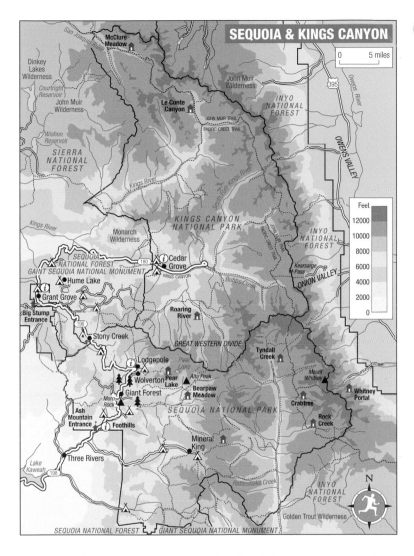

campgrounds, a maze of **hiking trails** for all abilities and a transport hub for shuttle buses out into the rest of Yosemite.

In **northern Yosemite**, everyone flocks to subalpine **Tuolumne Meadows** (pronounced Too-ol-uh-me), perched at 8600ft with a crisp, elemental atmosphere, stunning landscapes and some of the park's finest hikes. Walk to the ragged **Cathedral Range**, a place much loved by Yosemite's early champion, **John Muir**, who was the first to scale the dramatically pointed **Cathedral Peak**.

The spectacle continues in **southern Yosemite** around **Wawona**, little more than a lovely old wooden hotel and campground set beside a meadow. It has

Getting the most out of Yosemite

No temple made with hands can compare with the Yosemite. Every rock in its walls seems to glow with life.

John Muir, *The Yosemite*

Packed as Yosemite is with superlatives, it's hard to know where to start your visit – especially if you're not here for long. What follows is a brief list of some of the most popular and worthwhile sights and activities.

Two hours If you're just driving through, be sure to loop around Yosemite Valley, take photos from Tunnel View then either take a quick look at the giant sequoias in Mariposa Grove or drive the Tioga Road east through Tuolumne Meadows.

Half a day Make straight for Yosemite Valley and stroll to the base of Lower Yosemite Falls, hike some or all of the Mist Trail to Vernal Falls and gaze up at El Capitan from El Cap Meadow.

Full day Do all the half-a-day activities, add in the walk to Mirror Lake, visit the museum and Indian Village and, if driving, admire the late afternoon views from Tunnel View on the Wawona Road, then continue to Glacier Point for sunset and the stars after dark.

Two to three days Keen hikers shouldn't miss Half Dome, but they might also fancy the Four-Mile Trail or Upper Yosemite Falls Trail. Less ambitious visitors could float down the Merced River then repair to *The Ahwahnee* for a drink or a meal, and everyone should make side trips to Tuolumne Meadows and the Mariposa Grove at Wawona.

Over three days After three days in the park, you'll begin to feel like a local; consider hiking out to one of Yosemite's less visited corners (perhaps Hikes Y16, Y32 or Y42, covered in Chapter 4), taking a rock climbing course (see p.141) or visiting an area outside the park.

▶ Ranger talk at Glacier Point, Yosemite

a distinctly low-key feel enlivened by the proximity of the **Mariposa Grove**, one of the most awe-inspiring forests of **giant sequoias** found anywhere.

The immediate vicinity of Yosemite offers rich pickings, too, notably the other-worldly tufa towers rising from **Mono Lake**, to the east, and the picture-perfect ghost town of **Bodie** nearby. West of Yosemite, the Tuolumne and Merced rivers offer some exhilarating **whitewater rafting**, while south of the park the wild and rugged beauty of the Sierra continues into the **John Muir Wilderness** and the wonderfully remote **Mono Hot Springs**.

Yet more ravishing scenery awaits you in **Sequoia and Kings Canyon** national parks, home to two of the world's largest trees – the **General Sherman** and the **General Grant** – as well as **Kings Canyon** itself, where the Kings River rages during the spring snowmelt.

When to go

You can visit Yosemite, Sequoia and Kings Canyon at any time of year; choosing the best time to visit depends mostly on whether you've come for hiking, viewing waterfalls or winter activities. **Summer** is generally fairly hot and dry, while **spring** and **fall** are more variable, with comfortable temperatures everywhere except the high country. **Winter** means snowy trails and frozen waterfalls, though the frequent sunny days bring low-angled sun casting the cliffs and domes in a flattering light.

May and June are the prime months for viewing Yosemite Valley waterfalls and lowland hiking, though the high country is off limits: Yosemite's Glacier Point Road and Tioga Road, as well as the road into Kings Canyon, are all closed. The parks are busiest in **July and August**, when the days are warm, nights are starry, rivers and lakes are (just) warm enough for swimming, and most hikes are clear of snow. The more ephemeral waterfalls will have dried up, except after rain, which mostly comes in short **thunderstorms**.

◄ High-country backpacking, Kings Canyon National Park

Smarter than the average bear

You may never see a **black bear** anywhere else in California, but spend a few days in Yosemite Valley and you've a fair chance of spotting one, probably at night, breaking into a car or roaming the campgrounds looking for a free meal. Banging pans and yelling – from a safe distance, of course – will probably drive them off, but their dependence on human food has led to several bears being shot each year. Yosemite bears are not deterred by tent walls or car doors, and safe food **storage** is now mandatory in the park. As they say, "a fed bear is a dead bear", so do them and yourself a favour by keeping all food and smelly items – deodorant, sunscreen, toothpaste – either inside your room or in the metal lockers in campgrounds and parking lots, and at trailheads. If you don't, you can be fined up to $5000.

Out in the backcountry, campers must use portable plastic bear canisters to store food. Sows have taught their cubs to climb along slender branches to get at food, so the old method of hanging food seldom works. For more on bears and other local animals, see p.243.

Report all Yosemite bear sightings on ☎209/372-0322.

Yosemite's waterfalls will mostly be dry by **September and October**, which are otherwise excellent months to visit the parks, ending with a good display of fall colours. Crowds are smaller but most activities are still operating and there's plenty of hiking that's both cooler and dry under foot. **November** is getting marginal, with possible snowstorms and the high-country roads likely to close. **December to March** are the winter months, with cross-country skiing and skating in full swing; tyre chains are generally required. By **April**, Wawona and Yosemite Valley may well be free of snow, but late dumps are not uncommon and hiking is only in the lowlands.

◄ Grizzly Falls, Kings Canyon

Average daily temperatures and rainfall in Yosemite Valley

	Jan	Feb	Mar	Apr	May	Jun	Jul	Aug	Sep	Oct	Nov	Dec
Temperature												
Max/min (°C)	9/-3	13/-2	15/-1	18/2	23/6	28/9	32/12	32/12	31/8	23/4	14/-1	9/-3
Max/min (°F)	49/26	55/28	59/31	65/35	73/42	82/48	90/54	90/53	87/47	74/39	58/31	48/26
Rainfall												
mm	157	155	132	76	33	18	10	8	23	53	137	142
in	6.2	6.1	5.2	3.0	1.3	0.7	0.4	0.3	0.9	2.1	5.4	5.6

16

things not to miss

It's not possible to see everything Yosemite, Sequoia and Kings Canyon have to offer in one trip – and we don't suggest you try. What follows, in no particular order, is a selective look at highlights in and around the parks, including spectacular landscapes, thrilling activities and the best places to relax and relive the day's excitement. The highlights are arranged in five colour-coded categories, so you can browse through to find the very best things to see, do and experience. All highlights have a page reference to take you straight into the guide, where you can find out more.

01 **Hiking Half Dome** Page **108** • A steep cable "staircase" leads to the summit of Half Dome, a thrilling but exhausting hike ending high above Yosemite Valley.

02 **The Ahwahnee** Page **66** • Luxurious rooms, a cosy bar, sumptuous public spaces and classy dining make *The Ahwahnee* an essential stop.

03 **Tuolumne Meadows** Page **83** • The Sierra's most expansive meadows make a superb base for hiking in the surrounding mountains, but are also glorious for examining wildflowers or simply watching the day go by.

04 **Horseriding** Page **143** • Gentle but unforgettably scenic rides head from stables in Yosemite Valley, Tuolumne Meadows and Wawona.

12

05 **Waterfalls** Page **58** • Come in April, May or June to witness Yosemite's myriad waterfalls at their thundering best.

07 **El Capitan** Page **51** • Though stunning at first sight, El Cap's truly immense scale is only revealed when you spot the flea-like climbers on its face.

06 **Mineral King** Page **211** • Seek out some isolation in this quiet corner of Sequoia National Park, with superb high-country hiking.

08 **General Sherman Tree** Page **215** • Gaze up in awe at the world's largest tree, a 6000-ton monster in Sequoia National Park.

09 **Sunset at Glacier Point** Page **94** • The alpenglow on Half Dome and Clouds Rest assures stunning sunsets from Glacier Point.

10 **Kings River** Page **221** • Calm enough for swimming beside Muir Rock, in Kings Canyon, this river is a surging maelstrom just a short distance downstream, with some great waterfalls.

11 **Rock climbing** Page **139** • Climbers of all abilities will find boundless challenges both in Yosemite Valley and around the summertime crags of Tuolumne Meadows.

12 **Mariposa Grove of Giant Sequoias** Page 99 • It's always an honour to be among these forest giants, but better still at dawn or under a winter cloak of snow.

15

13 **Winter in Yosemite** Page **147** • Frozen waterfalls, pine boughs heavy with snow and a host of cold-weather activities make Yosemite a great winter destination.

15 Hiking the Mist Trail

Page **106** • Get drenched in spray following this fabulous hike to the top of Vernal Fall.

14 Moro Rock

Page **215** • Take a late afternoon stroll around Crescent Meadow then head up Sequoia's Moro Rock for superb sunset views.

16 Mono Lake

Page **153** • Outlandish tufa towers rise from the waters of Mono Lake, creating a sci-fi world on the semi-desert landscape of the Owens Valley.

Basics

Basics

Getting there

With well-maintained roads providing good access to Yosemite, Sequoia and Kings Canyon national parks, it's hardly surprising people opt to drive their own vehicles here. However, the combination of summer traffic congestion and the availability of pretty decent public transportation (some of it free) should make entering the parks by bus a more tempting option than it might sound. Several companies also run tours either solely to Yosemite, or visiting Yosemite as part of a longer circuit.

International and out-of-state visitors will probably want to **fly** to California, more than likely using the international airports in Los Angeles and San Francisco, then either renting a car at the airport or using public transportation from there. Fresno's airport is closer to all three parks and has car rental but no useful public transportation.

The following material focuses on Yosemite; we've covered **Getting to Sequoia and Kings Canyon** national parks in the box below.

By car

Contrary to popular belief, there is no restriction on driving your own vehicle into Yosemite. Indeed, **driving to Yosemite** is straightforward. Of the park's four road entrances, three are from the west and one traverses the Sierra Nevada from the Owens Valley in the east. The three western approaches are generally kept open all year (except immediately after snowfall), but the eastern approach (Hwy-120 East) over the 10,000ft Tioga Pass is closed all winter and

Getting to and around Sequoia and Kings Canyon national parks

There is no road access into **Sequoia and Kings Canyon National Parks** from the east, and only two roads from the San Joaquin Valley in the west. Many people loop through the parks, perhaps approaching on **Hwy-198** from **Visalia** (which has one very winding section limited to vehicles less than 22ft long) and leaving on **Hwy-180** bound for **Fresno**. In between runs the **Generals Highway**, a good tarmac road running through the heart of the parks, connecting two of the biggest sequoia trees, the General Sherman and the General Grant.

Most roads are generally kept open year-round, though **winter driving** regulations (see box, p.20) still apply. The Generals Highway is sometimes closed for several days after snowfall, and Hwy-180 into Kings Canyon itself is completely **closed** from mid-November to mid-April as there are many rockfalls and slips at this time of year.

It's possible to access at least parts of Sequoia and Kings Canyon by **bus**. Greyhound will get you to the town of **Visalia** (see p.168), departure point for the **Sequoia Shuttle** (☎1-877/287-4453, ⊛www.sequoiashuttle.com), the only bus service into the parks. From late May until mid-September the Sequoia Shuttle runs four times a day to Sequoia National Park from Visalia, with pickups at various hotels, the Convention Center and the Visalia Transit Center. The sixteen-seater buses (each with space for two bikes) depart Visalia at 7am, 8am, 9am and 10am for the run through Three Rivers (1hr), the Foothills Visitor Center (1hr 25min), Giant Forest Museum (2hr 30min) and Dorst campground (3hr). The **fare** is $7.50 each way and covers your park entry fee, making it a great deal. Advance **reservations** are essential. Buses from Sequoia to Visalia leave the Giant Forest Museum daily at 3.30pm, 4.30pm, 5.30pm and 6.30pm.

Within the twin parks there's a good network of **free shuttle buses** (see p.25) which will get you to many of the best sights and biggest trees.

Winter driving

All vehicles entering the national parks (including four-wheel-drives) are required to carry **tyre chains** whenever chain controls are in effect, most likely from November to April. Highway patrol occasionally checks compliance, especially if a storm is expected. Rental cars are not usually equipped with chains, but they can be rented (around $30 for up to a week) from service stations and auto parts shops around the region; shop around as deals vary considerably. Since you have to return rented chains to their source, many people find it more convenient to buy: a basic set for a compact car should cost under $60 from the same outlets, though prices roughly double for SUVs and pickups. Within the parks there are no chain rental facilities, but they're sold at the Yosemite Valley garage (around $55 for cars, $150 for trucks).

In snowy conditions, signs along the highway indicate the **restriction levels** on open roads; R0: all vehicles are required to carry chains; R1: snow tyres or chains; R2: 4WD or chains; R3: chains on all vehicles. Anyone not used to fitting chains should practise beforehand.

With no significant hills, Hwy-140 from Mariposa into Yosemite often stays open even if all other roads are snowed in, and it's usually the first to be ploughed. Hwy-120 West from Groveland is the Yosemite route most likely to have tyre chain restrictions after snowfall.

into spring. The park is around two hundred miles **from San Francisco** (just under 4hr), 310 miles **from Los Angeles** (6hr) and 340 miles **from Las Vegas** (8hr).

Approaching Yosemite

Drivers have a choice of **four roads into Yosemite**. All have concentrations of lodging and eating establishments close to the park boundary and your choice of route will most likely be determined by where you're starting. Towns along all four approach roads are covered in detail in Chapter 8.

From the west: Hwy-120 West

The most direct (though not necessarily the fastest) approach from the San Francisco Bay area to Yosemite is along **Hwy-120 West**, which can be picked up at Manteca, twelve miles south of Stockton, where the freeways I-5 and Hwy-99 meet. From there a fairly good road runs through tiny **Chinese Camp** to the attractive former gold-town of **Groveland**. With its supply of appealing lodging and restaurants, Groveland makes a great base for western Yosemite, particularly Hetch Hetchy, though Yosemite Valley is still an hour's drive away.

For the next twenty-odd miles there's little in the way of services except some accommodation, all oriented to Yosemite visitors.

The park entrance is at **Big Oak Flat**, where there's a small information station that's a good place to stop to check for both accommodation availability and wilderness permits.

From the southwest: Hwy-140

The fastest road into Yosemite from San Joaquin Valley in the west is **Hwy-140**, which cuts off Hwy-99 at **Merced**, an important transport interchange for Amtrak, Greyhound, and buses into the park. Although Merced has good lodging, including a HI hostel, it is really too distant from the park to make it a good base. A better bet is **Mariposa**, about an hour's drive from Yosemite Valley, or even **Midpines**, where there's an excellent backpacker hostel and lodge.

A major **rockfall** in 2006 closed the highway around ten miles west of the park entrance. A one-way traffic-light-controlled detour now allows traffic to bypass the slip but can add fifteen minutes to the journey.

You'll enter the park near **El Portal** at the **Arch Rock Entrance**, from where it's a short drive directly into Yosemite Valley.

From the south: Hwy-41

Approaching from Los Angeles and the southern half of California, you'll most likely follow **Hwy-41**, which enters Yosemite through the **South Entrance**, near Wawona and the Mariposa Grove of Giant Sequoias. At Fresno, turn off Hwy-99 onto Hwy-41, which runs for forty miles through the Sierra foothills to the bustling but functional **Oakhurst**. There's accommodation here and on the road into Yosemite at **Fish Camp**. At the South Entrance you have a choice of roads: right for the Mariposa Grove of Giant Sequoias; left for Wawona and the rest of the park.

From the east: Hwy-120 East

Visitors coming to Yosemite from Las Vegas or Death Valley during the summer and fall will enter Yosemite **from the east**: initially along **US-395**, which runs through the dry, sagebrush-covered hills of the Owens Valley, past Mammoth Lakes to Mono Lake and Lee Vining, and then along **Hwy-120 East**, which cuts west up the Lee Vining grade past a number of good campgrounds to the 10,000ft **Tioga Pass Park Entrance**. Tuolumne Meadows lies six miles ahead, but it's another hour and a half in the car to Yosemite Valley.

Note that Hwy-120 East – also known as the **Tioga Road** – is **closed by snow** in winter and spring, typically from mid-November (though late October is not unheard of) to somewhere between mid-May and mid-June; for snow conditions and road closures call ☎209/372-0200 or check ⓦwww.nps.gov/yose/planyourvisit/conditions.htm.

Renting a car

If travelling from out of state or from overseas, chances are you'll want to **rent a car**. For short visits the convenience is a boon, and even for longer hiking or rock climbing holidays rental rates are low enough that when shared between two or more people the cost isn't prohibitive.

The **type of vehicle** you choose is pretty much a matter of taste and budget, though there are a couple of things to consider. That convertible you had your eye on probably isn't the best when left overnight in a

Six steps to a better kind of travel

At Rough Guides we are passionately committed to travel. We feel strongly that only through travelling do we truly come to understand the world we live in and the people we share it with – plus tourism has brought a great deal of **benefit** to developing economies around the world over the last few decades. But the extraordinary growth in tourism has also damaged some places irreparably, and of course **climate change** is exacerbated by most forms of transport, especially flying. This means that now more than ever it's important to **travel thoughtfully** and **responsibly**, with respect for the cultures you're visiting – not only to derive the most benefit from your trip but also to preserve the best bits of the planet for everyone to enjoy. At Rough Guides we feel there are six main areas in which you can make a difference:

• Consider what you're contributing to the **local economy**, and how much the services you use do the same, whether it's through employing local workers and guides or sourcing locally grown produce and local services.

• Consider the **environment** on holiday as well as at home. Water is scarce in many destinations, and the biodiversity of local flora and fauna can be adversely affected by tourism. Try to patronize businesses that take account of this.

• Travel with a purpose, not just to tick off experiences. Consider **spending longer** in a place, and getting to know it and its people.

• Give thought to how often you **fly**. Try to avoid short hops by air and more harmful night flights.

• Consider **alternatives to flying**, travelling instead by bus, train, boat and even by bike or on foot where possible.

• Make your trips **"climate neutral"** via a reputable carbon offset scheme. All Rough Guide flights are offset, and every year we donate money to a variety of charities devoted to combating the effects of climate change.

Yosemite Valley parking lot with bears about. Even a hardtop isn't going to keep bears out if you've left something tempting inside, but a soft shell is inviting extra trouble. Generally an ordinary sedan works best, preferably something powerful enough to cope effortlessly with the hilly terrain. In the winter months it might be worth considering something with **4WD** and/or high clearance. You're not going to be off-roading in the national parks, but with 4WD you won't need to worry about tyre chains (unless it snows very heavily).

Most Sierra visitors flying into California will arrive at Los Angeles (LAX) or San Francisco (SFO) international airports, both of which have the full range of major **car rental companies**. At LAX, they're all based off-airport, with shuttle buses making frequent circuits from their depots to the terminals. At SFO the major companies – Alamo, Avis, Budget, Dollar, Enterprise, Fox, Hertz, National and Thrifty – have reservation desks on-site while smaller companies provide shuttles to their depots.

Closer to Yosemite, the best bet for rentals is the town of **Merced**, around eighty miles southwest of Yosemite Valley. You can travel here by Greyhound or Amtrak then pick up a car for exploring Yosemite for a few days. Expect to pay $30 a day for a compact and around $60 for a midsize SUV, both with unlimited mileage (plus tax and any insurance fees). Try Hertz, 1710 W Hwy-140 (☎209/722-4200, ⊛www.hertz.com), or Enterprise, 1334 W Main St (☎209/722-1600, ⊛www.enterprise.com). The latter is ten minutes' walk from the town's Transpo Center (where buses drop you) and offers three-day weekend deals for $20 a day providing you pick up on Friday or Saturday.

Major car rental companies

Alamo ☎1-877/222-9075, ⊛www.alamo.com
Avis ☎1-800/230-4898, ⊛www.avis.com
Budget ☎1-800/527-0700, ⊛www.budget.com
Dollar ☎1-800/800-3665, ⊛www.dollar.com
Enterprise ☎1-800/261-7331, ⊛www.enterprise.com
Hertz ☎1-800/654-3131, ⊛www.hertz.com
National ☎1-877/222-9058, ⊛www.nationalcar.com
Payless ☎1-800/729-5377, ⊛www.payless carrental.com

Rent-A-Wreck ☎1-877/877-0700, ⊛www.rentawreck.com
Thrifty ☎1-800/847-4389, ⊛www.thrifty.com

By air

Using a sequence of buses and trains (see below), it's possible to get from Los Angeles or San Francisco airports to any of the parks within a day. **Merced Airport** is the closest airport to Yosemite with regional flights, though the only scheduled services are daily flights from Las Vegas with Great Lakes (⊛www.flygreatlakes.com). The local YARTS bus service (see p.23) picks up on demand from the airport and runs to Yosemite, with pick-ups at the Merced Transpo Center.

The only other airport worth considering is **Fresno** (officially Fresno Yosemite International; ⊛www.flyfresno.org), some 95 miles south of Yosemite Valley and sixty miles west of Sequoia and Kings Canyon. Unfortunately there's no direct public transportation to any of the parks from the airport, but all the major car rental agencies are represented and you can be in any of the parks in around two hours. See below for airlines that fly direct to Fresno.

Flights to Fresno

Air ☎1-702/505-8888, ⊛www.allegiantair.com. Flights from Las Vegas.
American Airlines ☎1-800/433-7300, ⊛www.aa.com. Flights from Los Angeles, Dallas/Fort Worth and Guadalajara, Mexico.
Delta Airlines ☎1-800/221-1212, ⊛www.delta.com. Flights from Los Angeles, Portland, Salt Lake City and Seattle.
Horizon Air ☎1-800/547-9308, ⊛www.horizonair.com. Flights from Portland and Seattle.
United Airlines ☎1-800/241-6522, ⊛www.united.com. Flights from Los Angeles, San Francisco, Denver and Las Vegas.
US Airways ☎1-800/428-4322, ⊛www.usairways.com. Flights from Las Vegas and Phoenix.

By train

Unless you are very determined, **trains** are hopeless for getting to Sequoia and Kings Canyon, but Amtrak (☎1-800/872-7245, ⊛www.amtrak.com) can be combined with bus services for relatively easy access **to Yosemite**. The **nearest train station** is in **Merced**, where several rail services a day link with YARTS buses (see below) running straight to Yosemite Valley.

The most convenient combination is **from San Francisco**, with four daily departures to Merced, though only a couple of these connect tolerably with buses to Yosemite. The best is the early morning departure: Amtrak buses depart from the Ferry Building in San Francisco (7.05am), connect with trains across the Bay at Emeryville (7.40am), arrive at Merced in time to connect with YARTS buses (11am) and reach Yosemite Valley at 1.10pm.

On the return journey, the best bets are the YARTS departures at 10am and 4pm, which arrive at Merced Amtrak (12.35pm & 6.14pm) in time for the northbound train/bus combos (1.08pm & 6.42pm) which reach San Francisco at 4.40pm & 10.10pm.

From Southern California, Amtrak buses leaves Los Angeles' Union Station (4.10am & 10.45am) and connect with trains at Bakersfield (7.15am & 1.20pm), which reach Merced Amtrak (10.08am & 4.22pm) in time for YARTS departures (11am & 5.30pm) that arrive in Yosemite at 1.30pm and 8pm.

Leaving Yosemite heading south, departures at 10am and 4pm get you to Merced Amtrak (12.35pm & 6.14pm) in time for trains (12.59am & 7.06pm) which reach Los Angeles at 6.30pm and 1.05am the next morning.

Fares vary with demand and are best booked a few days in advance. Between San Francisco and Merced it costs roughly $25 each way, and from Los Angeles the fare is about $40 each way. Amtrak also sells tickets all the way to Yosemite (from $31 from San Francisco; $54 from Los Angeles), which usually work out slightly cheaper than buying the two legs separately.

By bus

Buses are the only form of public transportation that will get you right into the national parks. For Yosemite, there are year-round scheduled **Greyhound** services to Merced, eighty miles southwest of Yosemite Valley, from where you can catch the local **YARTS buses** into Yosemite National Park. In addition there's a summer-only YARTS service from Mammoth Lakes on the eastern side of the Sierra. Arriving by bus saves you

having to pay the park entrance fee. For Sequoia and Kings Canyon, there are Greyhound services to Visalia, where you can pick up the **Sequoia Shuttle** – for more details, see the box on p.19.

Greyhound

Greyhound (⊕1-800/231-2222, ⓦwww .greyhound.com) runs buses from all over California to Merced (see p.162), the only viable jumping-off point for Yosemite, and Visalia (see p.168), where you can get a bus into Sequoia National Park. **For Yosemite**, Greyhound is a little slower than the train and less convenient, with few services that directly connect with YARTS buses. **From San Francisco** there are typically three departures daily (4hr), with perhaps twice that number coming **from Los Angeles** (6–8hr), all calling at various towns along the way. **Fares** vary with demand: generally you can get a round-trip ticket to Merced from either San Francisco or Los Angeles for about $66.

Things are less convenient **for Sequoia National Park** with Greyhound services from both San Francisco (from $48 one way) and Los Angeles (from $27 one way) arriving in Visalia after the last Sequoia-bound bus has left: you'll need to spend the night in Visalia.

YARTS buses

The Park Service and local authorities have set up the Yosemite Area Regional Transportation System, or **YARTS** (⊕1-877/989-2787 or 209/388-9589, ⓦwww.yarts.com), as a way of encouraging people to leave their vehicles outside the park. While the service is excellent and quite cheap along the main Hwy-140 corridor from Merced into Yosemite Valley, it is less useful elsewhere with just a summer-only service from Mammoth Lakes over Tioga Pass and through Tuolumne Meadows to Yosemite Valley. No buses run along either Hwy-120 West from Groveland or along Hwy-41 from Oakhurst and Wawona.

Along the main route, Hwy-140 from Merced through Mariposa, Midpines and El Portal into the valley, **fares** include the park entry fee (potentially saving you $20) and each adult fare allows one child (12 and younger) to ride free: the round trip is $25 from Merced, $12 from Mariposa and Midpines, and just $7 from El Portal.

Some services have connections to Amtrak trains at Merced, and some buses are timed to coincide with the start of guided tours (see p.27) within the park. **Timetables** are available on the YARTS website and from visitor centres in the area. **From Merced**, there are four departures daily, picking up at the Merced Transpo Center and the Amtrak station (around 7am, 8.50am, 10.45am & 5.40pm), then calling at Mariposa (after 1hr) and Midpines (1hr 15min) before arriving in Yosemite Valley (after almost 3hr). In addition, a couple of early-morning services start their run in Mariposa, convenient if you're riding into Yosemite from Mariposa, Midpines or El Portal. All **drop off** at Curry Village, *The Ahwahnee*, and Yosemite Village before the final stop at *Yosemite Lodge*. **Tickets** can be bought on board. **Return services** leave the valley at 10am, 4pm, 5.20pm, 5.55pm and 8.35pm.

The summer-only YARTS service along Hwy-120 East **from Mammoth Lakes** through Tuolumne Meadows to Yosemite Valley is less useful for commuting into the park. There's only one service a day (Yosemite-bound in the morning, and Mammoth-bound in the afternoon) but it does mean you can stay in Mammoth or Lee Vining and make day-trips to Tuolumne Meadows that still allow enough time for a hike or two.

Tours and guided trips to Yosemite

Generally speaking, anything called a **sightseeing tour** that begins outside the park will involve you in an unsatisfying race through Yosemite Valley. The three organizations listed below, however, buck this trend with backpacker-oriented niche packages that keep costs low.

Tour operators based outside the park

Green Tortoise ☎1-800/867-8647, ⓦwww .greentortoise.com. With their roots going back to hippy bus tours from the early 1970s, Green Tortoise

offer a more alternative approach than most, using converted buses that facilitate a more communal atmosphere, and allow you to sleep on the bus (lying down) as you travel. They're geared towards active, outdoorsy types who enjoy camping out with limited privacy and pitching-in. You'll need to be flexible, must help with food preparation and should bring a sleeping bag and general travelling gear (but not a tent or cooking gear). Their two-day weekend trips (March–Sept; $141, plus $45 food fund) to Yosemite Valley and Mariposa Grove run roughly twice a month departing from San Francisco Friday evening at 9pm and returning around 7am Monday. The three-day trip (June–Sept; $209, plus $61 food fund) departs on Monday evening around 9pm, returning early Friday morning, and includes half a day in Tuolumne Meadows and time around Mono Lake. Both trips involve camping just outside the park boundary, free time for day hikes and a final fling at the *Iron Door Saloon* in Groveland (see p.157). The food fund covers almost all your meals and park entry fees.

Incredible Adventures ☎1-800/777-8464 or 415/642-7378, ⓦwww.incadventures.com. Based in San Francisco, this group runs three tempting tours to Yosemite using biodiesel fifteen-seater minibuses. The rushed one-day trip (daily departures all year 6am–9pm; $149) includes a quick whip around the main Yosemite Valley sights and gives you around three hours to explore and hike. The more satisfying three-day trip ($325; late-May to mid-Oct; departures Sun, Tues & Thurs) is a camping-based tour with everyone pitching in to prepare food. Trips spend two nights just outside the park, staying at the same campground each night and exploring by day, perhaps high-country hiking around Tuolumne or visiting the sequoias. Most meals are included in the trip price. You'll need your own sleeping bag or can rent one for $20. There's also a year-round two-day hotel-based trip ($309) staying at *Yosemite Cedar Lodge* (see p.177), with varied departure times throughout the year.

Yosemite Bug Bus Tours ☎1-866/826-7108, ⓦwww.yosemitebugbus.com. The *Yosemite Bug Rustic Mountain Resort* (see p.177), located a few miles outside Yosemite National Park, runs a number of excellent bus trips. Most frequent is the Two-Day-Two-Night Tour (all-year Mon, Wed & Fri; staying in a dorm $245; en-suite room $590 for two) starting in San Francisco and spending both nights at the *Bug*. Visits to Mariposa Grove, Sentinel Dome, Yosemite Valley and the Mist Trail are supplemented by swimming, meals and campfires at the *Bug*. For something more adventurous, go for the two-day Yosemite Backcountry Backpacking trips (June–Sept; $245–400), which involve exploring the high country and camping out in spectacular locations: see the website for details.

Getting around

The abundance of public transportation available in Yosemite and Sequoia/Kings Canyon is unusual for US national parks and makes leaving your vehicle behind a viable option. The following material focuses on Yosemite; we've covered Sequoia and Kings Canyon in the box on p.19.

YARTS services from the eastern entrance on Hwy-120 East and the western entrance on Hwy-140 run through the park to Yosemite Valley, where free **shuttle buses** ferry visitors around the main sights and accommodation areas at its eastern end. From here, **hikers' buses** fan out to Glacier Point and also Tuolumne Meadows, where there's another free shuttle service along the most popular section of Tioga Road. **Guided tours** range even further, with trips as far as Tuolumne Meadows and the southern section of the park, where a third free shuttle links Wawona to the Mariposa Grove of Giant Sequoias. Unfortunately, there is only very limited public transportation from Yosemite Valley to Wawona.

Despite all this choice, for some of the farther-flung parts, having a **car** is ideal. **Cycling** is also a viable option, and even **hitching is permitted** (though not encouraged): some hikers choose to walk one way then hitch back to their car, hotel or campground.

Shuttles and hikers' buses

At some point almost everyone visiting Yosemite uses one of the **free shuttle buses**. By far the most popular is the Yosemite Valley Shuttle Bus around the eastern end of Yosemite Valley, though other services around Tuolumne Meadows and Wawona are also very convenient. In winter, skiers and boarders can ride from Yosemite Valley to the skifield at no charge.

The Glacier Point and Tuolumne Meadows **hikers' buses** are both fee-charged services running in conjunction with the Glacier Point and Tuolumne tours. Consequently you get a full commentary, either all the way to the destination, or as far as your chosen trailhead.

Yosemite Valley Shuttle Bus

In Yosemite Valley, drivers should park at Curry Village or in the day-use parking area at Yosemite Village and get around on the frequent and free **Yosemite Valley Shuttle Bus**. These relatively quiet and low polluting diesel hybrids operate around the eastern end of the valley floor – we've marked shuttle stops with stars on our Upper Yosemite Valley map (see p.56). Services run counterclockwise on a loop that passes close to all the main points of interest, trailheads and accommodation areas. From May to September shuttles run roughly every ten to twenty minutes between 7am and 10pm to most sections of the valley, with slightly reduced frequency and hours at other times: see *Yosemite Guide* for the current details. Buses are designed with low floors for easy access.

El Capitan Shuttle Bus

To access the western end of Yosemite Valley use the free **El Capitan Shuttle** (June to early Sept daily every 30min 9am–6pm), which runs on a loop from the Valley Visitor Center (stop 5) along Northside Drive to El Capitan Picnic Area and El Capitan Meadow (for excellent views of the monolith), then back along Southside Drive past the Four-Mile Trailhead to stop 5.

Tuolumne Meadows Shuttle Bus

Getting around Tuolumne Meadows is best done on the handy and free **Tuolumne Meadows Shuttle**; for times and drop off/pickup points, see p.86.

Mariposa Grove and Wawona Shuttle

Travel between Wawona and the Mariposa Grove is best done on the free **Mariposa Grove & Wawona Shuttle Bus** – for full details, see p.98.

Wawona & Yosemite Valley Shuttle

With the arguable exception of the Grand Tour (see p.28), the only public transportation between Yosemite Valley and Wawona is this summer-only once-daily free **Wawona–Yosemite Valley Shuttle**. The bus leaves the *Wawona Hotel* at 8.30am and arrives at *Yosemite Lodge* a little over an hour later. The return journey leaves *Yosemite Lodge* at 3.30pm.

Tuolumne Meadows Hikers' Bus

Getting between Yosemite Valley and Tuolumne Meadows is straightforward. You can drive it in about ninety minutes, hike it in a couple of days along the John Muir Trail, ride the afternoon YARTS bus (see p.23) or catch the **Tuolumne Meadows Hikers' Bus** (mid-June to early-Sept; $14.50 one way, $23 round trip, kids 5–12 half-price, section fares available). Run in conjunction with the Tuolumne Meadows Tour (see p.28), it opens up the trails that lead off Tioga Road (hikes Y12–Y20) and plenty more from Tuolumne Meadows. The bus makes a 2 hours 10 minutes run from Yosemite Valley (leaving Curry Village at 8am, then *Yosemite Lodge* at 8.20am) to Tuolumne Meadows with stops at Crane Flat, White Wolf, *Tuolumne Meadows Lodge*, and anywhere else you request. The return journey leaves at 2pm, giving around three and a half hours in Tuolumne if done as a day-trip. If you need to be picked up en route, call a day or two in advance (☏209/372-1240) to let them know to expect you, then pay the driver when you board.

Glacier Point Hikers' Bus

A combined tour bus and trail access service, the **Glacier Point Hikers' Bus** (late May to Oct; $25 each way, seniors $23, kids $15, section fares available), runs from Yosemite Valley to Glacier Point and back (1hr 10min each way) and is particularly convenient for lazy hikers wanting to ride the bus up then hike down the Four-Mile Trail (Hike Y7), or for masochists to hike up and bus back. The bus is also useful for reaching the trailheads for Inspiration Point (Hike Y9), the Pohono–Panorama Trail Combo (Hike Y44) and the hikes off Glacier Point Road (hikes Y35–Y40).

There are three round trips daily, leaving *Yosemite Lodge* at 8.30am, 10am (not Oct) and 1.30pm, and departing Glacier Point at 10.30am, noon (not Oct) and 3.30pm. Section fares mean that you won't necessarily be paying the full Glacier Point fare for shorter rides.

Badger Pass Bus

During the winter months when the Badger Pass Ski Area is open, visitors staying in Yosemite Valley can travel there on the free **Badger Pass Bus** (Dec to early April daily). It leaves the valley each morning, calling at Curry Village (8am & 10.30am), Yosemite Village (8.10am & 10.40am), *The Ahwahnee* (8.15am & 10.45pm) and *Yosemite Lodge* (8.30am & 11am), arriving at Badger Pass an hour later. The return services leave Badger Pass at 2pm and 4pm, with extra services on busy days (particularly holiday weekends).

In addition, there's a new **Oakhurst Shuttle** to Badger Pass (mid-Dec to March Sat & Sun only; $10, including park entrance fee). It picks up outside Miller Mountain Sports, 40343 Hwy-41 in Oakhurst (7am) and Tenaya Lodge (8am), reaching Badger Pass at 9am. The return journey leaves Badger Pass at 3.45pm, reaching Oakhurst at 5.30pm.

Driving

Traffic congestion spoils everyone's fun, particularly in July and August, and the Park Service is doing what it can to reduce snarl-ups without cramping people's style unnecessarily. You can drive into Yosemite Valley, but there is a long-term strategy to reduce the number of parking spaces in the valley and get people to use the improved public transportation.

Visitors are encouraged to leave their vehicles in the surrounding towns, and ride buses (see p.23) into the valley. These are more tempting than they may sound, and for those staying outside the park and popping into the valley each day it definitely makes sense – there's more time for admiring the scenery, and you don't pay park entrance fees. This only really makes sense along the Hwy-140 corridor, with Mariposa, Midpines and El Portal being obvious bases. If you do **drive** into Yosemite Valley, be sure to leave your vehicle in one of the parking lots and use the free valley shuttle buses to get around.

For exploring areas outside the valley – Tioga Road, Glacier Point Road and Wawona – a car is very handy, with parking easier to find. Roads within the park are generally in good condition, but many are winding, with unnervingly steep drops to the side. The **maximum speed limit** is **45mph** (35mph in the valley) though often you'll be travelling much slower, maybe trapped behind some lumbering RV with no passing lanes in sight. The 55-mile drive from Yosemite Valley to Tuolumne Meadows might easily take two hours, and it is best to **be patient** and make frequent short stops to admire the view. Wherever you drive, try to keep your eyes on the road, and remember that others will be rubbernecking the scenery and may stop or pull out unexpectedly. Stop only at designated turnouts and pull well off the road. In winter and spring watch out for icy patches where the road is shaded by rocks or trees. For winter driving conditions and information on snow chains, see the box on p.20.

Cycling

While roads are narrow and grades are steep in much of Yosemite, **cycling** remains one of the most enjoyable ways to get around Yosemite Valley, where wide, flat roads are augmented by twelve miles of traffic-free asphalt **bike paths** at its eastern end. Elsewhere in the park, cycling can be pleasurable if you time your ride when there is minimal traffic – spring and fall are probably your best bets.

Most people just cycle gently between the main sights in the valley on single-speed **rented cruisers** ($9.50 per hour; $25.50 per day), available from the

Yosemite Lodge bike stand (summer daily from 9am to just before sunset; ☎209/372-1208) and the Curry Village bike stand (same times; ☎209/372-8319). Tandems are not available, but for those with kids there are six-speed bike and trailer combos ($16 per hour, $50.50 a day) and baby jogger **strollers** ($9.50 per hour, $21 a day). By law, anyone aged 17 or younger must wear a helmet ($5 per day).

Park regulations prohibit cycling off-road or along hiking trails, so you can forget about serious **mountain biking** within Yosemite National Park. More rewarding options lie just outside the park in the surrounding national forests. We've covered a couple of rides close to Hwy-140 near the Briceburg Visitor Center (see p.160). There's more to be found in the Stanislaus National Forest to the northwest, and a wealth of rides near Oakhurst, where there's the added benefit of all-terrain bike rental (see p.164).

Guided tours from Yosemite Valley

If time is short and you don't mind being herded around, you could join one of the **guided tours** from Yosemite Valley that let you see as many of the major sights as possible along with a breezy (and occasionally cheesy) commentary. All tours start from *Yosemite Lodge*, where you can buy tickets on the spot at the Tour Desk, though in July and August it pays to **buy a ticket** a couple of days in advance, either through the tour desk at any of the valley hotels or by calling ☎209/372-4386. Children 4 and under ride free; kids' rates are for ages 5 to 12 inclusive.

An additional tour – the **Big Trees Tram Tour** around the Mariposa Grove in the southern section of the park – is covered on p.99.

Valley-based tours

Glacier Point Tour Late May to Oct; 4hr; $41, seniors $35, kids $23. A round-trip bus tour from Yosemite Valley passing many of its most famous sights and spectacular vistas on the way to Glacier Point, climbing over 3000ft along the way. Buses depart from *Yosemite Lodge* at 8.30am, 10am (not in Oct) and 1.30pm daily. You'll get just over an hour at Glacier Point, but for those who want to stay longer, it can also be ridden one way in its role as the Glacier Point Hikers' Bus (see p.26). In addition there's a Stargazing Tour (June to early Sept daily 7–11.30pm; $41, seniors $35, kids $23), which is identical except you get time to join the sunset interpretive programme.

Grand Tour Late May to early Nov; 8hr; $82, seniors $69, kids, $46. An informative full-day bus tour visiting Glacier Point and Wawona, and including the Big Trees Tram Tour around the Mariposa Grove (see p.99). It departs from *Yosemite Lodge* at 8.45am and stops for lunch at Wawona, where you can eat lunch at the *Wawona Hotel* (additional $10 if bought when you book the tour). Only worthwhile if you're desperate to see as much as possible in one day.

Moonlight Tour May–Sept/Oct when full moon falls, 2hr; $25, seniors $23, kids $13. Essentially the Valley Floor Tour (see **below**) done in the evening on the four nights leading up to full moon, with departures from *Yosemite Lodge* at either 9.30pm or 10pm, depending on how late the moon rises. The enchanting silvery views make it worth enduring the annoying megaphone commentary.

Tuolumne Meadows Tour Mid-June to early Sept; 8hr; $23, kids $11.50. A there-and-back bus tour with stacks of photo opportunities at all the main Tioga Road viewpoints and sites of interest. A break allows over three hours for gentle hiking in Tuolumne Meadows. The tour is also the Tuolumne Meadows Hikers' Bus (see p.26) and can be used for one-way rides or for accessing the high country. Departs Curry Village at 8am then *Yosemite Lodge* at 8.20am.

Valley Floor Tour All year; 2hr; $25, seniors $23, kids $13, family rates available. A rather dull and predictable 26-mile tour along the valley roads on a kind of open-air flat-deck tram car with seats (or a bus from late Oct to April), with a fairly informative commentary on the famous landmarks, history, geology, flora and fauna. You get to visit or gaze at Yosemite Falls, Half Dome, El Capitan, Bridalveil Fall and Tunnel View (see p.91), which is otherwise hard to get to without a car (or a long walk). Best exploited on extremely rushed visits, the tour leaves from *Yosemite Lodge* every hour or so in summer, and twice a day in winter.

Hiking essentials

This book covers a wealth of superb hikes in the parks, from short and gentle meadow walks to major treks into the backcountry. The following advice will help you be prepared, get the most from your hike and come back satisfied, ready for another outing tomorrow.

Staying on track

Major trailheads and trail junctions in the parks all sprout a cluster of **signs** stating the distance to several prominent landmarks or destinations in each direction. In Yosemite many are stencilled metal affairs dating back to the 1950s. Most **trails** are easy to follow, and sometimes have fallen tree trunks aligned with the path to guide you. Where the trails cross bare rock, look for **cairns** (small piles of rocks also known as "ducks") marking the way. In addition, you may also come across a rectangle or letter "T" cut from the bark of trailside trees, remnants of an outdated practice of trailblazing.

It's hard to get lost if you stick to the trail, but that shouldn't stop you from carrying a **compass** and a detailed **topographic map** (see p.40) – essential if you're planning to go **off-trail**.

Safety

Safety on the trail is mostly common sense, but in an effort to reduce injuries the Park Service offers considerable precautionary information online (Ⓦwww.nps.gov/yose /planyourvisit/wilderness_safety.htm and www.nps.gov/seki/planyourvisit/trail-safety .htm). They make no attempt to keep track of hikers in the parks, so always let someone know where you're going (and tell

Equipment rental

Although it pays to come fully prepared for your hike, a fairly extensive range of camping equipment and clothing is available to buy in Yosemite Valley, and limited supplies can be found in Sequoia and Kings Canyon. In Yosemite, you can also **rent** outdoor equipment from the Yosemite Mountaineering School (☏209/372-8344) at the Mountain Shop in Curry Village, including overnight packs ($15.50), day-packs ($5.50), sleeping bags ($13), foam sleeping pads ($2.50), gaiters ($3), helmets ($7) and snowshoes ($22.50). Tents and rock climbing shoes are not available.

them when you get back), especially if hiking alone.

Before setting off, check the **weather forecast** at visitor centres or by phone (Yosemite ☏209/372-0200; Sequoia and Kings Canyon ☏559/565-3341). Sierra weather is generally stable, though short sudden summer and fall **thunderstorms** are quite common, especially in the afternoons. If you're caught in one, keep clear of exposed places, viewpoints and lone trees that are susceptible to lightning strikes. Regardless of the weather, you should always carry warm, waterproof clothing: **hypothermia** is a killer.

For all our hikes we've given an indication of the **normal hiking season**, when the trail is likely to be snow-free. It still pays, however, to check trail conditions through visitor centres or online (🌐www.nps.gov /yose/planyourvisit/wildcond.htm and www .nps.gov/seki/planyourvisit/trailcond.htm). In the high country it can still snow as late as June and as early as October. Besides inclement weather, other **potential backcountry hazards** include creatures big and small, from mountain lions to mosquitoes, along with the likes of poison oak; see "Health and backcountry dangers" (from p.33) for details.

What to take

Whether you're day hiking or off on a week-long trek, your most important decision is what to **wear**. Several layers of light clothing work best so that you can bundle up or strip off as required. Cotton is a liability when wet, so bring at least one layer of either wool or a "technical" synthetic material; always carry a light waterproof shell as well. Apart from the easiest excursions,

the hikes listed in the guide are mostly along rough paths. Day hikers carrying a light load may be happy with ordinary sneakers, but it's safer wearing **boots with ankle support**, preferably a relatively light pair. For summer hiking, heavy leather boots are overkill as you'll seldom come across wet or muddy terrain. Whatever you wear, be sure they're broken in, and wear good **socks**.

Always take more **food** than you think you'll need, and on longer hikes make sure you have some means of **water purification**. Also take a map, mosquito repellent, sunscreen, sunglasses and a wide-brimmed hat.

Backcountry equipment and packing

Many a backpacking trip has been ruined by taking the wrong **equipment** – take too little and you're unprepared, but too much can make each day a painful march. Getting it right is an art learned over many trips: the following won't make you an expert overnight, but it will help you avoid the biggest pitfalls.

What to wear

Wearing **layered clothing** is essential, as you must be able to adapt quickly to the varying conditions. In summer you'll be hiking in shorts and a T-shirt all day, then as soon as the sun goes down you'll be quickly scrabbling for that warmer gear, particularly at high-country campgrounds where temperatures drop rapidly. At places like Yosemite's Vogelsang in September you'll be in your sleeping bag an hour after the sun goes down.

Cotton is great when the weather is hot and dry (as it will often be in the main hiking

A hiking gear guide

Weather conditions and personal preferences dictate exactly what you'll need to take on a hiking trip, but the following checklist should point you in the right direction. Overnight hikers will need everything in the first two sections plus some of the additional overnight gear.

Day hiking
- strong hiking shoes or light boots
- good hiking socks
- waterproof coat
- water bottles
- sunscreen
- sunglasses
- sun hat
- water
- snacks and emergency food
- camera (optional)
- binoculars (optional)

Essential overnight gear
- wilderness permit
- map
- waterproof tent
- sleeping bag
- bear canister
- food (including emergency supply)
- water purifier
- stove and fuel
- pots, pans and utensils
- pocket knife
- shorts and a light shirt
- long-sleeved shirt
- warm, long pants
- fleece or down jacket
- light but warm hat and gloves
- first-aid kit
- waterproof matches or lighter
- flashlight (preferably a headlamp)
- garbage bag
- toilet paper (and Ziploc bags)
- mosquito repellent

Additional overnight gear
- sleeping pad
- soap/toiletries
- toothbrush and toothpaste
- small trowel (available for $3 from wilderness centres)
- tarp/ground cover
- journal
- entertainment: books, playing cards, etc
- camp shoes (light sandals work best)
- fishing gear (and licence)
- bathing suit
- flask

season), but it's virtually useless when wet and actually makes you feel colder, encouraging hypothermia. Always have a change of dry clothes handy. Try a light and comfortable base layer (next to the skin), preferably one of the modern fabrics that wicks away moisture and dries quickly when washed. If you carry two of these, rinsing one out each day, your hiking companions need never complain about your camping hygiene. In summer, you can probably do without a middle layer and just carry a warm, wind-breaking **outer layer** for when the sun goes down. This might be waterproof, or you may have an additional waterproof layer.

Overnight gear

Obviously you'll need a **tent**. John Muir may have been happy bedding down under the stars on newly hewn fir boughs with a raging fire nearby, but then he didn't mind waking up with a four-inch blanket of snow over him. Ideally you'll want a light, three-season tent that will stand up without having to be pegged out. Mosquito-proof mesh is good except when the temperature drops, so tents that allow you to zip over the mesh panels are good, though this adds to your load.

The cosy **sleeping bag** you use for car camping is likely to be too bulky for backpacking. Consider getting a light-weight, easily stored bag rated to 20°F, which should be fine for most uses. For a comfortable night's sleep, most people prefer to carry some form of **sleeping pad**. High-tech inflatable pads such as Therm-a-Rests are light and relatively luxurious, but it's worth considering a much cheaper closed-cell foam roll mat. They're almost as good at night, and much more useful for lunch breaks and lolling around the campground.

We've listed suggestions for the remaining gear you might want to bring along in the box opposite, but keep in mind that your pack will only get heavier with every step. Food in particular can weigh you down: eschew heavy packaging – especially bottles and cans – in favour of dried foods.

Water and waste disposal

In the vast majority of the backcountry there is no guaranteed safe **drinking water**, so hikers must be prepared to treat their supply (see p.35).

During the spring snowmelt there is no shortage of supply, but as the summer wears on creeks dry up and you should plan your hike with this in mind. That said, even creeks that aren't flowing often have stagnant pools that will satisfy your needs when necessary.

Except when using the vault **toilets** at Lower Yosemite Valley and Yosemite's High Sierra Camps, you're expected to **bury** human waste to protect water quality. It should be buried six inches deep in mineral soil at least 100ft (forty paces) from water-courses; portable plastic shovels are available from the wilderness centres for $3. Toilet paper must be packed out (not burned or buried); Ziploc bags are freely available in wilderness centres. When **washing**, be sure to carry water well away from the watercourse: even so-called "biodegradable" soaps pollute the water. All other waste – packaging materials, food scraps, etc – must be carried out. Do not burn or bury trash: **pack out what you pack in**.

Campfires and cooking

No special permits are required to light **campfires** in the backcountry, but to preserve the parks' delicate ecology and limit pollution you should try to manage without a fire, or at least build a small warming one rather than a large bonfire. Where they exist, **fire rings** should be used, and be sure to only use dead and down wood. There are seldom all-out fire bans, but fires are **banned at high altitudes** (9600ft in Yosemite; 9000–10,000ft in Sequoia and Kings Canyon parks depending on region) where trees grow slowly and suitable wood is scarce.

For cooking it makes sense to take a **camping stove** – fuel is available for most types of stove within the parks (see below). Bear in mind that airlines are increasingly wary about letting passengers carry these: the faintest whiff of fuel and they'll confiscate your equipment. Consequently those flying to Yosemite should consider their stove systems in advance. Stoves requiring fuel carried in a special pressurized bottle are particularly tricky as it's virtually impossible to rid them of all odours, and both the bottle and any pump are likely to be seized. Some airlines allow such equipment to be professionally cleaned then carried, but it's hardly worth the effort. A better bet is to rely on butane and propane gas stoves. You can't carry the fuel canisters, but at least there's no problem with carrying the stove itself.

Yosemite Valley's outdoor stores have a pretty good range of **butane** and **propane canisters** – including Gaz, MSR, Kovea and Primus – but in more remote stores, such as those in Tuolumne Meadows and Wawona, the stock is limited. If buying a new stove, get one that accepts several types of canister.

Gasoline is available in Tuolumne, Wawona and at Crane Flat but is not available in Yosemite Valley. More expensive **white gas** (such as Coleman Fuel) is just a refined type of gasoline, works well and can be bought in stores all over the park.

Trangia stoves burn **methylated spirits**, which is known in the US as **denatured alcohol** and can often be found in hardware stores. The Curry Village Mountain Shop has supplies.

Hiking and backcountry camping guidelines

- **Stay on the trail** Walk single file, avoid cutting switchbacks, and limit track-broadening by walking through any wet areas.
- **Pack out all trash** If you pack it in, pack it out. Some hikers even carry a plastic bag and pick up stuff dropped by less considerate souls.
- **Bury bodily wastes** Use the vault toilets found at most trailheads, but if you get caught short, bury waste six inches deep and over forty paces away from any stream or river.
- **Pack out toilet paper** Attempts to burn it have caused wildfires in the past.
- **Stand aside for horses** On some trails horses and mules are common. Stop on the side of the trail to let them pass.
- **Purify drinking water** See p.35.
- **Use existing campgrounds** Use the campgrounds in Little Yosemite Valley, next to High Sierra Camps and other spots that are regularly used.
- **Camp away from water and trails** Wherever you camp, make sure you're over forty paces away from lakes and streams, and out of sight of nearby trails.
- **Camp on firm ground** Avoid setting tents on fragile, untouched vegetation.
- **No "improvements"** Don't build windbreaks or new fire rings, dig trenches or cut vegetation for bough beds.
- **Limit campfires** Fires are banned above the tree line and are discouraged elsewhere. Use stoves, and if you must have a fire, burn only dead and down wood.
- **Wash clean** Avoid putting anything in the water. Carry washing water away from lakes and streams. Even "biodegradable" soap pollutes.
- **Be bear safe** Always store food and any odorous items in bear canisters unless you are preparing a meal.

Bear awareness

Yosemite Valley **bears** (see box, p.10) may be smart, but their Sierra backcountry cousins are no less adept at obtaining food from hikers. They're too timid to ambush humans, but unless you're happy to go hungry for the rest of your hike it is absolutely essential to correctly store your provisions overnight.

You may be familiar with the idea of **hanging food** in trees or the more advanced **counterbalance method** designed to prevent bears getting at your food. Neither are effective in the parks, where bears have learnt to obtain properly hung food and sows even teach their cubs to go out along thin branches that wouldn't hold the weight of a full-grown bear. Consequently, almost everyone overnighting in the backcountry is required to have a **bear-resistant food canister** (BRFC or just bear canister) – the only effective way for backpackers to store food in the wilderness. These three-pound plastic cylinders fit in your backpack and

store enough food for three to five days for one person. You typically leave them a short distance outside your tent at night. When first introduced, bears were determined to get at the contents and hikers would frequently find their canister several hundred feet away. Having repeatedly failed, bears now walk past your tent in the night and ignore the canister.

Hikers headed for campgrounds at Little Yosemite Valley, beside Yosemite's High Sierra Camps and several popular campgrounds in Sequoia and Kings Canyon may be able to use the *in situ* steel **bear-proof boxes** found there, but you increase your campground selection freedom by carrying a bear canister. In Yosemite, **rental** is $5 per trip (for up to a week; plus $90 deposit) and they can be rented from the Yosemite Valley Wilderness Center, the Crane Flat Store, the Wawona Store and the Hetch Hetchy Entrance Station. Reservations are neither available nor necessary, and canisters can be returned to any location after your trip: there's a $15 cleaning fee if you return one dirty. In Sequoia and Kings Canyon you'll pay $5 (plus $98 deposit) for up to fourteen days from visitor centres and ranger stations.

You can also **buy canisters** (several models from $43–75) from most wilderness centres and outdoor-oriented stores throughout the parks. If you own your own bear canister, make sure it is approved for use. A list of currently **approved canisters** for Yosemite can be found at ⓦwww.nps .gov/yose/planyourvisit/bearcanisters.htm.

Health and backcountry dangers

Most visitors leave Yosemite with little more discomfort than a sunburn or aching legs from hiking up Half Dome. Accidents, of course, do happen and it is sensible to take a few precautions. For starters, if injured or suffering any ill effects, get in touch with the Yosemite Medical Clinic in Yosemite Village (see p.40). Along with the safety advice given below, it's also worth being aware that altitude sickness (see box, p.87) can strike if you quickly travel from low to high altitudes and stay overnight.

Theft and threats to your **personal safety** are also rare, but as with anywhere that people congregate, there are risks: don't drop your guard just because you're on vacation.

Bears, rattlers and mountain lions

Visitors unfamiliar with bear territory often arrive in Yosemite with an irrationally heightened fear of the threat bears pose. Despite the presence of a grizzly bear on the California state flag, these majestic beasts have been extinct in California for almost a century and all bears in Yosemite (no matter what shade their fur) are **black bears**. In recent years, the Park Service has gone to great lengths to reduce the bears' reliance on human food and minimize human–bear contact. Consequently the bad old days when dozens of cars were broken into each night in Yosemite Valley are a thing of the past, and bears wandering through campgrounds are a little less common. You're encouraged to **report bear-related problems** and sightings on ☎209/372-0322. For more details see "Bear awareness" opposite, and our box on p.10.

Most visitors are thrilled to see bears, though fewer are keen on an encounter with a **rattlesnake**. There's no need to be especially fearful, but it definitely pays to keep an eye out for the thick-bodied Western rattlesnake (the only venomous snake you're likely to see). They're fairly common below 5000ft (and have been seen as high as 10,000ft), generally preferring moderate temperatures and even hunting at night in midsummer at lower elevations. You're most likely to encounter them in boulder-strewn areas where they warm themselves in the morning sun, or in the dappled shade of trees where their patchy markings camouflage them perfectly. Much of the hiking in Yosemite is above 5000ft where the risk is much reduced, but when hiking low down heavy footfalls generally ensure that snakes will keep out of your way. In particular, don't go turning over rotting logs and the like without checking for the presence of lounging snakes. If you get **bitten**, try to remain as calm as possible, stay put and send for help. The old advice to suck out the venom or tourniquet the limb is counterproductive and even gently binding the limb and using snakebite kits is no longer widely recommended. Get outside help as soon as possible.

Mountain lions (or cougars) live throughout the park but are rarely seen. Count yourself lucky if you catch sight of one but minimize the chance of an attack by grouping together and trying to appear as large as possible. Don't advance or run away, but retreat slowly, and if it attacks, fight back. Normal mountain lion prey doesn't do that, and the shock of being attacked themselves usually frightens them off.

Smaller critters and poisonous plants

Perhaps the most annoying of smaller critters is the **mosquito**. In summer they're around populated areas, particularly at dawn and dusk, but are particularly bad in the high country. If you're venturing backcountry, be sure to take long pants, a loose long-sleeved shirt and bug repellent. A number of "natural" non-DEET repellents are available in the park and work quite well, but when the going really gets tough you'll be glad of something with around thirty percent DEET.

Anyone who sits down to snack on a sandwich will soon be pestered by small critters, especially ground **squirrels**, Douglas' squirrels and the bushy-tailed Western Gray squirrel. More tiresome than dangerous, they do, however, carry rabies and other nasty diseases so don't encourage them.

In spring, hikers may be exposed to western-blacklegged **ticks** known to transmit the bacteria causing **Lyme disease**. Ticks lurk in moist, cool environments and may latch onto you as you brush through shaded grasses and shrubs, especially under oak trees. If you're walking in such areas, wear light-coloured clothing to show up any ticks, tuck long pants into your socks and apply tick repellent (available locally).

In the Sierra foothills (up to 5000ft), watch out for **poison oak**, with its oak-like grouping of three dark-green-veined leaves that secrete an oily juice. Simply brushing against it can induce a highly allergenic reaction: a nasty rash, intense itching and blisters are all common within twelve to 48 hours. Avoid touching it or coming into

contact with anything else that has touched it. If you do, washing immediately with water usually helps, though you're better off applying an oil removal product such as Tecnu as soon after contact as possible. In extreme cases, see a doctor.

Fire, ice and rock

Fire is both a natural hazard and a forest management tool used by the Park Service to reduce the risk of catastrophic fires. Those caused by human error and any blazes that threaten to destroy property are extinguished as soon as possible, but other wildfires are frequently left to burn, often for weeks. During summer and fall days, it's not unusual to see columns of **smoke** out in the Yosemite backcountry. At night, the cooling air draws the smoke down into Yosemite Valley, meaning hotel guests and campers rise to an oddly beautiful hazy world with beams of light filtering through the oaks. The smoke, however, can be irritating, particularly for elderly people and those with respiratory problems, who should avoid strenuous activity at such times. Usually the smoke clears by midday. More information on fire and its management (including details of fires currently burning) can be found at ⓦwww.nps.gov/yose/parkmgmt/fireman agement.htm.

One of the biggest health risks in Yosemite is **exposure** to the elements. With typically stable summer weather and mild nights it's tempting to head out hiking in just shorts and a T-shirt, but storms can arrive quickly and when they do temperatures drop rapidly, especially at altitude. Caught without shelter in wet, cotton clothes with the wind picking up is no fun at all and can quickly lead to **hypothermia**. Be prepared, and follow our hiking checklist on p.30.

Though there is little you can do except run, it's worth being aware of the potential for **rockfall**, particularly in Yosemite Valley (see box, p.55).

Safety around water

Every year people get into trouble trying to cross or swim in streams. It might sound obvious, but choose your **swimming spots** carefully. We've suggested a few good and relatively safe locales in Chapter 6, Summer activities (see p.145), but there are numerous other tempting swimming holes beside trails. Never swim or wade above **waterfalls**, even if the water appears calm. People are swept over falls almost every year when caught by unexpected currents – three in 2005 alone. In the spring, **snowmelt** turns Yosemite's **rivers** into raging torrents, often with underwater obstacles that can easily trap the unwary. At these times, stay away from river banks and avoid rock-hopping. Along the major trails, **streams** are all suitably bridged, but in places where there is no bridge look for a calm, safe spot to cross, and be prepared to turn back if you can't find anywhere suitable.

Swimming is best from July onwards: as the snowmelt abates the waters are safer, and by August the rivers are tolerably warm (at least on hot days). Most of all, **supervise children** closely when anywhere around water.

Water quality

Water from fountains and faucets throughout the park is invariably drinkable, but water taken from streams and lakes may contain disease-bearing organisms that can spread **giardia**. The official line is that all such water should be treated, though giardia is relatively uncommon and you may wish to chance it. That said, the consequence of contracting the disease are not pleasant at all, so choose your source carefully: rushing side streams are a better bet than lakes or large rivers which have a wide catchment.

Hikers should carry all the water they need or be prepared to **purify** it in some way. Options for the latter include carrying a giardia-rated water filter, dosing the water with iodine-based tablets or solutions, boiling the water for three to five minutes, or using an ultraviolet light irradiator.

To prevent the spread of disease, use toilets where provided. In other areas, **bury human waste** at least six inches deep at least forty paces away from any lake or stream, and carry out your toilet paper – double plastic bags should do the trick. All washing should be done a similar distance away from water.

Travel essentials

Campfires

Summertime air-quality restrictions limit **campfires** in Yosemite Valley to 5pm to 10pm from May to mid-October. Use only dead and down wood, or buy your firewood from one of the shops (around $8 a box). For ecological reasons, firewood must not be gathered in Yosemite Valley or above 9600ft elsewhere in Yosemite. In Sequoia and Kings Canyon restrictions vary but generally gathering firewood is banned above 9000ft. In the national forests surrounding all three parks you must obtain a free fire permit from the nearest ranger station.

Children

See "Kids", p.37.

Costs

Visiting Yosemite, Sequoia and Kings Canyon can be expensive. Accommodation, restaurant and tour **costs** are fairly high, and those on a brief visit might baulk at the $20 entrance fee. Outside the parks, prices are much the same as you might expect in rural California, though accommodation is still on the pricey side, especially in the peak summer months.

In contrast, much of what you'll be doing inside the parks is free. The scenery costs nothing, and many of the landmark sights are accessible by free shuttle buses. Once you've obtained the appropriate gear, hiking isn't going to dent the pocketbook, and if you're tackling overnight hikes (for which permits are free) then you camp in the backcountry for little or no charge. In addition, the Park Service runs numerous free ranger programmes and much of the evening entertainment costs little or nothing as well. In winter there's even a complimentary shuttle bus connecting Yosemite Valley with the Badger Pass ski area.

In Yosemite, if you're camping, preparing the majority of your meals yourself, and avoiding most fee-charging activities, you can scrape by on a **budget** of $20 a day per person. By staying in the cabins at Curry Village or *Housekeeping Camp*, or at the *Bug* hostel just outside the park, eating meals out at the cheaper places and perhaps going horseriding or taking a tour, you'll need to set aside $60–70 a day. If you're staying at *Yosemite Lodge* or the *Wawona Hotel*, you'll be paying $120–150 a day; and those sleeping in the luxury of *The Ahwahnee*, eating most meals there and not skimping on tours, can easily rack up a tally amounting to $400 a day.

In Sequoia and Kings Canyon you can survive on as little as $20 a day, though $60–70 would be much more comfortable, and spending $120–150 will afford some luxury.

Crime and personal safety

Yosemite, Sequoia and Kings Canyon are very **safe** places to visit; *Outside* magazine once claimed that the chances of being killed in an American national park are around two million to one, about the same as drowning in your own bath.

Of course you shouldn't cease to be vigilant just because you're on holiday: keep hold of those valuables and temptingly shiny cameras, smart phones and the like. For **emergencies** call ☏911; otherwise contact the nearest ranger.

Personal safety is under greater threat from the elements, flora and fauna, covered in detail under "Health and backcountry dangers" (see p.33).

Electricity

The US operates on 110V at 60Hz and uses **two-pronged plugs** with the flat prongs parallel. Foreign devices will need a plug adapter, though laptops and phone chargers automatically detect and cope with the different voltage and frequency. Other appliances will also require a transformer.

Entry requirements and park passes

All four roads entering Yosemite have **entrance stations** that are just a kiosk in the middle of the road staffed by rangers. These are usually open daily from 8am, in summer typically until 8pm, though only until 5pm at other times of year. When open you're required to stop and pay the park **entry fee** of $20 per vehicle (including all passengers), and $10 for each cyclist or hiker. The joint entry fee for **Sequoia and Kings Canyon** is also $20 ($10 for hikers and cyclists). One payment is good for seven days and there are potential savings with a number of annual passes. Passengers arriving by bus avoid any entry fee. In return for your fee you'll be given a handful of useful leaflets and one of the National Park Service's characteristically superb **maps**.

If the entrance station is closed, simply drive through (the parks themselves are always open), and pay your fee at one of the visitor centres, where you can also pick up the same leaflets. Rangers usually stop visitors leaving the park to check they've paid their fee.

Park passes

As well as the standard Yosemite entry tickets you can also buy a **Yosemite Pass** ($40) allowing unlimited visits for a year. The equivalent annual pass for Sequoia and Kings Canyon costs $30. If your visit is part of wider travels it may be worth investing in the **America the Beautiful National Parks and Federal Recreational Lands Annual Pass** ($80), valid for entry to all US national parks, national forests, national historic areas, national seashores and so forth for a year from the month of purchase. In addition, free lifetime access to all national parks is available to US citizens and residents 62 and over who buy the **Senior Pass** ($10), and US citizens and permanent residents with lifetime disabilities who obtain the **Access Pass** (free). The Senior and Access passes also give a fifty percent discount on camping fees in national parks: these are available at Yosemite entrance stations.

Gas

Around **Yosemite**, you'll find **gas** for a good price in Oakhurst, and moderate prices in Mariposa and Groveland. Within the park it's fairly expensive, though still cheaper than in Lee Vining or Groveland. It's available year-round inside the park at Crane Flat (the nearest to Yosemite Valley, 16 miles distant) and Wawona, and also at Tuolumne Meadows whenever Tioga Pass is open. Hours are printed in *Yosemite Guide* and all three gas stations have 24 hour operation with credit and debit cards.

There is no gas available in **Sequoia and Kings Canyon** national parks, but in the surrounding forests it's sold at Hume Lake, Stony Creek and at Kings Canyon Lodge on Hwy-180 into Kings Canyon. All are fairly pricey so fill up before entering the parks, perhaps in Visalia or Fresno.

Internet

Yosemite isn't that great for **internet access**, though you'll fare well enough in Yosemite Valley. *The Ahwahnee* has dataports in rooms and **wi-fi** throughout (guests only), while *Yosemite Lodge* has wi-fi in most places (free to guests; others $6 for 24hr). At Curry Village there's wi-fi in the guest lounge (currently free to all, though that may change).

The public **library** in Yosemite Village (Mon 8.30–11.30am, Tues 10am–2pm, Wed 8.30am–12.30pm, & Thurs 4–7pm) offers free internet access, but no wi-fi, on one of its three machines (limited to one 30min session per week), but opening hours are inconvenient if you want to be out doing stuff during the day. Demand is high and it's first-come-first-served so turn up early. The library is located just west of the Yosemite Museum in a building signed "Girls Club".

The only other public-use computers in Yosemite Valley are a handful of pay kiosks ($1 for 4min; bills accepted) at the daytime-only *Degnan's Café* in Yosemite Village (see p.188) and a couple more in the lobby of *Yosemite Lodge*. The park's only public internet access outside the valley is at the Bassett Memorial Library in Wawona (see p.98).

In **Sequoia and Kings Canyon** you'll find free wi-fi at the restaurant in Grant Grove, at *Wuksachi Lodge* and at We Three Bakery in Three Rivers. Otherwise head for Three Rivers Library, 42052 Eggers Drive (Wed & Fri 10am–1pm & 2–6pm, Thurs noon–5pm & 6–8pm), five miles south of the park entrance.

Kids

National parks are great places for **kids**, but as elsewhere it takes a little thought to maximize their (and your) enjoyment. Younger members of the family probably aren't going to thank you for dragging them (possibly literally) on long hikes with only a bit of boring scenery to look at. On the other hand, if you break up the hike with lake swimming, time spent looking at plants and animal tracks and some good old-fashioned play, you can all have a great day. Travelling with kids can be expensive, but many of the events and activities you'll want to go on are free, and those that are fee-charging – tours, shows, rentals, etc – usually have reduced **kids' prices**. Typically those aged 4 and under go free, while kids 5–12 inclusive go for half-fare, and teenagers must pay adult rates. Sometimes there are **family fares** that offer savings for two adults and two or more kids.

In **Yosemite**, one of the best ways to prepare for all this is to visit the **Nature Center at Happy Isles** (see p.70) which is specifically set up to introduce kids and their parents to what's out there alongside the trails. The staff here can introduce you to the **Junior Ranger** and **Little Cubs** programmes (see box, p.198), aimed at focusing young minds.

Most of the standard ranger programmes are suitable for children – stargazing, for instance, or learning about bears – but there are also free **child-oriented ranger programmes** and evening entertainment including campfire sing-songs and stories: see *Yosemite Guide* for the latest schedule. There's more fun to be had at the **Yosemite Museum**, including learning how to play Miwok stick games, handling animal furs native to Yosemite, and watching a **basket-weaving** demonstration. And in winter the Badger Pass Ski Area has an extensive programme for kids.

Parents might also want to keep their youngsters entertained with **books** (all available from the Yosemite Conservancy and most stores in Yosemite). Worthwhile examples include the native legends about the creation of El Capitan in *Two Bear Cubs*, the exploration of minuscule Yosemite in *The World of Small* (which comes with a magnifying glass), and *The Happy Camper Handbook*, an entertaining look at camping basics. It's also worth checking out the Park Services **Kids Zone** website (Ⓦwww.nps .gov/kidszone).

Guests at *Yosemite Lodge* and *The Ahwahnee* can organize a certified **babysitter**, though you'll need to reserve two weeks in advance and expect a substantial bill. Infants have to be 2 or older and be out of diapers.

In **Sequoia and Kings Canyon**, the Park Service runs a similar Junior Ranger Programme for those aged 5–12. Pick up a free booklet at any of the visitor centres and look in the park newspaper for child-oriented events such as hikes, nature walks and fireside chats. You can even earn yourself a Junior Ranger badge. The visitor centres all have entertaining displays, and the Giant Forest Museum is excellent, especially when combined with the family-oriented Beetle Rock Education Center across the road.

Laundry

See "Showers and laundry" on p.43.

Left luggage

Yosemite Lodge has a "bellman room" with limited space where nonguests can leave a backpack at no charge, but only during the day. For overnight storage, you'll find a few **lockers** (big enough for a medium-sized backpack) close to the pool and the shower block in Curry Village (75¢). The Wilderness Center, visitor centres, permit stations and ranger stations will not store food or equipment.

In Sequoia and Kings Canyon there is no formal system for left luggage.

Libraries

A public **research library** (usually Tues–Fri 8am–noon & 1–5pm) is situated upstairs from the museum entrance in Yosemite Village and contains all manner of Yosemite, backcountry and climbing information including recent **magazines** and daily **papers**. There's also a public library that opens for a few hours a day (see "Internet", p.37). Outside Yosemite Valley you'll find a library at Wawona (see p.98), and more in the gateway towns.

The nearest library to Sequoia and Kings Canyon is at Three Rivers (see p.37).

Living and working in Yosemite

Opportunities for **seasonal work** in Yosemite are fairly limited. Almost everything is run either by the Park Service or by DNC, the park concessionaire, both of which offer relatively low rates of pay in return for long hours that will probably include evenings, weekends and public holidays. In return you get a great location (with low-cost accommodation in a shared canvas tent), time off to explore, and a pretty decent social scene. The **best starting point** for a job search is Ⓦ www.nps.gov/yose/parkmgmt/jobs.ht, which contains links to most employers offering work in the park.

During the peak summer months (late-May to mid-Sept) **DNC** employs around 1800 people, mainly working in shops, restaurants and hotels. You might find yourself cleaning cabins and making beds, serving burgers or standing behind a cash register, most likely for a minimum wage or not much better. With all the form-filling, past employment verification, reference checks and pre-employment drug testing, recruiting is a time-consuming process so they expect you to stay a minimum of twelve weeks.

A list of **positions vacant** can be seen on their website (look for "Employment" under "About us" at Ⓦwww.yosemitepark .com) where you can also download an **application form**. There are no online applications, so you have to mail it in. Applications are accepted year-round, but for the summer positions it's wise to apply in February or March as they try to get positions filled by Memorial Day weekend at the end of May. Winter season jobs are posted on the website from September. Positions do become available at short notice, so impulsive types can just show up in person at DNC's Human Resources Department in Yosemite Village (Mon–Fri 9am–4pm; ☎209/372-1234) in the hope of finding something.

All employees are required to show their Social Security Card, but **international applicants** may be able to find something by contacting Intrax International (⊛www .experienceintrax.com) to see if there is a partner organization near you.

For jobs with the **National Park Service**, check out the NPS seasonal employment programme (⊛www.sep.nps.gov). There are usually more applicants than jobs available, especially at popular parks like Yosemite, and people with prior experience get priority, making it hard for first-timers to break in. All jobs are listed at ⊛www.usajobs.opm.gov, and all Park Service jobs are available only to US citizens. For Yosemite-specific jobs try the NPS's Yosemite Human Resources office on ☎209/379-1805 as they sometimes have jobs that haven't been advertised on the nationwide sites.

Volunteering

With assorted budget cuts, **volunteering** is becoming an increasingly important way to get crucial projects done. As a volunteer, apart from feeling good about giving something back, you get to hang out in the parks in convivial company.

In Yosemite, the easiest way to contribute is to join the **Habitat Protectors of Yosemite** (⊛www.nps.gov/yose/planyour visit/hapy.htm), a drop-in programme restoring habitat and removing invasive species (ie weeding). No registration is required, and there are no fees but kids under 14 must be accompanied by a parent. Three-hour sessions meet at the Yosemite Valley Visitor Center (Memorial Day to Labour Day Wed at 9am) and sometimes in Mariposa Grove.

US citizens and permanent residents can become **Work Week Volunteers** helping the

Yosemite Conservancy (see p.45; membership $25), typically working in groups of a dozen or so putting in four eight-hour days (with Wednesday off) on restoration and re-vegetation projects throughout the park. It can be back breaking work, but there are immediate rewards in seeing your handiwork repair a river bank or rehabilitate a meadow. Five one-week sessions are planned each summer with volunteers sharing a camp and being fed three hearty meals a day: there's a $150 fee to cover food costs. Schedules and application forms are available at ⊛www .yosemiteconservancy.org. Places are usually oversubscribed, so get your application in before the end of March to enter the lottery.

With more time at your disposal, consider becoming a **month-long volunteer**. You'll get a $10 daily allowance, free camping in Yosemite Valley, Wawona, or Tuolumne Meadows, and will be offered assorted discounts. Working five days a week through summer, volunteers are likely to be employed staffing information booths, assisting visitors at Happy Isles, as a docent at the Yosemite Museum, or helping at an outdoor adventure course in Tuolumne Meadows. Again, this is only open to US citizens and permanent residents.

The Park Service also accepts volunteers through their volunteer programme (⊛www.volunteer.gov/gov), which also has opportunities in **Sequoia and Kings Canyon National Parks**. This might involve staffing a campground or remote ranger station: apply early.

Mail

When it comes to sending those Ansel Adams posters home, you're well served at the **main post office** in **Yosemite Village** (Mon–Fri 8.30am–5pm, Sat 10am–noon), which also has general delivery (aka poste restante: Mon–Fri 8.30–9.30am & 11.30am–5pm). In addition, there's year-round service at *Yosemite Lodge* (Mon–Fri 12.30–2.45pm) and Wawona (Mon–Fri 9am–5pm, Sat 9am–noon) and summer-only service at Tuolumne Meadows (mid-June to mid-Sept Mon–Fri 9am–5pm, Sat 9am–1pm). The latter has general delivery for hikers on the John Muir and Pacific Crest trails. The **zip code** for the whole of Yosemite National Park is 95389.

In **Sequoia and Kings Canyon** there are post offices at Lodgepole Village (Mon–Fri 8am–1pm & 2–4pm; zip code 93262) and Grant Grove (Mon–Fri 9am–3.30pm, Sat 10am–noon; zip code 93263).

Maps

Armed with this Guide and the excellent **maps** of the parks that you're handed as you arrive, you'll have pretty much all the guidance you're likely to need, though hikers will want to get hold of more detailed maps (see below).

In **Yosemite**, consider buying one of the green and white concertina-folded maps published in cooperation with the Yosemite Conservancy, which use an angled projection to clearly show the rock formations and key features. These cover the main areas – Yosemite Valley, Tuolumne Meadows, plus Wawona and the Mariposa Grove ($3.95 each) – and are available in almost every shop and hotel in the park.

Anyone headed into the backcountry should obtain a **topographic map**. The best general hiking map is the double-sided 1:100,000 scale National Geographic *Trails Illustrated Yosemite National Park* map (No. 206; $12), which marks trail distances, and shows which wilderness areas are barred to camping and open fires. For those who need more detail, the same publisher produces four 1:40,000 maps covering the park ($10 each): Southwest covers Yosemite Valley, Half Dome and Wawona, and Northeast includes Tuolumne and the Saddlebag Lakes area.

In **Sequoia and Kings Canyon**, hikers should buy the double-sided 1:80,000 scale National Geographic *Trails Illustrated Sequoia Kings Canyon National Parks* map (No. 205; $12).

Medical assistance

Yosemite Medical Clinic (☎209/372-4637) has 24-hour emergency care and accepts appointments (Mon–Fri 8am–5pm). Consultations for minor ailments cost around $200, and medication is extra. Dental treatment (☎209/372-4200 for hours) is also available. The nearest **pharmacies** to Yosemite are in Mariposa and Oakhurst. Serious emergencies are medivaced to Modesto.

There are no medical services in Sequoia and Kings Canyon: for **emergencies** dial ☎911 or contact the closest visitor centre.

Money

While you can, of course, pay by **credit card** almost everywhere in the parks, for smaller expenses you'll want cash, accessible from 24-hour **ATMs** (typically charging $3 on each transaction). In **Yosemite** they're located in most of the park's stores and hotels; try Yosemite Village Store, outside the Yosemite Art & Education Center, in the lobby of *Yosemite Lodge*, inside the Curry Village Store, inside the Wawona Store or, just outside the park, at the *Yosemite View Lodge* in El Portal. There are **no banks** in Yosemite but the park concessionaire runs a **cheque cashing service** (Mon–Thurs & Sat 8am–3pm, Fri 8am–5pm, Sun 8am–1pm) in Yosemite Village in the lobby of the Yosemite Art & Education Center: they charge $5 for cashing each cheque.

In **Sequoia and Kings Canyon** there are no banks but you'll find ATMs at Lodgepole, Stony Creek, Grant Grove and Cedar Grove.

The gateway towns for all parks have full banking facilities, though nowhere nearby has provision for foreign currency exchange: those from outside the US should consider bringing US dollar **travellers' cheques**, which can be used like cash in shops, restaurants and hotels.

Pets

The best advice is to leave your dog at home. The national parks **discourage pets** by limiting where you can take them. All hiking trails and the backcountry are off-limits, dogs aren't allowed on shuttle buses or in any of the accommodation, restaurants or shops, and may not be left unattended in vehicles, tents or tied up anywhere. In **Yosemite** they can be taken (on a leash) anywhere on the Yosemite Valley floor, Nature Center at Happy Isles, Mirror Lake Parking Lot, Pohono Bridge and on paved paths not designated as a foot or horse trail. Seeing-eye and "hearing" dogs are generally exempt from these rules. Dogs are, however, allowed in all campgrounds except *Camp 4*, *Tamarack*

Flat and *Porcupine Flat*. Gentle dogs weighing more than twenty pounds can be boarded at the kennels at the stables by North Pines (May–Sept; ☎209/372-8348), provided you can supply evidence of immunization against rabies, distemper, parovirus and Bordatella.

Around **Sequoia and Kings Canyon**, suitably restrained dogs are allowed in all campgrounds and can be taken on trails in the surrounding national forests.

Phones

The easiest way to boast to family and friends about your ascent of Half Dome is by phone. **Mobile coverage** is only provided by Verizon, Sprint and AT&T, and even then coverage is patchy. Yosemite Valley is tolerably well covered but Wawona only has Verizon coverage. In the backcountry it's a lottery, though your chances are better at high points.

Public phones are found in a number of places around Yosemite, including Yosemite Valley, Wawona, Glacier Point and Tuolumne Meadows, as well as campgrounds and even popular trailheads. Keep a bunch of quarters handy for local calls, but for long-distance and international calls you should either get a calling card from your home phone service provider before setting out, or obtain one of the account-based **calling cards** from any of the park stores. Typically available in denominations of $5, $10 and $20, these can usually be topped up with a credit card when they run low.

In Sequoia and Kings Canyon you'll find public phones in most places where people congregate. Cell phone coverage is patchy to non-existent.

Photography

Yosemite is one of the most **photographed** places on earth. Ansel Adams (see box, p.68) spent more than half a century creating his splendid visual record of the park, and his work continues to inspire professional photographers and casual amateurs alike.

We've given a few pointers to help improve your shots (see below), but for more guidance you should join one of the free **Photography Walks** (four weekly in winter,

---

Tips for taking quality photos

Yosemite's scenery is so striking that it almost seems you could press the shutter without looking and still produce something to be proud of, but by following a few **pointers** you can quickly improve your strike rate.

- Take photos in the early morning and late afternoon when light is softer and longer shadows give scenes a greater sense of depth and texture.
- Animals are often easier to see at dawn or dusk, but be sure to use fast speed settings (400 ISO or more) when shooting in low light conditions.
- On sunny days avoid deep shadows by getting people to face the sun and remove their hat.
- With such vast sheets of granite and towering spires, it's important to give a sense of scale by including people or a building in the foreground.
- Keep shooting when the weather turns nasty – some of the best photos of Yosemite are taken during (or just after) storms, or with snow or mist all around.
- Avoid camera shake in low light levels by resting the camera against a railing or tree.
- Use a tripod whenever possible, even under good lighting conditions – if nothing else it helps you to concentrate on the perfect framing. Bring something lightweight but sturdy.
- Don't use a polarizing filter when shooting into the sun – streaks and flares can occur.
- On white-sky days, include less (or none) of the sky, choosing to concentrate on subjects close at hand. The softer light of overcast days is excellent for photographing the subtle textures in close-up.

daily in summer; check *Yosemite Guide* for details), run by the Ansel Adams Gallery (℡1-888/361-7622, ⓦwww.anseladams .com). These take place in Yosemite Valley, last an hour and a half, and look into exposure control and using different lenses. Sign up and meet at the Ansel Adams Gallery. The Park Service also runs free photo walks in Tuolumne in summer.

More committed photographers will learn a lot more on the galley's one-day **photography classes** (4hr; $95), which run three times a week in summer and cover topics such as "In the Footsteps of Ansel Adams" and "Using your Digital Camera". It's a substantial step up from those to the longer (non-residential) photography workshops dedicated to more specialist areas, such as the skills of platinum printing or crafting fine B&W prints (four days; $900) to learning about digital printing and colour management (four days; $1100). One-on-one **private lessons** cost $375 a half-day or $550 a day.

The Yosemite Conservancy (ⓦwww .yosemiteconservancy.org) runs some more mainstream multi-day field trips, ranging from a day honing skills in Yosemite Valley to three-day courses on, for example, fall photography ($360).

Equipment

What **camera gear** you take to Yosemite will largely depend on what you have and are familiar with. An SLR camera with suitable lenses will give the best results, but the extra weight can be a deterrent and only the more committed photographers will want to be lugging a couple of bodies, several lenses and a tripod around the backcountry. Of course, Ansel Adams carried a massive plate camera around with a dozen glass slides, but then he often took a mule as well. Point-and-shoot cameras can return incredible images. As ever, it all depends on where you point the camera and when you push the shutter.

For **photographic supplies** visit the Ansel Adams Gallery (p.65), which stocks tripods, memory cards and accessories along with a limited range of film.

Recycling

In Yosemite, just about everything imaginable – glass, plastic, cardboard, aluminium cans, newspapers, steel cans, automotive waste (batteries, oil, filters, anti-freeze, tyres), propane canisters and more – can be recycled at the **Yosemite Village Store Recycling Center** (summer daily 10am–5pm) and the **Curry Village Recycling Center** (summer daily 1–5pm). In addition, green **recycling receptacles** are located by many campgrounds, picnic areas and roadside pullouts. Locally bought beverage containers may be returned for a 5¢ deposit at all retail outlets.

Recycling within Sequoia and Kings Canyon is less well developed.

Senior travellers

Yosemite, Sequoia and Kings Canyon are well suited to senior travellers and there are some impressive discounts available. Foremost is the **Golden Age Passport** ($10) giving unlimited free access to all US national parks, available to US citizens and residents aged 62 and over: obtain one as you enter the park or at one of the visitor centres. Those in possession of the Golden Age Passport also get fifty percent discount on all camping in national parks. Some tours also have a small (10–20 percent) discount for seniors, but for things like bike rental and horseriding you'll be charged the full adult rate.

Getting around is fairly straightforward. You can drive close to most places you're likely to want to be, except in some places where you need to park then either walk a few hundred yards or catch one of the free **shuttle buses** (see p.25), which have low floors, making access easier.

Although there are medical facilities in Yosemite Village (see p.40) and some drugs are available over the counter in Yosemite stores, it pays to bring any **medication** you might need with you, or buy in one of the gateway towns on your way into the parks. You'll also need to be aware of your own level of **fitness** and choose your activities accordingly. It might sound obvious, but if it's a while since you've done much hiking or biking, be sure to build up slowly, perhaps trying one of the easy trails before stepping progressively up to the moderate and strenuous ones. **Altitude** can also be an issue, and while hikes around Yosemite Valley, Wawona, Hetch Hetchy and Kings Canyon aren't going to be a problem in this respect, those that head out of Yosemite Valley, and particularly those starting in Tuolumne Meadows and near Tioga Pass, all spend time above 8000ft and often top 10,000ft. At the very least you'll be out of breath and may suffer the effects of **altitude sickness** (see box, p.87). Lastly, those with breathing difficulties should avoid exertion at times when fires (see p.241) create a **smoke hazard**.

Showers and laundry

None of Yosemite's campgrounds has **showers**. To get clean in **Yosemite Valley**, visit the 24-hour facilities at Curry Village, which cost $4 and include the use of a towel (though outside peak times there's often no one in attendance to provide a towel or take your money). *Housekeeping Camp* also has public showers (daily 7am–10pm; $5 including towel). Alternatively, pay to use the pools at *Yosemite Lodge* and Curry Village (both $5, kids under 12 $3) and clean up while you're there. Showers are no longer available at *Tuolumne Meadows Lodge*. You'll find public coin-op **laundry** facilities at *Housekeeping Camp* (mid-April to mid-Oct daily 7am–10pm).

In **Sequoia and Kings Canyon** there are public showers at Lodgepole (summer daily 8am–1pm & 3–8pm; coin-op, 12 quarters for 10min), Stony Creek (mid-May to Sept daily 8am–7.30pm; $4 token for 10min), Grant Grove Village (all year daily 11am–4pm; 4 quarters for 3min) and Cedar Grove Village (summer daily 7am–1pm & 3–7pm; $3.50 for 10min). Lodgepole, Cedar Grove Village and Stony Creek have coin-operated laundries open daily 8am to 8pm in summer.

Taxes

Within the parks anything federally run is not subject to state tax, but you'll still have 8.75 percent tax added to meals, tours and most items bought in shops. We've excluded taxes from our accommodation price listings

For details on obtaining tourist information in **Sequoia and Kings Canyon** national parks, see p.205.

(as this is how most hotels quote their rates). Park campgrounds incur no taxes but you can expect to pay an additional 8–12 percent on all other accommodation.

Time

California runs on **Pacific Standard Time** (PST), which is eight hours behind GMT, and jumps forward an hour in summer (the second Sunday in March to the first Sunday in November). During most of this eight-month **daylight saving** period, when it is noon Monday in California it is 3pm in New York, 8pm in London, 5am Tuesday in Sydney, and 7am Tuesday in Auckland.

Tourist information

Upon entering **Yosemite National Park** you'll be provided with a free Yosemite map, the *Yosemite* annual booklet, and the seasonal *Yosemite Guide* listings newspaper, which has stacks of useful information including current museum, shop and restaurant opening hours. Yosemite Valley, Tuolumne Meadows and Wawona each have a **visitor centre** along with somewhere for overnight hikers to obtain wilderness permits.

While visitor centre staff field general questions about hiking in Yosemite, anyone planning serious treks and overnight camping trips should direct their enquiries to one of the **wilderness centres**, prime sources of backcountry information. In addition to issuing wilderness permits and providing advice on route planning and backcountry etiquette, they also sell maps and guidebooks and rent bear-resistant food canisters.

Yosemite is entirely encircled by the Stanislaus, Toiyabe, Inyo and Sierra **national forests**, in parts as scenic as the national park but considerably less regulated and virtually empty of visitors. In chapter 8 we've provided some information about the areas that immediately abut the park, but there's much more to uncover and the national forest ranger stations are the best place to start. Most of the **gateway towns** also have a visitor centre of some description; see the relevant town accounts in Chapter 8 for details.

Virtually everything within Yosemite, from transportation to accommodation, is organized through the five groups listed below under "**Useful contacts**" though you'll also find heaps of activities and programmes organized by the various **support groups** listed as well.

Visitor centres

Valley Visitor Center Yosemite Village. The park's main visitor centre is covered in detail on p.62.
Big Oak Flat Information Station At the park entrance on Hwy-120 West ☎209/379-1899; Easter–Sept daily 8am–5pm, Oct–Easter generally closed. Handy when arriving from the northwest, this small information station also has an accommodation-booking service and deals with wilderness permits.
Tuolumne Meadows Visitor Center Tuolumne Meadows. For visitor information in the north of the park. See p.87.
Wawona Visitor Center Wawona. For visitor information and wilderness permits for the southern part of the park. See p.98.

Wilderness centres

Valley Wilderness Center Yosemite Village ☎209/372-0745; mid-May to June & early Sept to mid-Oct daily 8am–5pm, July to early Sept daily 8am–5pm, closed in winter; shuttle stops 5 & 9. The foremost source of backcountry information, where a scale model of the park facilitates route planning. They specialize in hikes from Yosemite Valley trailheads, but the staff here has extensive knowledge of the entire park. During the winter months when the Wilderness Center is closed, wilderness permits are issued at the Valley Visitor Center.
Big Oak Flat Information Station Hwy-120 West ☎209/379-1967; April to mid-Oct daily 8am–5pm. Handy when entering the park from the northwest.
Hetch Hetchy Entrance Station Mid-April to mid-Oct daily 9am–5pm or longer. On the road to Hetch Hetchy and specializing in that area.
Tuolumne Meadows Wilderness Center Mid-May to June & early Sept to mid-Oct daily 8am–5pm; July to early Sept daily 8am–5pm; closed in winter. High country wilderness permits from an office near *Tuolumne Lodge*.

Wawona Visitor Center ☎209/375-9531; mid-May to mid-Sept daily 8.30am–5pm. Wilderness permits in the southern reaches of the park. Self-register when closed.

Ranger stations in the surrounding national forests

Groveland Ranger Station 24545 Hwy-120 West, 8 miles east of Groveland ☎209/962-7825, ⓦwww.fs.usda.gov/Stanislaus; Mon–Sat 8am–4.30pm Sun 8am–3.30pm, winter closed Sat & Sun. Covers the Stanislaus National Forest.
Mariposa County Visitor Center Mariposa ⓦwww.fs.fed.us/r5/sierra. A good source of information on the Sierra National Forest, which occupies Yosemite's southwestern flank. For full contact details, see p.162.
Mono Basin Scenic Area Visitor Center Just north of Lee Vining ⓦwww.fs.usda.gov/inyo. Covers the Owens Valley on the eastern side of the Sierra, and the Inyo National Forest. For full contact details, see p.155.
Yosemite Sierra Visitors Bureau Oakhurst. Like the Mariposa Country Visitor Center (**see above**), this is good for info on the Sierra National Forest. For full contact details, see p.164.

Useful contacts

Delaware North Companies Parks & Resorts (DNC) lodging reservations ☎801/559-4884, tour reservations ☎209/372-1240, ⓦwww.yosemite park.com. Resource for everything run by the park concessionaire – hotels, restaurants, tours, shuttle buses, etc.
Recreation.gov ☎1-877/444-6777 or 518/885-3639, TTY ☎1-877/833-6777, ⓦwww .recreation.gov. Advance Yosemite campground reservations.
Wilderness Permits ☎209/372-0740, ⓦwww .nps.gov/yose/planyourvisit/wildpermits.htm. For obtaining permits for overnight stays in the backcountry.
YARTS ☎1-877/989-2787, ⓦwww.yarts.com. Handles bus transport into Yosemite Valley from Merced, Mariposa and Mammoth Lakes.
Yosemite National Park recorded info on ☎209/372-0200, ⓦwww.nps.gov/yose. Resource for everything managed by the Park Service.

Support groups and organizations

Sierra Club ☎415/977-5500, ⓦwww.sierraclub .org. America's most powerful outdoor recreation and conservation group, founded by John Muir in 1892 and still active in the park with members serving as interpreters at the LeConte Memorial (see p.67). **Yosemite Conservancy** ☎1-800/469-7275, ⓦwww.yosemiteconservancy.org. In 2010, two long-standing organizations – the Yosemite Association and the Yosemite Fund – joined forces to create the Yosemite Conservancy, an educational, nonprofit organization dedicated to supporting the national park. It offers field seminars, assists the Park Service in its interpretive programmes, and sells Yosemite-related books and interpretive material (ⓦwww.yosemiteconservancystore.com). Members (mostly volunteers) staff a number of places around the park – the Nature Center at Happy Isles and the Mariposa Grove Museum among them – and run book stores in the visitor centres. They are also devoted to funding conservation and preservation projects in the park – managing wildlife, restoring habitat, repairing trails, providing educational exhibits. When staying in park lodging you have the option to donate to the Fund's "Dollar-per-night" programme with a voluntary $1 a day added to your bill going straight to the Yosemite Conservancy.

Yosemite Institute (YI) ☎209/379-9511, ⓦwww.naturebridge.org/yosemite. A private nonprofit organization fostering understanding of the natural and cultural heritage of Yosemite through environmental education programmes for school groups and individuals. Operating since 1971, they offer residential field science programmes for child and adult groups, often tailored to accommodate specific needs.

Travellers with disabilities

The National Park Service goes to great lengths to ensure that as much as possible of the park and its facilities are open and accessible to all. Full **information** is available on a downloadable brochure, ⓦwww.nps.gov/yose/planyourvisit/upload /access.pdf.

The park waives the entrance fee for travellers with disabilities: those eligible for the **Access Pass** (see p.36) get in free along with any passengers in the same vehicle. The Pass also gives a fifty percent discount on many fee-charging services, along with camping (provide your pass number when reserving).

There are disabled parking spaces close to most lodging and restaurants, and drivers can obtain a **Temporary Accessibility Placard** (from entrance stations and visitor centres) allowing the holder to drive on some roads normally only open to hikers and cyclists. This is particularly helpful for getting to Mirror Lake and along the Happy Isles Loop Road. Assistance is available at park gas stations during business hours.

When you want to leave your car behind, use the Yosemite Valley **shuttle buses**, which are all equipped with wheelchair lifts and tie-downs. Should you need them, manual **wheelchair rental** ($7.50 an hour, $11 a day) is available from the *Yosemite Lodge* (see p.67), along with a tandem bike for the visually impaired ($9.50 an hour, $25.50 a day) and hand-cranked bikes ($9.50 an hour, $25.50 a day).

Outside Yosemite Valley, some of the buses used for the Tuolumne Meadows shuttle service have wheelchair lifts: ask the driver for details.

If you have the choice, plan your visit outside the peak season: if nothing else, you'll find rangers and park staff have more time to assist you. Whenever you come, give the Park Service and your lodging as much notice as possible of your arrival. The Park Service may well be able to provide someone to help interpret ranger programmes for the hard-of-hearing (☎209/372-0296 or TTY ☎209/372-4726), and DNC will be able to ensure accessible **lodging** is available (TTY ☎559/255-2846). For TTY **camping** reservations call ☎1-877/833-6777.

Consult *Yosemite Guide* when you arrive, as the paper indicates **ranger programmes** accessible to those in wheelchairs with assistance, and also summer-only events with a sign language interpreter. The *Spirit of Yosemite* film (see p.62) has closed captioning and can be viewed with audio descriptions with a headset available from the visitor centre nearby. While pets are discouraged in the park, suitably leashed **guide dogs** can be taken into all park buildings and on trails except for horse/ mule trails.

For communications, the Valley Visitor Center has a TTY phone for incoming **calls** (☎209/372-4726). For outgoing calls, TTY payphones can be found inside the *Yosemite Lodge* lobby, at the Valley Visitor Center and at *The Ahwahnee*. The **ATM** at the Art & Education Center is set up for Braille use and has a socket for a headset.

None of the **hikes** we've listed in the guide is completely wheelchair accessible, though several (hikes Y1 and Y43, for example) can be managed with assistance.

Vehicle repairs

The Village Garage in Yosemite Village has a 24-hour towing service, sells propane until 4pm and is open for repairs (daily 8am–5pm; ☎209/372-8320).

Weather

For current conditions and forecasts (including road conditions) in Yosemite call ☎209/372-0200, or check ⓦwww.nps .gov/yose/planyourvisit/conditions.htm). The

contacts for Sequoia/Kings Canyon are ☎559/565-3341, ⓦwww.nps.gov/seki/plan yourvisit/weather.htm.

Weddings and religious services

The park concessionaire DNC (☎801/559-5050) is well set up for helping you get hitched in Yosemite. Services can be held outside *The Ahwahnee*, on the lawns around the *Wawona Hotel* or in the historic chapel; then the hotels make excellent places for the reception, especially *The Ahwahnee*. **Religious services** are held for various faiths at locations around Yosemite Valley: consult *Yosemite Guide* for service times, call ☎209/372-4831, or visit ⓦwww .yosemitevalleychapel.org.

Yosemite and around

Yosemite and around

Yosemite Valley

I n the minds of many visitors Yosemite National Park is **Yosemite Valley**, a four-square-mile nugget of mesmerizing landscape that never fails to impress no matter how many times you've visited. Perhaps because the whole always seems greater than the sum of its parts, Ralph Waldo Emerson felt that it was "the only place that comes up to the brag about it, and exceeds it".

Along the valley's narrow cleft you'll find the densest concentration of stupendous cliffs and waterfalls, with the face of **El Capitan** standing sentinel over the western entrance to the valley, and **Half Dome** looking imperiously on a couple of miles to the east. In between, **Yosemite Falls** plummets over the lip of the valley rim in a double cascade, which together form the highest fall in the US. Opposite El Cap, delicate **Bridalveil Fall** wafts down to the glossy rocks below, and during the spring snowmelt just about every other cliff sprouts a waterfall for a few weeks.

Through it all runs the **Merced River**, which rises in the high country around Merced Lake to the east. The river expends much of its youthful vigour before entering Yosemite Valley, where it meanders among meadows – forcefully in spring, sluggishly in summer and fall. Placid lily-flanked pools offer picture-perfect reflections of the cliffs and waterfalls, while sharp curves harbour sandy beaches that shelve into the cool waters making perfect swimming spots or pull-out points for leisurely float trips. Along the banks, mule deer and black bears forage amid black oaks and incense cedars.

Millennia of rockfall from the surrounding cliffs have formed talus slopes, at the foot of which, over the last century and a half, people have built the infrastructure for year-round habitation. **Yosemite Village**, at the eastern end of the valley, is effectively Yosemite's capital, home to the main visitor centre, wilderness centre, the **Yosemite Museum** and **Indian Cultural Exhibit**, the **Yosemite Cemetery**,

---

Avoiding the summer crowds

Most of Yosemite National Park is free of **crowds** year-round, but a few hotspots – **Tuolumne Meadows**, **Wawona**, and especially **Yosemite Valley** – get very congested in summer. Though the crowds may be less dense than some would have you believe, your appreciation of the park will be enhanced by following these few pointers:

Start early Aim to visit the most popular sights, particularly Lower Yosemite Fall and Bridalveil Fall, before 9am, when the low-angled light brings out the best in the scenery, and wildlife is most active.

Get off the beaten path The vast majority of visitors never stray more than twenty minutes' walk from their car and only visit the most popular sights.

Stay out late The hour or so before sunset is usually spectacular; the "golden hour" is no time to be in a restaurant or your hotel room.

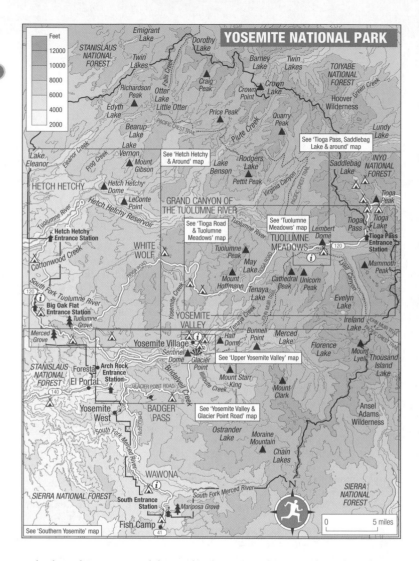

and a slew of restaurants and shops. There's accommodation nearby at the ordinary **Yosemite Lodge**, and the extraordinary **Ahwahnee**. Much of the rest of the accommodation is across the river on the southern, shaded side of the valley at **Curry Village**, with more places to eat and shop, and handy access to the family-friendly **Nature Center at Happy Isles**.

As it attracts the bulk of visitors, Yosemite Valley has the busiest **hiking** trails, some tracing the river gently along the valley floor, but most climbing steeply up the walls to the rim of the valley almost 3000ft above. Between these two extremes the many hikes from the popular **Happy Isles trailhead** step up in difficulty from one offering a distant view of Vernal Fall to the full-day blow-out to the summit of Half Dome.

With all the lodging, restaurants and the bulk of the trailheads concentrated at the eastern end of the valley, **getting around** is fairly easy. But with **Northside Drive** and **Southside Drive** (the main roads into and out of the valley) meeting in a confusion of one-way roads, you're better served by parking your vehicle and making extensive use of the free shuttle buses (see p.25).

El Capitan, Half Dome and the big cliffs

Everyone is stunned by their first view of Yosemite Valley, with the vertical grey walls of **El Capitan** and **Half Dome** dominating a wealth of magnificent granite architecture. A permanent backdrop to your time here, their constant presence grabs you every time you step out of a shop or restaurant, and continues to hold your attention with the shifting angles of sun and moon, ever-changing cloudscapes and, in winter, a heavy blanket of snow.

El Capitan

Whichever way you approach Yosemite Valley, your view will be blocked by **EL CAPITAN** (or *Tu-tok-a-nu-la* as it was known to the valley's native Ahwahneechee population), a vast monolith jutting forward from the adjacent

Ahwahneechee legends of Tu-tok-a-nu-la and Tis-sa-yak

To Yosemite's native Ahwahneechee people, El Capitan is known as **Tu-tok-a-nu-la**, or "measuring worm", after the chant of the inchworm that rescued two bear cubs. The story goes that in the time of the animal people, the two bear cubs slipped away from their mother and went for a swim in the river. Afterwards they dozed off on a flat rock nearby, and while sleeping the rock grew higher and higher up until the bear cubs scratched their faces on the moon. Their mother was distraught and asked her animal friends, but none had seen the cubs. Eventually the crane spotted them and all the animals rallied around to try and help. The field mouse, rat, fox, raccoon, mountain lion and all the other animals tried so hard to scale the slippery surface that their feet left dark scratches on the rock near its base. Still, none could make any progress until the inchworm fronted up. The other animals all laughed at his bravado, but off the little worm went, painstakingly making his way up the rock all the while chanting "Tu-tok, tu-tok, tu-tok-a-nu-la". The inchworm finally reached the summit, awoke the still-sleeping cubs and guided them back to the ground and safety. All were overjoyed, and to honour the inchworm they named the rock after his song.

At the other end of Yosemite Valley, equally dramatic mountain-forming was going on. A woman named **Tis-sa-yak** and her husband Nangas lived on the arid plains to the east, but had heard tell of the wonders of the valley of Ahwahnee. As they journeyed west, Tis-sa-yak carried a heavy basket of acorns and a baby carrier. Nangas followed with his bow and arrows. Tired, hungry and thirsty after the long journey, Nangas lost his temper and struck Tis-sa-yak who fled up the valley spilling acorns, which eventually grew into the oaks we see today. Reaching Mirror Lake, she drank it dry, which further enraged the thirsty Nangas who hit her again. The gods were greatly displeased and vowed to permanently separate them. When Tis-sa-yak was cornered by Nangas, she turned and flung the basket at him, at which moment they were turned to stone, she as Half Dome with the tears of remorse streaking her face, and he on the opposite side of the valley as Washington Column with Basket Dome above.

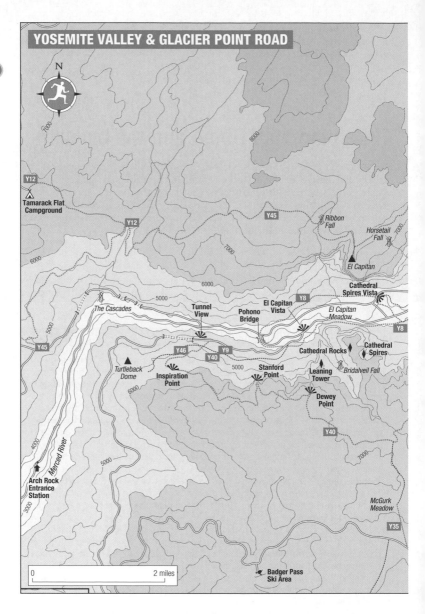

YOSEMITE VALLEY & GLACIER POINT ROAD

N

Tamarack Flat
Campground

Y12

Y12

Y45

Ribbon
Fall

Horsetail
Fall

El Capitan

The Cascades

Tunnel
View

Pohono
Bridge

El Capitan
Vista

Y8

Cathedral
Spires Vista

El Capitan
Meadow

Y8

Y45

Turtleback
Dome

Y46

Y40

Inspiration
Point

Y9

Stanford
Point

Cathedral Rocks

Cathedral
Spires

Leaning
Tower

Bridalveil Fall

Dewey
Point

Merced River

Y40

Arch Rock
Entrance
Station

McGurk
Meadow

Y35

0   2 miles

Badger Pass
Ski Area

cliffs and looming 3593ft above the valley floor. Though there are cliffs in Alaska, Canada's Baffin Island and Pakistan that are bigger, "The Captain" remains one of the largest pieces of exposed granite in the world, a full 320 acres of grey-tan rock. It is seemingly devoid of vegetation and is so sheer it's a wonder anyone ever considered climbing it let alone making it the holy grail of rock climbing worldwide. El Cap's enormous size isn't really apparent until you join the slack-jawed tourists craning their necks and training binoculars and

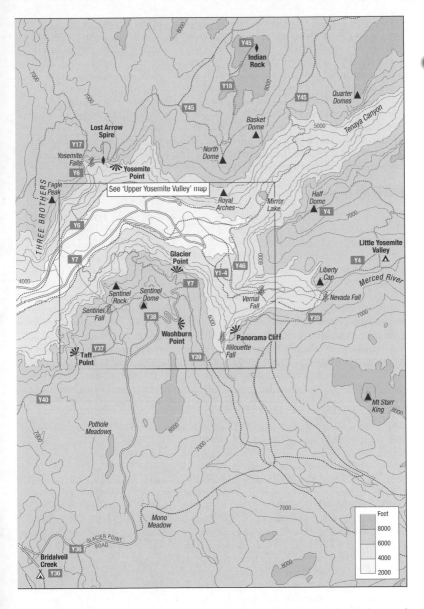

See 'Upper Yosemite Valley' map

cameras on the rock climbers on the face. Eventually you'll pick out flea-sized specks inching up what appears to be a flawless wall, though closer inspection reveals a pattern of flakes, fissures and small ledges. The most accessible sequences are connected by what is probably the most famous rock climbing route in the world, **The Nose**.

Straight on, El Cap looks almost flat, but it really has two principal faces that meet at The Nose to form a kind of prow. To the left is the **Salathé Wall**, distinguished by a massive heart-shaped indentation a third of the way up. To the right is the **North American Wall**, with its 1000ft-high patch of dark rock that looks remarkably like a map of North America. Follow it down to the bottom of the dark stain and you'll find El Cap's only significant vegetation, a 100ft **ponderosa pine** rooted in the cracks and hunkered under an overhang.

A long, thin pullout at the base of El Cap allows drivers to stop and gawp, while the adjacent **El Cap Meadows** are quite delicate and you're discouraged from walking out onto them (though few seem to take much heed). Geologists will tell you that El Cap formed in the same way as most of the granite around here, cooling slowly underground to leave a solid lump of hard rock, smoother and more uniform than rock found almost anywhere else. The Ahwahneechee offer a less prosaic explanation (see box, p.51).

Half Dome

Impressive though El Capitan is, for most people it is **HALF DOME** (*Tis-sa-yak*) that instantly grabs their attention. A stunning sight topping out at 8842ft, it rises almost 5000ft above the valley floor, smoothly arching from northeast to southwest but cut off on each side. Its 2000ft-high northwest face is only seven degrees off vertical, making it the **sheerest cliff in North America**. According to a member of the 1849 Walker Party, it "looked as though it had been sliced with a knife as one would slice a loaf of bread", and to English naturalist and adventurer, Joseph Smeaton Chase, it was a "frightful amputation".

It's easy to imagine that the "other half" of the dome was hewn away by a massive glacier, but actually it's faulting in the rock that is primarily responsible for its shape. The relatively young plutonic rock from which Half Dome is formed cooled slowly below ground under intense heat and pressure around a hundred million years ago, and in the latter phase of this process the basic half-dome took shape. Subsequent glaciers merely shifted away any debris from the base of the gradually crumbling face.

Ambitious hikers can make it to the shallow saddle of Half Dome's thirteen-acre summit and back in a day (see p.108). The final 400ft of the demanding ascent are tackled by way of a steep steel **cable staircase** hooked on to the rock's curving whale back. The first ascent of this route was made in 1875 by Scottish sailor and Yosemite Valley blacksmith, **George Anderson**, who spent a week drilling a series of eyebolt holes using home-made drill bits. Daubing his feet in pine pitch and grit to get better purchase on the smooth rock, he attached ropes as he went to afford protection on the 45-degree slope. Standing on one eyebolt as he drilled the next one higher up, he in effect became Yosemite's first technical climber. Andersons' pegs and ropes were upgraded to cables in 1919 using donations from the Sierra Club, and then replaced in the 1930s by the Civilian Conservation Corps as part of a Depression-busting work programme. This remained the only way to the top until climbers forged new routes from 1931 onwards.

Once at the summit, the brave can inch out towards the edge of the projecting lip for a vertiginous look straight down the near-vertical face. While the cables remain all year, the cable supports and wooden slats only stay in place from late May to mid-October, making a winter ascent extremely difficult. Keep clear of the summit if there are any signs of impending storms; lightning can occur at any time of year and Half Dome receives strikes during almost every thunderstorm. There have been fatalities.

Peaks and domes of the valley rim

The sheer scale and presence of El Capitan and Half Dome put everything else in their shadow, but part of what makes Yosemite Valley so stunning is the wealth of wildly striking **cliffs** and **spires**. Anywhere else these would be star attractions but here they're often relegated to a supporting role. As naturalist John Muir (see box, p.60) put it, "every attempt to appreciate any one feature is beaten down by the overwhelming influence of all the others".

The north side

Entering Yosemite Valley along Southside Drive, your best views are of the rock formations on the north side of the valley, dominated by El Capitan. To the right (east), the **Three Brothers** step in symmetry up the valley wall, triple gables which were given their name by John Boling, who led the second expedition of the Mariposa Battalion in 1851. The story goes that Boling had a brief to chase out the Ahwahneechee, but the tribe had got wind of his imminent arrival and made themselves scarce. They left behind five scouts who were subsequently captured just east of El Capitan. Three turned out to be sons of Ahwahneechee chief Tenaya, and Boling couldn't help but name the rocks the Three Brothers. Their individual names haven't stuck and we now simply have **Lower Brother**, **Middle Brother** and **Eagle Peak**, which at 7779ft tops the peaks along the north side.

After some more broken, lower-angled terrain you reach the sheer face bisected by Upper Yosemite Fall (see p.59), and to its right the **Lost Arrow Spire**. This

---

And the walls came tumbling down

Yosemite's robust granite accounts for the sheer verticality of the valley's cliffs, but no matter how hardy, the rock is not immune to gravity, and in the past 150 years over six hundred **rockfalls** have been recorded. Forces within the granite, and the levering effect of freezing and thawing in cracks and joints, gradually peel away the outer layers, often dramatically. Evidence is visible both on the valley floor and on its walls, where white patches are left by the detached rock, most of it originating over 2200ft up, above the scour line of the last glacier to come through Yosemite Valley some twenty thousand years ago.

One of the largest recorded rockfalls occurred in 1987 at **Middle Brother** when 1.4 million tons of rock broke loose, leaving a huge pile of talus right to the edge of Northside Drive. Signs still advise drivers not to stop along that section of road. Then, in 1996, a 500ft-long slab of granite arch cut loose from cliffs below Glacier Point. After sliding over a ledge an estimated 68,000 tons went into a 1700ft freefall before hitting the ground at 270mph, generating a huge blast of wind which uprooted trees in a huge arc, only just missing the Nature Center at Happy Isles. The scattered trees destroyed a nearby footbridge over the Merced River and everything was coated in a two-inch-thick layer of grey dust. One tree killed a hiker and a dozen were injured. In 1999 a climber was killed and tent cabins in Curry Village were damaged by rock sweeping down Glacier Point Apron, then in 2008 one ranger was killed and three Curry Village guests were slightly injured by falling rock. Since then, 233 cabins (around a third of the total) have been closed and are likely to be removed.

Records show that only fourteen people have lost their lives as a result of falling rock in Yosemite, but it always pays to be alert, especially below steep cliffs. Many rockfalls occur in spring, when there's plenty of water around and the daily freeze–thaw cycle is at its most destructive. Physical damage caused by recent rockfalls has alerted the Park Service to the less than prudent building policies of the past and informs much of the thinking behind the Yosemite Valley Plan (see p.236).

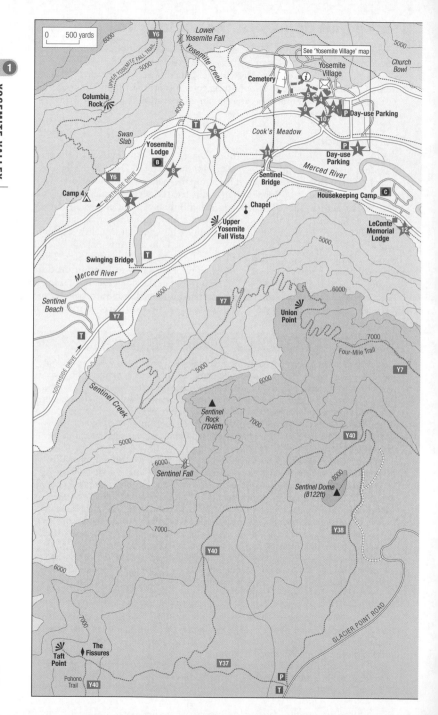

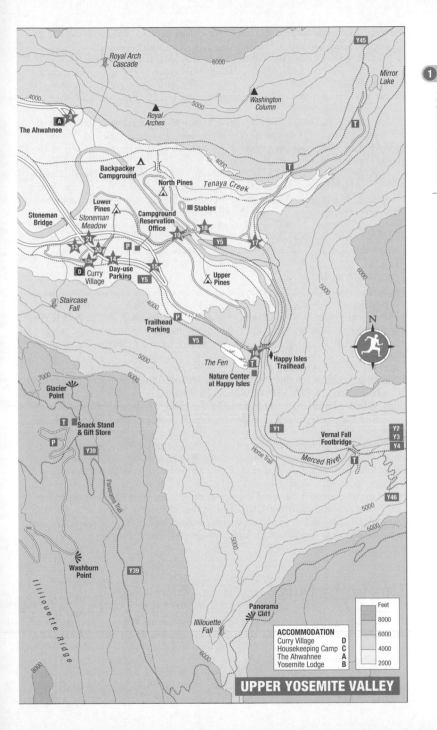

Royal Arch
Cascade

6000

Mirror
Lake

Washington
Column

4000

5000

Royal
Arches

The Ahwahnee   A

Backpacker
Campground

North Pines

Tenaya Creek

4000

Stables

Stoneman
Bridge

Lower
Pines

Stoneman
Meadow

Campground
Reservation
Office

19   18

Y5

17

13

20

21

6000

P

15

Y5

Curry
Village

D   13a

14

Day-use
Parking

Upper
Pines

Staircase
Fall

4000

5000

Trailhead
Parking

P

Y5

16

T

← Happy Isles
Trailhead

5000

The Fen

Nature Center
at Happy Isles

N

7000

Glacier
Point

6000

Snack Stand
& Gift Store

T

P

Y39

Y1

Vernal Fall
Footbridge

Y2
Y3
Y4

Panorama Trail

Horse Trail

Merced River

T

Y46

5000

6000

Washburn
Point

Y39

Illilouette Ridge

8000

Panorama
Cliff

Illilouette
Fall

6000

ACCOMMODATION
Curry Village   D
Housekeeping Camp   C
The Ahwahnee   A
Yosemite Lodge   B

Feet

8000
6000
4000
2000

UPPER YOSEMITE VALLEY

thousand-foot-high column is completely detached from the rock wall for its uppermost 200ft, forming a slender pinnacle, its summit almost level with the top of the cliff. Barely visible throughout the middle of the day, the pinnacle is only clearly revealed in the low-angled morning and afternoon sunlight when it casts a shadow against the cliff behind. Occasionally you'll see climbers making a spectacular Tyrolean traverse using ropes strung out in space to regain the cliff from the top of the spire.

Yet further east, behind *The Ahwahnee*, lie the **Royal Arches**, a series of rock bands against the cliff face that overhang in places like giant raised eyebrows. In spring **Royal Arch Cascade** streaks down the cliff to the left; for the rest of the year it's just a black smudge.

Above the Royal Arches swells the smooth hemisphere of the **North Dome** (7525ft), which seems to be kept from sliding off the valley rim by the rocky shoulder of **Washington Column**. Viewed from the south rim of the valley, this formation is supposed to resemble the profile of George Washington, though few can spot the likeness. Almost detached from the cliff, Washington Column stands where Yosemite Valley doglegs up Tenaya Canyon, forming an enduring buttress that provided an early test piece for 1930s climbers.

The south side

From Washington Column, **Tenaya Canyon** runs toward Tuolumne Meadows, its southeastern side almost entirely formed by the smooth mile-high sheet of rippled granite that sweeps up to the summit of **Clouds Rest**, at 9926ft the highest peak visible from Yosemite Valley. It got its name from the cloud perched over its summit when the valley was first visited by the Mariposa Battalion on March 28, 1851.

Moving back downstream, Half Dome looms large. It's separated from the rest of the valley cliffs by the Merced River, which sweeps down Merced Canyon over Nevada and Vernal falls (see p.61). West of the river, Curry Village hunkers 3000ft below **Glacier Point**, the two separated by a smooth, steeply angled quarter-cone of rock known as **Glacier Point Apron**, scene of major rockfalls in 1996 and 1999 (see box, p.55).

The next large geological feature is the 3000ft **Sentinel Rock**, a petrified watch-tower standing guard over the south side of Yosemite Valley. The texture of its fissured flat face catches the afternoon sun beautifully, especially when viewed from the Four-Mile Trail (Hike Y7, p.110) which climbs the valley wall to the west. Looming above is **Sentinel Dome**, casting its eye west past the overlook of **Taft Point** to the magnificent **Cathedral Spires** and **Cathedral Rocks**, directly opposite El Cap. Just around the corner is Bridalveil Fall, and above it, the **Leaning Tower**, a vast slab of rock overhanging by twenty degrees.

The waterfalls

If there's one star in the Yosemite firmament that shines brighter than the rock architecture it's the stupendous **waterfalls** that stream down the canyon walls. Several are among the highest in the country, and nowhere else in the world is there such a spectacular array of cascades concentrated in such a small area. Come **in spring** or early summer and the cascades will be at their snowmelt best, though many dry up by August or September, and after a mild winter some might not make it beyond July.

The highest is the spectacular **Yosemite Falls**, but **Bridalveil Fall, Ribbon Fall, Horsetail Fall** and **Sentinel Fall** are hardly less impressive, and the combination of them all streaming into Yosemite Valley beats any individual cascade. Tucked away up the Merced River canyon, **Vernal Fall** and **Nevada Fall** make up for in power what they lack in height.

Yosemite Falls

At 2425ft, **Yosemite Falls** (or *Cholok*, "the fall"; shuttle stop 6) is widely claimed as the fifth-highest in the world, and the highest in North America. It's a somewhat spurious assertion since it's actually two falls, separated by a couple of thousand feet of churning rapids and chutes known as **Middle Cascade** that drops a total of 675ft. Nonetheless, the 1430ft **Upper Yosemite Fall** and the 320ft **Lower Yosemite Fall** are magnificent, especially in May and early June when runoff from melting snow turns them into a foaming torrent. Cast your eyes up to the top where the water drops a short way (actually almost 100ft) then part of the flow hits a lip, forcing plumes of water out into space and breaking up the flow so even a gentle breeze fans it out over a broad expanse of the cliff. When the falls are at their most powerful, a steady breeze blows from the base of the lower fall, pushed along by the force of the air drawn down with the water. If you're in Yosemite at full moon in spring and early summer, be sure to head for the base of Lower Yosemite Fall by night, where the spray creates shimmering **moonbows**.

The flow typically dries up entirely by mid-August, but leaves a dark stain of algae and lichen to mark the spot. In winter the falls begin to flow again, but just enough to build up a 200–300ft **ice cone** of frozen spray and fallen blocks of ice at the base of the upper fall.

Of course, John Muir couldn't resist an ascent and reported it in *The Yosemite*:

Thus I made my way nearly to the summit, halting at times to peer up through the wild whirls of spray at the veiled grandeur of the fall, or to listen to the thunder beneath me; the whole hill was sounding as if it were a huge, bellowing drum. I hoped that by waiting until the fall was blown aslant I should be able to climb to the lip of the crater and get a view of the interior; but a suffocating blast, half air, half water, followed by the fall of an enormous mass of frozen spray from a spot high up on the wall, quickly discouraged me. The whole cone was jarred by the blow and some fragments of the mass sped past me dangerously near; so I beat a hasty retreat, chilled and drenched, and lay down on a sunny rock to dry.

The shuttle bus stops along Northside Drive at the start of a flat, quarter-mile, wheelchair-accessible asphalt trail which winds through the incense cedars and ponderosa pines to the base of the lower fall, where a bridge crosses Yosemite Creek – an area always crowded with video camera-wielding tourists and kids playing among the rocks.

In the middle of the forest, a side trail leads to a viewpoint of Lower Yosemite Fall created a century back by early hoteliers who hacked down a passage through the trees so that their guests could see the falls from the hotel.

Bridalveil Fall

Perhaps the most sensual waterfall in the park is the 620ft **Bridalveil Fall**, a slender ribbon at Yosemite Valley's western end, which in Ahwahneechee goes by the name of *Pohono* or "spirit of the puffing wind". While Bridalveil seldom completely dries up, it's best seen from April to June when winds blow the cascade outwards up to 20ft away from its base and draw the spray out into a delicate lacy veil. The spray-shrouded viewing platform near the base of the fall is at the end of

John Muir

John Muir was one of nature's most eloquent advocates, a champion of all things wild who spent ten years living in Yosemite Valley in the 1870s, and the rest of his life campaigning for its preservation. Born in Scotland in 1838, he had an austere upbringing which prepared him well for the life he chose. After his family moved to the United States when he was 11, he grew up in Wisconsin where he later worked as a mechanical inventor until, aged 27, he nearly lost an eye in an accident. The incident galvanized his desire to search for something outside the normal run of things. Noting in his diary, "All drawbacks overcome…joyful and free…I chose to become a tramp", he set off on a **thousand-mile trek** to the Gulf of Mexico by "the wildest, leafiest, and least trodden way" laden only with a New Testament, a volume of Keats' poems, Milton's *Paradise Lost* and a plant press. Dry bread and a twist of tea leaves were his sustenance, so he often slept hungry under the stars.

Arriving in Florida, he contracted malaria then spent time recuperating in Cuba. He then continued via Panama to California, supposedly for a short stay before doubling back to his real goal, South America. On arrival, he asked for "anywhere that is wild", and was pointed towards the Sierra; he is said to have shouted for joy when he first saw **Yosemite Valley**. So began months of camping and exploration with little more than a ragged blue notebook and a blanket. Often there was no particular destination since every path both posed questions and provided the answers, and every step was as rich as the last. Each night he'd chop down a few spruce branches for a bed then build a roaring fire to keep himself warm. Even in winter he'd be out, sometimes waking up under a mantle of snow. He later wrote "As long as I live, I will ever after hear waterfalls and birds and winds sing. I'll acquaint myself with the glaciers and wild gardens, and get as near to the heart of the world as I can".

In 1869 he spent the summer helping a shepherd **grazing sheep** in Tuolumne Meadows, a practice he soon learned to hate for the trampling damage their hooves caused to the delicate meadows. Later that year Muir moved to Yosemite Valley where he worked as a **sawmiller**, carpenter and part-time guide, living in a sugar pine shack he built himself. Unlike most of the valley's other residents, he stayed year-round, eschewing the wintertime comforts of the Bay Area in favour of the place that made him content. This, and his desire to spend every waking moment exploring the mountains and waterfalls, made him something of an eccentric and put him outside Yosemite's social circles. He was regarded as nothing more than a "mere sheepherder" by the literary and scientific cognoscenti who came in search of enlightenment. Only gradually did Muir's star rise, largely thanks to the unflagging promotion of his Oakland friend, Jeanne Carr. She dispatched Berkeley geologist **Joseph LeConte** to visit him, and word of Muir's intelligence and understanding of

an easy quarter-mile path from a parking lot four miles west of Yosemite Village. The shuttle bus doesn't go this far west, so unless you visit on the Valley Floor Tour (see p.28) you'll have to drive, cycle or come on foot.

Other falls

Come to Yosemite Valley in April or early May and you'll see numerous other falls, including the slender 1612ft **Ribbon Fall**, the highest single-drop waterfall in Yosemite (and indeed in North America). It tumbles down the cliffs to the west of El Capitan and with its small, low-lying catchment is always the first waterfall to dry up each spring.

Moving round to the eastern side of El Cap you'll have to be here in winter or early spring to catch the 1000ft **Horsetail Fall**, famous for its glowing display during any clear sunset for a few weeks in mid-February. As the last rays of the

Yosemite Valley gradually got out. Even his hero, essayist and poet Ralph Waldo Emerson, visited him and began to spread the word.

Muir dubbed the Sierra Nevada the **"Range of Light"**, and spent years developing his theory of how glaciers shaped the range. After Carr's constant imprecations, Muir quit his sawmill job in 1871 and began to write up some of his copious notes ensconced in *Black's Hotel* in the valley. His first article, *Yosemite Glaciers*, was printed in the *New York Tribune* later that year and subsequent pieces gradually won him academic acceptance. The classic journal-based books for which he is known today – especially *My First Summer in the Sierra* and *The Yosemite* – were written much later, but mostly tell of his exploits at this time.

It was November 1872 before Muir returned to the city for the first time, signalling a gradual weaning off Yosemite, though the Sierra never left his heart. He **married** Louie Wanda Strentzel, nine years his junior, in 1880 when he was almost 42. They lived in Martinez, northeast of Oakland, and had two children, Wanda and Helen. Though Muir was a loving father, it seems he wasn't there all that much, often disappearing for weeks into the Sierra, taking off to Alaska, visiting Europe or making trips to Asia.

Muir was desperate to protect his beloved landscape from the depredations of sheep grazing, timber cutting and homesteading, and through magazine articles and influential contacts goaded Congress into **creating Yosemite National Park** in 1890. To act as a kind of watchdog for the new national park, two years later he set up the **Sierra Club**, an organization whose motto "take only photographs; leave only footprints" has become a model for like-minded groups around the world.

From the mid-1890s Muir was increasingly spending his time writing his books, but in November 1903, President **Theodore Roosevelt** asked to meet Muir. The pair managed to slip Teddy's minders and spent four happy days camping rough in the high country. Suddenly Muir had a very powerful ally, one who set aside five more national parks during his term, though this wasn't enough to save Hetch Hetchy from being drowned (see box, p.79). Still, the publicity actually aided the formation of the present National Park Service in 1916, which promised – and has since provided – greater protection.

Muir finally visited South America at the age of 74, almost fifty years after California had waylaid him. He died in 1914, aged 76, an event some claim was hastened by his failure to save his beloved Hetch Hetchy.

Muir's name crops up throughout California as a memorial to this inspirational figure, not least in the 211-mile **John Muir Trail** which twists through his favourite scenery from Yosemite Valley south to Mount Whitney, and the **John Muir Wilderness**, California's largest, located southeast of Yosemite.

setting sun catch the cascade they create an ephemeral orange backlight that makes it looks like it's on fire. On the south side of Yosemite Valley, **Sentinel Fall** cascades off the valley rim beside Sentinel Rock, falling a total of 2000ft in a series of stairstep drops.

Two of the park's most striking falls are actually much shorter than these giants, and are guaranteed to be still active (though past their best) in September and October. Sequestered away from the road up the Merced River canyon, they can only be seen on foot from Happy Isles (see hikes Y1–4, beginning p.103). It's a relatively easy walk to get a distant glimpse of the 317ft **Vernal Fall**, a vertical curtain of water perhaps 80ft wide that casts bright rainbows as you walk along the wonderful Mist Trail. It requires much more commitment to hike steeply upstream as far as the 594ft **Nevada Fall**, but it's worth the effort for a close look at this sweeping cascade that drops vertically for half its height then fans out on the apron below.

Yosemite Village and around

Very much the heart of activity in the valley, **YOSEMITE VILLAGE** is not really a cohesive "village" at all, but a scattered settlement of low shingle-roofed buildings tucked away among the pines and black oaks where mule deer wander freely.

There wasn't much here at all until the 1930s when tastes changed and people decided they preferred the warm side of Yosemite Valley to the cool. Most hotels and shops were formerly on the shady south side of the valley close to the chapel, but virtually everything has now moved here.

Basically a service centre for visitors as well as a home for park employees, you'll find yourself returning time and again during your visit. Yosemite's **main visitor centre** is here along with shops, restaurants and cafés, banking facilities, internet access and a post office. Close to the visitor centre you'll also find the **Ansel Adams Gallery**, and beyond it the **Wilderness Center** (see p.44), essentially the visitor centre for backcountry hikers.

The other main centres of activity on this side of the valley are the restaurants and rooms at **The Ahwahnee**, half a mile to the east, and all manner of facilities at **Yosemite Lodge**, a similar distance west.

Valley Visitor Center

The first stop for most people is the **Valley Visitor Center** (daily: June–Sept 9am–7.30pm, Oct–May 9am–5pm or 6pm; ☎209/372-0299; shuttle stops 5 & 9), a single-storey river-stone building that is pretty much the hub of Yosemite Village. Besides having a good **bookshop**, this is your main source of visitor **information**, and though the staff are often at full stretch it's good for picking up maps, checking the weather forecast and learning about the week's ranger programmes. With a brief to help interpret Yosemite, the centre gives a quick overview of the park by means of an excellent relief map of Yosemite Valley, followed by displays on geology, flora, fauna and the people who have populated the place. Run your finger over examples of the different types of granite found throughout the park, learn about the role of fire, and cast your eyes at photos of early inhabitants and the explorers and entrepreneurs who quickly replaced them. Hagiographic treatment is awarded to key players such as Galen Clark, Ansel Adams and David Brower.

Save time for the free 23-minute film *Spirit of Yosemite* (Mon–Sat 9.30am–4.30pm or later, Sun noon–4.30pm or later), which screens every half-hour in the West Auditorium, immediately behind the visitor centre. Expensively made and with a somewhat overblown commentary, it's still well worth seeing for the great images of the park through the seasons.

Hikes from Yosemite Village and Curry Village

Yosemite's **fifty best hikes** are covered in chapters 4 and 5. For our coverage of **day hikes** from Yosemite Village and Curry Village see hikes Y1–Y7 (from p.103), and for **overnight hikes** see hikes Y46 and Y47 (from p.134). These trails are among the busiest in the park, so hike early, late, or out of season if you want to avoid too much company.

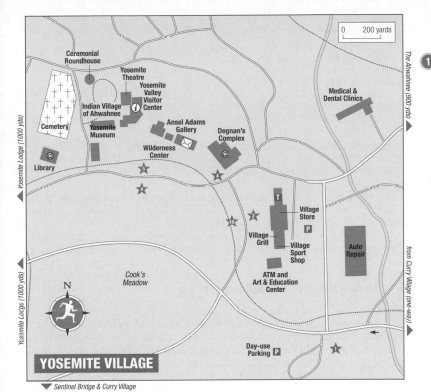

0   200 yards

The Ahwahnee (900 yds)

Medical & Dental Clinics

Ceremonial Roundhouse

Yosemite Theatre

Yosemite Valley Visitor Center

Indian Village of Ahwahnee

Yosemite Museum

Ansel Adams Gallery

Degnan's Complex

Wilderness Center

Cemetery

Library

Village Store

Village Grill

Village Sport Shop

Auto Repair

Cook's Meadow

ATM and Art & Education Center

from Curry Village (one-way)

Yosemite Lodge (1000 yds)

Yosemite Lodge (1000 yds)

N

Day-use Parking

YOSEMITE VILLAGE

▼ Sentinel Bridge & Curry Village

Yosemite Museum

Immediately west of the visitor centre is the two-storey **Yosemite Museum** (daily 9am–5pm; free; shuttle stops 5 & 9), its entrance flanked by a cedar-bark tipi and a hefty 9ft **slice of a giant sequoia**, the rings suitably marked with significant dates going back to its sapling days in 923 AD. The museum's small but diverting collection of artefacts focuses on Native American heritage, specifically the local Ahwahneechee and their neighbours, the Mono Lake Paiute, with whom they traded and sometimes intermarried.

The objects on display illustrate the tribes' way of life and how it has changed since their first encounters with whites in the 1850s. There's little mention of the abominable way they were treated, with the exhibits instead concentrating on **basketwork**, one of the few crafts to flourish post-contact. Fine examples include a superbly detailed 1930s Mono Lake Paiute basket almost 3ft in diameter which took close to three years to make, and its even larger Miwok/Paiute equivalent painstakingly created by the celebrated basketmaker Lucy Telles. She appears with her basket in a photo next to a cabinet of more of her work. The intricate patterns of chevrons, red squares and black triangles were traditionally fashioned from sedge root and bracken fern root around a willow frame, and similar techniques are demonstrated by Ahwahneechee artisans throughout the day.

A couple of **feather-trimmed dance capes** also warrant a look, as does the buckskin dress worn by natives in the 1920s and 1930s during demonstrations of basket-weaving and dance. Though completely alien to the Miwok tradition, the

Plains-style buckskin clothing and feather headdresses fulfilled the expectations of the whites who came to watch. Kids will enjoy being able to touch samples of animal fur native to the region, and can learn how to play Miwok stick and dice games.

The white man's history is remembered through an immensely detailed hotel **guest register** from the long-gone *Stoneman House* hotel, which operated from 1887 to 1896 near the current site of Curry Village.

At the entrance to the museum there's a store (see p.200) selling finely wrought native crafts and jewellery, and upstairs hides a good research library (see p.38).

Indian Village of Ahwahnee

Wander through the Yosemite Museum (or, when closed, around its western side) to join a self-guided trail through the **Indian Village of Ahwahnee** (always open; free), a compact reconstruction of a Miwok village built in the 1920s as a venue for native dances on the former site of the largest native village in Yosemite Valley. An explanatory booklet available on site (*The Miwok in Yosemite*; 50¢) is rendered somewhat redundant by numerous signs describing the buildings and the uses of various plants such as black-oak acorns, which were ground into flour on a pounding rock and later made palatable by several washings to leach out the tannin. In the villages of all Sierra Indians the **acorn granary** was an essential repository of the principal source of carbohydrates. The granary here exhibits the usual features: high to keep it away from animals and bark-sheltered to keep the acorns dry.

The focal point of the Indian Village is its largest building, the semi-subterranean **ceremonial roundhouse** built in 1992 to replace a 1970s model. You can only peer into the gloomy interior, almost 50ft across and crowned with a low-pitched cedar-bark roof that is of a design common in the post-contact period. The roundhouse is still used for ritual purposes by local Ahwahneechee throughout the year, as is the working **sweathouse** built in 1989 just behind the roundhouse. Traditionally used to rid hunters of human odours before a hunt, it's heated by an oak fire with each hunter spending a couple of hours inside before ritually bathing then rubbing down with scented bark and brush to disguise any remaining smells.

Along with a few traditional bark shelters, there's a Miwok cabin exhibiting strong Euro-American influence, which illustrates how native builders often had to make do with poorer or scavenged materials, building directly on the ground with a central fire pit and smoke hole in the roof. There are plans to improve the interpretation of the lives of Yosemite's native people but as yet it remains undecided whether this will be on the existing "village" site or west of the *Camp 4* campground on the site of the last Ahwahneechee settlement in Yosemite Valley.

Edging out the Ahwahneechee

The **Ahwahneechee**, a subtribe of the Southern Miwok people, have to some degree occupied Yosemite Valley for three thousand years, gathering acorns and trading them for obsidian arrowheads. While three dozen inhabited sites have been identified, it's thought that there were seldom more Ahwahneechee here at any one time than the few hundred discovered by the Mariposa Battalion when they entered Yosemite Valley in 1851. Many members of the tribe were killed trying to escape capture, and the rest were temporarily bundled off to a reservation in California's Central Valley before being allowed to gradually filter back to Yosemite. Claims that the Ahwahneechee had signed away their land were never upheld, but the tribe became fragmented and marginalized in the increasingly white valley. After the formation of the Park Service in 1916, the Indians became a sideshow, providing visitor entertainment disguised as cultural revival, and designer basket-making flourished.

Behaviour that the rangers deemed to be unacceptable was punished, and unsanitary living standards were used as an excuse to re-house natives away from their traditional villages. By the late 1920s the Ahwahneechee had been confined to one large village near the foot of Yosemite Falls; nevertheless a new park superintendent sought their virtual eviction. Those whose claims to residency couldn't be denied eventually settled in cramped new cabins constructed west of *Camp 4* in the early 1930s. By the 1950s, only those with permanent jobs in the park could stay, and in 1969 the last remaining residents were re-housed once again and the village razed. A few Ahwahneechee still live in government housing in the park (some working as interpreters at the museum and Indian Village), but most live outside, returning primarily for ceremonial occasions.

Yosemite Cemetery

Anyone interested in Yosemite's history, or simply drawn to graveyards, should visit the **Yosemite Cemetery** (always open; free), fifty yards west of the Yosemite Museum. A peaceful spot in the shade of oaks and incense cedars, it holds some three dozen graves, including a few poorly marked Ahwahneechee burial sites. The better-marked graves are all of early white settlers who attempted to farm Yosemite Valley, and often died in its isolation. Most of the headstones, dating back to the mid-1800s, are identified by horizontal slabs of rock, some etched with crude or faded writing. Notables include **James Lamon**, who died in 1875 after establishing what is now known as Curry Orchard (an apple orchard which still bears fruit in the Curry Village), and Yosemite's first guardian, **Galen Clark** (1814–1910), whose grave is marked by an irregular hunk of granite with his name and dates inscribed on one smooth, weathered face. Clark honoured Lamon by planting a sequoia beside his grave, then selected half a dozen sequoia saplings for his own resting place. Altogether five sequoias survive, though none is especially large. The visitor centre stocks the detailed *A Guide to the Yosemite Cemetery* (see "Books", p.251).

Ansel Adams Gallery

Anyone with even the slightest interest in **photography** should devote some time to the **Ansel Adams Gallery** (daily: June–Aug 9am–6pm, Sept–May 9am–5pm; Ⓦ www.anseladams.com; free; shuttle stops 4, 5 & 9), which specializes in the work of the world-renowned photographer. Originally known as Best's Studio, this is the park's oldest concession-holder, owned by Harry Cassie Best who first set up shop as a landscape painter in the Old Village below Sentinel Rock in 1902. Ansel Adams used to drop by to practise the piano but eventually his interests shifted to Best's daughter, Virginia, whom he married in 1928. By the 1930s the business had relocated to its current site and as Adams became more famous it eventually took his name. It's still in family hands, run by Ansel and Virginia's grandson, Matthew.

Understandably, the gallery specializes in work by Adams, from postcards, calendars and photographic books to posters (from $30) and high-grade photographic prints ($225 for a 10in by 8in unframed image), produced by Alan Ross, a disciple of Adams who's been printing his work since the 1970s. Adams' successors are also represented, and there's usually a display of prints by some notable landscape photographer currently working in the field. The gallery also has a healthy selection of outdoors and ecology-based books on the Sierra and the greater American West, as well as a reasonable choice of novels. Photographers' needs are also catered for (see p.199) with equipment and film sales plus free group photography lessons.

The Ahwahnee

Heading east from Yosemite Village you soon leave the bustle behind, the pace calming appreciably as you approach the sedate confines of **The Ahwahnee**, the park's most distinguished hotel – worth a visit even if your budget doesn't stretch to staying in the plush rooms, dining in the restaurant (see p.187) or sipping a cocktail in the bar (see p.187). It's a pleasant ten-minute walk from the village, or a short shuttle ride (stop 3); once there, free hour-long **tours** (see p.195 for times) introduce you to the hotel's history, architecture and its role in the national park.

Standing an imposing six storeys above the meadows below the Royal Arches, this National Historic Landmark is definitely the most architecturally successful building in Yosemite Valley: a harmonious synthesis of a grand European hotel and a backwoods cabin, built in 1927 to attract wealthy tourists, something it still does fairly effortlessly. Over the years royalty, heads of state and film stars have graced the hotel with their presence, including JFK, Greta Garbo and Queen Elizabeth II.

A young Los Angeles architect named **Gilbert Stanley Underwood** was instructed to make the hotel blend into the valley – something achieved by making the building a third of the size of the original specification, and by staining and wood-graining the cast concrete to make the exterior look like huge redwood beams.

Inside, amid the stately baronial-style common areas on the ground floor, the finest room is the **Great Lounge**, hung with grand chandeliers, and bookended by matching fireplaces large enough to live in (and blazing in winter). As with most of the hotel, the lounge is decorated with Native American motifs, Miwok basketware, and some wonderful rugs and oriental carpets. French doors open both sides to let in the summer breeze, and the sofas are a perfect place to relax, especially at 4pm when tea and cookies are served for guests to piano accompaniment. If you think the room looks familiar, it was used as the model (though not the actual location) for the interiors of the *Overlook Hotel* in Stanley Kubrick's *The Shining* – coincidentally, exterior shots of the film's haunted hotel are of Oregon's famed *Timberline Lodge*, another of Gilbert Stanley Underwood's designs.

At the southern end of the Great Lounge, the Solarium opens out to the grounds, and provides access to the **Mural Room** with its frieze of forest plants and animals, and the **Winter Club Room**, where old photos of skiing, ski-jumping and tobogganing line the walls. Back in the lobby, look out for the delicate Yosemite watercolours by Swede Gunnar Widforss.

Through the quieter seasons of the year *The Ahwahnee* continues to lure well-heeled guests for special events based on gormandizing, imbibing and general revelry (see p.196). You don't have to stay at *The Ahwahnee* to attend most of the events, but to overnight elsewhere would undermine the spirit of the whole occasion: accommodation packages are generally available through the park concessionaire, DNC: check on ⓦwww.yosemitepark.com under "Special Events" and see p.172 for general information on **staying** here.

Yosemite Lodge

A fair proportion of Yosemite Valley's visitors find themselves staying west of Yosemite Village at **Yosemite Lodge** (officially *Yosemite Lodge at the Falls*; shuttle stop 8), built on the site of a US cavalry post which operated from 1906 to 1914. Some of the barracks were soon converted for use as a hotel (which opened in 1915) and several original buildings remained until the 1950s. All you see now is a fairly modern complex of low buildings, open year-round with 245 rooms, a couple of restaurants, a bar, grocery and gift shops, tour desk, a public swimming pool, a post office, bike rental and an outdoor amphitheatre used for slide shows and presentations (nightly in summer). All this is very convenient if you're staying here or across the road at the *Camp 4* campground, but otherwise you may only come here to visit the *Mountain Room Restaurant*, the bar or, perhaps, one of the ranger programmes at the amphitheatre. For more information on staying at Yosemite Lodge, see Accommodation, p.173.

Curry Village and eastern Yosemite Valley

At some point, everyone finds themselves at the eastern end of Yosemite Valley, either to hike the **Mist Trail**, explore the **Nature Center at Happy Isles**, stroll to **Mirror Lake** or visit the **stables** (see p.143). For many Yosemite visitors this is also "home", as the main campgrounds are here along with the permanent cabins of *Housekeeping Camp* and the tent cabin complex of **Curry Village**. The main **Southside Drive** runs through the area and is plied by frequent **shuttle buses** that always run to Curry Village and the campgrounds, and from early April to late October also make a loop past Happy Isles and the Mirror Lake trailhead.

LeConte Memorial Lodge

From the southern side of Sentinel Bridge, Southside Drive runs along a narrow strip between the foot of cliffs and the Merced River to *Housekeeping Camp* (see "Accommodation", p.173). Across the road is the **LeConte Memorial Lodge** (May–Sept Wed–Sun 10am–4pm; free; ⓣ209/372-4542, ⓦwww.sierraclub.org /leconte; shuttle stop 12), a small, rough-hewn, granite-block structure where the **Sierra Club** maintains displays on the Club's history, runs a conservation library and has a corner for kids with books and educational games. There's also a fascinating relief map of Yosemite Valley dating back to around 1885, and changing displays on topics relevant to the work of the Sierra Club. Their evening programmes (usually Fri–Sun; free) are a little more highbrow than those elsewhere in the park and might include a slide show or talk by some luminary: check *Yosemite Guide* for details.

Ansel Adams

Few photographers have stamped their vision on a place as unforgettably as **Ansel Adams** has done with Yosemite Valley. He worked all over the American West, but it is here that he did much of his most celebrated work: icons of American landscape photography such as 1944's *Clearing Winter Storm*; *Jeffrey Pine, Sentinel Dome* from the following year; and *Moon and Half Dome* from 1960.

Adams once said "Sometimes I think I do get to places just when God's ready to have somebody click the shutter", but this ignores the years he spent toting his 10in x 8in view camera – and forty pounds of tripods, filters, lenses and glass plates – up Yosemite's steep gullies, and days spent waiting for that perfect moment. For some, Adams' images are dispassionate, perhaps too perfect and naïve for the modern world, and seemingly at odds with their creator, a man whom one critic described as "as friendly, twinkle-eyed, excitable, and enthusiastic as a warm puppy".

Born in 1902 into a moderately wealthy San Francisco family, Adams was given his first camera – a Box Brownie – when he was fourteen, on his first trip to Yosemite. Though classically trained as a concert pianist, he claimed that he knew his "destiny" on that first visit to Yosemite. His mother pleaded "Do not give up the piano! The camera cannot express the human soul!" to which Adams replied "Perhaps the camera cannot, but the photographer can." Soon he turned his attentions to the mountains, returning every year and taking up a job as custodian of the Sierra Club headquarters.

He first made his mark in 1927 with *Monolith, The Face of Half Dome*, his first successful **visualization**. Adams believed that before pressing the shutter, the photographer should have a clear idea of the final image and think through the entire photographic process, considering how lenses, filters, exposure, development and printing need to be used to achieve that visualization. This approach may seem obvious today, but compared to the hit-and-miss methods of the time, it was little short of revolutionary. Visualization was made easier by applying the **zone system** of exposure calculation which, though not new, was codified and promoted by Adams as the basis for his teaching. This blend of art and science divides the range of possible tones into ten zones, each given Roman numerals, from velvet black (I) through middle grey (V) to pure white (X), and allows precise tone control, something Adams felt was key to full expression through photography. This also marked Adams' transition from a nineteenth-century pictorial approach – soft focus and middle tones characterized by the desire to emulate painting – to a cleaner, more modernist "straight photography".

In 1932 Adams joined forces with like-minded photographers such as Edward Weston and Imogen Cunningham to form **Group f/64**, which was soon criticized for being out of step with the social documentary photography fashionable in the class-conscious aftermath of the stock market crash. French photographer Henri

---

The Lodge itself was built by the Sierra Club in 1903 to commemorate one of its founding members, **Joseph LeConte** (1823–1901), who had died in Yosemite Valley and had expressed a wish to be buried there, but his relatives felt the family plot in Oakland was more appropriate. An eminent geologist, Le Conte was an early supporter of John Muir's glaciation theory on the creation of the Yosemite Valley.

Originally constructed in Camp Curry, where it served as the valley's first visitor centre and marked the northern terminus of the John Muir Trail, the Lodge was rebuilt to the original design (and fitted with the existing steep-pitched Tudor roof) in its current location in 1919. As the Sierra Club's Yosemite headquarters, it was managed for a couple of summers in the early 1920s by **Ansel Adams**, who was happy to do anything if it meant he could spend more time in Yosemite Valley.

Cartier-Bresson later declared "The world is going to pieces and people like Adams and Weston are photographing rocks." Adams held to his belief that the primal aspects of the earth had as much value as photographing breadlines, though that didn't stop him sensitively photographing Japanese Americans in internment camps during World War II.

As Adams fine-tuned his artistic theories through the 1930s, the idea of photography as fine art was still considered novel. Adams was therefore delighted when, in 1940, he was made vice chairman of the newly established **Department of Photography** at New York's Museum of Modern Art (MoMA). There was still very little money in photography and Adams continued to take commercial assignments, often producing promotional shots for the Yosemite Park and Curry Company and menu photos for *The Ahwahnee*. Commercial and personal work through the 1940s and 1950s earned Adams an ever wider audience. While still demanding the highest standard of reproduction, he had now tempered his perfectionism and allowed his work to appear on postcards, calendars and posters. By now, Adams was virtually a household name and for the first time in his life – in his early seventies – he began making money to match his status as the grand old man of Western photography.

His final triumph came in 1979, when MoMA put on the huge "Yosemite and the Range of Light" exhibition, which won him a *Time* magazine cover story. That same year, he was asked to make an official portrait of President Jimmy Carter – the first time a photographer had been assigned an official presidential portrait – and was subsequently awarded the nation's highest civilian honour, the Medal of Freedom.

Throughout his life, Adams had another great passion, one that he pursued with the same fervour as photography: **conservation**. Back in 1932, the artist had a direct hand in creating Kings Canyon National Park. Two years later he became a director of the **Sierra Club**, a position he held until 1971, overseeing several successful environmental campaigns. He never quit campaigning for the cause of conservation, and, after an interview in which he suggested he'd like to drown Ronald Reagan in his own Martini, agreed to meet the president to promote the environmental cause.

In his final years, Adams tired of printing the same old "greatest hits" and devoted his time to producing master sets of his best work for selected museums and galleries, and writing his autobiography. He died on April 22, 1984, aged 82, and has since become even more honoured. The mountain which had been widely known as Mount Ansel Adams since 1933 now bears that name officially, and a huge chunk of the High Sierra south of Yosemite National Park is known as the Ansel Adams Wilderness.

Curry Village

After Yosemite Village, the park's largest concentration of visitor facilities is at **CURRY VILLAGE** (shuttle stops 13, 13a, 13b, 14, 20 & 21), a rambling area of canvas tent cabins and wooden chalets centred on a small complex of restaurants, shops, pay showers and an outdoor amphitheatre hosting ranger programmes and evening shows. There's also a winter ice rink, a rock climbing school, bike rental and a kiosk renting rafts for use on the nearby Merced River.

The "village" is the direct descendant of **Camp Curry**, which was established in 1899 by David and Jeannie Curry, who were keen to share their adopted home in Yosemite Valley and charged just $12 a week for a "good bed, and a clean napkin

The Firefall

Hard to believe now, but for decades local hoteliers struggled to lure tourists to Yosemite Valley, even trying toboggan rides near Curry Village and organized bear feeding at the open dump in Church Bowl. From the beginning of the twentieth century to the late 1960s, the biggest draw was the spectacular **Firefall**, which took place every summer evening (and a couple of times a week in winter) at the end of Camp Curry's evening entertainment programme.

As the music and vaudeville acts went through their routines, guests gazed up at Glacier Point, 3200ft above, where a **fire** made from ten barrow-loads of red fir bark could be seen lighting the night sky. As the show drew to a close, the stentorian voice of camp owner David Curry would boom out "Hello Glacier! Is the fire ready?" The faint reply of "The fire is ready!" would waft back down, and at Curry's instruction "Let the Fire Fall!" the smouldering pile of embers would be raked over the cliff to create a **thousand-foot fiery cascade** that seemed to fall almost directly on the guests (but actually landed harmlessly on a ledge). The Firefall, accompanied by a solo rendition of *The Indian Love Call* or *America, the Beautiful*, always took place at exactly 9pm, though one night in the early 1960s the proceedings were delayed for half an hour while President Kennedy finished his drink at *The Ahwahnee*.

The event was so popular that spectacle-seekers crossed counties, clogged Yosemite Valley roads, and trampled meadows to stake out the best vantage points. Though the cinders never caused a serious fire, the Firefall was eventually deemed inappropriate for a national park; the last one took place on January 25, 1968. Talk to older park visitors who grew up with the Firefall and you'll uncover a deep fondness for the spectacle. A sense of what it was like can be gleaned from a presentation that forms part of Tom Bopp's "Vintage Songs of Yosemite" show (see p.198), or seek out the 1954 Humphrey Bogart flick, *The Caine Mutiny*, which features a seven-second sequence.

every meal". Their first six guests stayed in tents below Glacier Point, but amenities soon improved with a dance hall, tennis courts, croquet lawns, and evening entertainment which culminated in the **Firefall** (see box above). Through the Currys' daughter, Mary Curry Tressider, the business stayed in family hands until 1970 but is now run by the park concessionaire.

The village isn't a place for sightseeing, though you can wander through the ageing apple trees of **Curry Orchard**, planted in the 1860s by Yosemite Valley's first year-round white resident, James Lamon, on a site that now serves as the Curry Village parking lot. The trees are past their best, but they still bear fruit that is collected by volunteers so it doesn't attract bears to the area. Further sites of historic interest are visited on the **Legacy of Curry Village** trail, a half-hour stroll around Curry Village's precincts past signs explaining the likes of the Firefall and the old toboggan run.

Nature Center at Happy Isles

Throughout the summer, shuttle buses continue from Curry Village along a car-free loop around the very eastern end of Yosemite Valley. First stop is the **Nature Center at Happy Isles** (early May to mid-Sept daily 10am–4pm or longer; free; shuttle stop 16), a modern, river-stone and cedar-shingle building amid the pines on the site of a 1927 trout hatchery. It houses the most **family-friendly** set of displays in the valley, and is the base for the park's Junior Ranger Program, aimed at kids aged 7–13 (see p.198). Highlights include a mock-up section of forest that comes complete with stuffed examples of animals that make

Yosemite their home – woodpeckers, owls, a coyote, a porcupine, pine martens, flying squirrels, a raccoon, even a mountain lion perched on a rock as though waiting to pounce. Hands-on exhibits allow you to touch the casts of animal footprints and feel how hunks of rough granite get weathered to river pebbles and eventually sand. There's also an "After Dark" section with a diorama featuring the animals that make up the Yosemite night shift, and an exhibit on a year in the life of a bear.

At the rear of the Nature Center, be sure to check out the **rockfall exhibit** (unrestricted entry) where a number of explanatory panels highlight the pulverized rock and flattened trees that resulted from the 1996 rockfall (see box, p.55). The air blast laid waste to everything up to the viewing spot, but already large bushes are beginning to recolonize the talus slope, now barely visible behind the new-growth trees. Short trails nearby explore the various ecosystems around about – riparian, forest, talus and fen.

Towards the Merced River, a couple of bridges lead out to the **"Happy Isles"** themselves, a string of three wooded islets first described in 1885 by Yosemite guardian W. E. Dennison: "No one can visit them without for the while forgetting the grinding strife of this world and being happy". A bit optimistic perhaps but hanging out at the swimming holes on a hot summer's afternoon is certainly very relaxing.

Five minutes' walk away, on the eastern side of the Merced River by the road bridge, lies Yosemite Valley's most important trailhead. From here the **Mist Trail** (see Hike Y2, p.106) heads up to Vernal Fall, the **Half Dome Trail** (see Hike Y4, p.108) continues to the summit of Half Dome, and the **John Muir Trail** (see Hike Y46, p.134) spurs off to the Tuolumne high country.

Mirror Lake

The lure of Half Dome reflected in the glassy waters of Tenaya Creek makes **Mirror Lake** (*Ahwiyah*, or "quiet water") one of Yosemite's most popular sights, approached along a flat, mile-long footpath from shuttle stop 17. Really just a wide spot in a stream, Mirror Lake is subject to seasonal variations and is best visited in spring and early summer when it's nearly bursting its banks. May is particularly spectacular with the dogwood blooms at their best, and reflected in this compellingly calm pool.

Long thought of as a lake in the process of turning into a meadow, ecologists now consider Mirror Lake a pool in a seasonal stream. Either way, there is little, if any, water left by August or September, but it's pleasant enough just wandering or biking along the broad asphalt path to admire the woods or gaze at the wondrous rock formations all around. Find the right spot and you can photograph Half Dome reflected in its meditative stillness – an uplifting sight to behold.

The lake's moneymaking potential was spotted early on and a toll road was installed here in the 1860s. A decade later there was a boathouse beside the lake, an inn and even a dance pavilion built out over the water. To raise the water level and improve the boating, the natural rock dam was built and the bottom dredged, a practice not halted until 1971. The area is now free from the trappings of early entrepreneurial ventures, but the self-guided **Mirror Lake Interpretive Trail** helps you identify the site of the dance pavilion and the location of an icehouse used to store winter-harvested ice for the summer demand. There's also extensive coverage of Native American use of the area, including the harvesting of bracken fern for the black elements in basketware.

Exploring the Yosemite Valley loop road

The matchless beauty and variety of Yosemite Valley can't be fully appreciated from the developed areas around Yosemite Village and Curry Village, and you really need to explore further either on foot or along the road system. Two roads make up an eleven-mile one-way loop through the valley, with the westbound **Northside Drive** hugging the base of El Capitan and the Three Brothers, and the eastbound **Southside Drive** running parallel below Bridalveil Fall and Sentinel Rock. Set aside half a day, allowing time to take photos, have a picnic lunch in some sylvan spot beside the Merced River, or hike the western end of the valley by following Hike Y8 (see p.111).

Northside Drive

Northside Drive heads west from Yosemite Village, initially along a two-way road with the open expanse of **Cook's Meadow** on the left and, on the right, regenerating **black oak woodland** blocking views towards **Lower Yosemite Fall**, indicated by wayside marker V3 (see box opposite). Immediately beyond the Lower Yosemite Fall (shuttle stop 6) and *Yosemite Lodge* you pass the *Camp 4* walk-in campground and the Upper Yosemite Fall trailhead (V5), followed half a mile on by **Rocky Point** (V6), a mountain of boulders left by a major rockfall in 1987 (see box, p.55).

Drive on for a mile and a half to reach **Devil's Elbow**, a loop in the Merced River where the bank is being restored after the area was reclaimed from its earlier role as a parking lot. An unobtrusive cedar-rail fence keeps visitors back from the river bank while regeneration of native willows and cottonwoods gets under way. At either end of the restoration area there are sandy **beaches**, good for swimming once the spring snowmelt abates. Opposite is the appropriately named **Cathedral Spires Vista** pullout, and a short trail leading to the base of El Capitan where climbers begin their multi-day ascents.

It's just a few hundred yards further to **El Capitan Bridge** (a possible return route over the Merced River to Yosemite Village) and **El Capitan Meadow** (V8), an open field with stupendous views of El Capitan itself (see p.51), which towers above, and Cathedral Spires across the valley. Walking on the meadow is discouraged as it's becoming heavily impacted from thousands of people keen to spy on El Cap climbers. At the western end of the meadow you can still pick out the abandoned route of **Old Big Oak Flat Road**, a very early toll road that climbs the valley wall to the west.

Another quarter-mile on, the road suddenly dips (V9) as it descends a recessional moraine left by the last glacier to occupy Yosemite Valley. The Merced is swift here, as witnessed through a break in the trees revealing great views of Bridalveil Fall (V10). The river then slows again at **Valley View**, where you do indeed get a tremendous long view towards Half Dome.

Hwy-120 West and Hwy-140 now continue out of Yosemite Valley, or you can turn left and double back along Southside Drive towards Yosemite Village.

Hikes from the western end of Yosemite Valley

For our coverage of **day hikes** starting from the western end of Yosemite Valley, see hikes Y8 and Y9 in Chapter 4 (from p.111), and for **overnight hikes** see hikes Y44 and Y45 in Chapter 5 (from p.133). These hikes are considerably quieter than those starting at the eastern end of the valley.

Wayside markers

Around Yosemite Valley and along roads throughout the park, you'll see **wayside markers** with a letter and a number: V1–V27 in Yosemite Valley, G1–G11 along Glacier Point Road, T1–T39 along Tioga Road, and so on. These correspond to entries in the Park Service's *Yosemite Road Guide* (see "Books", p.251), which is useful for the completist, though you'll find that everything of importance is amply covered in the relevant section of our text. We've mentioned the nearest marker to points of interest where relevant.

Southside Drive

Approaching Yosemite Valley along Hwy-120 or Hwy-140 you enter a one-way system at **Pohono Bridge**, which crosses the Merced and passes the small **Fern Spring** (V12) on the right. The road soon reaches the edge of **Bridalveil Meadow** where a marker (V13) records the spot where, on May 17, 1903, President Theodore Roosevelt and John Muir camped together and nutted out the conservation measures Muir felt were needed in the park. Muir (and presumably the surroundings) obviously had some effect, because several of his proposals were enacted over the subsequent years.

At the eastern end of the meadow, Hwy-41 comes in from Wawona. Turn right here for the parking lot for **Bridalveil Fall**, or left to continue the circuit. Next stop is **El Capitan Vista**, a broad section of road where RVs and buses regularly line the parking bays on both sides of the road for one of the most celebrated views of the big stone. It looks its best early and late in the day when lower-angled light plays on the sheer granite walls, highlighting its features.

Cathedral Spires (V15) rise up on your right as you drive a mile or so on to a small side road to **Cathedral Beach picnic area** and **Three Brothers Vista** (V16). Another mile on, a side road leads to two more excellent waterside picnic areas, **Yellow Pine** and **Sentinel Beach**, the latter one of the nicest and most convenient picnic spots in the park.

Across the road a sign marks the trailhead for the **Four-Mile Trail** to Glacier Point (Hike Y9, p.112). In the mid-nineteenth century this was the location of Lower Yosemite Village, home to Camp Ahwahnee and Yosemite Valley's original hotel, *Leidig's*, which saw its first tourists in 1856. The hotel was just a few muslin sheets stretched over a wood frame and is now long gone, but the name survives as Leidig's Meadow, reached across a very sturdy bridge from the **Swinging Bridge Picnic Area**.

Half a mile on, you get the first really startling view of Yosemite Falls from **Upper Yosemite Fall Vista** (V19), then reach the interdenominational **chapel**, (see p.46), a suitably alpine-looking structure with its vertical wooden battens, steep-pitched roof and short steeple. The oldest building in the park still in use, the chapel was built in 1879 close to the base of the Four-Mile Trail, and later

Moving on from Yosemite Valley

From the western end of Yosemite Valley: Big Oak Flat Road heads northwest (see p.76), where you can pick up the Tioga Road (Hwy-120 West; see p.80); Hwy-140 heads west out of the park towards Mariposa (covered on p.159); and Hwy-41 (see p.90) heads south past Tunnel View to Wawona, with a spur to Glacier Point (see p.91). No roads run east from Yosemite Valley: to get to Tuolumne Meadows follow our description for Tioga Road, above.

moved three-quarters of a mile to its current site. It's the last remaining building of the old Yosemite Village, once the main settlement in the valley, with a store, post office, park headquarters, hotel, saloons and three photographers' studios. The site was chosen for its shade on hot summer days, but tastes changed and during the 1930s most services were transferred to the sunnier and warmer northern side of the river. Several of the old buildings have ended up in the Pioneer Yosemite History Center in Wawona (see p.97).

A hundred yards further on, turn left over **Sentinel Bridge** to return to Yosemite Village, or continue straight ahead for Curry Village and eastern Yosemite Valley.

2

Northern Yosemite

Only ardent hikers prepared to spend several days in the backcountry get to see the true remoteness of **Northern Yosemite**, a vast expanse of angular peaks and glaciated valleys stretching beyond the northern park boundary to the Hoover and Emigrant wildernesses. But between these wilds and the relative civilization of Yosemite Valley lies some of Yosemite's finest scenery, made accessible by **Tioga Road**, which virtually bisects the park from east to west. Snowbound and impassable for all but the five warmest months, the road climbs up through densely forested high-country to the open grasslands of **Tuolumne Meadows**, surrounded by the polished granite domes and with a southern horizon delineated by the saw-tooth crest of the **Cathedral Range**. It's a gorgeous and relaxing place to hang out, free from the bustle of Yosemite Valley but with access to the only significant cluster of visitor facilities in the park's northern half.

There are opportunities to go horseriding, swimming in chilly but alluring alpine lakes, fishing in the Tuolumne River or simply picnicking among the meadow wildflowers – but the real draw for most people is **hiking**. Nowhere else in the park is such fabulous hiking country so close at hand or so easy to reach: starting at an elevation of 8600ft, most of the hikes don't require a huge altitude-gaining slog at the start. For a selection of the **best trails** in the area, turn to chapters 4 (day hikes) and 5 (overnight hikes), where you'll find full details of our favourites, from a short stroll to the effervescent **Soda Springs**, to the two-day hike along a section of the **John Muir Trail** between here and Yosemite Valley.

East of Tuolumne Meadows, Tioga Road tops out at the 10,000ft **Tioga Pass**, the park's eastern boundary and the heart of a historic mining area. To the west of Tuolumne, the best of the Tioga Road scenery is around **Olmsted Point**, where everyone stops to photograph the barren granite walls of Tenaya Canyon, and **Tenaya Lake**, surrounded by glacier-smoothed domes typically populated by rock climbers. Elsewhere, bumpy side roads spur off to wooded campgrounds and pass numerous trailheads, some feeding down to the northern rim of Yosemite Valley while others thread their way to alpine lakes and the sequoias at **Tuolumne Grove**.

The only other road-accessible section of Northern Yosemite is **Hetch Hetchy**, once said to be the match of Yosemite Valley, but now controversially filled by the Hetch Hetchy Reservoir. It's an attractive area, nonetheless, particularly in spring when three lovely **waterfalls** burst into life among abundant wildflowers.

Big Oak Flat Road and northwestern Yosemite

Considering the quality of road access, the northwestern corner of Yosemite receives surprisingly few visitors. Plenty of people drive through the region along Hwy-120 on the way from the Bay Area but few stop for long, except for a quick photo from one of the viewpoints or a leisurely stroll down to the **Merced Grove** of **giant sequoias**. If they stop for any length of time it's likely to be at **Hetch Hetchy**, notorious for being the only major dam in a national park, but still of interest as a springboard to hikes in the north of the park.

Yosemite Valley to Crane Flat

To get to the northern reaches of Yosemite from Yosemite Valley, drive northwest along **Big Oak Flat Road**, which starts climbing as soon as it spurs off Hwy-140 at the valley's western end. There are great cliff views along the way as the Merced River rapidly drops away to your left; notice how the river leaves behind the U-shaped Yosemite Valley and takes on the classic V-shape of an unglaciated river canyon.

After a couple of short tunnels lie two spectacular springtime waterfalls right beside the road. John Muir felt that the first, **Cascade Creek** (wayside marker B2), was fittingly named, writing "as far as I have traced it above and below our camp it is one continuous bouncing, dancing, white bloom of cascades." The less dramatic **Tamarack Creek** takes its name from the lodgepole pines hereabouts, which early visitors thought looked like the eastern tamarack. The two creeks join forces just downstream and plummet 500ft into Merced River canyon as **The Cascades**. From here you can also look across the valley to **Elephant Rock**, a granite lump vaguely resembling a great pachyderm.

Almost half a mile on, **Valley Portal** (B3) offers an excellent vista of the western half of Yosemite Valley. The longest of the three tunnels on this road runs almost a mile from here to a view of **Merced River canyon** (B4) and Half Dome. **Big Meadow Overlook** (B6), four miles on, affords views of the silted-up lake bed of Big Meadow, once used to grow hay to feed packhorses and now an important foraging area for the locally rare great grey owl. Four miles down a graded but unmade road on the edge of Big Meadow stands the private settlement of **Foresta**, around 150 homes on a plot of land that was grandfathered into the park when it was created. It was a gorgeous spot until a 1990 wildfire swept through and burned virtually everything here along with 23,000 surrounding acres. The greenery is gradually returning and most of the houses have been rebuilt, mostly to luxurious standards. The only reason to come here is if you're going to stay (see p.175). Big Oak Flat Road continues to climb over the next couple of miles, levelling off around 6200ft at **Crane Flat**, a small meadow where you'll find the Crane Flat Store and gas station and, across the road, *Crane Flat* campground. Here Tioga Road (Hwy-120 East) branches off from Big Oak Flat Road, heading east towards Tuolumne Meadows: our account of this route continues on p.80.

Merced Grove to Big Oak Flat Entrance

Just over three miles west of Crane Flat along Big Oak Flat Road, a small pull-out provides parking for the **Merced Grove** of **giant sequoias**, which, with only a couple of dozen trees, is smaller and less spectacular than the Mariposa and Tuolumne groves. In compensation, it's the least visited of all the groves, and being satisfyingly free from barriers and signs is all the more appealing. A broad, sandy **trail** (1hr 30min–2hr round-trip; 3 miles; 600ft ascent on the way back) takes you to a dense cluster of five trees heralding the main section of the grove, set around the shuttered and gabled **Merced Grove Cabin**. Built in 1935 to exhibit the "highest evolution of log cabin construction", and now restored, it's closed to the public, but you can admire its bold exterior, featuring a hipped, shingled roof and log window boxes. It's managed by the Yosemite Institute (see p.45), and if a group is present you may get to peek inside. Beyond the cabin the grove thins out after one final 15ft-diameter sequoia with a huge hemispherical burl across its entire width.

Continuing west on Big Oak Flat Road, **North Country View** (B11) gives a great view of Hetch Hetchy reservoir far below, filling the valley behind the dam. A couple of miles past the overlook stands the park's **Big Oak Flat Entrance** (B12), where you'll find a small **Information Station** (Easter–Sept daily 8am–5pm, Oct–Easter generally closed; ℡209/379-1899) with a desk for obtaining wilderness permits, a free phone for reserving Yosemite lodging, a campground reservations office (April to mid-Oct 8am–5pm), a few drink machines and toilets. Across the road, the *Hodgdon Meadow* campground (see p.183) sits on the site where Jeremiah Hodgdon and his family ran a horse and stage waystation until the 1890s, making the best of their location beside the original Big Oak Flat Road into Yosemite.

A mile west of the Big Oak Flat Entrance, **Evergreen Road** heads north and re-enters the park on the way to Hetch Hetchy. Our coverage of Hwy-120 West is on p.156.

Hetch Hetchy

John Muir's passion for Yosemite Valley was matched, if not exceeded, by his desire to preserve **HETCH HETCHY** (open dawn–dusk only, unless you have a wilderness permit), which he considered to be every bit as beautiful as Yosemite Valley. At 3800ft it's around the same height as the Yosemite Valley floor and was described by Muir as "one of nature's rare and most precious mountain temples", with grassy, oak-filled meadows and soaring granite walls.

When Hetch Hetchy came under threat from power and water supply interests in San Francisco in 1901, Muir began a twelve-year losing battle for its preservation (see box, p.79). Eventually, in 1913, the cause was lost to a federal bill paving the way for the Tuolumne River to be blocked by the **O'Shaughnessy Dam**, creating the slender, eight-mile-long **Hetch Hetchy reservoir**. The dam, completed in 1923 and raised to its current height in 1938, drowned the meadows under a couple of hundred feet of water.

Despite Muir's stirring admiration of Hetch Hetchy, it's hard to imagine that it was ever the equivalent of Yosemite Valley. The meadows may well have been very beautiful, but the rocks all around could never quite equal Yosemite's majesty. It is certainly no match now, and with so much wonderful countryside competing for visitors' attention elsewhere in the park, it isn't so surprising that Hetch Hetchy is little visited. That said, the view up the reservoir from the middle

---

Hetch Hetchy hikes

Yosemite's **fifty best hikes** are covered in chapters 4 and 5. For trails from Hetch Hetchy, see hikes Y10 and Y11, from p.112. The relatively low altitude and light snow cover in this part of the park encourage early spring hiking, when the waterfalls and wildflowers are at their best.

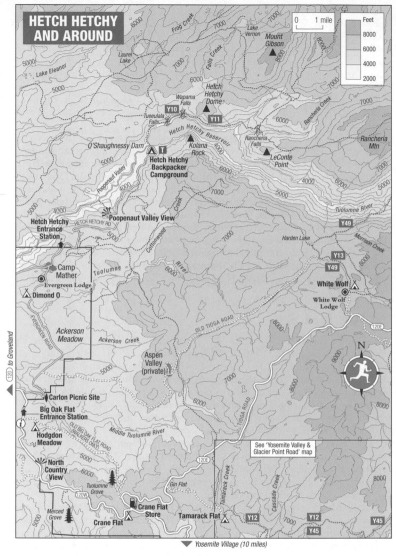

▼ Yosemite Village (10 miles)

of the dam is stunning, with the bell-shaped dome of **Kolana Rock** dominating on the right and providing an active breeding ground for endangered **peregrine falcons**. Across the water, two beautiful falls drop over a thousand feet from the cliffs on the north side, both of them accessible on relatively easy hikes (see hikes Y10 & Y11, from p.112). The voluminous **Wapama Falls** roars away in its dark recess in dramatic contract to **Tueeulala Falls** (pronounced TWEE-lala), described by Muir as a "silvery scarf burning with irised sun-fire". Both are at their best from April to early June: Tueeulala Falls is usually dry by early June, with Wapama Falls hanging on for a couple more months.

The battle for Hetch Hetchy

"Dam Hetch Hetchy! As well dam for water-tanks the people's cathedrals and churches, for no holier temple has ever been consecrated by the heart of man."

John Muir, *The Yosemite*

As early as 1867 the burgeoning city of San Francisco, perched at the end of a dry peninsula, began searching for a dependable water supply. In 1900 the US Geological Survey recommended Hetch Hetchy valley as a potential source, where a relatively small **dam** would hold back a large body of water. San Francisco mayor James Phelan concurred, but **John Muir** and his cohorts, instigating the first environmental letter-writing campaign to Congress and obtaining support from most of the country's influential newspapers, initially defeated the proposal.

At the time conservationists split into those favouring total preservation of "one of Nature's rarest and most precious mountain temples", and those advocating "wise use". Dam advocate William Kent described Muir as "a man entirely without social sense", while Muir retaliated by labelling his adversaries "mischief-makers and robbers" and "temple destroyers, devotees of ravaging commercialism".

The environmentalists eventually lost the battle in 1913 when commercial interests persuaded President Wilson to sign the Raker Act, allowing for the construction of the **O'Shaughnessy Dam**, which was built between 1914 and 1923. The *New York Times* reported "The American people have been whipped in the Hetch Hetchy fight", no one more so than Muir himself, who died dispirited in 1914.

Though Muir and company failed to stop the dam, their work led to the creation of both the National Park Service and the Sierra Club (see p.44), the latter a long-time advocate of **undamming Hetch Hetchy** and returning it to its original state. Since Muir's day, the construction of the huge Don Pedro reservoir (downstream from Hetch Hetchy) means that San Francisco's water supply would barely be affected; the bigger stumbling block would be the loss of power generation. With power shortages and rolling blackouts in recent years the proposal looks set to remain an environmentalists' pipe dream for the time being.

For more on the issues around Hetch Hetchy consult the appropriate section of the Sierra Club site (ⓦwww.sierraclub.org/ca/hetchhetchy) or visit the site of the campaigning organization, Restore Hetch Hetchy (ⓦwww.hetchhetchy.org).

Long before it was drowned by the reservoir, Hetch Hetchy valley was scoured out by glaciers, which ground down the valley between ten thousand and two million years ago. Their route was followed by the Tuolumne River, a passage used by Miwok peoples, who named the area "Hatchatchie" after a type of grass with edible seeds once common hereabouts. **Wildflowers** are still abundant in the region in spring – look for bright California fuchsia, waterfall buttercups in trickling cascades and shooting stars in damp meadows – along with California black oak, incense cedar, ponderosa pine and big leaf maple.

The only **facilities** at Hetch Hetchy are toilets, drinking water, phone and a backpacker campground (wilderness permit required), which makes a good starting point for treks into the near-deserted northern reaches of the park. As the reservoir forms part of San Francisco's water supply, swimming and boating are not allowed, and **fishing** is only permitted from the shore if live bait isn't used.

Approaching Hetch Hetchy

The road into Hetch Hetchy (initially Evergreen Road, then Hetch Hetchy Road) cuts off Hwy-120 West a mile outside the Big Oak Flat Entrance, and twists north through the Stanislaus National Forest and then the park for a total of sixteen miles to the O'Shaughnessy Dam. It is generally accessible without chains from mid-April to mid-October. A mile off Hwy-120 West, you pass the **Carlon Picnic Site** (with picnic tables, toilets and stream water) where you cross the South Fork of the Tuolumne River.

Another mile or so on, the forest opens out at **Ackerson Meadow**, once used by an early prospector for growing hay to sell to transport companies in Yosemite Valley. Six miles north off Hwy-120 West is the *Dimond O* campground (see p.185); continue a mile to *Evergreen Lodge* (see p.175) and **Mather**, a former sheep ranch and later a stop on the railroad during the construction of the O'Shaughnessy Dam. It's now the San Francisco Recreation Camp, open to San Francisco residents by lottery. Turn right here to enter the park at the **Hetch Hetchy Entrance** (closed dusk–dawn), with a kiosk acting as the **ranger station** where you can pick up wilderness permits.

The Hetch Hetchy Road climbs gently through **Poopenaut Pass** (H2) to reveal a view of the Grand Canyon of the Tuolumne River, the Hetch Hetchy reservoir and dam, and Wapama and Tueeulala falls. From **Poopenaut Valley View** (H3), a mile on, you can see Poopenaut Valley below the dam, where a few cabins remain from the small sheep and cattle herding settlement that once thrived there. It's a further three miles to Hetch Hetchy.

Tioga Road: Crane Flat to Tenaya Lake

Snow-covered and impassable for more than half the year, **Tioga Road** (Hwy-120 East: usually open late May–early Nov) runs 46 miles from Crane Flat through some of Yosemite's most breathtaking **high-country scenery** to the park's sole eastern entrance at the 9945ft Tioga Pass, the highest road pass in California. Along the way it traverses alpine tundra and subalpine forests, cuts through glaciated valleys, and crosses the sublime Tuolumne Meadows. Throughout these varying zones are trailheads for numerous hikes and great places to stop, such as **Olmsted Point**, with its tremendous views of Half Dome and Clouds Rest, and chilly **Tenaya Lake**, where the brave can go for a swim from sandy beaches.

Tioga Road roughly follows a trading route used by the Mono Lake Paiute, which in 1883 was turned into the Great Sierra Wagon Road, opened by the Great Sierra Consolidated Silver Company, who needed to transport machinery and supplies to their mines around Tioga Pass. Though realigned frequently over the years, parts of this road were still used until 1961. You can get a sense of what travel was like in those times by exploring short sections of the old route which spur off to the May Lake trailhead and *Yosemite Creek* campground.

Facilities along Tioga Road are limited to a handful of campgrounds, and the lodge, restaurant and store at White Wolf (both generally open mid-June–early Sept), before you get to Tuolumne Meadows. If you're planning to spend a few days exploring out this way, be sure to stock up with supplies in Yosemite Valley or at the Crane Flat Store.

Entering Yosemite from the east

If you're entering Yosemite National Park **from the east**, through Lee Vining, note that the sections of this chapter covering Crane Flat to Tioga Pass should be read in reverse order. Those driving to the Tioga Road **from Yosemite Village** should follow our coverage first of Northside Drive (see p.72), and then of Big Oak Flat Road (see p.76).

For our coverage of **day hikes** accessed off Tioga Road, see hikes Y12–Y20 in Chapter 4 (from p.113), and for **overnight hikes** see Hike Y48 in Chapter 5 (p.136). Most of these trails are usually under snow from November to early June.

Tuolumne Grove

Just half a mile north of the intersection of Big Oak Flat Road and Tioga Road at Crane Flat sits the first major sight in this direction, the trailhead for the **Tuolumne Grove** of **giant sequoias** (open all year, but usually snowbound from late November to April; free). With just a few dozen trees, it's far less impressive than the Mariposa Grove but is closer to Yosemite Valley and has the distinction of being the grove spotted by pioneer Joseph Walker and his party when they first entered Yosemite in 1833.

Access to the grove is on foot along a root-buckled asphalt road that once formed part of the **Old Big Oak Flat Road**, built in 1874 at a time when it took a day and a half of travel to get here from San Francisco. This stretch of the old road is inaccessible to vehicles (including bikes) but sees plenty of foot traffic on the way to the grove. The first sequoia is a mile down the road from the parking lot and marks the start of a mile-long loop trail that passes several more magnificent big trees. The huge **fallen giant** was known as the Leaning Tower Tree until, weakened by successive fire scars then laden with snow, it tumbled in 1983. Now hollow and fairly rapidly crumbling away, you can still crawl through. Nearby, the charred remains of a **tunnel tree** are distinguished by the car-sized hole that was bored through and undoubtedly contributed to the tree's early demise. There were once several drive-through trees in California, though most have either toppled or access has been forbidden.

Beyond the sequoia grove, the long-abandoned Old Big Oak Flat Road continues about four miles on to the *Hodgdon Meadow* campground, opposite the Big Oak Flat Entrance; again, cars, bikes and other vehicles are prohibited. The road takes its name from the former gold-mining town just west of the park border that once had a population of three thousand.

Tamarack Flat to White Wolf

Three miles east of the Tuolumne Grove parking lot, a drivable but winding and potholed section of the Old Big Oak Flat Road leads three miles southeast to the primitive *Tamarack Flat* campground (see p.183). Immediately past the turn-off, **Gin Flat** (T3) marks the spot where a bunch of delighted cowboys happened upon a barrel of gin lost off a passing wagon.

The next five miles run through a fire-scorched patch of forest, then parallel to the South Fork of the Tuolumne River to **Smoky Jack** (T6), the former site of a simple campground which got its name from John Connel, who originally employed John Muir to tend his flocks. Much of the next four miles passes through an almost pure stand of **red fir forest** to the delightful, grass-fringed **Siesta Lake** on the right. Beyond, a narrow side road leads a mile north of Tioga Road to **White Wolf**, a lodge (see p.174), restaurant (see p.190), campground (see p.184) and very small store (mid-June to early Sept daily 8am–8pm), which gets its name either from a misidentified coyote that happened by in the old days or a local chief. Surrounded by lush meadow and forests, it's a good base for easy hikes to Harden and Lukens lakes (see hikes Y13 & Y14, p.114).

Back on Tioga Road, a third of a mile east, a rough section of the Great Sierra Wagon Road heads five miles southeast down to the *Yosemite Creek* campground. The road was built in 1883 for taking machinery up to mines around Tioga Pass, and is still passable in ordinary vehicles. Hike Y15 (p.114) to the top of Yosemite Falls starts at the campground.

Clark Range View to Clouds Rest View

Beyond the White Wolf and Yosemite Creek crossroads, the Tioga Road leads into the high-country proper: 8000ft up, with trails heading off from the road to alpine lakes and craggy peaks. These lofty destinations are visible a couple of miles on from the **Clark Range View** (T11), offering extensive views south to the 11,522ft **Mount Clark** with its sharp-ridged back resembling the pointy plates of a giant stegosaurus. The first guardian of the 1864 Yosemite Grant, Galen Clark, would undoubtedly be proud to be honoured with such a fine specimen.

To the east of the viewpoint lies the broad-shouldered grey granite mass of **Mount Hoffmann** (10,850ft), the geographical centre of the park and one of John Muir's favourite summits. The peak was named for Charles F. Hoffmann, chief topographer of Whitney's California State Geological Survey, who initially appraised the area's topography. Its angular peak was never subjected to the ravages of glacial action, and stands in contrast to the smooth slabs of its lower flanks. When Tuolumne Meadows was 2000ft under an ice sheet, it was the surrounding Hoffmann Range that divided the flowing ice into two distinct glaciers, one carving out the Tuolumne Canyon and Hetch Hetchy, and the other grinding down the Tenaya Canyon to sculpt Yosemite Valley.

The **Western Juniper** interpretive sign (T12), another mile and a half along, celebrates this relatively common tree which grows on rocky ridges in the sub-alpine forest and can live up to a thousand years. A road cutting a third of a mile on (T14) reveals a particularly clear example of **exfoliating granite**, the onion-like layers peeling off over the millennia in the same process that has created all Yosemite's domes, and indeed continues today, gradually reshaping the landscape.

Three miles on, Tioga Road crosses Yosemite Creek, which crashes over Yosemite Falls seven miles downstream. A further four miles from the crossing, *Porcupine Flat* campground immediately precedes the 100-yard **Sierra Trees Nature Trail** (T18), along which are marked the various trees whose habitats overlap at this intersection of several climatic zones: Jeffrey pine, western white pine, lodgepole pine, white fir and California red fir.

From here it's half a mile to the **North Dome Trailhead** (T19; Hike Y16, p.115), then a further mile to where a gap in the trees reveals the magnificent **Half Dome View** (T20), with Mount Starr King lurking behind the great, grey monolith. It's a little over another mile to **May Lake Junction** (T21), where a bumpy two-mile side road leads to the road-end trailhead for **May Lake** (Hike Y19, p.116), a popular, pleasant hour-plus stroll that can be extended to the top of Mount Hoffmann, one of the park's great viewpoints.

Back on Tioga Road, it's a mile to **Clouds Rest View** (T23), where you can gaze in awe at the vast, smooth sheet of granite sweeping at 45 degrees from the base of Tenaya Canyon 5000ft up to the 9926ft summit ridge of Clouds Rest. In case you were wondering why no trails seem to follow **Tenaya Canyon**, it is deemed too dangerous, with some sections requiring ropes.

Olmsted Point to Tenaya Lake

Almost two miles east of Clouds Rest View an expansive vista opens out at **Olmsted Point**, named after Frederick Law Olmsted, first chairman of the

Yosemite Park Commission and joint architect of New York City's Central Park. Undoubtedly the most outstanding viewpoint from Tioga Road, it offers long views down Tenaya Canyon towards Clouds Rest and Half Dome, and up the canyon to Tenaya Lake with the sculpted, smooth monoliths of Tuolumne beyond. A quarter-mile trail leads to the top of a nearby dome where even more stupendous views await.

In the early 1960s when the Tioga Road was being re-aligned, Ansel Adams fought against routing the next section of highway past the cold, clear waters of the mile-long **Tenaya Lake**. He failed and the road now skirts the northern shore of this beautiful alpine tarn, which fills a hollow gouged out by the Tenaya Branch of the ancient Tuolumne Glacier. The lake takes its name from the native chief captured here by the Mariposa Battalion in 1851. The Ahwahneechee knew the lake as Py-wi-ack, or "Lake of the Shining Rocks", an apt description as its entire basin exhibits abundant evidence of glacial polish. Arrive in the early morning or evening and it can be a wonderfully peaceful place to appreciate the granite scenery and perhaps dangle a fishing pole.

As it skirts the lake, the road passes **Sunrise Lakes Trailhead**, marking the start of hikes Y18 and Y20 (see p.116), then runs beside the sandy **beach** at **Murphy Creek**, where there's a small parking area that's popular on hot days. The **swimming** is good here, but generally deemed better at the far end of Tenaya Lake, where a long strand is excellent for those afraid to brave the chilly waters.

You're now deep into **granite dome** country, which continues for the remaining five miles to Tuolumne Meadows. Overlooking Tenaya Lake on the north side of Tioga Road, you may see climbers tackling the relatively gentle slopes of **Stately Pleasure Dome**, presumably named by some fan of Coleridge's "Kubla Khan". Further on, **Pywiack Dome** rises above the south side of the road with a large pine growing out of its steepest face. **Mendicott Dome** is behind that, and further still is the blunt visage of **Fairview Dome**, the largest of them all. Rounding a bend, the low **Pothole Dome**, to the north, heralds the open expanse of Tuolumne Meadows.

Tioga Road: Tuolumne Meadows

The alpine area around **TUOLUMNE MEADOWS** – the "meadow in the sky" in the local Miwok tongue – has a very different atmosphere from that of Yosemite Valley, 55 miles (about ninety minutes' drive) away. Here, at 8575ft, it is much more open; the light is more intense, and the air has a fresh, crisp bite courtesy of temperatures fifteen to twenty degrees lower. There can still be good-sized blasts of carbon monoxide at peak times, however, as this is the main high-country congregation point for visitors, and the only accommodation base in the area within easy reach of the park's eastern entrance at Tioga Pass.

The meadows themselves are the largest in all of the Sierra; twelve miles long, between a quarter and half a mile wide, and threaded by the meandering

Tuolumne Meadows hikes

For our coverage of **day hikes** from Tuolumne Meadows, see hikes Y21–Y30 in Chapter 4 (from p.117), and for **overnight hikes** see hikes Y49 and Y50 in Chapter 5 (from p.137). Bear in mind that these trails are usually under snow from November to early June.

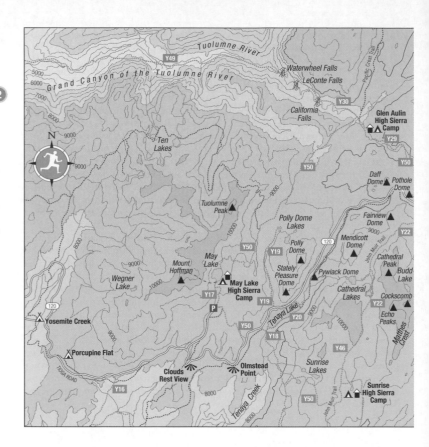

Tuolumne River. Snow usually lingers here until the end of June, forcing the **wildflowers** to contend with a short growing season. They respond with a glorious burst of colour in July, a wonderful time for a wander. The distinctive glaciated granite form of **Lembert Dome** (see Hike Y27, p.120) squats at the eastern end of the meadows gazing across the grasslands towards its western twin, **Pothole Dome** (Hike Y21, p.117), which makes for a great sunset destination.

It is abundantly clear why in 1869 John Muir asserted that "this is the most spacious and delightful high pleasure-ground I have seen…and though lying high in the sky, the surrounding mountains are so much higher, one feels protected as if in a grand hall". A little fanciful perhaps, but there's no denying that the mountain scenery is particularly striking to the south, where the **Cathedral Range** offers a horizon of slender spires and knife-blade ridges. This is best seen from **Soda Springs**, where the angled protuberant spire of **Unicorn Peak** evokes the mythical beast's horn. To its right is **Cathedral Peak**, a textbook example of a glaciated "Matterhorn", where glaciers have carved away the rock on all sides leaving a sharp pointed summit.

Tuolumne is a focal point for **hikers** who find the higher altitude makes this a better starting point than Yosemite Valley, and use it as a base from which to fan out into the surrounding High Sierra wilderness. The store here is the first provisioning point for southbound hikers on the **John Muir Trail** (see p.135),

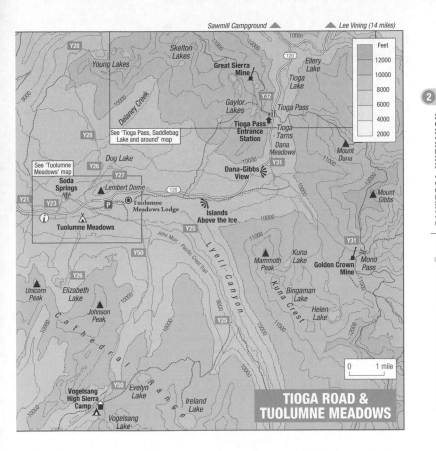

who typically take two days to get here from Yosemite Valley then start heading southeast towards Mount Whitney. Come in July and you may meet through-hikers on the 2650-mile **Pacific Crest Trail** from Mexico to Canada, who'll be restocking for the next leg of their five-month journey.

Soda Springs and Parsons Memorial Lodge

If you've only got a short time in Tuolumne, take a stroll across the meadows to **Soda Springs**, one of the area's most popular and rewarding short **hikes**. It's included as part of Hike Y23 (see p.118), but can also easily be visited by following a section of the old carriage road that spurs across the meadow three hundred yards east of the visitor centre (see p.87). This takes you straight to the naturally carbonated springs, described in 1863 as "pungent and delightful to the taste". And so it is, though the Park Service discourages drinking, warning of potential surface contamination. By 1885 the area was being homesteaded by the insect collector and so-called "hermit of the Sierra", **Jean–Baptiste Lembert**, who raised goats on 160 acres and erected a small enclosure surrounding the springs, of which only the low walls now survive.

The area around the springs became one of the favourite camping spots of John Muir, who appreciated its location on a slight rise with a great view of the

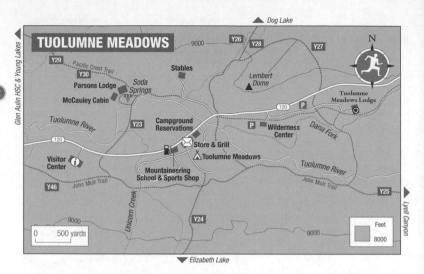

meadows and the jagged Cathedral Range to the south. Noting the devastating effect sheep were having each summer when these "hoofed locusts" were herded up to the meadows from the lowlands for pasture, the avid conservationist, urged on by magazine editor **Robert Underwood Johnson**, campaigned for Tuolumne's protection as part of a newly created Yosemite National Park. Muir wrote two articles for *Century Magazine* outlining his proposal, and in the fall of 1890 Congress passed a bill along the lines that Muir advocated.

Muir's subsequent fight to save Hetch Hetchy (see box, p.79) was supported by high-country guide Edward Taylor Parsons, whom the fledgling Sierra Club honoured posthumously by building the rugged but elegantly proportioned **Parsons Memorial Lodge** (July to early Sept daily 10am–4pm; free) right by the springs. Managed by the Yosemite Conservancy, its single room houses displays on local environmental and campaigning issues, and hosts frequent talks and demonstrations (see *Yosemite Guide* for details). The adjacent **McCauley Cabin** was built by the McCauley brothers, who bought Lembert's homestead after his death in 1897. It was subsequently sold to the Sierra Club who used it as a summer camp from 1912 to 1973, after which the Park Service bought it; the cabin is now closed to the public.

Tuolumne practicalities

Tuolumne is the sort of place you might base yourself for several days (or even weeks), heading out on long hikes or strolling the meadows taking photos, botanizing, or just lying in the sun by the river. You'll certainly not be pampered while staying here, but you can sleep and eat fairly well. Facilities are inconveniently scattered along a two-mile stretch of road, so visitors without their own vehicles will need to avail themselves of the **free Tuolumne Meadows Shuttle** (mid-June to mid-Sept daily 7am–7pm). This makes an eleven-mile run every half hour heading west from Tuolumne Meadows Lodge, passing the Tuolumne Visitor Center and several important trailheads to Tenaya Lake and the fabulous viewpoint at Olmsted Point. The last bus leaves Olmsted Point at 6pm. Four times a day (9am, noon, 3pm and 5pm) the route is extended and the bus runs six miles eastbound from Tuolumne Meadows to the park entrance at Tioga Pass, opening up a handful of excellent hikes; the last bus leaves Tioga Pass at 5.15pm.

Altitude sickness

Though unlikely, it's possible to suffer **altitude sickness** 8600ft up in Tuolumne Meadows, especially if you spend the night here after coming up in one day from much lower elevations. You'll certainly feel short of breath, but older people and those with heart and lung diseases should consider spending at least one night in Yosemite Valley (4000ft) to acclimatize, and avoid high-fat foods and alcohol. If you find yourself suffering from headaches, nausea, shortness of breath, irritability and general fatigue, the only solution is to descend.

The westernmost building of interest is the **Tuolumne Meadows Visitor Center** (mid-June to Sept daily 9am–5/6pm; ℡209/372-0263), which concentrates on information on the north of the park, and sells books, maps and gifts. It contains moderately interesting displays on alpine wildflowers (divided into four characteristic zones of the region: forest, meadow, riparian and rocky), local geology and the area's human history. Kids get to touch bear fur, feel rams' horns and pick up a large but featherweight lump of Mono Lake pumice. The wood and granite building was constructed by the Civilian Conservation Corps in 1934 in a style recalling Yosemite pioneer buildings, and was later used as a work crew mess hall.

It's over half a mile east to the **gas station** (mid-June to early Oct daily 9am–5/6pm & 24hr with credit card) and Tuolumne Mountain Shop, which sells outdoor gear and **climbing** paraphernalia, and doubles as the summer home of the Yosemite Mountaineering School (see box, p.103). Next door a large, white plastic shed houses the fast-food style *Tuolumne Meadows Grill* (see p.189) and the Tuolumne Meadows Store (June to early Nov daily 8am–8pm), which stocks a reasonable selection of hiking and camping supplies, Coleman fuel, camping gas canisters, basic groceries, ice, booze and firewood, and has a small **post office** (mid-June to early Oct Mon–Fri 9am–5pm, Sat 9am–1pm). The huge *Tuolumne Meadows* campground (see p.183) is tucked behind, with the reservation office a hundred yards or so east of the store. Across the Tuolumne River it's another half mile past the Lembert Dome parking area to the **Wilderness Center** (see p.44) and another few hundred yards down a side road to the tent cabins and hearty meals of *Tuolumne Meadows Lodge* (see p.174 & p.189).

Hike, or drive, a mile down the road beside Lembert Dome to reach the Tuolumne Meadows Stables (see p.143), which offers **horseriding** from a couple of hours to several days.

Tioga Road: Tioga Pass and the road to Lee Vining

At Tuolumne Meadows the Tuolumne River splits into two forks, the southerly Lyell Fork tracing the floor of Lyell Canyon towards Mount Lyell, while the Dana Fork runs six miles east to Dana Meadows and the park entrance at Tioga Pass. Tioga Road follows the Dana Fork past the **Islands above the Ice** pullout where there's a distant view of Cockscomb, Unicorn and Echo Peaks silhouetted against the horizon, though partly obscured by young pines. Mount Gibbs (12,764ft) and the park's second-highest peak, Mount Dana

TIOGA PASS, SADDLEBAG LAKE AND AROUND

Dana Meadows (1 mile) ▼ *& Tuolumne Meadows (6 miles)*

(13,053ft), are both visible a mile further at **Dana–Gibbs View** (T36), from where you can admire their reddish ferriferous tinge, a striking contrast to the ubiquitous grey Yosemite granite.

Just past a stand of lodgepole pines, these mountains appear again as a backdrop to **Dana Meadows**, a quarter-mile wide and studded with erratics deposited by the ancient Tuolumne Glacier, the largest glacier in the Sierra Nevada, which receded twenty thousand years ago. Huge lumps of ice left behind as it receded formed a series of kettle lakes known as **Tioga Tarns**, now an extremely attractive collection of pools in boggy land beside the fledgling Dana Fork. At the eastern end of Dana Meadows, the road climbs the last few feet to **Tioga Pass** (T39), immediately preceded by the trailhead for the hike to Gaylor Lakes (see Hike Y32, p.123).

For in-depth details of Tioga Road **closures** at the pass, see p.21.

Hikes around Tioga Pass

For our coverage of hikes starting near or just over Tioga Pass, see hikes Y31–Y33 in Chapter 4 (from p.122), all of which reach altitudes of over 10,000ft with relatively little effort.

Lee Vining Grade

You might imagine that Tioga is a Miwok or Paiute word, but it actually means "where it forks" in Iroquois, a name appended by a native of Tioga County in New York State, who was then living in the area.

Leaving the park you cross into the **Inyo National Forest** and quickly begin the rapid descent down what is known as the **Lee Vining Grade**, a steep and fast road that descends the heavily glaciated Lee Vining Canyon, dropping over 3000ft in six miles from lodgepole-pine studded meadows to low sage-covered hills. Beyond lies the small town of **Lee Vining** (see p.153) on the shores of **Mono Lake**.

Interpretive panels at **Tioga Lake Overlook**, less than a mile along, discuss the one-time town of Bennettville and introduce the work of early twentieth-century conservationist **Aldo Leopold**, whose thoughts on natural history and his "land ethic" are continued on more signs down the valley. A mile on, just past the *Tioga Lake* campground, the partly paved, quarter-mile **Nunatak Nature Trail** makes a pleasant place for a break among lodgepole and whitebark pines. Signs use the views of Mount Dana and the Dana Plateau – both untouched by the Lee Vining Glacier twenty thousand years ago – to illustrate the creation of nunataks, angular pinnacles free of glacial erosion.

Half a mile further on, the *Tioga Pass Resort* offers rooms (see p.175) and has a good diner (see p.190). It sits right by the *Junction* campground (see p.184), from where a mile-long trail (350ft ascent; starting just by the pay station) runs to the former silver-mining town of **Bennettville**. The town flourished for two years from 1882 and was then abandoned, though it saw brief flurries of activity in 1888 and 1933. A couple of wooden shacks – the former assay office and a livestock wintering barn – can still be seen. Through the trees to the west you can glimpse the tailings and mine entrance: follow the obvious short trail to reach them.

The *Junction* campground also marks the start of a three-mile gravel road past the *Sawmill* campground (see p.184) to **Saddlebag Lake**, a gorgeous area which is popular with **trout** fishers and opens up access to hiking in the 20 Lakes Basin (see Hike Y33, p.123). At the road end there's the first-come-first-served *Saddlebag Lake* campground (see p.184) and the Saddlebag Lake Resort (roughly July–Sept daily 7am–7pm; Ⓦwww.saddlebaglakeresort.com), a 1930s former hunting lodge which is now an all-in-one store and boat rental place (fishing boats $60 for 5hr) with a good diner. They also run a **ferry** service to the far end of the lake (every 30min; $11 round trip).

Back on Tioga Road, you continue down the Lee Vining Grade, gradually gaining views of Mono Lake, and in the last few miles before Lee Vining pass side roads leading to a handful of Forest Service campgrounds collectively known as the *Lee Vining Creek* campgrounds (see p.185).

3

Southern Yosemite

Roughly a quarter of the park's total area, **southern Yosemite**'s broad swathe of sharply peaked mountains extends from the foothills in the west twenty miles to the Sierra crest in the east. This section of the park is predominantly rugged country, though most visitors only see the thickly forested and more forgiving landscape of its very eastern fringes, accessed along **Wawona Road**.

In the 1860s and early 1870s Wawona Road was the stagecoach route from the San Joaquin Valley into Yosemite Valley, a harrowing journey typically broken up at the meadow-side homestead of Wawona. This is still where visitors to the southern part of the park stay, either at the campground or in the *Wawona Hotel*, with its sweeping lawns and broad verandas. In recognition of Wawona's historic importance, it was elected as the site for the **Pioneer Yosemite History Center**, a well-designed open-air museum with cabins and significant commercial buildings rescued from around the park and amassed beside the South Fork of the Merced River. Interesting though it is, the museum plays second fiddle to the **Mariposa Grove** of **giant sequoias**, part of the original 1864 Yosemite Grant that also set aside Yosemite Valley for preservation. Around five hundred enormous trunks make this easily the largest of Yosemite's three sequoia groves, and the most varied, with trees that have been hollowed out by fire, grown together, fallen over and bored through to create a car-sized passage. While the Mariposa Grove suffers slightly from its own popularity, it still outshines Wawona's nine-hole **golf course**, the horseback trips from the **stables** and general outdoor pursuits at hand in southern Yosemite.

Partway along Wawona Road, **Glacier Point Road** cuts east through forests past the winter sports nexus of **Badger Pass Ski Area**, to the park's **viewpoint** *par excellence* at **Glacier Point**, right on the rim of Yosemite Valley and level with the face of Half Dome. It's a justly popular spot, especially at sunset when it seems as if half the park's visitors are here hoping to catch the last rays glinting off the distant **Sierra crest**.

South from Yosemite Valley: Tunnel View and beyond

Wawona Road (Hwy-41) leaves the Yosemite Valley loop road near Bridalveil Fall and immediately starts to climb past a number of breaks in the trees which occasionally open up to reveal stunning views of the valley, the best being from

Tunnel View, a mile and a half up the road. Here, the whole of Yosemite Valley unfolds before you with El Capitan and Sentinel Rock standing as guardians to what lies beyond, notably Half Dome. From here it's easy to imagine the valley swamped by its primordial lake, which gradually filled in to leave the existing flat floor.

The view will be immediately recognizable to anyone familiar with the Ansel Adams image *Clearing Winter Storm*, with El Capitan and Sentinel Rock struggling to free themselves of cloud as Bridalveil Fall shines clearly on the right. Adams actually took the shot one rainy December day from **Inspiration Point**, a few hundred feet up the hill above Tunnel View. To get there, he would have used the original stagecoach road between Yosemite Valley and Wawona that was the regular route until 1933. Parts of it remain and can be seen by hiking the fairly steep first mile or so of the trail to Inspiration Point (see Hike Y9, p.112) starting just across the road from Tunnel View.

Yosemite Valley View and the road to Wawona

Tunnel View immediately precedes a 0.8-mile tunnel – the longest in the park – ending at **Yosemite Valley View**, where visitors bound for Yosemite Valley get their first glimpse of El Capitan and Half Dome. Above the road is the exfoliated granite form of **Turtleback Dome**, and across the valley are falls known simply as **The Cascades**. Although you're not actually much higher here than in Yosemite Valley, the vegetation has already changed. Black oaks have been left behind and the ponderosa pines are joined by cinnamon-barked incense cedar, tall, slender Douglas fir, low, scrubby manzanita and canyon oak.

The next six miles pass through scorched forest to a road junction known as **Chinquapin**, from where Glacier Point Road breaks off to the northeast. South from Chinquapin towards Wawona, a side road soon spurs a mile off to the right to **Yosemite West**, a private development just outside the park's western boundary that's not worth visiting unless you plan to stay at one of the B&Bs there (see p.175).

Back on Wawona Road it's an eleven-mile descent to Wawona, almost entirely through evergreens so thick they seldom reveal any views. Just before Wawona you pass the *Wawona* campground, site of the first park headquarters from 1891 to 1906, and a small riverside picnic area.

Glacier Point Road

The sixteen-mile-long **Glacier Point Road** (usually open mid-May to late Oct) branches off northeast from Wawona Road and provides the principal access to **Glacier Point**, arguably the finest viewpoint in the whole park. There's also some great hiking country hereabouts, with 7000ft trailheads saving hikers the grinding haul out of Yosemite Valley.

In winter the first five miles of the road are kept open to provide access to the **Badger Pass Ski Area** (chains are sometimes required); the only reason to stop before that is for the view down some 4500ft to Merced Canyon from a lookout (wayside marker G1) a couple of miles along. Theoretically, you can see down to the San Joaquin Valley and even to the Coast Mountains, but suitably clear days are rare.

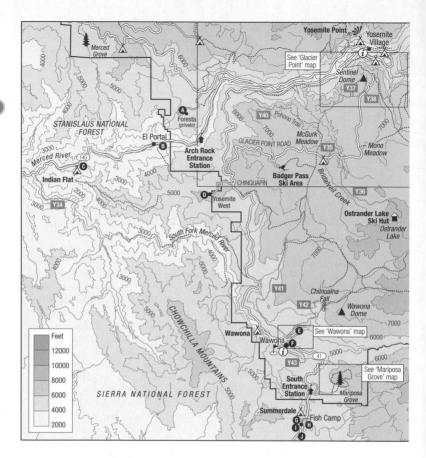

Badger Pass Ski Area

Three miles past the viewpoint is the **Badger Pass Ski Area** (for full coverage see Chapter 7, Winter activities), California's oldest skifield, established in 1935 at a time when the National Park Service was eager to attract as many visitors to Yosemite as possible. With a handful of short tows, a predominance of beginner and intermediate terrain, and superb cross-country skiing and snowshoe trails, it makes a great and unpretentious family destination. Once the tows stop and the snows melt, Badger Pass gets shut up until the next winter season.

Beyond Badger Pass to Washburn Point

Three miles past Badger Pass, through forests brimming with red fir, sits the **McGurk Meadow** trailhead (see Hike Y35, p.124), immediately followed by the *Bridalveil Creek* campground (see p.184), located a quarter of a mile south off Glacier Point Road. Bridalveil Creek begins its life at **Ostrander Lake** (see Hike Y36, p.124) and eventually plummets over Bridalveil Fall before joining the Merced River.

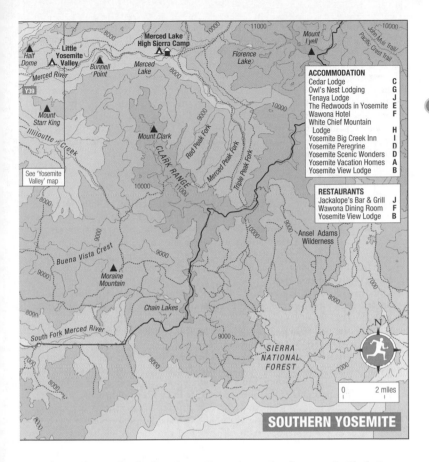

ACCOMMODATION
Cedar Lodge   C
Owl's Nest Lodging   G
Tenaya Lodge   J
The Redwoods in Yosemite   E
Wawona Hotel   F
White Chief Mountain
 Lodge   H
Yosemite Big Creek Inn   I
Yosemite Peregrine   D
Yosemite Scenic Wonders   D
Yosemite Vacation Homes   A
Yosemite View Lodge   B

RESTAURANTS
Jackalope's Bar & Grill   J
Wawona Dining Room   F
Yosemite View Lodge   B

SOUTHERN YOSEMITE

Almost three miles further along Glacier Point Road you reach **Clark Range View** (G6) where the 11,522ft Mount Clark can be identified by the avalanche trail down its face and into the forest below. To the left is the domed **Mount Starr King** (9092ft), named for the Unitarian pastor who did much to alert America to the wonders of Yosemite through his writings in 1860. At **Pothole Meadows** (G7), a couple of miles later, 5ft-diameter natural depressions fill with snowmelt in spring and early summer.

The sight of **Sentinel Dome** from the G8 marker may tempt you to tackle Hike Y38 (see p.126) from a trailhead parking lot just ahead. The mile-long trail leads to the 8122ft gleaming granite scalp of Sentinel Dome, topped by the remains of a gnarled Jeffrey pine. A second trail from the lot (Hike Y37, p.125) leads west to **Taft Point**, a fine vantage on the rim of Yosemite Valley, with views across to El Capitan. Nearby, the valley rim's granite edges have been deeply incised to form

Hikes from Glacier Point Road

Yosemite's **fifty best hikes** are found in Chapters 4 and 5. For our coverage of hikes from Glacier Point Road, see hikes Y35–Y40 in Chapter 4 (from p.124).

the **Taft Point Fissures** and, with care, you can peer down hundreds of feet. Far fewer people follow this trail, perhaps because of the vertiginous drops all around, only protected by the flimsiest of barriers in one spot.

Glacier Point Road soon launches into a descending series of steep **switchbacks** marking the last two miles to Glacier Point. Stop halfway along at **Washburn Point** for a striking side view of Half Dome. From here you're looking at the vertical face side-on, helping make the granite monster look remarkably slim in profile. Below lies the Merced River canyon, where you can clearly see the so-called "Grand Staircase" of Nevada and Vernal falls with the smooth dome of Liberty Cap rising above. To the right Mount Clark and the rounded summit of Mount Starr King stand out.

Glacier Point

The most astonishing views of Yosemite Valley are from **GLACIER POINT**, the top of an almost sheer cliff 3214 precipitous feet above Curry Village, thirty slow and twisting miles away by road. From the lookout, the valley floor appears in miniature far below and Half Dome fills the scene at eye level, backed by the distant snowcapped summits of the High Sierra. From here, Half Dome stands with its face angled slightly towards you, a stance that looks gorgeous when bathed in alpenglow just after sunset.

Right from the early days of tourism in Yosemite, Glacier Point's amalgam of boulders, pines and granite-formed viewpoints was a powerful lure. The **Four-Mile Trail** from Yosemite Valley was one of the earliest to be created, and even before the first road was constructed in 1883, visitors were coming up on mule-back to stay here (see box opposite).

The hotels have gone, but 150 years of tourism have left their mark with a network of viewpoints linked by smooth, asphalt pathways through the scattered pines. To learn something of the forces that created the wondrous landscape, drop in briefly at the open-sided **Geology Hut** on the eastern side of Glacier Point, then continue north to the valley rim to inspect the **Overhanging Rock**, which reaches way out over the void. Postcards found in every park store depict scenes of performers poised on the end of the rock doing handstands or

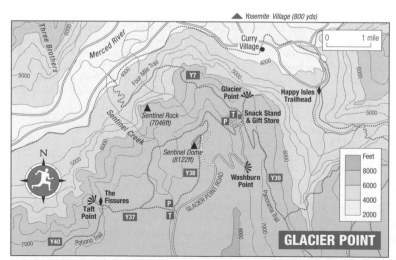

precarious ballet steps. In one early promotional stunt, someone even drove a Dodge out onto the end. The rock is supposedly off-limits, though that doesn't seem to deter those with something to prove from wandering out there to be photographed with Half Dome in the background. Nearby, where the main approach path meets the valley rim, the number 1982 on a metal railing marks the spot where the red fir bark fire was constructed then raked over the edge to create the **Firefall** (see box, p.70).

Practicalities

Though it's enjoyable to drive up here or ride the shuttle bus from Yosemite Valley, the moment of arrival at Glacier Point is much more rewarding if you hike to it on the very steep Four-Mile Trail (Hike Y7, p.110). Most people take a couple of photos, raid the **gift store** (daily June–Oct 9am–6pm), grab something from the **snack stand** (daily June–Oct 9am–4pm), and then leave. But it's worth spending a couple of hours in the area, perhaps hiking to the summit of Sentinel Dome (there's a trail from here as well as that described in Hike Y38) then returning to watch the lowering sun cast its golden hue over the mountainscape. After dark the crowds will disappear and you'll have time for reflection as the moon casts its silvery glow on the surface of Half Dome. On most summer evenings, the remodelled 150-seat granite amphitheatre overlooking Half Dome hosts free ranger-led talks. The half-hour **Sunset Talk** (usually on something topical) is frequently followed on Friday and Saturday evenings by the hour-long "Stars over Yosemite", explaining the mysteries of the night sky: see *Yosemite Guide* for details.

Oddly, the park concessionaire sees fit to close the gift store and snack stand well before a large number of people arrive for sunset, meaning there are no facilities for late arrivals. Pack accordingly, especially if you're staying for an astronomy talk: you may find it hard to get served dinner if you get back to the valley after 9pm.

Life at Glacier Point

By the mid-1870s Yosemite Valley was seeing around a thousand visitors a year, a tiny number by today's standards, but enough to justify the creation of the **Four-Mile Trail** from the valley to Glacier Point. Though built under the masterful eye of one John Conway, it was financed by James McCauley who then used the trail to transport materials for **The Mountain House**, a hotel built in 1876. Early guests would stand at the edge of the precipice, impressed by the sheer scale of the drop to the valley floor below. Some tossed things off, one visitor exclaiming "even an empty box, watched by a field-glass, could not be traced to its concussion with the valley floor". McCauley would then front up with a **hen** under his arm and toss it off. As she fluttered to a speck, and then disappeared altogether, the visitors would turn aghast to McCauley who, with a wave of his hand, would dismiss their fear claiming the chicken was used to it and made the enforced journey every day during the summer season. Apparently it walked back up, visitors occasionally encountering the chicken on the trail.

By 1917, *The Mountain House* was joined by the **Glacier Point Hotel**, and visitors could stay in grand style, lounging on the veranda which looked east with the best views to Half Dome. Both stayed open over the summer months, and in winter caretakers would protect the properties, shovelling snow and feeding winter visitors who skied or snowshoed in from Badger Pass (much as they do today). Both hotels **burned down** in 1969, and revised park authority policies didn't allow either to be rebuilt.

Wawona

In the southern half of Yosemite, everyone heads for **WAWONA**, beside the South Fork of the Merced River, 27 miles south of Yosemite Village on Hwy-41. Though Wawona is at the same altitude as Yosemite Valley (around 4000ft) it has a completely different feel, more open and surrounded not by granite domes and spires, but by dense forest and meadows. There's also a considerably more relaxed pace here with visitors playing a round of golf, ambling around the **Pioneer Yosemite History Center** or hopping on the free shuttle bus that runs the seven miles to the **Mariposa Grove** of **giant sequoias**, and guests lounging around the grounds of the *Wawona Hotel*.

For those feeling more active, a handful of **hikes** start in the area and the Wawona Stables (see p.143) offer short and full-day **horseback rides**. The area's best **swimming hole** is close by the **Swinging Bridge**: follow Forest Drive for two miles to the Seventh Day Adventist Camp, where you branch left for a quarter of a mile along a dirt road then park and walk five minutes to a deep, crystal-clear pool with big white boulders.

Some history

The meadows of Wawona were originally known as *Pallachun*, or "good place to stop" to Native Americans making their way from the Sierra Nevada foothills to Yosemite Valley. Here they hunted game and gathered acorns and basket-making materials, until their lifestyle was destroyed by the 1851 arrival of gold miners and the Mariposa Battalion (see "History", p.232). In 1856, 160 acres of the area were homesteaded by 42-year-old **Galen Clark**, who had suffered a severe lung haemorrhage and headed for the hills to live out his last days, but ended up surviving until he was 96. The area's giant sequoias had been "discovered" as early as 1851, but it wasn't until 1857 that Clark and trail-building entrepreneur Milton Mann thoroughly documented the big trees. Clark called the forest "Mariposa Grove" and renamed his homestead **Big Trees Station**.

Close to the current site of the *Wawona Hotel*, Clark ran a sawmill and blacksmith's shop, and provided for visitors travelling the original carriage road from Mariposa to Yosemite Valley. When Mariposa Grove became part of the Yosemite Grant in 1864, Clark was made guardian. He sold Big Trees Station in 1874 to the Washburn brothers who built the original *Wawona Hotel*, which burned down four

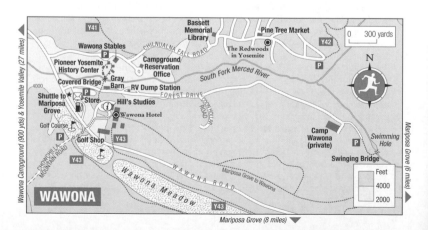

Wawona hikes

For our coverage of hikes accessed from Wawona and around, see hikes Y41–Y43 in Chapter 4 (from p.127).

years later. By 1879, the existing main building was built, the meadow was fenced for grazing animals, and produce was grown for hotel guests. Within three years, the area's name had changed again, this time to **Wa-wo-nah**, the local Indian name for the big trees, and the sound of the call of their guardian spirit, the owl.

In the early twentieth century the Washburns' son Clarence persuaded his parents to build a golf course to lure the newly car-mobile visitors. By 1925, planes were landing on the meadow, and there were daily mail and passenger flights until 1932 when the Wawona area was incorporated into Yosemite National Park. As with many national parks, areas that were previously occupied became "inholdings" where residents were entitled to remain living. One such homesteaded section lies along Chilnualna Falls Road about a mile from the *Wawona Hotel*. You'll see it if you head to the start of the Chilnualna Fall trail (Hike Y42, p.128) and may even choose to stay there in the private homes of *The Redwoods in Yosemite* (see p.174).

Wawona Hotel

Pretty much everything in Wawona revolves around the landmark *Wawona Hotel*, California's second-oldest hotel (after the *Coronado* in San Diego). It started out in 1876 as a small cluster of white-painted, wooden buildings, but was soon joined by the Washburn brothers' main two-storey building with its encircling broad verandas and scattered chairs. The entire complex is set in expansive grassy grounds with incense cedars and ponderosa pines all about.

The hotel (see "Accommodation", p.174) boasts a small **swimming pool** for guests only, a **tennis court** open to all (free for guests, otherwise $2.50; free racquets from the golf shop), and a **nine-hole golf course** with fairways sprawled across the meadows, just over the road. The course is open to the public (mid-April to Oct; $41.50 for 18 holes, $25.50 for 9, plus optional cart rental $22.50 for 18 holes, $17.50 for 9; ☎209/375-6572). There are slightly cheaper green fees on weekdays. Alternative tees turn this into a par seventy eighteen-hole course, with grazing mule deer as an added obstacle. The site of Galen Clark's first residence is marked behind the seventh green.

Pioneer Yosemite History Center

Though most of Yosemite's historic buildings have been lost to fire or simply knocked down, around a dozen have been gathered together at the **Pioneer Yosemite History Center** (self-guided walking tour all year; free), two minutes' walk north of the *Wawona Hotel*. Though well executed, it can be a little pedestrian except when (funding permitting) park staff dress in period costume and open up some of the History Center's buildings.

Most of the structures were brought here in the early 1960s and arranged either side of the **covered bridge**, which spans the South Fork of the Merced River. The bridge was originally built by Galen Clark in 1868, but was covered in 1878 (to prevent snow build-up in winter). All Yosemite-bound traffic used to come this way, and though a modern bridge nearby now takes the strain, age has taken its toll. Now restored, the bridge is open to pedestrians and wagon rides only.

On the bridge's south side, the large **Gray Barn** was used for harnessing up the carriages and now contains a couple of early stagecoaches, horse tack and a 1916 toll board – the six-mile journey from Wawona to the Big Trees cost a horse and rider twelve cents. The remaining relocated buildings are clustered on the north side of the bridge, centred on the **Wells Fargo office**, once the hub of telegraph and booking services in Yosemite Valley. Also of interest are a dank, stone building which was once used as a primitive jail; **Degnan's bakery**, run in Yosemite Valley by an Irish couple who baked a thousand loaves a day along with doughnuts, muffins and cookies; and the cabin belonging to **George Anderson**, the valley blacksmith made famous for his original ascent up Half Dome (see p.54). Throughout the summer, free **blacksmithing demonstrations** are held here (check *Yosemite Guide* for times).

Something of the spirit of life in Yosemite in the late nineteenth century can be gleaned on fun, ten-minute **Horse-Drawn Stage Rides** (late June to early Sept Wed 2–4pm, Thurs–Sun 10am–noon & 2–4pm; $4, ages 3–12 $3), which start outside the old Wells Fargo office.

Wawona practicalities

Wawona is just over an hour's drive south of Yosemite Valley and a shade under five miles north of the park's South Entrance. There's no convenient public transportation to Wawona from Yosemite Valley or anywhere outside the park, though you could visit Wawona and the Mariposa Grove on the guided Grand Tour from the valley (see p.28). The parking lot at Mariposa Grove is often full, so, once in Wawona, make use of the free **Mariposa Grove & Wawona Shuttle Bus** (mid-April to early Oct daily 9am–6pm) which runs frequently from the Wawona Store to Mariposa Grove. There's an intermediate stop at the South Entrance, so drivers entering the park from the south can park here and ride the shuttle to the Mariposa Grove, then pick up their vehicle on the way back. The last bus back leaves the grove at 6pm. The shuttle is also handy for hikers who want to ride one way then hike back to Wawona, downhill all the way (see box, p.100).

Information and wilderness permits are available from the **Wawona Visitor Center** (mid-May to mid-Sept daily 8.30am–5pm; ℡209/375-9531), housed in Hill's Studio, once the workshop of landscape painter Thomas Hill. Snacks, camping supplies and a limited range of **groceries** are available from the Wawona Store (daily: June–Aug 8am–8pm; Sept–May 8am–7pm), and from the **Pine Tree Market** (similar hours), a mile along Chilnualna Falls Road. The Wawona Store also has a **post office** (Mon–Fri 9am–5pm, Sat 9am–noon), and the Bassett Memorial **Library**, 7971 Chilnualna Falls Rd (late May to early Sept Mon–Fri 1–6pm, Sat 10am–3pm; early Sept to late May Wed–Fri 1–6pm, Sat 10am–3pm), has free **internet access**.

Evening **entertainment** hereabouts is limited. Most nights each week there's a **ranger campfire programme** at the campground (open to all; free; check *Yosemite Guide* for details), but if the opportunity arises don't miss the show put on by **Tom Bopp** (April–Oct Tues–Sat 5.30–9.30pm; Nov–March some weekends; free) in the *Wawona Hotel* lounge. A fixture since 1983, Tom mostly just plays the piano as guests drink cocktails and wander in to dinner, but roughly twice a week (check with the hotel for details) he performs an hour-long interpretive session. While bashing out songs from Yosemite's past (mostly vaudeville, but anything goes) on a piano once used to accompany the Firefall at Curry Village (see box, p.70), he reels slides pertinent to the pieces being played. Pitched for all ages, some might find it all a bit cheesy, but Tom's obvious passion and enthusiasm always carry the evening.

Mariposa Grove

The biggest and most spectacular stand of **giant sequoias** in Yosemite is **MARIPOSA GROVE** (snowbound in winter, but open at all times; free), at the end of Mariposa Grove Road, two miles east of the park's South Entrance. Eight-foot diameter ponderosa pines and huge cedars are dwarfed by approximately five hundred mature sequoias, some up to 3000 years old, spread over an area roughly two miles by one mile. You can see sequoias all around the entrance area parking lot at an altitude of 5500ft, but to see the best, you really need to walk – not far, but all the trails lead gradually uphill. The sequoias straggle across a hillside gaining 1500ft from the **Lower Grove**, home to most of the biggest trees, to the **Upper Grove** where there's a greater concentration of sequoias but fewer really enormous specimens.

First explored by Galen Clark in 1857, the Mariposa Grove and Yosemite Valley were jointly set aside as the **Yosemite Grant**, the world's first public preserve, in 1864. This afforded some protection at a time when sequoias were being cut for lumber and generally mistreated: one tree in the Calaveras Grove, north of Yosemite, died after its bark was stripped for display on the East Coast and in Britain. Clark was appointed as the first guardian, but wasn't able (or willing) to prevent tunnels being cut through two of the trees during his guardianship. Mariposa Grove was finally incorporated into Yosemite National Park in 1916.

Cars are now banned from the grove, but anyone with a modest level of fitness should have no trouble exploring some of the two and a half miles of well-maintained **trails** on foot: take your time heading uphill and enjoy the quick stroll back down at the end. If you can't cope with the terrain, join the hour-and-a-quarter-long **Big Trees Tram Tour** (June–Oct daily 9am–5pm, every 20min; $25.50, seniors $24, ages 5–12 $18; ☏209/375-1621) and get towed along a paved road on a flat-deck trailer with seats. Headphone narration comes in several languages. There are stops at the Fallen Monarch, Grizzly Giant and Clothespin Tree, and you're allowed to get off at the museum and board a later tour if you

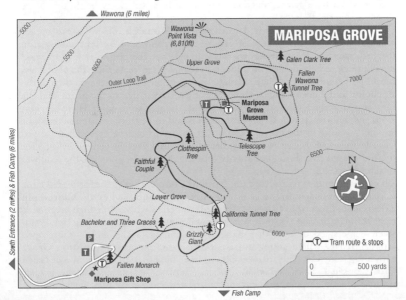

Hiking the loop: Mariposa Grove to Wawona

Throughout much of the year, visitors travelling from Wawona to Mariposa Grove are encouraged to use the free Mariposa Grove & Wawona Shuttle Bus. Rather than take the bus in both directions, consider riding the shuttle to the grove, exploring at leisure, then hiking back to Wawona. It's not an especially spectacular hike by Yosemite standards, but it's downhill all the way and gives you the flexibility to stick around Mariposa Grove after the last shuttle bus has gone.

The hike from **Mariposa Grove to Wawona** (6.5 miles one way; 2–3hr; 2000ft descent) is a pleasant forest walk signposted off the grove's Outer Loop Trail. After 0.7 miles, a left fork is signed to Wawona. Continue steadily downhill through trees allowing sylvan views of Wawona Dome and the Wawona basin. After an hour or so you come to a small roadside parking bay and, at a trail junction two hundred yards beyond, take the left fork and follow it along a broad, undulating ridge used by horses. Keep going straight to reach the hotel for a well-earned cocktail on the veranda.

wish, though at busy times you may have to wait for a place. **Tickets** can be bought at the Mariposa Gift Shop, by the parking lot (April–Oct daily 9am–6pm), which also sells a limited range of **snacks**.

Mariposa Grove suffers slightly from its own popularity, so you should try to **arrive early or stay late** to avoid the crowds. A winter visit can be fantastic, though you'll need snowshoes or cross-country skiing equipment. You can even camp here in the snowy season (see p.147).

Grove highlights

After a century and a half of tourism, Mariposa Grove is presented as something of a sequoia freak show. While it's impressive enough just coming face-to-bark with these giants, throughout the grove unusual trees are singled out for attention – ones which have grown together, split apart, been struck by lightning, or are simply staggeringly large.

In the Lower Grove signs lead to the **Fallen Monarch**, made famous by the widely reproduced 1899 photo of cavalry officers and their horses standing atop the prostrate tree. No one knows when it fell, but the tannin-rich heartwood doesn't seem to have deteriorated much in the hundred years since the photo was taken. Following the path beyond the elegant cluster of four trees known as the **Bachelor and Three Graces**, you arrive at the largest tree in the grove (and the fifth-largest in the world), the **Grizzly Giant**, thought to be somewhere between 2700 and 3500 years old. Its lowest branch is said to be thicker than the trunk of any non-sequoia in the grove, a claim that is easy to believe even when viewed from 100ft below. Adjacent is the **California Tunnel Tree**, bored out in 1859 for stagecoaches to pass through, but only accessible to pedestrians since the road was realigned in 1932.

It's a ten-minute walk to reach the **Faithful Couple**, two trees that seeded close to one another and appear to be united. A bit further up the hill, the **Clothespin Tree** is indeed shaped like an old-fashioned clothespin with a 40ft-high inverted V right through its base where it was hollowed out by fire. Continuing uphill you reach a final stand of trees that marks the beginning of the slightly more open **Upper Grove**, where you'll also come upon the one-room **Mariposa Grove Museum** (June–Oct daily 10am–4.30pm; free), built in 1930 on the site of Galen Clark's original cabin. It contains modest displays and photos of the mighty sequoias, and sells Yosemite- and woodland-related books and educational materials.

Most visitors don't go much further so you'll have more peace and quiet as you stroll up to the **Telescope Tree**, where you can walk into the fire-hollowed base and peer up the length of the trunk to a tiny disc of sky. A little further on you'll see the **Wawona Tunnel Tree** lying beside the trail where it fell under a heavy load of snow in 1969. The tunnel dated from 1881 when the Yosemite Stage and Turnpike Company paid the Scribner brothers $75 to enlarge an old burn scar to a tunnel 26ft long, 8ft high and up to 8ft wide.

If you've still got the energy, tackle the half-mile spur trail to **Wawona Point**, at 6810ft the highest point in the grove, for a great panorama of the High Sierra and along the South Fork of the Merced River.

Day hikes in Yosemite

However magnificent the roadside scenery, it is no substitute for striking out on foot along some of the eight hundred miles of **hiking trails** weaving through Yosemite National Park. The solitude and scenic grandeur quickly get their hooks into you, and many people are so aptivated by the experience they end up doing far more hiking than they ever imagined.

Novice hikers may want to join one of the excellent guided day hikes, but it is really very easy to head out on your own along one of the less strenuous walks we've listed. More **experienced hikers** may feel restricted by our day-hiking recommendations and should flip straight to Chapter 5, Backcountry hiking and camping. Everyone should read our "Hiking essentials" section on p.28.

Gentle hikes can be undertaken without leaving Yosemite Valley floor, but to get away from the crowds you only need to tackle any path with a bit of a slope. Some of the finest and most accessible trails, including the stunning **Mist Trail** and the demanding route up **Half Dome**, start from the **Happy Isles trailhead** at the eastern end of Yosemite Valley. In other areas of the park, **Tuolumne Meadows** has the greatest concentration of high-country walks, though there are also plenty along **Tioga Road** and several more around **Wawona** and at **Hetch Hetchy**.

Since **wilderness permits** are **not required** for day hikes, you need only get yourself to the trailhead and set off. In Yosemite Valley there is no trailhead parking, so you must park in one of the day-use lots and ride the free **valley shuttle** (see p.25) to the trailhead. Elsewhere in the park, either ride the Glacier Point or Tuolumne Meadows **hikers' buses** (see p.26), or drive your own vehicle to the trailhead; you'll usually find enough parking, along with steel **bear-resistant lockers** in which you must stash any food and scented toiletries.

How tough is the hike?

All fifty hikes in this guide have been given a rating in one of four categories:

Easy Generally a walk of up to a couple of hours on relatively smooth surfaces across flat or gently sloping ground.

Moderate A hike with some gradient but on well-maintained trails, taking up to several hours.

Strenuous A tougher proposition on fairly steep and occasionally rough ground, usually consuming most of the day.

Very strenuous A trek of at least eight hours negotiating steep terrain on uneven ground.

Estimated **walking times** assume a short break every hour or so but do not take into account lunch breaks or picnic stops.

Remember to pack out all **trash**, bury **bodily waste** at least six inches deep and 100ft from any water, and stand quietly aside for **horseback riders**. For the longer walks you'll want to carry a hiking map (see p.40 for more on maps).

Hikes from Yosemite Valley: Happy Isles trailhead

The hikes in this section all start from the **Happy Isles trailhead**, at the eastern end of Yosemite Valley (shuttle stop 16). They all initially follow the Merced River, and each hike builds on the previous one.

Y1 Vernal Fall footbridge

Difficulty Easy
Distance 1.6 miles round trip
Estimated time 1hr
Elevation gain 500ft ascent
Season Accessible all year, though falls are best in May and June
Trailhead location Map p.106, shuttle stop 16 near the Nature Center at Happy Isles
Comments Beautiful scenery but sometimes crowded

If you don't have time for the Mist Trail (see Hike Y2), try this moderately steep path over broken asphalt to a perfect pine-framed view up the Merced River to Vernal Fall. It follows part of the John Muir Trail (JMT: see box, p.135), starting

---

Guided day hikes

If you're uncertain of your ability to navigate, fancy a little commentary about the journey, or are just looking for some companionship, the answer might be to join a **guided hike**. As well as their rock climbing instruction (see p.141) and backcountry hikes (see p.134), the **Yosemite Mountaineering School** (℡209/372-8344, ⓦwww .yosemitemountaineering.com) runs a series of organized group hikes mostly from late May to early September. You'll be teamed up with other hikers and will be led by a knowledgeable guide. The school's guided day hikes include:

Cliffs and Climbers Hike A great taster, spending a couple of hours or so ferreting around the base of cliffs where rock climbers ply their trade. Guides tell tales of colourful characters and their exploits. $10 per person; under 10s free.

Discovery Hike Head out for three to four hours, perhaps following a gentle loop trail around the eastern end of Yosemite Valley (similar to Hike Y5), or hiking from Tunnel View to Inspiration Point (Hike Y9). The emphasis is on appreciating the scenery, flora, fauna and local history. $20 per person; under 10s free.

Adventure Hike Six hours of exploration giving the group time to explore more extensively. $40 per person; under 10s free.

Custom Hikes Hikes tailored to your needs and tastes. Rates are for half a day ($58 a head for 3–7 people, $160 total for 1–2); an eight-hour day ($75–86 a head for 3–7 people, $96 for two); or an extreme ten-hour day ($125 a head for 3–7 people, $290 total for 1–2).

Companies based outside the park also run guided hikes in the park. One of the best is **Yosemite Guides** (℡1-866/922-9111, ⓦwww.yosemiteguides.com), based at *Yosemite View Lodge* on Hwy-140 (see p.177), who offer five-hour naturalist-led walks. Try the High Country Trails ($65) or the Sunset Walk ($70), which explores the valley rim around Sentinel Dome. Also worth checking out is the extensive programme of specialist hikes run by the **Yosemite Conservancy** (ⓦwww.yosemite .org; see p.45)

Yosemite's best day hikes

Hike	Name	Grade	Length (miles)	Time (hr)	Ascent (feet)	Season	Waterfalls	Best in spring	Wildlife	Wildflowers	Kid-friendly	Swimming	Solitude	Views	History
	YOSEMITE VALLEY														
Y1	Vernal Fall footbridge	Easy	1.6	1	500	All year	✓				✓				
Y2	Mist Trail to the top of Vernal Fall	Moderate	3.0	2–3	1100	All year	✓								
Y3	Mist Trail to the top of Nevada Fall	Strenuous	7.0	5–8	1900	May–Nov	✓								
Y4	Half Dome	Very strenuous	17.0	9–12	4800	Late May to mid-Oct									
Y5	Eastern Valley Loop	Easy	2.6	1–2	50	All year	✓	✓			✓			✓	
Y6	Upper Yosemite Fall	Strenuous	7.0	4–7	2700	April–Dec		✓				✓			✓
Y7	Four-Mile Trail to Glacier Point	Strenuous	4.8	2.5–4	3200	Mid-May to Oct							✓	✓	✓✓
Y8	Western Valley Loop	Easy	6.5	2.5–3.5	350	All year							✓	✓	
Y9	Inspiration Point	Moderate	2.4	1.5–2.5	600	Mid-May to Oct									✓
	HETCH HETCHY														
Y10	Wapama Falls	Easy	5.0	2–3	400	Mid-April to Nov	✓	✓		✓	✓		✓		
Y11	Rancheria Falls	Moderate	14.5	5–8	800	Mid-April to Nov	✓	✓		✓			✓	✓	
	TIOGA ROAD														
Y12	El Capitan from Tamarack Flat	Strenuous	16.5	7–10	1240	June–Oct				✓	✓		✓	✓	
Y13	Harden Lake	Easy	6.0	2–3	270	June–Oct				✓	✓		✓	✓	
Y14	Lukens Lake	Easy	1.6	1	200	June–Oct					✓				
Y15	Yosemite Falls from Yosemite Creek	Strenuous	12.0	5–7	700	June–Oct	✓				✓	✓			
Y16	North Dome from Porcupine Creek	Moderate	9.0	4–6	650	June–Oct			✓					✓	✓
Y17	May Lake	Easy	2.5	1	400	June–Oct					✓	✓			
Y18	Clouds Rest from Tenaya Lake	Strenuous	14.5	7–10	1800	June–Oct				✓				✓	✓
Y19	Polly Dome Lakes	Easy	5.0	2–3	500	Late June–Oct				✓		✓		✓	
Y20	Tenaya Lake circuit	Easy	3.0	1–1.5	50	June–Oct					✓	✓			

TUOLUMNE MEADOWS & TIOGA PASS

	Hike	Difficulty	Distance	Time	Elevation	Season
Y21	Pothole Dome	Easy	0.5	1	200	June–Oct
Y22	Cathedral Lakes	Moderate	8.0	3–5	1000	June–Oct
Y23	Soda Springs and Parsons Lodge	Easy	4.0	2	50	June–Oct
Y24	Elizabeth Lake	Moderate	4.8	3–5	900	June–Oct
Y25	Lyell Canyon	Easy	11.0	4–5	100	June–Oct
Y26	Dog Lake	Easy	3.2	1.5–2.5	600	June–Oct
Y27	Lembert Dome	Moderate	3.7	2–3	850	June–Oct
Y28	Young Lakes	Strenuous	13.5	7–10	1500	June–Oct
Y29	Glen Aulin	Moderate	11.0	6–8	600	June–Oct
Y30	Waterwheel Falls	Very strenuous	17.5	8–12	2100	June–Oct
Y31	Mono Pass	Moderate	8.0	4–6	1000	June–Oct
Y32	Gaylor Lakes and the Great Sierra Mine	Moderate	3.0	2–3	500	June–Oct
Y33	Saddlebag Lake and 20 Lakes Basin	Moderate	8.0	3–5	600	July–Oct

HWY-140 & GLACIER POINT ROAD

	Hike	Difficulty	Distance	Time	Elevation	Season
Y34	Hite Cove Trail	Moderate	7.0	3–5	300	Feb–Oct
Y35	McGurk Meadow	Easy	1.6	1	150	Mid-May to Oct
Y36	Ostrander Lake	Strenuous	12.6	5–7	1600	Mid-May to Oct
Y37	Taft Point and the Fissures	Easy	2.2	1	250	Mid-May to Oct
Y38	Sentinel Dome	Easy	2.2	1	250	Mid-May to Oct
Y39	Panorama Trail	Moderate	9.0	6–8	800	Mid-May to Oct
Y40	Pohono Trail	Strenuous	13.8	5–8	2800	May–Oct

WAWONA & MARIPOSA GROVE

	Hike	Difficulty	Distance	Time	Elevation	Season
Y41	Alder Creek	Strenuous	12.0	5–7	1700	April–Nov
Y42	Chilnualna Fall	Strenuous	8.2	4–6	2400	Mid-May to Oct
Y43	Wawona Meadow Loop	Easy	3.5	1–2	100	March–Dec

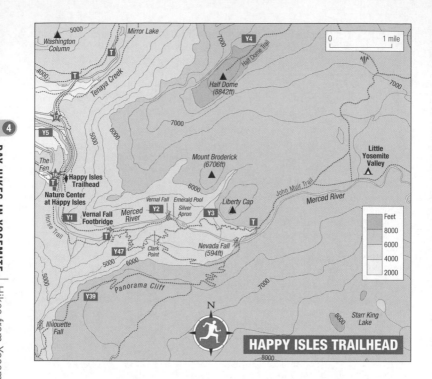

HAPPY ISLES TRAILHEAD

just east of the road bridge over the Merced River. The path leads upstream past a detailed trail distance sign and starts climbing. There are plenty of chances to catch your breath, as breaks in the pines and black oaks reveal the churning river below and views up to the 370ft **Illilouette Fall** lurking in the shadows of Illilouette Canyon. The fall is formed by Illilouette Creek, which drains the country west of Glacier Point Road then plunges over what is known as **Panorama Cliff** to join the Merced River below.

The trail continues to a footbridge over the Merced from where you'll get a great view of **Vernal Fall**. With the river crashing over huge boulders in the foreground it's a dramatic vantage point, usually crowded with people photographing their friends with the falls in the background. Vernal Fall gets its name from the Latin for spring, and the 317ft fall indeed looks its best during the spring snowmelt when the curtain of water is perhaps eighty or a hundred feet wide.

There are toilets and drinking water at the footbridge. Return the way you came.

Y2 Mist Trail to the top of Vernal Fall

Difficulty Moderate
Distance 3 miles round trip
Estimated time 2–3hr
Elevation gain 1100ft ascent
Season Accessible all year; the falls are best in May & June but run year-round
Trailhead location Map p.106, shuttle stop 16 near the Nature Center at Happy Isles
Comments Fairly crowded and you can expect to get drenched in spring

If you only do one hike in Yosemite, this should be it. During the spring snowmelt this short walk really packs a punch as it twists up a path so close to **Vernal Fall** that a rainbow often frames the cascading water, and hikers get drenched in spray; bring a raincoat or plan to get wet. Though hardly dangerous, the Mist Trail demands sure footing and a head for heights.

Start by following Hike Y1 to the Vernal Fall footbridge, after which the crowds thin appreciably. Continue 150 yards past the bridge to a junction where the John Muir Trail (and all the mule traffic) goes right. Take the pedestrian-only left-hand path marked **Mist Trail**, which starts climbing steadily along a fairly narrow path built over large wet boulders. If you're lucky, the sun will be playing on the spray thrown up by the roaring falls, creating beautiful rainbows. Railings protect you from the edge and provide support for the final haul up slippery steps cut into the rock. At the top of the fall you can rest on the smooth slabs beside the deceptively placid **Emerald Pool**. Water flows into the pool over the **Silver Apron**, a thirty-yard-wide shelf of slick rock that looks very tempting as a slide. Rocks in the pool at the bottom have caused numerous injuries and signs ban both sliding and swimming. People still swim, but rangers are increasingly keen to stop people diving onto the submerged rocks or getting swept over the falls, which happens almost every year.

Either retrace your steps to the trailhead, or return via the JMT (slightly longer but easier), reached along the path leading uphill from near the footbridge just above the Silver Apron.

Y3 Mist Trail to the top of Nevada Fall

Difficulty Strenuous
Distance 7 miles round trip
Estimated time 5–8hr
Elevation gain 1900ft ascent
Season May–Nov; falls are best May & June, good fall colours Oct & Nov
Trailhead location Map p.106, shuttle stop 16 near the Nature Center at Happy Isles
Comments Crowds thin towards Nevada Fall where you get a high-country feel

This hike expands on Hike Y2, adding an extra 800ft of ascent and taking in more expansive views of the high country, including a **close-up view** of the 594ft **Nevada Fall**, higher and perhaps even more striking than Vernal Fall. It takes its name from the Spanish for snowy (as in Sierra Nevada, "snowy range") and forms a relatively narrow cascade falling vertically for half its height then fanning out on a steep, smooth granite apron for the remaining 300ft.

Follow Hike Y2 as far as the Silver Apron then cross the footbridge immediately above it. Except on the busiest summer weekends you'll have few fellow hikers as you wind through the forest, passing a flat spot which, from 1870 until 1897, was the spray-drenched location of *La Casa Nevada*, also known as *Snow's Hotel*. Guides apparently used to boast of being able to show their clients 11ft of snow, even in summer. They then introduced them to the 6ft-tall Albert Snow and his 5ft wife, Emily.

The path then follows a series of switchbacks climbing up the side of Nevada Fall with the rounded peak of **Liberty Cap** rearing above. Roughly level with the top of Nevada Fall you meet the JMT (toilets). Half Dome hikers turn left here, but turn right and you'll soon reach the Merced River at the top of Nevada Fall. Peer over the lip at the cascade below from one of numerous excellent viewpoints, then relax on the smooth grey slabs of rock while tucking into your lunch. Some vigilance is required to stop the squirrels spiriting away your sandwiches. Once again, the pools look very tempting, but swimming is banned, for good reason.

For the return journey, rejoin the JMT and continue downhill passing an intersection with the Panorama Trail (Hike Y39). The JMT now cuts across a cliff face, the path almost carved into the rock face with dripping overhangs above and a solid stone wall separating you from the vertiginous drop. This section can be icy in spring before the summer sun warms the shady corners. The trail then eases with some great views of Half Dome, and across Yosemite Valley to the park's northern reaches.

Y4 Half Dome

Difficulty Very strenuous
Distance 17 miles round trip
Estimated time 9–12hr
Elevation gain 4800ft ascent
Season Late May to mid-Oct; cable stays are removed from Half Dome in winter (note permit restrictions – see box below)
Trailhead location Map p.106, shuttle stop 16 near the Nature Center at Happy Isles
Comments Understandably the park's most popular hard hike; well worth the effort, providing you can get a reservation

The summit of Half Dome is the most alluring target of ambitious day hikers, who are rewarded with stupendous views from the broad, flat top almost 5000ft above Yosemite Valley floor. The route is a full-day undertaking and hikers should start at the crack of **dawn**, initially following either Hike Y3 to the top of Nevada Fall or following the JMT to the same point; for variety take the other route on the way down. From the junction of the two trails, follow the JMT as it skirts the backcountry campground in **Little Yosemite Valley** and follows Sunrise Creek steeply uphill. Split off the JMT along the **Half Dome Trail**, passing the **last water** on the track (a small spring half a mile past the junction on the left), then reaching the base of Quarter Dome. Steep steps lead up across smooth slabs until you reach the base of **Half Dome** with **steel cables** and wooden slats lashed to its extremely steep curved back. This is the only way to ascend the last four hundred vertical feet to the summit, and short sections are at an intimidating angle of sixty degrees. The steps are removed in mid-October to discourage winter ascents and reinstalled at the end of May. At the base of the cables you'll probably find a pile of free-use **gloves** left behind by hikers. The Park Service regards this as trash and requests people take their gloves home with them, but they are nice to protect tender hands while gripping the rough cables. Do not approach the summit if there's thunder around (commonly late afternoons from August to October), as both the peak and steel cables attract **lightning bolts**.

At the summit, you're rewarded by magnificent views across Yosemite Valley to Basket Dome and North Dome, right to Clouds Rest and left along the valley towards El Capitan. Anyone concerned about their outdoor credibility will want to edge out to the very lip of the abyss – known as "The Visor" – and peer down the sheer 2000ft northwest face. You have now earned yourself the right to buy a "I climbed Half Dome" T-shirt from the Village Store.

Half Dome permits

In an attempt to control overcrowding on the final cables section of the Half Dome route, the Park Service has instituted an interim **permit system**. In 2010 this required anyone wanting to use the cables on a Friday, Saturday, Sunday or a federal holiday during the entire mid-May to October cables season to obtain a permit. Costing only a couple of dollars, four hundred were available for each day, but the entire quota was **sold out within ten minutes** of becoming available. This has forced people to hike up on other days, and daily numbers sometimes peak at 1200, creating dangerous congestion. It is possible that, in future, the quota system will be applied every day of the week through the season. Get the latest on obtaining a permit at ⓦwww.nps.gov/yose/planyourvisit/hdpermits.htm.

Wilderness permit holders may be able to get a permit to ascend the cables if Half Dome is part of their itinerary.

Hikers were once allowed to camp on the Half Dome's summit, but the few trees which hung on soon became firewood, sanitary facilities on bare granite proved near impossible, and the rare Mount Lyell salamander was not given the protection it needed. Camping is now forbidden, but it is possible to do Half Dome as an **overnight hike** by spending the night at Little Yosemite Valley around halfway up: be sure to reserve wilderness permits early as the quota is taken up fast, particularly for weekends.

Hikes from Yosemite Valley: the rest of the valley

The hikes in this section start at the eastern end of Yosemite Valley and move west. The main features on these walks are discussed in depth throughout Chapter 1.

Y5 Eastern Valley Loop

Difficulty Easy
Distance 2.6-mile loop
Estimated time 1–2hr
Elevation gain 50ft ascent
Season All year
Trailhead location Map p.106, main parking lot at Curry Village
Comments A gentle stroll around Curry Village and the Happy Isles area close to most of the campgrounds

This gentle hike weaves through some of the most populated sections of the park, but is surprisingly peaceful as it loops around the eastern end of Yosemite Valley past its main features and some attractive riverside scenery.

Starting from the main parking lot at Curry Village, head east along the broad path that runs between tent cabins until you reach the shuttle road. Turn right, and then almost immediately go right again into a parking lot used by overnight hikers. From the lot's eastern corner, a dirt track cuts half a mile through incense cedars and ponderosa pines to a swampy area known as **The Fen**, its soggy ecosystem explained by an interpretive panel. A trail from here leads you to the Nature Center at Happy Isles, beside the Merced River, where there's an impressive view of **North Dome** and Washington Column. Take a few minutes to visit the nature centre (see p.70) and don't miss the display on rockfall around the back. Cross the Merced on the road bridge and turn left to follow the dogwood-shaded river bank, gradually veering further left as you approach the valley stables; there are especially good views of Upper Yosemite Fall along this stretch. At the stables, walk over Clark Bridge then immediately turn right into the **Lower Pines campground** and follow the campground roads to the far northwestern end. Here a narrow path cuts through trees to Stoneman Meadow. Cross over the long boardwalk and continue straight to return to Curry Village.

Y6 Upper Yosemite Fall

Difficulty Strenuous
Distance 7 miles round trip
Estimated time 4–7hr
Elevation gain 2700ft ascent
Season April–Dec, but best in spring and fall when it isn't too hot
Trailhead location Map p.56, Camp 4 parking lot accessed from shuttle stop 7
Comments Very popular trail but rewarding both physically and scenically – Columbia Rock makes a far easier destination than hiking the whole way to the top of the fall

This perennially popular, energy-sapping hike climbs steeply to the north rim of Yosemite Valley with great views of Upper Yosemite Fall for much of the way, and the opportunity to sit virtually on the edge of the fall and gaze down at the Lilliputian activity below in Yosemite Village. The south-facing slopes catch the sun for most of the year, quickly melting most snowfall and keeping this trail open when others are snowbound. This also means you'll want to get an early start in summer, when it's best to set off by 7am.

The hike starts behind *Camp 4*, and quickly climbs through glades of canyon live oak. You'll probably want to catch your breath a couple of times in the first half-hour until the trail gradually bends to the right and eases. Breaks in the trees reveal the valley far below, but the best vista is saved for **Columbia Rock** (if you only hike this far it's 2 miles round trip; 2hr; 1000ft elevation gain), from where Half Dome dominates to the east.

Beyond Columbia Rock the trail descends gradually until you round a corner revealing the full majesty of **Upper Yosemite Fall** – all 1430ft of it – straight ahead. During the meltwater period, the power and volume of the water become increasingly apparent as you draw nearer. In the morning light, the cascade casts ever-changing shadows against the rock wall, and you can also pick out **Lost Arrow Spire** standing apart from the cliff face to the right of the fall.

Climbing again, the track gradually pulls out of the trees into the full force of the sun just as the switchbacks get really steep. This is where you'll wish you'd got up an hour earlier. When you get into some shady Jeffrey pines and red firs, a sign points to the top of the fall just a couple of hundred yards away.

There are numerous vantage points at the top, but the best is just to the right of the fall (facing downstream), where you can follow a narrow path to a rock shelf below, very close to the top of the fall. In July and August the low water flows combine with Yosemite Valley winds to frequently blow the spray back over the shelf. If you've got lots of stamina, consider exploring **Yosemite Point**, a mostly level mile from the top of Upper Yosemite Fall, and perhaps **Eagle Peak**, a two-mile hike from the fall with an ascent of 1100ft.

A popular alternative to a tiring day hike is to come up in the cool of the afternoon and **camp** up here, though regulations dictate you'll need to be a quarter-mile back from the valley rim. Wilderness permits are required, and can be tricky to obtain for summer weekends (see p.132). To return to Yosemite Valley, retrace your steps.

Y7 Four-Mile Trail to Glacier Point

Difficulty Strenuous
Distance 4.8 miles one way
Estimated time 2hr 30min–4hr one way; 5–8hr round trip
Elevation gain 3200ft ascent
Season Mid-May to Oct or Nov
Trailhead location Map p.56, on Southside Drive, two miles west of Curry Village
Comments One of the more popular valley rim hikes and steep enough to be best avoided in the summer heat; ambitious hikers can combine the Four-Mile Trail with the Panorama Trail (see Hike Y39) for a very strenuous full-day circuit

Glacier Point can be reached by car and the hikers' bus but neither approach is as rewarding as hiking the very popular **Four-Mile Trail**, which climbs the southern wall of Yosemite Valley, ascending switchbacks the whole way. Originally constructed in 1872, the track was financed by James McCauley, who intended it as a toll route to his hotel at Glacier Point. Remodelled and lengthened since, it now starts from a trailhead parking lot accessible by the El Capitan shuttle. Alternatively, get off the Yosemite Valley shuttle at stop 7 and walk west along

Northside Drive, then take the paved bike and footpath half a mile across the valley to the trailhead.

The trail surface has been largely neglected, leaving a lot of broken asphalt underfoot. This is now covered in sand, making it fairly slippery; consequently it is safer to hike up than down. The trail starts steeply, but you're in shade for much of the way, and views become ever more expansive as you rapidly gain height. After about an hour, you'll reach the first really fantastic **views** of Half Dome, Cathedral Rocks, Tenaya Canyon and Washington Column. Further up, you're level with the near-sheer face of **Sentinel Rock**, its fissures cast in relief by the afternoon light. Soon you'll leave the last of the switchbacks behind and skirt some small cliffs with Yosemite Valley far below and Yosemite Falls on the far side. After a brief descent, the final forested climb brings you to **Glacier Point**, and a well-earned ice cream.

Either return the way you came or ride the Glacier Point Hikers' Bus back to Yosemite Valley (last departure 3.30pm). Better still, arrange for friends to drive round and meet you for sunset at Glacier Point, making this a wonderful hike to do in the late afternoon.

Y8 Western Valley Loop: El Capitan and Bridalveil Fall

Difficulty Easy
Distance 6.5-mile loop
Estimated time 2hr 30min–3hr 30min
Elevation gain 350ft ascent
Season All year, but perhaps best for fall colours in Oct & Nov
Trailhead location Map p.52, El Capitan Bridge, three miles west of Yosemite Village
Comments Though never far from a road, this is a serene way to tour Yosemite Valley's western end – take a picnic

This fairly long but easy and usually peaceful hike visits the meadows and viewpoints at the western end of Yosemite Valley, involving intimate encounters with El Capitan, Cathedral Spires and Bridalveil Fall. The trail largely parallels the road but is a lot more pleasurable than the equivalent stop-start sightseeing drive, and being shaded makes it a good hike on a hot day.

Drive or take the El Capitan shuttle to El Capitan Bridge, then walk east for a couple of hundred yards along a path beside Northside Drive. When you cross over to the north side and into the forest on the trail marked "Bridalveil Fall 4.1", **El Capitan**'s North American Wall will be straight ahead, and you'll soon cross climbers' paths leading to El Cap's base. Continuing west with the road about fifty yards off to the left, the trail bridges Ribbon Creek, which is dry in late summer but violent in spring when Ribbon Fall (just upstream) is in full flow.

Just past a view of Bridalveil Fall, you'll cross **Pohono Bridge** to the southern side of Yosemite Valley following a track that sticks close to the Merced River. You are now headed upstream with the river on your left. Don't bother crossing the road to see Fern and Moss springs, and instead press on to Bridalveil Meadow, keeping close to the road until you meet Wawona Road coming in from the right. After visiting **Bridalveil Fall**, pick up the wide path that heads east, parallel to Southside Drive. A sign announcing 5.5 miles to Curry Village marks the start of the only significant climb on the walk, which gradually ascends a moraine to reveal great treetop views across to El Cap. It is pleasant undulating walking for the next half-hour or so until you reach the "El Capitan 1.4" sign, where you'll turn left and follow a footpath north across Southside Drive. After wandering through young ponderosa pines you'll be back at El Capitan Bridge.

Paths along both sides of Yosemite Valley link up with the loop described here, making it possible to form an **extended loop** from *Yosemite Lodge* or Curry Village of 11–12 miles.

Y9 Inspiration Point

Difficulty Moderate
Distance 2.4 miles round trip
Estimated time 1hr 30min–2hr 30min
Elevation gain 600ft ascent
Season Mid-May to Oct when it is generally free of snow
Trailhead location Map p.52, Tunnel View, a mile and a half west of Bridalveil Fall
Comments Shun the roadside viewpoint crowds for the peace of one of Yosemite's great vistas

This short but taxing hike leads you away from the crowded viewpoint at Tunnel View and takes you to Inspiration Point, an even more magnificent spot for viewing Yosemite Valley, not least because you'll most likely be alone. This is where Ansel Adams came to shoot his famous "Clearing Winter Storm".

Inspiration Point was once easily accessed from the main road from Wawona to Yosemite Valley, and there's still a disused asphalt track visible, but few people come this way now. Head up in the late afternoon, switchbacking steeply through manzanita, oak and conifer woods with plenty of glorious wayside viewpoints, making use of good photo opportunities to catch your breath. Cross the asphalt road and continue uphill for another ten minutes or so. Inspiration Point isn't marked, but the magnificent **view** through a clearing in the trees announces your arrival. Return the way you came.

Hikes from Hetch Hetchy

There's really not a great deal to do at **Hetch Hetchy** except go hiking. Fortunately a couple of excellent hikes cross the O'Shaughnessy Dam and head along its northern shore to some fine waterfalls. They're at their best in spring, when the higher reaches of the park are still under a mantle of snow.

Y10 Wapama Falls

Difficulty Easy
Distance 5 miles round trip
Estimated time 2–3hr
Elevation gain 400ft ascent
Season Mid-April to Nov, but best in spring when the falls are in spate
Trailhead location Map p.78, where Hetch Hetchy Road meets the O'Shaughnessy Dam
Comments Great waterfall views for very little effort

This is a relaxing trail in a quiet corner of the park, following the north shore of Hetch Hetchy reservoir and ideal for accessing the foaming **Wapama Falls**. Low altitude and a southerly aspect ensure that the path is clear of snow early in the season, which coincides with the falls' best display from late April to June; it generally dries up by August.

Park your vehicle beside O'Shaughnessy Dam and cross its concrete curve, gazing across the reservoir at the hefty bell-shape of **Kolana Rock**. At the far end of the dam a short tunnel brings you to the trail, which flows mostly on level terrain just above the water. The hike is especially nice in the spring, when wildflowers are abundant, and for a few weeks **Tueeulala Falls** plunges down the cliff to the left of the trail, its veils of spray wafting onto the path until it dries up in mid-June. At all times keep an eye out for **rattlesnakes** that might be camouflaged in fallen leaves dappled by the shade of live oaks. Further on, **Wapama Falls** drops 1400ft from the valley rim in two steps before pouring over rocks as a braided stream, all best seen from a couple of footbridges on the route.

After you've had your fill of the falls, either head back the way you came, or continue a further five miles to Rancheria Falls (Hike Y11).

Y11 Rancheria Falls

Difficulty Moderate
Distance 14.5 miles round trip
Estimated time 5–8hr
Elevation gain 800ft ascent
Season Mid-April to Nov, but best early in the season
Trailhead location Map p.78, where Hetch Hetchy Road meets the O'Shaughnessy Dam
Comments More effort than Hike Y12 but rewarded by great scenery

As an extension of Hike Y10, this hike is similar in character but more arduous, and with a gorgeous springtime reward in the form of Rancheria Falls. From Wapama Falls, the trail climbs towards the base of **Hetch Hetchy Dome**, eventually reaching a magnificent viewpoint high above the water and directly opposite Kolana Rock. Here you can look back to the dam, and up the lake towards your goal (still an hour and a half ahead) where **Rancheria Falls** courses down over smooth rock, the flow disturbed by shelves, ledges and scattered rocks that get in the way. **Overnighters** can camp at the backcountry site beside the falls. Return the way you came.

Hikes from the Tioga Road

The hikes in this section are listed in trailhead order from Crane Flat east to Tuolumne Meadows.

Y12 El Capitan from Tamarack Flat

Difficulty Strenuous
Distance 16.5 miles round trip
Estimated time 7–10hr
Elevation gain 1240ft ascent on the way back
Season June–Oct
Trailhead location Map p.78, at Tamarack Flat campground, four miles east of Crane Flat
Comments Hike to this little-visited summit without climbing The Nose

While the summit of El Cap is the goal of some of Yosemite's most spectacular and intense rock climbs, it is also accessible by trail from Tamarack Flat, three miles off Tioga Road. Begin hiking along a disused section of the Old Big Oak Flat Road at the eastern end of *Tamarack Flat* campground, crossing Cascade Creek after a couple of miles. Continue downhill for another half mile or so to a point where a log jam forces you left onto a narrower path which climbs steadily for almost three miles, following a ridge to the diminutive Ribbon Meadow. There are potential **campgrounds** where you cross Ribbon Creek, just before the rim of El Capitan Gully gives you your first really good views of Yosemite Valley.

El Capitan dominates the scene ahead, its sheer face topping out not with a plateau but with a surprisingly steep slope rising back from the lip to a domed summit. The trail skirts the top and continues east along the valley rim, with just a few cairns marking the way down to the lip. Watch your footing as you head to the edge for tremendous views up Yosemite Valley towards Tenaya Canyon and Half Dome, and across to the face of Sentinel Rock and the knife-blade ridge of Mount Clark. Return the way you came.

Y13 Harden Lake

Difficulty Easy
Distance 6 miles round trip
Estimated time 2–3hr
Elevation gain 270ft ascent
Season June–Oct
Trailhead location Map p.78, at White Wolf campground, 15 miles east of Crane Flat and 25 miles west of Tuolumne Meadows
Comments One of Yosemite's finest wildflower walks

What this hike lacks in scenic splendour it easily makes up for in the glorious profusion of **wildflowers**, good from late June to August but especially vibrant in July. Heading north on the gravel service road from *White Wolf*, follow signs for **Harden Lake**, which bring you alongside a tributary of the middle fork of the Tuolumne River where the banks shimmer with the blue, pink, purple and white of lilies and lupins. Elsewhere in the area the red and yellow flowers of columbine mix with the delicate pink of Lewis' monkey flower. The lake itself fills a pleasant enough forest clearing, and you've got the walk back to look forward to.

Y14 Lukens Lake

Difficulty Easy
Distance 1.6 miles round trip
Estimated time 1hr
Elevation gain 200ft ascent
Season June–Oct
Trailhead location Map p.78, 17 miles east of Crane Flat and 23 miles west of Tuolumne Meadows
Comments Meadows and a beautiful lake are an easy hike from White Wolf

Colourful displays of delicate flowers make this easy hike a hit in July, with the added benefit of a beautiful destination in the form of the serene **Lukens Lake**. Partly filled with photogenic semi-submerged logs, Lukens Lake is bounded at one end by meadows, where lush growth creates a waist-high grassland thick with **wildflowers**. The path winds through red fir and white pine forest from a trailhead on Tioga Road, but is also accessible directly from *White Wolf* campground (see p.184) along a well-signposted track. Both camping and fires are prohibited here and even picnicking isn't always pleasant with the summertime menace of mosquitoes: bring repellent. Walk back the way you came.

Y15 Yosemite Falls from Yosemite Creek campground

Difficulty Strenuous
Distance 12 miles round trip
Estimated time 5–7hr
Elevation gain 700ft ascent on the way back
Season June–Oct
Trailhead location Map p.84, at Yosemite Creek campground, 15 miles east of Crane Flat then 5 miles down a dirt road
Comments An unusual (and gentler than normal) approach to a popular destination

The top of Yosemite Falls is a justly popular hiking destination from Yosemite Valley, but you can cut out much of the ascent by using this alternative approach from *Yosemite Creek* campground, five miles off Tioga Road. A longer hike, but on primarily gentle terrain, it follows Yosemite Creek as it cuts its way first through forest, then down small granite canyons choked with rocks.

The path starts beside a trail-junction sign by the campground's entrance, and heads south, slowly descending through woods until reaching a section where

Yosemite Creek is confined between high banks; take a few minutes to watch smooth sheets of water break up over cascades then calm themselves in deep blue pools. Broad sandy areas alternate with thicker forest and offer a few potential **campgrounds** along the way as you cross Blue Jay Creek and eventually pass a trail junction for Eagle Peak. Half a mile on you'll encounter exhausted hikers ascending the Upper Yosemite Fall trail. Join them for the final couple of hundred yards to **Upper Yosemite Fall**, best viewed from a wonderful viewpoint (see Hike Y8). There are potential side trips to **Yosemite Point** and **Eagle Peak** before returning the way you came.

Y16 North Dome from Porcupine Creek

Difficulty Moderate
Distance 9 miles round trip
Estimated time 4–6hr
Elevation gain 650ft ascent on the way back
Season June–Oct
Trailhead location Map p.84, 25 miles east of Crane Flat and 15 miles west of Tuolumne Meadows
Comments Great Yosemite Valley views from this little-visited dome

It's almost all downhill from Tioga Road to the top of North Dome, giving this hike the unusual distinction of approaching a Yosemite Valley viewpoint from above. From the Porcupine Creek trailhead, you'll plunge into pine and fir forest broken up by occasional meadows. Follow signs for North Dome and start climbing as the forest begins to open out to reveal expansive vistas. A little over an hour from the start a sign points along a five-hundred-yard spur trail to **Indian Rock**, a slender rock arch perhaps thirty or forty feet across; not much by Utah standards, but an unusual feature in granite. Return to the track and drop steeply along Indian Ridge with Basket Dome off to the left, until you reach **North Dome**. Here, perched high above the Royal Arches and Washington Column, you find yourself face to face with the enormous bulk of Half Dome. Clouds Rest, too, is prominent, and the daily activity of Curry and Yosemite villages goes on below, with only the distant sounds of shuttle buses to disturb the tranquillity.

Be sure to keep some reserves of energy for the uphill walk back, or plan to turn this into an overnight hike by **camping** at the low saddle behind North Dome, though finding water can be a problem once the last of the snow has melted.

Y17 May Lake

Difficulty Easy
Distance 2.5 miles round trip
Estimated time 1hr
Elevation gain 400ft ascent
Season June–Oct
Trailhead location Map p.84, 2 miles north of Tioga Road, some 27 miles east of Crane Flat and 15 miles west of Tuolumne Meadows
Comments The prettiness of May Lake is easily surpassed by the views from the summit of Mount Hoffmann

This short hike is one of the most popular outside Yosemite Valley, chiefly for its destination, the gorgeous crystal-clear May Lake, huddled in the shadow of looming Mount Hoffmann, and home to the most accessible of the High Sierra Camps (see p.182).

From the trailhead, two miles north of Tioga Road, it's a short but fairly steep hike through woods and open granite-boulder fields with great views down Tenaya Canyon towards Clouds Rest and the back of Half Dome. As the trail levels out you'll see **May Lake**, reached through the scattered tents of a camping area. Nearby, prime lakeside positions are occupied by the white tent cabins of the High Sierra Camp, which uses lake water for its supply; swimming is not allowed, but you're free to fish.

Anyone keen to see just why the summit of **Mount Hoffmann** was one of John Muir's favourite spots in the park can continue along a three-mile track to the top. It's moderate to tough going, but thoroughly rewarding. Return the way you came.

Y18 Clouds Rest from Tenaya Lake

Difficulty Strenuous
Distance 14.5 miles round trip
Estimated time 7–10hr
Elevation gain 1800ft ascent
Season June–Oct
Trailhead location Map p.84, 31 miles east of Crane Flat and 9 miles west of Tuolumne Meadows
Comments Great views of Half Dome and the Cathedral Range

The easiest and most popular approach to Clouds Rest is from Tenaya Lake; it is still a strenuous undertaking but involves only a third of the ascent you'd have to negotiate if starting in Yosemite Valley.

From the trailhead at the western end of Tenaya Lake you first cross a small creek and then turn south through meadows before beginning to climb to the rim of **Tenaya Canyon**. Follow Clouds Rest signs past a junction that leads to the Sunrise Lakes High Sierra Camp, and drop down to a little meadow near the foot of Sunrise Peak. The small creek at the lowest point is your last chance for water. Ascend until you pass another trail junction, then continue through white pine as the knife-edge peak of **Clouds Rest** comes into view. At the base of the summit ridge a poorly signed path marked by cairns on bare rock rises to the top. Alternatively follow the horse trail that skirts the ridge on the southern side, then join a better-marked track from the western end of the ridge. Either way, be sure to watch your footing around the summit. The **views** from Clouds Rest, the highest peak visible from Yosemite Valley, are breathtaking: Half Dome dominates to the west, the Cathedral Range bristles to the east, and below you a wave of smooth granite sweeps down to the base of Tenaya Canyon. Either return the way you came or continue over the top of Clouds Rest and loop back along a section of the JMT.

Y19 Polly Dome Lakes

Difficulty Easy
Distance 5 miles round trip
Estimated time 2–3hr
Elevation gain 500ft ascent
Season Late June–Oct
Trailhead location Map p.84, 32 miles east of Crane Flat and 8 miles west of Tuolumne Meadows
Comments Pleasant hike with evidence of glacial action underfoot

From a trailhead midway along the north side of Tenaya Lake, this gentle and little-used track follows **Murphy Creek** through lodgepole pine forest to its source at **Polly Dome Lakes**. Polly Dome itself rises above, and there's good camping all about. Much of the second half of the hike is across rock slabs with abundant evidence of glacial action. The area is littered with erratics, and the polished surface is punctuated by "percussion marks" where boulders embedded in the base of the glacier have gouged their signature of multiple matching divots in the rock. The lake makes a good spot for a picnic before heading back the way you came.

Y20 Tenaya Lake circuit

Difficulty Easy
Distance 3 miles round trip
Estimated time 1hr–1hr 30min
Elevation gain 50ft ascent
Season June–Oct; Aug and early Sept are warmest for a dip
Trailhead location Map p.84, 33 miles east of Crane Flat and 7 miles west of Tuolumne Meadows
Comments Great views all round and even a beach

One of the easiest hikes along Tioga Road is this circuit of **Tenaya Lake**, which mostly stays out of the trees with open vistas of granite domes the whole way. It starts at the picnic area at the eastern end of Tenaya Lake, where sunbathers loll on a beach.

The hike loops around the southern side of the lake, with views across the water to the climbers' playground of **Stately Pleasure Dome**. It's a riot of wildflowers in summer. The route rejoins Tioga Road at the major trailhead at Tenaya Lake's western end, from where you can either retrace your steps or complete the lake circuit by hiking along the road.

The hike can be accessed from Tuolumne Meadows by riding the free Tuolumne Meadows shuttle (see p.86), and if you time your walk right, riding the shuttle back from the far end thereby avoiding the road section.

Hikes from Tuolumne Meadows

The hikes in this section are listed in sequence moving west to east.

Y21 Pothole Dome

Difficulty Easy
Distance 0.5 miles round trip
Estimated time 40min–1hr
Elevation gain 200ft ascent
Season June–Oct
Trailhead location Map p.84, 38 miles east of Crane Flat and 2 miles west of Tuolumne Meadows
Comments A perfect, photogenic sunset hike

This short but fairly steep walk ascends **Pothole Dome**, which marks the western limit of Tuolumne Meadows. The relatively small dome commands great views of the meadows, Cathedral Range and virtually all of the High Sierra, seen to best effect in the hour before sunset. A ten-minute walk around the base of the dome is followed by a short, stiff scramble up bare granite: wear the stickiest shoes you have. The more-or-less level summit is a lesson in glaciation. The rock here is **porphyritic granite**, its fine granular structure embedded with feldspar crystals an inch or two long. As glaciers ground over the rock, it was planed smooth leaving a beautiful mosaic that shimmers in the low light. Notice, too, the glacial erratics deposited on the summit, now elegantly juxtaposed with stunted pines.

Y22 Cathedral Lakes

Difficulty Moderate
Distance 8 miles round trip
Estimated time 3–5hr
Elevation gain 1000ft ascent
Season June–Oct
Trailhead location Map p.84, 39 miles east of Crane Flat and a mile west of Tuolumne Meadows
Comments A justly popular hike with views of Cathedral Peak from several angles

A candidate for the best Tuolumne day hike, this route follows several miles of the JMT as far as **Cathedral Lakes**, a pair of gorgeous tarns in open alpine country with long views to a serrated skyline.

From the trailhead just west of the Tuolumne Meadows visitor centre, the path climbs moderately steeply through lodgepole forest and small meadows. The blunt end of Cathedral Peak seen from this early section of the trail is barely recognizable as the same spiky two-pronged mountain you'll see further on. Its aspect changes as you continue through rolling woods to a junction at three miles. Here, a half-mile side trail leads to **Lower Cathedral Lake**, a divine spot lodged in a cirque now partly filled with lush meadows, and split by a ridge of hard rock polished smooth by an ancient glacier. Looking back the way you came, the twin spires of **Cathedral Peak** catch the afternoon light beautifully and, on still days, may be reflected in the lake's waters.

Return to the JMT, turn right and continue for half a mile to reach **Upper Cathedral Lake** at 9585ft. There's a more open feel here, though you're still ringed by mountains: the truncated ridge of Tressider Peak to the south, Echo Peaks rising up to the east, and Cathedral Peak always drawing your eye to the northeast.

There's great **camping** at both Lower and Upper Cathedral lakes. Return the way you came.

Y23 Soda Springs and Parsons Lodge

Difficulty Easy
Distance 4 mile loop
Estimated time 2hr
Elevation gain 50ft ascent
Season June–Oct
Trailhead location Map p.86, Tuolumne Meadows visitor centre
Comments Visit the highlights of Tuolumne Meadows on this easy loop hike

This is an easy meander around some of Tuolumne Meadows' best and most accessible features. Start from the visitor centre and walk about three hundred yards east along Tioga Road before turning left on a track across the meadow, which was once part of the original Tioga Road. While it's a pleasant walk at any time, in June and July the **wildflower** display along here is superb – look out for penstemon, shooting stars, yellow goldenrod and white pussytoes. On the meadows' far side, you cross the Tuolumne River beside a small path leading up to **Soda Springs** and **Parsons Lodge** (see p.85). From here, take the wide path following signs for Tuolumne Meadows stables and the Lembert Dome parking lot; it is essentially a nature trail, lined with panels explaining flora, fauna, glaciation and a little history. An alternative route from Soda Springs picks up a narrow unmarked riverside trail winding upstream past beautiful small rapids and pools. The two routes meet close to the base of Lembert Dome from where you can walk to the visitor centre along the road, or ride the shuttle bus, saving a two-mile walk.

Y24 Elizabeth Lake

Difficulty Moderate
Distance 4.8 miles round trip
Estimated time 3–5hr
Elevation gain 900ft ascent
Season June–Oct
Trailhead location Map p.86, at the Tuolumne Meadows campground
Comments Steep granite slopes hem in this pretty lake

Scrambling up Unicorn Peak

If you've an interest in **scrambling** (see p.142), don't pass up an assault on the needle summit of **Unicorn Peak**, a round trip of about three hours from Elizabeth Lake (Hike Y24). Just use a little common sense and keep heading uphill until you can go no further. From the top there are great views of Cockscomb, Cathedral Peak, Echo Peak and the end of Matthes Crest.

One of the more popular day hikes around Tuolumne Meadows, this trail culminates where the idyllic Elizabeth Lake nestles in a hollow scooped out by an ancient glacier, surrounded by pine trees.

The trailhead is at the back of the *Tuolumne Meadows* campground, most easily found using a free campground map from the kiosk near the entrance. The trail soon crosses the JMT and climbs steadily through forest, steeply at first and then more gradually alongside Unicorn Creek. Shortly after the track bridges Unicorn Creek you arrive at the glistening waters of **Elizabeth Lake**, perhaps not quite as exquisite as Cathedral Lakes (Hike Y23), but still a gorgeous spot surrounded by steep, craggy mountains and ringed by paths which provide access to spots ideal for fishing, a picnic, or, for the brave, a swim. There's no camping at the lake, and you'll have to return by the same route.

Y25 Lyell Canyon

Difficulty Easy
Distance 11 miles round trip
Estimated time 4–5hr
Elevation gain 100ft ascent
Season June–Oct
Trailhead location Map p.86, Tuolumne Meadows campground
Comments Follow the John Muir Trail as far as you feel like

This long but gentle and virtually level walk follows the John Muir and Pacific Crest trails (see box, p.135) through the somewhat misnamed **Lyell Canyon**, a quarter-mile-wide valley flanked by wooded slopes rising a couple of thousand feet on either side. There's no real destination, so if you don't fancy hiking the full eleven miles, just go as far as you please then retrace your steps.

Pick up the JMT at the eastern end of the *Tuolumne Meadows* campground, where you immediately start following the **Lyell Fork** of the Tuolumne River, climbing very slightly as you pull out of the forest and into more open country.

Donohue Pass

The **John Muir Trail** runs for twelve miles through **Lyell Canyon** (Hike Y25) to the 11,000ft **Donohue Pass**, where it leaves the park. Robust hikers can make it from Tuolumne Meadows to Donohue Pass and back in a day, climbing 2000ft in the last three miles through some stunning alpine scenery with views of the park's highest mountain, Mount Lyell, and its attendant glacier. Around nine miles from Tuolumne Meadows you reach Lyell Base Camp (9040ft), a popular waystation for John Muir Trailers and a base for assaults on Mount Lyell and Mount McLure. Here the valley loses its bottom and the stream you've been following disappears into a rocky chasm, heard but unseen from the trail, which cuts away to the right. Climb through woods to about 10,000ft, where Mount Lyell comes into view, and continue across more alpine country to Donohue Pass.

The river courses hurriedly amid fields thick with wildflowers in early summer, but by September is reduced to a steady trickle through grasses burned golden by the high-country sun. Swimming in the river is particularly nice (if cold) in late summer, and anytime of year there's decent wildlife-spotting with a little patience. The broad-shouldered **Mammoth Peak** is initially almost directly ahead, and as the trail swings to the south you get distant views to some of Yosemite's highest peaks; in fact, the further you go, the better the mountain scenery.

Y26 Dog Lake

Difficulty Easy
Distance 3.2 miles round trip
Estimated time 1hr 30min–2hr 30min
Elevation gain 600ft ascent
Season June–Oct
Trailhead location Map p.86, Lembert Dome parking area
Comments Meadows, mountain views and a great destination for a picnic lunch; can be easily combined with Hike Y27 (4.5 miles total; 2hr 30min–4hr; 900ft ascent)

This relatively easy there-and-back hike ends at the small, attractive Dog Lake, where you might linger for a picnic lunch, an afternoon with a book, or maybe a bracing swim.

From the Lembert Dome parking area follow a trail through trees across a flat patch of polished granite and keep heading right at a series of trail junctions. The climb then turns steep, but only for a mile or so, until you fork left for an easy stroll to **Dog Lake**. The right fork goes to the summit of Lembert Dome (Hike Y27). Find a spot to relax amid the lodgepole pines and small patches of meadow, or continue right around the lake for good views back to the Cathedral Range. The circumnavigation is easier in late summer when it is drier underfoot.

Y27 Lembert Dome

Difficulty Moderate
Distance 3.7 miles round trip
Estimated time 2–3hr
Elevation gain 850ft ascent
Season June–Oct
Trailhead location Map p.86, Lembert Dome parking area
Comments Hike up the back of Tuolumne's most prominent dome

Lembert Dome is the most prominent feature on Tuolumne Meadows' perimeter, and with broad summit views and interesting glacial features along the way, this is an essential hike.

Follow Hike Y26 as far as the trail junction where the Dog Lake path bears left. At this point head right, initially steeply but with the gradient easing until you reach the northeast corner of **Lembert Dome**. Here a series of cairns marks the fairly steep route across bare rock to the summit. After exploring the exposed stunted pines, glacial erratics and long views across Tuolumne Meadows and up Lyell Canyon, return to the trail and turn right for the descent to Tioga Road. Cross the road to the wilderness centre, where you can pick up a track running west and back to your starting point.

Y28 Young Lakes

Difficulty Strenuous
Distance 13.5 miles round trip
Estimated time 7–10hr
Elevation gain 1500ft ascent
Season June–Oct
Trailhead location Map p.86, Lembert Dome parking area
Comments A long day-trip or excellent overnight camping destination from Tuolumne Meadows

Spectacular vistas of the Cathedral Range and the trio of beautiful glacial tarns that are **Young Lakes** make a suitable reward for your hiking efforts. From the Lembert Dome parking area follow signs for Dog Lake (Hike Y26) for the first mile and a half. At a trail junction, follow the Young Lakes sign to some wide-open meadows bordered to the east by Mount Dana and Mount Gibbs. After a long and steady climb over a forest ridge and past a granite dome you emerge on a hillside studded with stunted trees and backed by the gap-toothed Ragged Ridge. Here you get a grandstand view back across Tuolumne Meadows to the whole of the **Cathedral Range**. Nowhere else do you get such an incredible panorama for relatively little effort. Mount Lyell and its acolytes stand above everything else at the left, and scanning right you can pick out Unicorn Peak, Echo Peak, Cathedral Peak, Fairview Dome and the distant Mount Hoffmann.

After a short ascent the trail descends for a while and then climbs again up forested moraine to the first of the lakes, with barren rocky ridges all around. Take a break beside the water's edge before exploring higher up (using informal and unsigned trails) where two smaller lakes nestle in marshy meadows. Though an excellent day hike, Young Lakes also makes a great backpacking destination with ideal lakeside **camping**. Following the trail on the way back you've got that fantastic view straight ahead.

Y29 Glen Aulin

Difficulty Moderate
Distance 11 miles round trip
Estimated time 6–8hr
Elevation gain 600ft ascent on the way back
Season June–Oct
Trailhead location Map p.86, Lembert Dome parking area
Comments Glorious hike with the tumbling Tuolumne River for company all the way

This there-and-back hike to **Glen Aulin** is one of Tuolumne's finest, following the Tuolumne River as it cascades its way to a beautifully situated High Sierra Camp and campground.

From the trailhead at Lembert Dome, hike along the broad, flat path to Soda Springs then follow signs for Glen Aulin along a good track that's made less pleasant by the evidence of all the mule traffic headed for the High Sierra Camp. With lodgepole pines all about, the trail begins to dip slowly, the trees often pulling back to reveal fabulous views of the surrounding mountains. The river, too, is wonderfully picturesque all the way. Frenetic during the snowmelt in early summer, the water courses down the canyon over house-sized boulders, slithers over slickrock and eases into deep, bottle-green pools lined with polished river stones. By fall the torrent subsides, making the pools between the cataracts calm enough for bathing. The classic photo stop is at **Tuolumne Falls**, the most vertical drop along this stretch, and there are more cascades as you continue further downstream, with the descending trail switchbacking to **White Cascade** and the High Sierra Camp. Press on a few hundred yards downstream to Glen Aulin itself where shallows provide access to a deep pool below a marvellously sculpted rock chute. Here you can rest a while before embarking on the long uphill hike back.

Y30 Waterwheel Falls

Difficulty Very strenuous
Distance 17.5 miles round trip
Estimated time 8–12hr
Elevation gain 2100ft ascent on the way back
Season June–Oct, but best in June and early July
Trailhead location Map p.86, Lembert Dome parking area
Comments A big day out with waterfalls galore

This hike is an extension of Hike Y29, continuing past Glen Aulin, following the Tuolumne River as far as Waterwheel Falls. Beyond Glen Aulin the trail passes a two-mile-long almost unbroken series of cascades, officially called **California Fall**, **LeConte Fall** and **Waterwheel Falls**. In reality, each fall tumbles into another with little to distinguish where one ends and another begins. As the path winds down alongside, you get occasional views before Waterwheel Falls themselves, where a couple of midstream rocks on a smooth chute throw the snowmelt torrent 20ft up into the air like a pair of paddle-wheels. Though never especially steep, the hike back along the same trail is tiring, so leave plenty of time.

Hikes from Tioga Pass and around

The hikes in this section are listed in trailhead order from Tuolumne Meadows east towards Tioga Pass and Lee Vining.

Y31 Mono Pass

Difficulty Moderate
Distance 8 miles round trip
Estimated time 4–6hr
Elevation gain 1000ft ascent
Season June–Oct
Trailhead location Map p.84, 4.5 miles east of Tuolumne Meadows and 1.5 miles west of Tioga Pass
Comments Trade in granite and waterfalls for old miners' shacks and red rocks

Some old miners' cabins, delightful alpine tarns and mountain scenery geologically distinct from most of the park make this an intriguing day hike. Plus, there are opportunities for camping in Inyo National Forest just over Mono Pass, an area with a beautiful high-country meadow right on the Sierra crest, overlooked not by granite but by the iron-rich red rocks of Mount Gibbs and Mount Lewis which lured late nineteenth-century miners here.

The hike starts six miles east of the Tuolumne Meadows store, and climbs steadily pretty much all the way, alternately passing through meadows and lodgepole forest. After three miles you'll reach the tree line and then break out into open country before closing in on the 10,600ft **Mono Pass**. Several small lakes mark the pass and make a pleasant lunch spot. Mine hounds should retrace their steps for a couple of hundred yards and head south for ten minutes along an unmarked path. This drops briefly then climbs over a ridge to reach what remains of the **Golden Crown Mine**, just five primitive and strikingly weathered but well-preserved cabins. Enjoy fossicking around then head back the way you came.

Y32 Gaylor Lakes and the Great Sierra Mine

Difficulty Moderate
Distance 3 miles round trip
Estimated time 2–3hr
Elevation gain 500ft ascent
Season June–Oct
Trailhead location Map p.88, right at Tioga Pass, 6 miles east of Tuolumne Meadows
Comments High-country hiking with lovely views and some mine ruins

A couple of pretty alpine lakes in open country above the tree line and the opportunity to explore some meagre silver-mine workings make this a particularly rewarding short walk. The lakes can be fished, but there's no camping in this area.

From the trailhead right beside the Tioga Pass entrance station, the track is initially quite steep, and unless you're accustomed to being at 10,000ft you'll quickly become breathless. At the crest of a blunt ridge there are views back to the scattered pools in Dana Meadows, and north beyond Granite Lake to the Sierra crest. The path then drops down into the shallow **Gaylor Lakes** basin, almost entirely filled by the lower Gaylor Lake. Bear right around the lake and start climbing gently towards the upper of Gaylor Lakes, with Gaylor Peak on your right. After skirting the left side of this lake, climb a ridge to reach the ruins of a stone cabin, virtually all that remains of the **Great Sierra Mine**. A hundred yards on, just on the park boundary, you'll find a couple more dilapidated stone huts and the vertical shaft that briefly sustained the mine. Rest a while admiring the view, then hike back the way you came.

Y33 Saddlebag Lake and 20 Lakes Basin

Difficulty Moderate
Distance 8-mile loop
Estimated time 3–5hr
Elevation gain 600ft ascent
Season July–Oct
Trailhead location Map p.88, right by Saddlebag Lake Resort
Comments Pretty alpine scenery on the easiest hike that gets you above 10,000ft

Though just outside the national park, this is one of the best (and most popular) hikes on the eastern fringes of Yosemite. It heads around Saddlebag Lake and 20 Lakes Basin, a moderate trail with some gorgeous views of alpine lakes. Lingering snow in shaded areas means it's probably best left until July, or even September if you have a major aversion to mosquitoes. You're already above 10,000ft when you start so you may want to take it easy, though the several short hills only add up to 600ft of ascent.

The less ambitious can just make a circuit around **Saddlebag Lake** (4 miles; best done counterclockwise) but the best of the scenery is beyond over the easy Lundy Pass in **20 Lakes Basin**. First up is little Hummingbird Lake (where there are a few campgrounds) – genuine **wilderness camping** only an easy hour from the trailhead. Continuing past Odell Lake you reach Helen Lake, where the trail continues around to the left. Rocky shorelines, wildflowers and whitebark pines characterize the area around Shamrock Lake and on to **Steelhead Lake**, where a short side trip visits the abandoned Hess Mine. Complete the circuit past Waso and Greenstone lakes then along the western shore of Saddlebag Lake. You can skip the somewhat dull walk beside Saddlebag Lake by using the **ferry** (see p.89).

A hike from Hwy-140

Y34 Hite Cove Trail

Difficulty Moderate
Distance 7 miles round trip
Estimated time 3–5hr
Elevation gain 300ft ascent
Season Feb–Oct but best Feb–April and sometimes closed July–Sept because of fire risk
Trailhead location Map p.92, on Hwy-140 beside Savage's Trading Post
Comments One of the finest wildflower hikes in the Sierra

If you're in Yosemite Valley between February and April (or heading there along Hwy-140 through the Merced River Canyon), find time to hike the **Hite Cove Trail**, highly regarded throughout the Sierra for its **wildflowers**. Some sixty varieties have been recorded, and if you time it right the orange California poppies are sensational. Poison oak (see p.34) is almost equally common in the river canyon and there may be **rattlesnakes**, so keep your eyes peeled.

This popular hike follows the South Fork of the Merced River, initially across private land and eventually to the former site of **Hite's Mine**, a small town that produced over $3 million in gold. The story goes that when prospector John Hite was caught in a snowstorm he was nursed back to health by Maresa, the daughter of a Miwok chief, who later showed him the rich quartz vein. John later married her sister, Lucy, used Chinese labour to extract the gold and became very rich.

Hikes from Glacier Point Road

The hikes in this section are listed in trailhead order from Chinquapin east to Glacier Point.

Y35 McGurk Meadow

Difficulty Easy
Distance 1.6 miles round trip
Estimated time 1hr
Elevation gain 150ft ascent on the way back
Season Mid-May to Oct
Trailhead location Map p.52, 9 miles east of Chinquapin and 7 miles southwest of Glacier Point
Comments Visit a pretty meadow and a slice of old Yosemite

McGurk Meadow makes a peaceful destination for this stroll through lodgepole pine forest. The trail starts almost opposite the entrance to *Bridalveil Creek* campground, and visitors staying there can walk straight from their site. Otherwise, park a couple of hundred yards east of the trailhead at a small turnout, then head into the forest. Descend gently until you notice a tumbledown summer sheepherders' cabin. Wildflower-filled **McGurk Meadow** is just beyond.

Y36 Ostrander Lake

Difficulty Strenuous
Distance 12.6 miles round trip
Estimated time 5–7hr
Elevation gain 1600ft ascent
Season Mid-May to Oct
Trailhead location Map p.52, 9 miles east of Chinquapin and 7 miles southwest of Glacier Point
Comments A fairly tough hike is rewarded by an often deserted lake flanked by a rugged, stone lakeside lodge

Best known as a winter cross-country skiing destination, **Ostrander Lake** makes an equally good summer goal, either as a day hike or to **camp** near the waterside Ostrander Ski hut, which is managed by the Sierra Club. Originally known as Pohono Lake, Ostrander Lake feeds Bridalveil Creek, which enters Yosemite Valley as Bridalveil Fall (or Pohono). Whatever you call it, it's a fine spot nestled in a hollow with the rocky exfoliating scarp of Horse Ridge on the far side.

From the trailhead on Glacier Point Road, about a mile east of *Bridalveil Creek* campground, the path is initially flat as it winds through lodgepole forest burned in 1987 and where the saplings are already over 7ft high. After three miles the trail begins a steady climb, which continues until just before the lake. Occasionally you emerge from the forest onto the bare rock slopes that run down from Horizon Ridge, the route waymarked by small cairns. As you crest the ridge, breaks in the trees allow views of Half Dome, the Clark Range and Mount Starr King. A final descent brings you to the lake and **Ostrander Lake Ski Hut** (for winter bookings see p.150), built in rustic style with heavy beams and chunky rock, and named after Harvey Ostrander, a sheep herder who had a cabin near Bridalveil Fall. The hut was constructed in 1940 by the Civilian Conservation Corps at a time when it was hoped to turn Yosemite into a premier ski resort. Head back the way you came.

The Ostrander Lake trail can also be accessed from the southern end of *Bridalveil Creek* campground: head towards the horse camp and just before you cross Bridalveil Creek turn right. After about a mile and a half a trail bears left to link up with the Ostrander Lake Trail.

Y37 Taft Point and the Fissures

Difficulty Easy
Distance 2.2 miles round trip
Estimated time 1hr
Elevation gain 250ft ascent on the way back
Season Mid-May to Oct
Trailhead location Map p.94, 14 miles east of Chinquapin and 2 miles southwest of Glacier Point
Comments Stand astride a fissure with hundreds of feet of air between your legs; this hike can be easily combined with Hike Y38 (5 miles, 2–3hr; 600ft ascent) using a couple of miles of the Pohono Trail

For such an easily accessible and wonderfully scenic spot overlooking Yosemite Valley, Taft Point is surprisingly little visited – all the more reason to hike this trail.

From the Sentinel Dome parking area the dusty and undulating path heads west across a meadow, descending all the while. As you enter a patch of forest you cross a small creek where wildflowers flourish in the damp margins, then descend more steeply until you emerge from the trees just before Taft Point: the **fissures** are just to the right, the prow of **Taft Point** itself just beyond. Unlike crowded Glacier Point with its walkways and barriers, Taft Point has just a flimsy railing in one spot to protect you from the vertiginous drops all around. A hundred yards to the right, the granite edges have been deeply incised to form the **Taft Point Fissures**, narrow 30ft slices carved out of the valley rim where you can stand astride a gap with hundreds of feet of air between your legs.

You can't see Half Dome from Taft Point, but that's more than compensated for by the view of the monstrous face of El Capitan, the staircase of the Three Brothers, and the slender white streak of Upper Yosemite Fall. Following the same trail back you'll have Sentinel Dome straight ahead.

Y38 Sentinel Dome

Difficulty Easy
Distance 2.2 miles round trip
Estimated time 1hr
Elevation gain 250ft ascent on the way back
Season Mid-May to Oct
Trailhead location Map p.94, 14 miles east of Chinquapin and 2 miles southwest of Glacier Point
Comments Justly popular short hike with great Half Dome views – it's a pity the famed pine tree has gone

The most popular hike for Glacier Point visitors is to the gleaming granite scalp of Sentinel Dome; the floor of Yosemite Valley isn't visible from the summit, but just about everything else is. Sentinel Dome is directly accessible from the Glacier Point parking lot, but most people set off from a trailhead two miles back along Glacier Point Road. From here, the track crosses sandy ground with little shade; bring plenty of water as you won't find any at the trailhead. **Sentinel Dome** becomes visible on the left and the trail gradually curls around towards it, following waymarkers and getting progressively steeper. The final push to the summit takes you up the east side, the lowest angled (but still steep) approach.

Now you're 1000ft higher than Glacier Point and views extend to the park boundary in almost every direction, with Half Dome dominant to the east. The summit is crowned by what's left of a famous **Jeffrey pine**. Well known from Ansel Adams' atmospheric 1940 image prosaically titled "Jeffrey Pine – Sentinel Dome", the tree still bore cones until the mid-1970s when a drought and old age finally killed it off. Its skeletal form stood until its root system finally collapsed in 2003, leaving the fallen spindly trunk gradually succumbing to the elements.

Y39 Panorama Trail

Difficulty Moderate
Distance 9 miles round trip
Estimated time 6–8hr
Elevation gain 800ft ascent, 4000ft descent
Season Mid-May to Oct
Trailhead location Map p.94, at Glacier Point
Comments Catch the bus to Glacier Point then hike back along this trail – a Yosemite classic

One of Yosemite's oldest routes, the **Panorama Trail** passes the top of the otherwise inaccessible **Illilouette Fall**, skirting above the Panorama Cliff with its views down towards Glacier Point Apron and Happy Isles.

The Panorama Trail links Glacier Point with the top of Nevada Fall, and can either be tackled as a there-and-back trek from Glacier Point, or combined (as we've done here) with the John Muir Trail to make a one-way hike from Glacier Point to the Happy Isles trailhead in Yosemite Valley. Either ride the Glacier Point hikers' bus to Glacier Point, or go for a very strenuous day hiking up the Four-Mile Trail (Hike Y7) and down the Panorama Trail (14 miles; 8–12hr).

Just south of the gift and snack store at Glacier Point, a large sign announces the start of several hiking routes. Follow directions for the Panorama Trail and start a two-mile-long descent to Illilouette Creek. The surrounding fire-damaged forest provides little shade, but has regrown a hardy understorey of chinquapin (with its distinctive chestnut-like fruit) that provides ideal cover for California blue grouse. Beyond the junction with the trail to Mono Meadow, switchback down into the forest, keeping an eye out for a short path on the left which leads to one of the only places with a good view of Illilouette Fall. The route soon crosses Illilouette Creek near some cascades and rock chutes just above the fall. It's a perfect spot for a break, but camping is not allowed.

Climbing steeply away from the fall, the track passes the unsigned but fairly obvious **Panorama Point** and continues up until **Nevada Fall** comes into view. After a trail junction you descend on switchbacks to meet the JMT. Before turning left to head down to Yosemite Valley, it's worth detouring right a quarter of a mile to the top of Nevada Fall.

Y40 Pohono Trail

Difficulty Strenuous
Distance 13.8 miles round trip
Estimated time 5–8hr
Elevation gain 2800ft ascent
Season May–Oct
Trailhead location Map p.94, at Glacier Point
Comments Infrequently hiked trail past several great Yosemite Valley views

The **Pohono Trail** ties together all the viewpoints along the south rim of Yosemite Valley, emerging from the forest periodically for magnificent vistas, each one significantly different from the last. Often tackled as part of a longer backpacking trip (see Hike Y44), the Pohono Trail can be done in a day, either combining it with the Four-Mile Trail to form a very strenuous loop or using the Glacier Point hikers' bus for one leg of the journey. Neither the starting nor finishing points are close to where you're likely to be staying, so transport considerations are paramount.

From Glacier Point, signs guide you onto the Pohono Trail, which initially ascends through forest then skirts the north side of Sentinel Dome, seen on the left. Occasionally views can be glimpsed through the trees, but none prepare you for **Taft Point** and its fissured fringes (see Hike Y37). For the next couple of miles you drop down to **Bridalveil Creek**, a good spot to take a break, bathe and refill water bottles. Late in the season many creeks dry up, so this may be your last decent supply. Climbing out of the watershed, ignore the trail cutting south to *Bridalveil Creek* campground, and continue back to the valley rim at **Dewey Point**, distinguished by several isolated rocky viewpoints accessible with a little easy scrambling. The end of the trail at Wawona Tunnel is visible below and to the left, still over four miles away. Press on to nearby **Crocker Point**, where you can look directly across to the top of El Cap, and down on Bridalveil Fall. **Stanford Point**, another half-mile on, offers a slightly different perspective before you begin the final forested descent. The last viewpoint is **Inspiration Point** (see Hike Y9) from where it's a mile down to the Tunnel View parking area.

Hikes from Wawona and Mariposa Grove

The hikes in this section are listed north to south following Wawona Road. (For details on the two- to three-hour hike from Mariposa Grove back to Wawona, see p.100).

Y41 Alder Creek

Difficulty Strenuous
Distance 12 miles round trip
Estimated time 5–7hr
Elevation gain 1700ft ascent
Season April–Nov
Trailhead location Map p.92, on Chilnualna Fall Road
Comments Solitude and cascading water are your rewards here

Alder Creek Trail faces south and is mostly at low elevation, so it sheds its layer of snow early in the season making it perfect for energetic springtime hikers, especially those keen to catch the first of the wildflowers. At any time of year it's a lovely but little-used path steadily climbing a forested ridge to a **100ft fall** on **Alder Creek**.

The route starts on Chilnualna Fall Road and follows a former railbed used for extracting timber from the area's enormous trees. This is initially fairly open country with long views to distant ridges, but as the trail ascends the forest gradually hems you in. After almost three miles the track meets a side path down to Wawona Road, but the Alder Creek Trail continues uphill, crosses into the Alder Creek watershed and finally reaches the falls themselves. This is a great place to relax, and makes a good **camping** spot if you're thinking of exploring the area further.

Y42 Chilnualna Fall

Difficulty Strenuous
Distance 8.2 miles round trip
Estimated time 4–6hr
Elevation gain 2400ft ascent
Season Mid-May to Oct
Trailhead location Map p.92, on Chilnualna Fall Road
Comments Stiff but rewarding hike with swimming options; avoid the midday sun

South-facing and at low elevation, the Chilnualna Fall trail is perfect in early spring and fall. Though it gets quite hot on summer days, you can cool off in deep pools along **Chilnualna Creek**.

The route starts 1.8 miles along Chilnualna Fall Road: if you hit a gravel road you've gone too far. The first few hundred yards of ascent is among granite boulders alongside roaring cascades, where the water continues to carve out channels and hollows in the rock. Moving west, away from the river, you continue ascending through manzanita, deer brush and bear clover, and return briefly to the river before again looping west to a point with long views down to Wawona and across the valley to Mariposa Grove. All along the way, **wildflowers** bloom throughout spring and early summer. Finally the trail rejoins the creek at the top of **Chilnualna Fall**, an intimidating spot where snowmelt gathered in the high country thunders down into the narrow chasm below your feet. Catch it in early spring when the spray clings onto the walls in an organ pipe accumulation of icicles.

Take a break here, but don't turn back yet. Instead, continue upstream to yet more tumbling cataracts; take care where spray coats the slick riverside rock, making it very slippery. Return the way you came.

Y43 Wawona Meadow Loop

Difficulty Easy
Distance 3.5 miles round trip
Estimated time 1–2hr
Elevation gain 100ft ascent
Season March–Dec, but best for wildflowers April–June
Trailhead location Map p.96, at the *Wawona Hotel*
Comments Best for wildlife and wildflowers around the fringes of Wawona's golf course

This circuit of **Wawona Meadow** is the easiest of the walks around Wawona, popular with cyclists, horses and even Wawona dog walkers. It's mainly of interest for the plethora of **wildflowers** bursting forth in April, May and June.

From the *Wawona Hotel*, cross Wawona Road and follow the paved footpath through the golf course to a small parking area. The road straight ahead is the Chowchilla Mountain Road, first pushed through to Wawona in 1856 as a toll trail from Mariposa to Yosemite Valley. Four years later, Galen Clark developed it into a stage road to lure coaches to his hotel at Clark's Station (now Wawona). Don't follow Chowchilla Mountain Road, but instead turn left and follow the loop trail with the Wawona golf course on the left. This soon gives way to meadows as the route follows a fire road through ponderosa pine and incense cedar. Keep an eye out for wildlife, especially mule deer, which favour the forest margin.

After almost circumnavigating the meadow, the trail meets Wawona Road, which you'll cross to return to the *Wawona Hotel*.

Backcountry hiking and camping in Yosemite

There's no denying the appeal of spending the night under the open skies with the last rays of sun glinting off the granite domes and a pearlescent alpenglow silhouetting the tall pines. Add in a hearty meal, hard-earned after a day **hiking** up past thunderous waterfalls, and you have a recipe for a magical experience. By **camping** out you'll also open up the majority of Yosemite's **backcountry**, essentially anywhere more than a mile from a road. The seven detailed backcountry itineraries that follow cover some of the most popular **overnight trails** and, with the accompanying advice, will give you all the grounding you need for a lifetime of exploring the rest of Yosemite's eight hundred miles of trail.

Much of the backcountry is pristine, with very little evidence of human impact. The exceptions are **Little Yosemite Valley**, at the top of Merced Canyon, which sees almost a quarter of all wilderness travellers, and the five **High Sierra Camps**

Yosemite's best overnight hikes

Hike	Name	Grade	Length (miles)	Time
Y44	Pohono–Panorama Combo	Very strenuous	23.0	2–3 days
Y45	North rim of Yosemite Valley	Very strenuous	30.0	2–3 days
Y46	John Muir Trail	Strenuous	20.0	2 days
Y47	Merced Lake HSC	Very strenuous	27.0	2–3 days
Y48	Ten Lakes	Strenuous	22.0	2 days
Y49	Grand Canyon of the Tuolumne	Very strenuous	28.0	2–3 days
Y50	The High Sierra Camp Loop	Moderate	47.0	6 days

(see box, p.182), semi-permanent clusters of frame tents designed to cater to those who don't relish lugging a tent and cooking gear. All six places have adjacent primitive campgrounds (free) with pit toilets, bear boxes and a water source.

Before heading out on your selected overnight hike, be sure to obtain a **wilderness permit** (see box, p.132) and read our **Hiking essentials** section on p.28. Hikers leaving from Yosemite Valley, or using one of the hikers' buses to get to the start of the trail, must park their vehicles in the **backpackers' parking area** between Curry Village and Happy Isles: you receive a dashboard parking permit when you get your wilderness permit. In Tuolumne Meadows, backpackers need to park beside the wilderness centre, and should note that vehicles are not allowed to remain overnight at Tioga Road trailheads (including Tuolumne Meadows) after mid-October, effectively ruling out overnight hikes starting here at that time. When hiking in other areas of the park, you can often leave your vehicle right at the trailhead.

Backcountry information and practicalities

Backcountry information is best gleaned at one of the **wilderness centres** (see p.44), particularly those in Yosemite Valley and Tuolumne Meadows, which are both close to numerous trailheads. They'll help you sort out a wilderness permit and enlighten you on backcountry safety and etiquette. Wherever you go, be sure to **leave an accurate itinerary** with family or friends, as it will be their responsibility to initiate a search if you do not return as scheduled. Several of the hikes we've listed start and/or finish away from the park's main centres and you'll find it convenient to make use of Yosemite's **hikers' buses** (see p.25), which run from Yosemite Valley to Glacier Point and Tuolumne Meadows.

Maps and selecting a backcountry campground

With trails so well marked, you may find that the maps in this book along with the Yosemite map provided when you enter the park are all the guidance you need, but most serious hikers will feel naked without a decent **topographic map**. For recommendations see "Travel essentials" on p.40.

Once out in Yosemite's backcountry, you are free to camp wherever you wish, subject to a few limitations. In the more popular sections of the park, though,

Ascent (feet)	Season	Waterfalls	Best in spring	Wildlife	Wildflowers	Kid-friendly	Swimming	Solitude	Views	History
3600	Mid-June to Oct	✓		✓				✓	✓	
5700	Late May–Oct	✓					✓	✓	✓	
6100	June–Oct	✓		✓			✓		✓	
3300	June–Oct	✓		✓	✓		✓	✓	✓	
4500	June–Oct			✓			✓		✓	
4000	June–Oct	✓					✓	✓		
8000	June–Sept	✓		✓	✓		✓		✓	✓

Wilderness permits

Anyone planning to spend the night in the backcountry (including at High Sierra Camps) must obtain a **wilderness permit**. Each trailhead has a daily quota, with sixty percent of permits available in advance and the rest available on a first-come-first-served basis the day before your first planned hiking day. Remember that quotas apply to the **trailhead** (rather than destination), and you may find that you can start from a slightly different spot and still do largely the hike you wanted to.

Outside busy times (or for less popular trailheads) it's usually easy enough to obtain an **on-the-spot permit** (free) in person early on the day before you want to start hiking. Line up outside any of the wilderness centres or information stations (see p.44), though preferably the one nearest to your trailhead. If you can't get a day-before permit for your desired trailhead, put your name on the waiting list. You'll need to return **after 10am on the day you plan to leave**. Any advance permits not picked up by this time then become available to those on the waiting list.

During the busiest period, from mid-July to the end of August, you should **reserve in advance** for all trailheads. Most summer weekends are also busy enough to justify making reservations for those hikes beginning at popular trailheads such as Happy Isles and Upper Yosemite Falls in Yosemite Valley, May Lake along the Tioga Road, Sunrise Lakes at the western end of Tenaya Lake, and Cathedral Lakes, Rafferty Creek and Lyell Fork from Tuolumne Meadows.

Advance wilderness permits ($5 per person plus $5 per group reservation) are available from 24 weeks to two days ahead of your trip. Check availability online at Ⓦwww.nps.gov/yose/planyourvisit/wildpermits.htm, though sadly there is no online booking. Download a form, fill it in and fax (yes, fax) it to Ⓕ209/372-0739.

With the exception of campgrounds beside the High Sierra Camps and the one in Little Yosemite Valley, **bear canisters** are now required throughout the backcountry area of Yosemite. Almost everyone seeking a wilderness permit will need to rent a bear canister (see p.32) or show they already have one.

In winter (mid-Sept to mid-May), when demand is at its lowest, there is no need to reserve in advance, and wilderness centres are closed. Free wilderness permits are available at several places: the visitor centre in Yosemite Valley, the ski hut in Tuolumne Meadows, and the ranger station at the Badger Pass Ski Area. Winter hikers starting near Wawona and Big Oak Flat can self-register outside the nearest visitor centre.

Climbers spending the night on a wall are not required to have a wilderness permit, but it is illegal to camp at the base of a wall, and when bivvying at the summit all park regulations must be followed. Unless it's in a bear canister, food must be hung a full rope length up or down the climb.

you're encouraged to aim for and camp in existing **primitive campgrounds**, each with fire rings and some form of water source (which may need to be treated). The most popular such areas are Little Yosemite Valley (on the John Muir Trial just south of Half Dome), and beside the five High Sierra Camps (see p.182).

Away from these areas, you're free to set up camp almost anywhere as long as the following **backcountry regulations** are met.

Do not camp within four miles of any settlement (principally Yosemite Valley, Tuolumne Meadows, Hetch Hetchy, Glacier Point and Wawona), within one mile of any road, or less than a quarter of a mile from the Yosemite Valley rim. In addition, select a site at least 100ft from any watercourse, away from fragile and untrammeled vegetation, and out of sight of hikers on nearby trails. In practice, many commonly used sites don't meet all these criteria, but you should make sure yours does: the rules are designed to ensure everyone has a quality wilderness experience.

Hikers' passage into and out of the backcountry is eased by the existence of drive-to **backpacker campgrounds** (no reservations necessary; $5) in Yosemite Valley, Tuolumne Meadows, White Wolf and Hetch Hetchy. Here, hikers with valid wilderness permits have a place to camp for their last night before a trip and a place to stay when turning up late in the day after several days' hiking.

Overnight hikes

The following hikes cover a wide spread of Yosemite's topography and anyone keen enough to complete the lot can consider themselves enough of a Yosemite expert to venture into the really wild country in the very north of the park. We've listed these hikes according to their trailhead location; Yosemite Valley first, then Tioga Road and finishing with Tuolumne Meadows.

Y44 Pohono Trail–Panorama Trail Combo

Difficulty Very strenuous
Distance 23 miles one way
Estimated time 2–3 days
Elevation gain 3600ft ascent, 4000ft descent
Season Mid-June to Oct
Trailhead location Map p.52, Tunnel View, a mile and a half west of Bridalveil Fall
Comments Hike the entire south rim of Yosemite Valley with a welcome break at Glacier Point

This hike combines the **Pohono Trail** (Hike Y40, here tackled in reverse) with the **Panorama Trail** (Hike Y39) to take in a full west-to-east span of Yosemite Valley's south rim, without resorting to messy shuttle transfers. It is not entirely a wilderness experience – the two trails meet at Glacier Point – but this does have the advantage of assuring hikers access to food, potable water and flush toilets along the way. Be aware that there is **no camping** within four miles of Glacier Point. A good strategy is to catch the Glacier Point hikers' bus as far as the Pohono trailhead at Tunnel View, then camp early before Glacier Point's exclusion zone (Bridalveil Creek makes a good spot). The second day is long, passing through Glacier Point for supplies before hiking the Panorama Trail, perhaps camping a short distance off the trail at Little Yosemite Valley. Day three can then be spent exploring (maybe hiking up) Half Dome and finally descending along the Mist Trail or John Muir Trail. By pacing yourself this way you'll always be camping by water, a significant consideration in late summer.

Y45 North rim of Yosemite Valley

Difficulty Very strenuous
Distance 30 miles one way
Estimated time 2–3 days
Elevation gain 5700ft ascent, 6700ft descent
Season Late May to Oct
Trailhead location Map p.78, Big Oak Flat Road, 6 miles southeast of Crane Flat
Comments Lots and lots of unpopulated miles and great Yosemite Valley views

The summit of El Capitan, Eagle Peak, the top of Upper Yosemite Fall and North Dome can all be linked together in one lengthy traverse of Yosemite Valley's **north rim**. Apart from the section near the top of Yosemite Fall, you'll see few people, making this a more solitary undertaking than the rest of the overnight hikes listed here. Though possible throughout the summer and fall, timing is everything: too early and you'll have to cope with patches of snow; too late and most streams will have dried up. July and August are the most suitable months.

Guided overnight hikes

Yosemite Valley-based **Yosemite Mountaineering School** (☏209/372-8344, ⓦwww .yosemitemountaineering.com) not only runs guided day hikes and rock climbing courses, but also leads **guided backpacking trips** (late July to mid-Sept only). Trips start from the Mountain Shop in Curry Village and include transportation from Curry Village to the trailhead, all meals, tents, stoves, pans, water filters and wilderness permits; all you need is your personal gear plus a backpack and sleeping bag (both available for rent, see p.29). Along with the trips listed below, **custom trips** going wherever you want them to can be arranged; typical rates are $133 per day, per person for groups of 4–7; $138 each for three; $160 per day for two; and $256 per day if solo. All camping equipment and food is included.

Learn to Backpack Aimed at backpacking neophytes, this is a two-day trip carrying tent, sleeping bag and all food, typically leaving Yosemite Valley and hiking for 3–4 miles. Prices start at $200 a head ($276 each for three; $320 for two; $512 for one).

Young Lakes to Mount Conness trip A three-day trip north of Tuolumne Meadows with a relatively easy first day to the campground near Young Lakes (our Hike Y28). The second day is spent hiking up the 12,590ft summit of Mount Conness (ropes not needed). Around four trips are scheduled each summer, all leaving on Friday morning and returning on Sunday afternoon. Rates are $300 per person assuming a group of four or more.

Tuolumne Meadows to Yosemite Valley A four-day scheduled trip from Tuolumne Meadows to Yosemite Valley (more downhill than up), mostly avoiding the John Muir Trail and taking in Vogelsang Pass and Merced Lake. The trip includes a rest day with an optional hike up Half Dome. The four annual trips all start on Thursday morning and return on Sunday afternoon. Rates are $400 per person assuming a group of four or more.

The best bet is to start at the trailhead on the Big Oak Flat Road, two hundred yards uphill from the Foresta turn-off: in season you can get there on the Tuolumne Meadows hikers' bus. The route crosses a couple of minor streams then meets a disused section of Old Big Oak Flat Road (Hike Y12) and follows it downhill for a little over half a mile. Logs across the road mark the resumption of the track, which climbs to the summit of **El Capitan**, then undulates along the valley rim with a short spur trail to the summit of **Eagle Peak**. A short descent brings you to the top of **Upper Yosemite Fall**, where there are numerous camping spots located a quarter-mile back from the rim. Even when Yosemite Fall is dry, water can be obtained from deep pools above it.

The way ahead climbs out of the valley cut by Yosemite Creek to reach **Yosemite Point**, then heads away from Yosemite Valley rim to sidle around the head of Indian Canyon. Follow signs for **North Dome** and make a short detour to its summit. You then double back and head south again for the steep descent down Snow Creek which eventually brings you past Mirror Lake and back to the Yosemite Valley settlements.

Y46 John Muir Trail: Yosemite Valley to Tuolumne Meadows

Difficulty Strenuous
Distance 20 miles one way
Estimated time 2 days
Elevation gain 6100ft ascent, 1500ft descent
Season Late June to Oct
Trailhead location Map p.106, shuttle stop 16 near the Nature Center at Happy Isles
Comments Yosemite's most famous overnight hike

Several routes from Yosemite Valley lead to Tuolumne Meadows, but one of the best, and certainly the most popular, follows the **John Muir Trail** (JMT): reserve a permit early. In two fairly easy days you'll be rewarded with some of the best hiking available, with views to match. The track starts at the Happy Isles trailhead and follows the Merced River to Nevada Fall, mostly keeping away from the river and switchbacking up the canyon wall before traversing along the head of the fall. The major features of this region are discussed in hikes Y1–Y3, which follow the Mist Trail, parallel to the JMT.

The John Muir and Pacific Crest trails

Yosemite is traversed by two of the best-known **long-distance trails** in the western United States: the John Muir and Pacific Crest trails. The 211-mile **John Muir Trail** links the Happy Isles trailhead in Yosemite Valley with the 14,497ft summit of Mount Whitney, the highest peak in the contiguous 48 states. Along the way it passes through Tuolumne Meadows and Lyell Canyon, leaves the park at Donohue Pass and continues through the John Muir and Ansel Adams wildernesses and Sequoia and Kings Canyon National Parks before reaching Whitney's peak. It is all beautiful country with 13,000ft and 14,000ft peaks, alpine meadows and pure, rushing streams.

The trail is traditionally tackled from south to north (with a net descent of 4000ft), and the bulk of people still go this way, but it's worth considering going north to south: the terrain is easier around Yosemite so you can break yourself in gently, and gradually get accustomed to the higher altitudes further south. At the end of the trail you still have another eleven miles down to Whitney Portal trailhead (a 6000ft descent) making a total of 222 miles. Most hikers cover eight to twelve miles a day, making it a **three-week trek**. July and August are the most popular months, when temperatures are warmest and there's little chance of snow. It's pretty much a wilderness experience, so you'll need to carry everything on your back, though every few days there's an opportunity to buy food or pick up supplies you've sent ahead. For more information check ⊛ www.pcta.org/about_trail/muir/over.asp and obtain the *Guide to the John Muir Trail* by Elizabeth Wenk (see "Books", p.252).

The **Pacific Crest Trail** is a much more serious undertaking, running 2650 miles from Mexico to Canada through the Mojave Desert and across all the major western ranges, following the JMT through southern Yosemite then striking through the north of the park. Expect everything from scorching deserts in southern California to damp, old-growth rainforests in the Pacific Northwest and the arctic-alpine country of the Sierra Nevada.

Every year a couple of hundred people attempt the entire trail in one season – so-called "thru-hikers" – starting at the Mexican border in early spring and hiking north, always keeping a week or two behind the receding snowline. Around fifty successfully turn up at the Canadian border just before winter sets in. Most take five to six months in all, assuming a pace of around twenty miles a day and including a reasonable number of (much needed) rest days. PCT hikers can often be found at the Tuolumne Store in early July, ripping into the food parcels they shipped to the post office.

It often takes longer to plan the trip than to do the hike, and timing is all-important, especially if you don't want to worry about carrying an ice axe or crampons. You'll also want to start off with a good level of physical fitness, and should consider honing skills covered in Ray Jardine's *The Pacific Crest Trail Hiker's Handbook*. One such skill is keeping clean in cold water: you might only get half a dozen hot showers over the entire route.

Typically, wilderness permits are issued by the agency (National Park, State Park, National Forest or whatever) that manages the area in which you start your hike, and are valid for the entire hike no matter where you roam. For hikers covering over five hundred miles, **permits** can be issued by the Pacific Crest Trail Association (☏916/285-1846, ⊛ www.pcta.org), which is a superb source of information.

From Nevada Fall, the JMT skirts around Liberty Cap to reach the popular wilderness campground (and composting toilets) at **Little Yosemite Valley**. Soon after, the trail becomes more peaceful as most hikers head for the summit of Half Dome. The JMT now follows Sunrise Creek, climbing fairly steeply to crest a ridge revealing your first startling views of the Cathedral Range. A short descent leads to the **Sunrise Lakes High Sierra Camp**, beautifully set by a meadow overlooked by Merced Peak and with a striking view of Mount Clark to the south. There's a wilderness campground beside the camp, basic supplies are generally available, and if you've booked in advance you can even eat your meals here.

Edging around the meadow, the trail continues into mixed country of forests and meadows to the shallow saddle of **Cathedral Pass** and a virtually unsurpassed view of the stegosaurus back of the **Cathedral Range**: Cathedral Peak, Echo Peaks and the sinuous Matthes Crest. It's all beautifully set off by **Upper Cathedral Lake**, the next significant feature along the way. From here, the trail follows Hike Y22 in reverse to the trailhead. Immediately before the trailhead, turn right and follow the JMT parallel to Tioga Road for the last two miles to Tuolumne Meadows.

Y47 Merced Lake High Sierra Camp

Difficulty Very strenuous
Distance 27 miles round trip
Estimated time 2–3 days
Elevation gain 3300ft ascent
Season June–Oct
Trailhead location Map p.106, shuttle stop 16 near the Nature Center at Happy Isles
Comments Lovely meadows and cascades (with plenty of swimming opportunities), and the chance to summit Half Dome

Though **Little Yosemite Valley** is one of the park's gems, few bother to explore its three miles of glacier-sculpted 2000ft walls, lush meadows and feathery waterfalls. It's too far from the Happy Isles trailhead to allow full exploration in one day, so is best tackled by spending a night or two at **Merced Lake**, either camping or at the High Sierra Camp. Tack on an extra night at the *Little Yosemite Valley* campground and you could also summit Half Dome.

From Happy Isles follow hikes Y1–Y4 as far as the *Little Yosemite Valley* campground. Here you leave the Half Dome and JMT hikers and follow the Merced River as it winds its way across mostly level ground around the massive lump of **Bunnell Point**. The river slithers over **Bunnell Cascade**, one of many falls, gorges and slides along this active part of the Merced. The meadows of **Echo Valley**, just beyond, herald the liveliest stretch of the river, a mile-long tumbling torrent where springtime eddies have hollowed out great bathing spots. Merced Lake lies a bit further along, with the campground and High Sierra Camp just a bit further, though neither sits right by the lake. The campground has a treated water supply and toilet, and the High Sierra Camp has a limited range of supplies, and can offer meals to those who've booked in advance.

Y48 Ten Lakes

Difficulty Strenuous
Distance 22 miles
Estimated time 2 days
Elevation gain 4500ft ascent, 3500ft descent
Season June–Oct
Trailhead location Map p.84, 20 miles east of Crane Flat and 20 miles west of Tuolumne Meadows
Comments A one-way overnighter requiring transport, but well worth the extra effort

It's hard to say exactly which of the multitude of lakes make up the **Ten Lakes**, but you'll hardly care when camped out in this beautiful environment. The hike starts on the north side of Tioga Road, approximately twenty miles east of the Crane Flat road junction, and initially follows Yosemite Creek, crossing side streams and alternating between forest and open manzanita for a few miles. Climbing all the way you pass the pretty **Half Moon Meadow** (where camping is possible), and the junction for a two-mile side trip to **Grant Lakes**. After a total of five miles on the main trail you top out at Ten Lakes Pass, affording fabulous views down into the **Grand Canyon of the Tuolumne River** and to the innumerable mountains beyond.

Descending, you soon catch the first four of the ten lakes strung out in a sequence that earns them the occasional title of the Paternoster Lakes for their similarity to the beads on a rosary. Most people camp over the next few miles on spots near (but not right next to) one of the lakes. Throughout summer you won't be alone, but you can usually find a peaceful enough spot.

After joining the South Fork of the Tuolumne River, the trail climbs again, almost reaching 10,000ft on the shoulder of Tuolumne Peak before descending towards May Lake. As you enter the forest before May Lake, look out for tiny **Raisin Lake**, which makes a good spot for a dip: note that swimming is not allowed in May Lake. From May Lake follow Hike Y17 back to the May Lake parking lot.

The hike is slightly inconvenient in that it ends ten road miles from the starting trailhead: either organize a driver, shuttle cars, or time your finish so that you can walk the extra two miles to Tioga Road in time to meet the Yosemite Valley-bound YARTS or Tuolumne hikers' bus (see p.26) back to your vehicle.

Y49 Grand Canyon of the Tuolumne River

Difficulty Very strenuous
Distance 28 miles one way
Estimated time 2–3 days
Elevation gain 4000ft ascent, 4800ft descent
Season June–Oct
Trailhead location Map p.84, Lembert Dome parking area at Tuolumne Meadows
Comments One of the longest river hikes in the park; remote and rewarding

The **Grand Canyon of the Tuolumne River** is probably the most-used overnight backpack route north of Tioga Road, but you'll see far fewer fellow hikers here than in the popular areas between Yosemite Valley and Tuolumne Meadows. It is unlike other hikes in the park, following a single river for over twenty miles as it cuts deep into a granite canyon, alternately erupting into wild cascades, then easing to deep, bottle-green pools. Vegetation changes from stunted lodgepole pines to lowland forests then back to alpine up the relentless 4000ft climb out to White Wolf.

The hike is best divided into three sections, with nights spent at Glen Aulin and Pate Valley. With the trail wedged between river and cliff for much of the way, there are few other legal places to camp, though the authorities have a grudging acceptance of the use of "heavily impacted" sites where hikers have obviously camped before.

From Tuolumne Meadows the first five miles follow Hike Y29 to the **Glen Aulin High Sierra Camp** and campground; good sunbathing and swimming possibilities abound a quarter of a mile downstream. Beyond the camp you're on ground covered by Hike Y30 as far as **Waterwheel Falls**. Just beyond that is the confluence of the Tuolumne River and Return Creek, an attractive, shaded spot with an impacted camping area. You now climb away from the river for a couple of hours as it negotiates **Muir Gorge**.

It's then a steep descent to Register Creek where a pleasant waterfall makes a good place to recover. Ten minutes after Register Creek you cross Rodgers Creek and rejoin the Tuolumne at a collection of attractive impacted camping spots.

Here, down below 5000ft, the canyon traps the heat of summer, allowing black oak to predominate and encouraging **rattlesnakes** to sunbathe: keep your eyes peeled. The trail levels out beside languid pools as you approach **Pate Valley** and a legal camping spot ideal for recuperating before tomorrow's big ascent.

A mile after crossing the Tuolumne you start uphill on a series of switchbacks. Towards the end of summer there's no flowing water along the way, though several streams have stagnant pools that can be pressed into service; fill up whenever possible. About halfway up you cross the biggest stream, **Morrison Creek**, then five minutes beyond arrive at a camping spot with nice views down to Hetch Hetchy and **Kolana Rock**. After a final series of switchbacks the terrain eases and, after a couple of trail junctions, hits **Harden Lake**, a pleasant waterside camping area. From here it's three miles to **White Wolf**, described in reverse in Hike Y13.

Y50 The High Sierra Camp Loop

Difficulty Moderate
Distance 47 miles one way
Estimated time 6 days
Elevation gain 8000ft total ascent and descent
Season Camps open late June to early Sept
Trailhead location Map p.84, at Tuolumne Meadows Lodge
Comments The classic tour of the Yosemite high country

The most civilized way to spend time in Yosemite's backcountry is to make a **loop of the five High Sierra Camps** (which we shorten here to HSC; see box, p.132), all situated at least 7000ft up and linked by a wonderful high-country circuit that passes through some of the very finest landscapes the park has to offer. If you're unlucky with the HSC lottery or simply prefer to rough it a bit more, the campgrounds beside each camp make convenient and beautifully sited alternatives. All have toilets and most have potable water. Locations are spaced just six to ten miles apart (eight on average), making it an easy circuit, especially if you're not carrying camping gear.

Most people start in Tuolumne Meadows and make a counterclockwise loop, perhaps spending the first night at *Tuolumne Meadows Lodge* (actually an original High Sierra Camp, though with vehicle access it is now rather different). The first stop is the **Glen Aulin HSC**, reached along a dramatic stretch of the Tuolumne River by following Hike Y29. From there, the route doubles back slightly to join a trail heading southwest, eventually depositing you at the **May Lake HSC**, exquisitely sited by the lakeshore with Mount Hoffmann reflected in its waters. Follow the day hikers down to a parking area, then cross the road to pick up through forest to Tioga Road. From here, turn left to get to the Sunrise trailhead at the western end of Tenaya Lake. You now pick up Hike Y18 as far as Sunrise Lakes junction; turn left to get to the **Sunrise Lakes HSC**, also with a nice lakeside location.

From Sunrise Lakes, follow the JMT half a mile north, then turn right and swing south for eight miles to Echo Valley where you meet Hike Y47 for the delightful final two miles to the **Merced Lake HSC**. For many the next day is the toughest, only eight miles but with a 3000ft elevation gain to the **Vogelsang HSC**, perched high in alpine country with gorgeous tarns and barren mountains all around. There's a choice of routes: the shorter, steeper and more popular **Fletcher Creek** trail to the west, and the quieter and more scenic **Lewis Creek** track to the east. From Vogelsang it's a relatively easy amble down through forests and meadows beside Fletcher Creek to meet a section of the JMT for the final mile or so into Tuolumne Meadows.

6

Summer activities in Yosemite

While hiking is by far the park's most popular summer activity, it is by no means the only one. Anyone seeking more adventure can get off trail **scrambling** up the more accessible peaks, experience technical **rock climbing** with the Yosemite Mountaineering School, or try a little summer snow climbing on the park's highest peaks.

Most people are content with more sedentary pastimes: **horseriding**, gentle **rafting** down the Merced River, or lolling on its banks occasionally indulging in a little gentle **swimming**. It's also great fun **cycling** around Yosemite Valley floor, something we've covered under "Getting around" on p.27, and Wawona even has a **golf course** (see p.97). Note that off-road **mountain biking** is forbidden inside Yosemite National Park, but there's good riding just outside the park, near Briceburg and around Mammoth Lakes (for both, see p.160).

Rock climbing and scrambling

Even for the most sluggish couch potato it's hard to visit Yosemite without becoming fascinated by the antics of **rock climbers**, particularly in Yosemite Valley, where the sound of climbers calling out to one another is often heard around the base of the cliffs. Though it's always courteous to ask, climbers are generally happy to have an audience. Some of the most accessible areas in the valley for **watching climbers** in action are: Swan Slab, just north of *Yosemite Lodge*; Church Bowl, between Yosemite Village and *The Ahwahnee*; and El Cap Meadow. In Tuolumne Meadows, walk to the base of Lembert Dome where there are almost always ropes strung up the cliff. In addition, there are sometimes interpretive shows as part of the ranger programme; check *Yosemite Guide* for details.

You'll also catch people **bouldering**, a kind of low-level climbing without ropes where the thrill is in tackling ridiculously hard moves while barely leaving the ground, and **scrambling**, also rock climbing without ropes, but practised on less steep sections of the high peaks.

Climbing practicalities

The main rock climbing **season** runs from April to October, with most of the action concentrated in Yosemite Valley outside the summer months of July to

The Yosemite Decimal System

It is human nature to want to classify, and hikers and climbers are especially keen to measure their achievements, if only to gauge how to progress. It is for these people that the **Yosemite Decimal System** (YDS) was developed. It essentially divides all vertical endeavours into six categories of increasing difficulty:

Class 1 General hiking along well-established trails, both flat and steep. The fifty hikes listed in this guide are all Class 1.

Class 2 Cross-country hiking requiring some route-finding and using hands for balance over rough ground or over fallen trees.

Class 3 Both hands are required to get over rough, steep ground. Some may want a rope in case of a fall.

Class 4 As for Class 3 but on steeper terrain where a fall would likely cause serious injury or death. Most people will want to be roped.

Class 5 Free rock climbing grades – see below.

Class 6 Aid climbing, where climbing hardware and the rope are used to climb the cliff, not just for protection.

In practice, classes 1 and 2 are seldom used while 3, 4 and 6 get mentioned in some hiking and rock climbing guides. The only class that is widely used is Class 5. Historically this was divided into ten subclasses – 5.0, 5.1 up to 5.9 – but as rock climbs got harder new grades were invented – 5.10, 5.11, etc – with each class subdivided into four letter categories. The world's hardest climbs are now 5.15b: the hardest climb in Yosemite is a route named "Meltdown", in a remote part of Yosemite Valley, provisionally graded 5.14c.

The class of each rock climb (or hike) is defined by its hardest section. A simple hike with a short section of steep scrambling may be Class 3, and a rock climb that is generally 5.8 but has one 5.11a move will be classed as 5.11a. Rock climbs are typically rated (and named) by the first person to climb the route, though the rating may be adjusted as subsequent ascents are made and other climbers pass judgement on how hard it is.

September. When it gets too hot, climbers often migrate to the cooler Tuolumne Meadows, which sees the majority of the climbing from July to September. In spring and fall, virtually all climbers stay at the bohemian **Camp 4**, near *Yosemite Lodge*, a trampled, dusty and noisy site often entirely taken over by climbers. It's relatively cheap, with a great sense of camaraderie, and an excellent **bulletin board** for teaming up with climbing partners, selling gear, organizing a ride and the like. Normally you can only stay for seven nights at a stretch, but from mid-September to April you're allowed to settle in for a month.

Boulderers are especially well supplied with a bunch of great rocks near the campground, including the famous Columbia Boulder right at the heart of *Camp 4*. On its overhung eastern side, one route, "Midnight Lightning" – given the extremely hard bouldering grade of V7 – defeats most who spend their afternoons trying to ascend it.

Attempts to ease long-standing tensions between climbers and park rangers include discussions over free coffee between climbers and the "**climbing ranger**". These typically take place beside Columbia Boulder on Sunday mornings in spring and fall, and in Tuolumne in summer: check notice boards for times. Another good source of general **information** about the climbing scene, along with discussion of climbing ethics and details of the latest closures either for rockfall or ecological reasons, can be found at Ⓦ www.nps.gov/yose/planyourvisit /climbing.htm.

Websites, guidebooks, gear and lessons

There's a wealth of information on climbing in Yosemite, particularly on the **web**, where Terra Galleria (ⓦ www.terragalleria.com/mountain/info /yosemite/index.html) is a helpful resource for rock climbers, with everything from suggestions for beginners to the latest beta on aid routes. It has great photos and useful links as well.

We've listed climbing and bouldering **guidebooks** on p.252, principally the Falcon Guides by Don Reid, and Chris McNamara's Supertopos series. To catch

Climbing lessons and guided tours

The following lessons, run by the **Yosemite Mountaineering School** (April to mid-Nov; ☏ 209/372-8344, ⓦ www.yosemitemountaineering.com), follow a logical progression and can be taken in sequence to achieve a high level of proficiency. Try to reserve at least a few days in advance, especially in August. Prices given below are per person, and vary according to the size of the group.

Group climbing lessons

All classes last around **seven hours**, and start at 8.30am either from the Mountain Shop in Curry Village or from the Tuolumne Sport Shop in Tuolumne Meadows. All climbing equipment is provided except for climbing shoes, which can be rented ($8.50 a day).

Go Climb a Rock Here's where you start. Seven hours learning the ropes, so to speak. $117 for three or more people, $156 for two, and $217 for one.

Crack Climbing Much of the climbing in Yosemite follows crack lines: you'll get nowhere without some basic skills in this area. Ideal for gym climbers hitting the rock for the first time. $118 for three to five people, $158 for two, and $217 for one.

Anchoring Learning how to safely set up anchors to facilitate multi-pitch climbing. $118 for three to five people, $158 for two, and $217 for one.

Leading and Multi-pitch Climbing Do away with the security of a top-rope and start leading. Now you're really climbing. $140 for three people, $165 for two, and $235 for one.

Self-rescue and Aid Climbing Start your training for The Nose learning the basics of aid climbing. $118 for three to five people, $158 for two, and $217 for one.

Big Wall Climbing Seminar A two-day seminar covering all you need to know to make an assault on one of Yosemite's mightier cliffs. These take place on nine weekends throughout the summer: check the website for details. $280 for three people, $330 for two, and $470 for one.

Private classes and guided climbs

Small group or individual guiding on some of the world's finest rock routes allows you to test your limits without overstepping the mark, and is available for all skill levels. These are effectively private lessons and are often booked weeks in advance in midsummer.

3/4-day Up to six hours of climbing covering six to eight pitches. What you tackle depends very much on the ability of the party. $135 each for three people, $158 for two, and $221 for one.

Full-day Eight hours covering around eight pitches, or a shorter route with a long walk-in. $192 each for three people, $210 for two, and $283 for one.

Extreme day A big ten-hour day out. $237 each for two people, and $317 for one.

Overnight climbs Dream of that big wall, but never thought you could do it? El Capitan goes for $4466 over six days, while Half Dome costs $3616 for five days. Maximum two climbers per guide.

Banned in the park

It often seems that the Park Service takes a dim view of adventure sports; hardly surprising when they have to organize rescues, and then pick up the pieces (sometimes literally). While rock climbing has become a mainstream activity, its very nature seems to encourage an anti-authoritarian streak, and relations between the climbing community and the park authorities have always been strained.

With this in mind it should come as no surprise that **BASE jumping** was banned in Yosemite virtually as soon as it came on the radar screen. The sport first hit the headlines in 1978 when free-fall photographer Carl Boenish and some friends jumped off El Capitan and produced a film of their escapades. The Park Service did experiment with legal jumps for a couple of months in 1980, but the rules were so badly abused that a complete ban has been in place ever since. That doesn't stop people jumping, even though they risk a large fine, jail time and confiscation of their equipment. Still, that's nothing compared to the risk of things going wrong; and they do. Some have hit the rock face, while one jumper in 1998 drowned in the Merced River while trying to escape from rangers after a successful jump.

That same year there was even a day of civil disobedience when BASE jumpers did a deal with the Park Service where they would jump and voluntarily surrender in return for reduced fines. As a BASE jumping promo it backfired badly when one jump veteran, in full view of the media, failed to open her chute and died. Undoubtedly jumps still take place, but it is a secretive pursuit.

Dan Osman wanted to up the ante even further and pioneered **free falling**, using a cat's cradle of climbing ropes, pulleys and anchors to allow huge jumps that would be halted just a few feet above the ground. Often dubbed crazy, or worse, Osman had spent ten years gaining a reputation for fearlessness, always pushing the boundaries. His antics had begun to crop up on extreme videos – *Masters of Stone 4* for example – and even commercials. The Park Service was not amused, though his sport remained legal. On a November evening in 1998, Osman was standing atop the Leaning Tower about to make his biggest jump, a free fall of 1100ft designed to be stopped just 150ft above the deck. He called friends on his mobile from the top then jumped: several seconds later his friends were still waiting for his usual exalted shouts.

something of the spirit of the scene, read Steve Roper's *Camp 4* (see p.250), which should be available at the Mountain Shop in Curry Village.

Rock climbing **gear** is available from the Tuolumne Meadows Sport Shop (summer only), and the well-stocked and competitively priced Mountain Shop in Curry Village (daily 8am–6pm or later). For a more organized introduction to the climber's craft or to brush up on a few skills, engage the services of the **Yosemite Mountaineering School** (see box, p.141, for details), based at the Curry Village Mountain Shop from spring to fall. During the warmest months (late June to Aug), they also operate from Tuolumne Meadows Sport Shop, located in the gas station near the Tuolumne Meadows Store. Private lessons can be arranged in both locales, weather permitting.

The school also offers instruction in **summer snow climbing**, an essential skill for backcountry adventurers, covering safe travel through snow country, avalanche avoidance, and the use of ropes and ice axes on steep terrain. Trips are on-demand and are priced at private guiding rates (see box, p.141).

Scrambling

Anyone who likes to get off trail but lacks the skill or inclination to go rock climbing should consider **scrambling**, essentially low-grade rock climbing on terrain where you feel tolerably comfortable without a rope. All you need is a head for heights, a pair of strong boots and a detailed topographic map of the area, plus the ability to read and understand it. Just be sure you know your abilities, and discuss your proposed route with a ranger in one of the wilderness centres before you start.

With so many exposed ridges and dramatic peaks in Yosemite, it is beyond the scope of this book to cover scrambling in any detail, but an obvious starting point is Tuolumne's **Cathedral Range** – scrambling heaven. Here, in 1869, the 31-year-old John Muir scaled Cathedral Peak and never commented on any difficulties encountered. Even by modern climbing standards, most people would want a rope to scale the final summit block, but scramblers can easily reach the spectacular saddle between the true summit and its attendant Eichorn Pinnacle. Cast your eyes along the horizon from here and numerous other possibilities present themselves: Unicorn Peak from Elizabeth Lake, Echo Peaks, and much more.

Horseriding

Yosemite has a long heritage of **horse** travel. Ahwahneechee natives went on foot, but when the Mariposa battalion first entered Yosemite Valley they were pursuing the Ahwahneechee on horseback. Until the development of stage roads, and the eventual arrival of automobiles, all long-distance travel was by horse or mule, and the tradition continues today with three sets of stables accommodating everyone from beginners to those prepared to tackle a six-day circuit of the High Sierra Camps.

Yosemite's stables

Unless you're bringing your own horses and gear into Yosemite, **horseriding** is limited to trips from the three stables. There are two-hour rides (several daily; $60), four-hour rides (8am & 1pm; $80) and full-day rides ($119).

For beginner-oriented short rides you can usually just show up, but **reservations** (℡ 209/372-8348, Ⓦ www.yosemitepark.com) are recommended for longer excursions. Either way, you can generally expect a stately walk along some trails with few, if any, opportunities to even break into a trot – it's more about being on horseback in fabulous surroundings. No experience is necessary, but all riders need to be at least seven years old, over 44 inches tall and weigh less than 225 pounds, and should additionally wear long pants and closed-toed shoes. Be sure to arrive at least 45 minutes early to complete paperwork and get matched up with an appropriate horse, or, more likely, mule.

The most extensive facilities are at **Yosemite Valley Stables** (late April to Sept), which offers two-hour rides into Tenaya Canyon up to Mirror Lake; four-hour rides along the John Muir Trail, with views of Vernal and Nevada falls; and strenuous all-day rides (Sun only) to Quarter Dome on the shoulder of Half Dome.

In the summer months, splendid scenic riding can be done from the **Tuolumne Meadows Stables** (late June to Sept), which offers two-hour rides around Tuolumne Meadows and along Young Lakes trail (see Hike Y28) to a perfect vista of the Cathedral Range and Mammoth Peaks; four-hour rides along the Tuolumne River; and all-day outings to Waterwheel Falls.

In the south of the park, **Wawona Stables** (early May to Sept) offers perhaps the least scenic range of horseback trips, including two-hour rides around the Pioneer Yosemite History Center and Wawona Meadows; half-day rides (June & July only) on the Chilnualna Falls trail (see Hike Y42); and full day rides into Mariposa Grove by arrangement.

Horserideing is also available just **outside the park** near the southern entrance at Fish Camp with Yosemite Trails Pack Station, (℡559/683-7611, ⓦwww .yosemitetrails.com). Along with daily one-hour ($40) and two-hour ($80) rides, they run an entertaining five-hour ride ($140) into the Mariposa Grove of giant sequoias a couple of days a week.

High Sierra saddle trips

An excellent way to spend several days in the high country is to join one of the **High Sierra saddle trips** (July to early Sept; ℡801/559-4909), four- and six-day journeys with professional guides and packers who look after your mount and tend to the mules that carry the gear. They're based at Tuolumne Meadows Stables and make a loop of the High Sierra Camps (see box, p.182) with all accommodation and meals included in the price: $1018 for four days (Tues & Sun departures) and $1602 for six days (Sun departures). Customized guided excursions can also be arranged with groups of three to five paying $270 a day for a guide/packer and $129 a day for each pack mule.

Going it alone

The park service makes considerable provision for people bringing horse and pack animals into the park. You're allowed on most of the park's trails, and there are seasonal **stock camps** at Wawona, Tuolumne Meadows and Bridalveil Creek, with each site accommodating six people and six head of stock, and costing $25. Reservations for horse sites can only be made over the phone on ℡877/444-6777. Rules and regulations can be found at ⓦwww.nps.gov /yose/planyourvisit/stock.htm.

Anyone wanting to rent animals and equipment outside the park for use in Yosemite should contact either Eastern High Sierra Packers Association (ⓦwww .highsierrapackers.org) or West Side Packers (ⓦwww.easternsierrapackers.com).

Rafting and canoeing

While commercial whitewater rafting isn't permitted in Yosemite National Park, there's still plenty of opportunity for **messing around in boats**, chiefly on the relatively calm waters of the Merced River in Yosemite Valley. At Curry Village you can **rent** rafts (late May to late July; $26 per adult per run, $16 for under-13s; ℡209/372-4386), which hold up to four adults and come with buoyancy aids, and two paddles so that you can guide yourselves around fallen trees and sand banks. There's no hurry, so make a day of it by taking lunch then getting onto the river at Sentinel Bridge, from where you float three miles down to El Capitan and ride the free transport back to Curry Village. Kids must weigh at laest 50 pounds to go in the rafts.

There are no other watercraft rental facilities in the park, but if you bring your own canoe, kayak or **inflatable plaything** you are free to use the Merced River between Stoneman Bridge and Sentinel Beach (daily 10am–6pm) and the South Fork of the Merced in Wawona from Swinging Bridge down to the *Wawona* campground (daily 10am–6pm). The Park Service gives the okay once spring flows abate. In the high country the only feasible venue is Tenaya Lake, which lends itself to exploration by kayak or canoe, though it's exposed in windy conditions.

Top-class **whitewater rafting** takes place outside the park from April to late June on the Merced River (Class III–IV; see box, p.160) and the Tuolumne River (Class III–V; see box, p.158).

Active Yosemite

**T-shirts on sale in Yosemite urge you to
"Go climb a rock!" and certainly the park is
a climber's paradise. But Yosemite offers
plenty of other great ways for anyone to
get active – from horseriding or gentle
rafting to swimming and, of course, hiking.
Shamefully, some visitors barely stray from
the roads, shunning the hundreds of miles
of well-maintained hiking trails that thread
the entire park. They miss out on fabulous
waterfalls tucked away up side canyons,
magnificent Sierra vistas, refreshing swims
in high-country lakes and the subtleties of
the park's meadows and wildflowers.**

Hiking

The only way to really get to know Yosemite is to strike out on foot, and with eight hundred miles of trails the park can occupy a lifetime of **hiking**. The majority of visitors see only a handful of the most popular trails, but they're fashionable for good reason. Bagging the five hikes we've listed below will quickly introduce you to a wonderful cross section of Yosemite's finest features.

The rest of the park is left to hardy souls heading out into the **backcountry**, explored by a mere one percent of Yosemite's annual four million visitors. Join them and you can walk for days only seeing a handful of people, camping alone with just that big starry sky for company.

Backcountry hiking in Yosemite ▲

Camping in the park, near Isberg Lake ▼

Five favourite hikes

▶▶ **The Mist Trail** (Hike Y2, p.106): Precarious spray-drenched steps beside one of the park's finest waterfalls make this the best short-ish hike in Yosemite.

▶▶ **Half Dome** (Hike Y4, p.108): The summit in a day is a big effort, but well worth it for the haul up the steep cables and great views from the vertiginous summit.

▶▶ **Cathedral Lakes** (Hike Y22, p.117): Relatively easy subalpine hiking to gorgeous lakes and sublime views of Cathedral Peak.

▶▶ **Waterwheel Falls** (Hike Y30, p.122): Head into northern Yosemite past numerous wonderful cataracts and swimming holes. Best done overnight.

▶▶ **The High Sierra Camp Loop** (Hike Y50, p.138): Superb multi-day hike through the Yosemite high country, with optional stays in seasonal tent cabins.

Horseriding

It's hard to beat arriving at your mountain-girt campground after a hot day on the trail, unhitching saddles and leading your pack animals down to the river to drink, then heading back to the tents for a meal that's far more luxurious than anything hikers would be prepared to carry.

Most of Yosemite's backcountry trails are open for **horseriding**, so getting out into the wilderness doesn't have to involve backpacking-style hardship. It's an altogether more relaxing experience, evocative of early pioneering times when travelling with horses and mules was standard practice. Such trips can be organized through the stables in Yosemite and through pack outfitters based just outside the park.

In practice, most people take a more spontaneous approach, just riding for a few hours for the sheer joy of being on horseback. Each of Yosemite's three **stables** – in Yosemite Valley, Tuolumne Meadows and Wawona – offers two-hour trips following river banks or heading out across meadows in magnificent scenery. Half-day trips stray further afield and give you a chance to really get used to your steed. If you're saddle-hardened, go for a full-day trip, like the ride up to **Quarter Dome**, at the base of the final ascent to **Half Dome**.

▲ Enjoying Yosemite from a saddle

▼ A ranger-led snowshoe walk

Snowshoeing and skiing

With its silent blanket of pure white snow, and visitor numbers at a fraction of their summertime peak, winter is a fine time to be in Yosemite. Closed roads limit access to the high country, but that makes the destination all the more appealing for those prepared to head out on **cross-country skis** or **snowshoes**.

Most people make straight for the modest downhill slopes of **Badger Pass** where you can rent gear and take lessons. The classic trip is then to journey along the snowbound Glacier Point Road to **Glacier Point** itself, where the winter-gripped Sierra stretches to the horizon in every direction, and you can look straight down on the skaters at the Curry Village ice rink in Yosemite Valley. There are even organized trips that stay overnight at Glacier Point for that moonlit vista of Half Dome.

Whole books have been written on cross-country skiing routes through the Yosemite backcountry, and with your own gear the options are limitless, especially if you're prepared to snow-camp. In fact, one of the winter highlights is a night spent in **Mariposa Grove** with massive sequoias all around, their gargantuan boughs weighed down by a fresh dump of powder.

Badger Pass Ski Area ▲

Rafting on the Merced, inside the park ▼

Rafting

Enjoying the scenery **on the water** in Yosemite is a leisurely affair. Pick a sunny day, stock up with supplies for your journey, bring along your swimsuit and assorted aquatic toys and settle in for a stately drift past the towering cliffs and spires of the valley walls. A few ripples provide a hint of adventure, but this is more about **cruising** downstream, occasionally dipping your paddle in the water, rolling over the stern for a refreshing dunking, then pulling up at a sandy beach for a picnic. Of course, if you've got friends in an adjacent raft, pirate-boarding antics are pretty much essential.

If you're after something wilder, **Class III–V rapids** await you just outside the park boundary at El Portal, on a livelier stretch of the Merced.

Swimming

Your enthusiasm for **swimming** in Yosemite will be dictated largely by your pain threshold: the park's rivers, streams and lakes are generally icy-cold. Even in the middle of summer the languid waters of the two most popular swimming rivers – the Merced River in Yosemite Valley and the South Fork of the Merced River in Wawona – could hardly be called warm. Still, when the sun is beating down and temperatures are in the nineties, half a day at one of the riverside beaches can become very alluring. The period from mid-July to mid-September is best, when the days are hot and early season snowmelt has abated: perfect for washing away the sweat of tired hikers.

Be aware that **currents** can still be deceptively swift and submerged logs can be a hazard. Always keep away from tempting pools above waterfalls: in 2005 alone, three people died in this way, and over two hundred people have either drowned or gone over Yosemite waterfalls since 1870. Remember that kids should have some form of flotation device on them or nearby.

As well as the natural swimming areas listed below, there are public outdoor **swimming pools** (mid-May to mid-Sept daily 11am–5pm; guests free, others $5) at *Yosemite Lodge* and Curry Village. Both the *Wawona Hotel* and *The Ahwahnee* have pools as well, though these are only open to guests.

Yosemite's top natural swimming spots

Yosemite Valley and Little Yosemite Valley

Clark Bridge Proximity to the *North Pines*, *Lower Pines* and *Upper Pines* campgrounds makes this Merced River swimming hole a perennial favourite. Watch for strong currents early in the season.

Housekeeping Camp A pleasant beach and swimming spot frequented mostly by *Housekeeping Camp* guests.

Sentinel Beach A lovely and peaceful spot just off Southside Drive.

Merced Lake to Little Yosemite Valley There are dozens of gorgeous swimming spots along this lively backcountry stretch of the Merced River.

Northern Yosemite

Tenaya Lake The lake boasts cool waters at 8000ft, but there's a lovely beach at the northeastern end, and a more secluded one at Murphy Creek on its north side.

Glen Aulin Trail The water is too pushy here in spring and early summer, but come this way (following Hike Y29) in fall and you'll find numerous beautiful swimming holes.

Southern Yosemite

Wawona Campground The South Fork of the Merced River makes an ideal, gentle and popular place for watery frolics in summer.

Swinging Bridge A gorgeous and relatively little-used pool just over a mile upstream from Wawona.

Outside the park

Mono Lake By being salty and very alkaline, Mono Lake allows you to float like few other places: see p.153.

Hot springs Hot springs in the Owens Valley are covered on p.153.

Fishing

Yosemite isn't really a **fishing** destination. None of the rivers and lakes is stocked (though many once were), and over half of Yosemite's lakes have no fish at all. That said, there's some pretty decent trout fishing along the 58 permanent streams, notably at lower elevations such as along the Merced River in Yosemite Valley and along the Tuolumne River above the Hetch Hetchy reservoir. The Merced offers enjoyable fishing all summer and into the winter, where the descendants of hatchery-raised brown and rainbow trout are the main attraction.

To fish, anyone sixteen or over needs a California sport fishing licence (one day $13.40; two days $20.75), which must be visibly attached to your upper body. These are sold at the Tuolumne Meadows store, the Wawona store and the Sport Shop in Yosemite Village, which has the best supply of fishing **gear**. It's open season year-round on lakes and reservoirs, and the stream- and river-fishing season (the last Sat in April to Nov 15) excludes Frog Creek and Lake Eleanor, which both open on June 15.

Bag limits vary with location, and you should check with the Park Service rangers, but along the popular Happy Isles to Pohono Bridge stretch of the Merced, you can only fish with artificial lures or flies with barbless hooks. A daily bag of five brown trout is permitted, but rainbow trout are strictly catch-and-release. For more details visit Ⓦ www.nps.gov/yose/planyourvisit/fishing.htm, where there's a link to the California Department of Fish and Game.

Keen fishers might consider engaging the services of Sierra Fly Fisher (Ⓣ 559/683-7664, Ⓦ www.sierraflyfisher.com), who run personalized catch-and-release **fly fishing trips**. A full day costs $400 for the first two people and $110 each for additional fishers; half a day goes for $275 plus $50 for each extra person.

7

Winter activities in Yosemite

From sometime in November until around the middle of April much of Yosemite is cloaked in a mantle of snow and looks even more magical than it does the rest of the year. Anywhere over 5500ft has an almost continuous coating during these months, but even in lowland areas like Yosemite Valley, pines and cedars are frequently bowed with the weight of snow, waterfalls glisten with icicles, and Half Dome is topped by a thick white cap. The cold days are often sunny, though conditions can change rapidly with clouds rolling in only to pull back, revealing tantalizing glimpses of snowcapped peaks.

If your vehicle is equipped with tyre chains, you can experience Yosemite Valley, Wawona and a limited number of other areas from the road, but to fully appreciate Yosemite at its seasonal best you'll need to indulge in some **winter activities**. Much of the action at this time takes place at the **Badger Pass Ski Area**, but skaters glide around the outdoor **ice rink** in Curry Village, and **snowshoe** and **cross-country ski** enthusiasts have virtually the whole park at their disposal. In practice, most gravitate to the snow play areas at Crane Flat and Mariposa Grove, where you can ski among the giant sequoias and even camp out under their towering canopy.

Downhill skiing and snowboarding

Yosemite isn't really about **downhill skiing and snowboarding**. The park's only tows are those at the family-friendly **Badger Pass** (see box, p.148), which is seldom crowded, and has runs best suited for beginner and intermediate skiers. The **vertical drop** is a modest 800ft, with ten runs fed by five lifts (one triple-chair,

---

Winter wilderness camping

Winter backcountry regulations are essentially the same as for summer. You still need a wilderness permit (advance reservations not needed) and those leaving Yosemite Valley must reach the valley rim before camping. The Tuolumne Grove of giant sequoias is still off-limits, but in winter (Dec to mid-April) you can **camp in Mariposa Grove** as long as you are uphill from the Clothespin Tree. Although bears do spend long periods sleeping, they don't hibernate and can be after your food at any time.

Badger Pass

The **Badger Pass Ski Area** (generally mid-Dec to March daily 9am–4pm; ☎209/372-1000) lies at 7200ft, a forty-minute drive from Yosemite Valley on the road to Glacier Point. It's home to Yosemite's only **downhill ski area** and is the park's gateway to subalpine cross-country activities, specifically **cross-country skiing** and **snowshoeing**, with 350 miles of skiable trails (90 of them marked) and 25 miles of machine-groomed track fanning out into the backcountry. Expect **temperatures** in the 30–60°F range (-1 to 16°C).

In winter, Glacier Point Road is kept open as far as Badger Pass, which is accessible by a free one-hour **shuttle** starting from Curry Village (8am & 10.30pm), calling at Yosemite Village (8.10am & 10.40am), *The Ahwahnee* (8.15am & 10.45pm) and *Yosemite Lodge* (8.30am & 11am). Shuttles depart Badger Pass at 2pm and 4pm. There's also a weekend shuttle from Oakhurst ($10, including park entry).

Once there, you'll find gear rental, a tuning shop and a couple of basic **restaurants** – the *Off-the-Grill* and the *Snowflake Room* – that'll keep you supplied with burgers, sandwiches, pizza slices, salads, sodas, beer and wine without breaking the bank.

The best source of advance **information** is ⓦwww.BadgerPass.com, which includes full details of facilities, rental prices, lessons and trips, along with links to the snow report and any special deals. People travelling with **children** will appreciate the Badger Pups Den (9am–4.30pm; $10 an hour, $95 a day), a kind of crèche for kids aged three to nine that only requires you to provide and eat lunch with your kids. Those aged 4–6 can also attend one-hour group ski lessons (one lesson $49; two lessons $69).

three double chairs and one cable tow). Only around fifteen percent of the terrain is suitable for advanced skiers.

Lift tickets cost $42 a day at weekends ($35 midweek), with a one-ride ticket going for $5 and a full-season pass $492. Half-day tickets (12.30–4.30pm) are $33/30, and there are kids' tickets (7–12 years inclusive) costing half the adult rate. Seniors (65 and up) get a free lift pass on weekdays but pay almost the full adult fare on weekends and holidays. **Equipment rental** costs $31 (ages 12 and under $22) for downhill skis, boots and poles; $35 (kids $25) for snowboarding gear.

Beginners and those needing to brush up on their technique should enlist the services of the **Badger Pass Ski School**, which has been providing ski instruction for over seventy years. Novices should take the **Guaranteed Learn-to-Ski Package** ($69, kids aged 7–12 $59), with two two-hour group lessons plus ski rental and beginners' lift ticket: there's also a snowboarding equivalent ($79, kids $69). Those looking to improve their technique will want the **Next Step Package** with a two-hour lesson, gear rental and a full lift ticket. There are skiing ($88, kids $58) and boarding variants ($92, kids $62). In addition, one-hour **private lessons** are charged at $80 for one person, $112 for two and $136 for three.

Cross-country skiing

Perhaps the best way to get a true impression of Yosemite in winter is to head out **cross-country skiing** into the backcountry. Seeing the domes, spires and meadows cloaked in a mantle of snow from some viewpoint miles from anyone else is an experience to treasure. Almost the entire park is open to skiers, though most activity is concentrated around areas with easy access to winter facilities, particularly Badger Pass (see box, p.148), with its gear rental, lessons and guided trips. Touring skis, boots and pole **rental** goes for $23 (ages 12 and under $11), and you'll pay a few dollars more for skate skis, and a couple more again for telemark gear.

Complete **beginners** should take the Learn to Ski/Board Package (daily 10am; ski $69, board $79), which includes gear rental and two consecutive two-hour group lessons. Tuition in telemark skiing ($36, $46 including rentals) is also available. One-hour private lessons cost $37 for the first person and $20 each for up to three others.

You're free to follow the groomed trails that meander through the forests around Badger Pass, and perhaps tackle a **self-guided trip to Glacier Point Hut** (room and board $120). Reservations are essential and a minimum of six skiers is needed to justify opening the hut for the night. Experienced skiers might also want to join a **guided day tour** ($116 each for 4–7 people), designed to improve your off-track skills.

Elsewhere in the park, most of the cross-country action happens at **Crane Flat** and in the **Mariposa Grove**, each of which has marked trails for all levels of ability ranging from a half-mile loop to sixteen-mile backcountry epics. Maps are available from visitor centres and ranger stations. More advanced skiers and snowshoers might want to tackle **Snow Creek Trail** from Yosemite Valley to Tioga Road, near Tenaya Lake. You must be competent in backcountry winter travel, winter camping and avalanche assessment, and you'll need to register at the Yosemite Valley Visitor Center. Alternatively, consider joining one of the excellent **guided overnight trips** run by the Cross-country Ski Center; see the box below for details.

Snowshoeing

Snowshoeing isn't much harder than walking, and if you're in Yosemite in winter you should grasp the opportunity it gives to explore the backcountry. Anywhere that's open to cross-country skiers – virtually the whole park – is potential snowshoeing territory: just don't walk in the tracks the skiers have carefully

---

Guided cross-country ski trips

The following **trips** are run by the Cross-country Center & Ski School (☎209/372-8444): book several weeks in advance if possible.

Glacier Point Overnight Ski Trip This is one of the park's most popular intermediate-grade cross-country trips, and deservedly so with the chance to sleep at Glacier Point and wake up to a winter sunrise over Half Dome. Under skilled guidance you negotiate a 21-mile round trip along Glacier Point Road to Glacier Point, where there's a new ski hut, with dormitory accommodation and hearty meals provided. Your personal gear and a sleeping bag (rentals available) are all you need. They need a minimum of three people; rates are $350 per person for one night and $550 for two nights.

Snow Camping Learn the basics of snow travel (ski or snowshoe) and winter camping skills on this guided overnight trip. You'll need previous ski or snowshoe experience and will have to carry a pack carrying some of the food and communal camping equipment (supplied). Bring or rent skis or showshoes. Three-person minimum; $292 each.

Trans-Sierra Ski Tour An excellent advanced intermediate six-day ski tour through the Sierra Nevada, journeying from the east to the Ski School hut in Tuolumne Meadows then exploring the pristine high-country. You'll need to be fairly fit to enjoy this. Three-person minimum; $876 per person.

Tuolumne Meadows Hut Tour This six-day tour is slightly less demanding than the Trans-Sierra Ski Tour but still includes several days skiing around Tuolumne Meadows. Two tours starting Sunday in late March and/or early April; $876 per person; three-person minimum.

Ostrander Ski Hut

Skiers and snowshoers who fancy a night out but don't relish sleeping in a tent or joining one of the guided trips might like staying at the stone-built **Ostrander Ski Hut** (🌐 www .yosemiteconservancy.org), nine miles southeast of Badger Pass. The hut is open from just before Christmas to early April and costs $32 per person per night ($52 on Fri & Sat nights): reserve through the Yosemite Conservancy (☎ 209/372-0740; Mon–Fri 8.30am– 4.30pm Pacific time). Weekends and holidays are in high demand: if you want to stay at these times, mail in your request (downloadable form on website) before the beginning of November to be entered into the lottery for spaces.

Whenever you go, take everything you need for camping. The trail to the hut can be treacherous in winter and visitors need to be prepared to snow camp if caught in bad weather along the way.

grooved. Snowshoes can be rented ($22.50 all day, $18.50 half-day) at Badger Pass (see box, p.148), where Park Service naturalists lead frequent two-hour **snowshoe walks** (free; snowshoe rental $5) teaching about the dynamics of snow, and plant and wildlife adaptations to winter. On the four evenings leading up to full moon (if clear) there are two-hour **Full Moon Snowshoe Walks** (Jan–March; $5 with your own snowshoes, otherwise $18.50) involving over two miles of walking up a ridge to a viewpoint: check *Yosemite Guide* for times and sign up at the *Yosemite Lodge* Tour Desk (☎ 209/372-1240).

In the rest of the park you are limited only by your imagination and your knowledge of winter wilderness travel and survival, route finding and avalanche safety. The hiking trails (see chapters 4 & 5) are obvious candidates for those sufficiently skilled, but most snowshoers head for the winter trails at Crane Flat and Mariposa Grove, both described on maps available from the visitor centres. For anything ambitious you'll need winter camping equipment, the main exception being the Ostrander Ski Hut (see box above).

Snowtubing, sledding and ice-skating

Badger Pass has traditionally been a little stuffy in its approach, but it has now fashioned a new groomed area for **snowtubing**, where young kids can ride specially designed inner tubes. Two-hour sessions run daily from 11.30am and 2pm and cost $15 per person per session. **Sledding** is not allowed at Badger Pass, but is permitted at the snow play area at the *Crane Flat* campground. Here sledding, tobogganing and inner-tubing are all encouraged. There are no rentals, so bring your own toys.

Though plenty of enthusiasts ski and snowshoe around Yosemite Valley, the most popular winter activity is **ice-skating** at the open-air rink at Curry Village (typically mid-Nov to mid-March; ☎ 209/372-8341). Two-and-a-half-hour sessions cost $8 (kids $6; skate rental $3) and run daily from 3.30pm & 7pm with additional sessions from 8.30am and noon on Saturday, Sunday and holidays. Comforts include a warming hut, a fire pit and a snack service.

8

Around Yosemite

The beauty of the Sierra doesn't stop at the boundaries of Yosemite National Park. Surrounding areas can be just as stunning, regulations for camping, hunting and fishing are often more relaxed, and people are usually far more scarce. Even if Yosemite remains your sole goal, heavy demand for accommodation within the park means you may well find yourself staying just outside or in the surrounding towns.

Head **east of Yosemite** (over the summer-only Tioga Pass) to explore two of the finest sights in the region: ethereal **Mono Lake**, whose shoreline is dotted with contorted tufa towers set in an open land of sagebrush, and **Bodie**, probably the West's most evocative ghost town, often cited as the coldest town in the country. Don't miss the chance to warm up afterwards at one of the area's rustic **hot springs** hidden away in the Owens Valley.

There's less of an immediate appeal to the area **northwest of Yosemite**, along Hwy-120 West, though you'll find a good range of accommodation, particularly in the picturesque old gold town of **Groveland**. Anyone seeking the region's wildest **whitewater rafting** should head straight for the nearby Tuolumne River, while tamer alternatives can be found along the Merced River, **west of Yosemite** along Hwy-140. Close by is the former gold town of **Mariposa**, which, with its good places to stay and eat and relative proximity to Yosemite Valley, makes an appealing base if you need to stay outside the park. Further out, **Merced** is mainly useful as a transport interchange, though it does have a convenient hostel.

South of Yosemite, functional **Oakhurst** serves as a handy launch pad for the park's southern reaches, and provides access to wonderful country around **Bass Lake** and in the **John Muir Wilderness** – though you'd want to shift camp if you plan to explore the remote area around **Mono Hot Springs**.

Further south still, you're into Sequoia and Kings Canyon National Parks (see Chapter 13), which both have accommodation, though you may prefer to base yourself in either **Fresno** or **Visalia**, the latter with a bus service into the parks.

East of Yosemite: Mono Lake and Bodie

Snow typically blocks the Tioga Road (Hwy-120 East) from early November until late May, cutting off the bulk of Yosemite National Park from the eastern Sierra. For the rest of the year, the Tioga Road and the area around Mono Lake and Bodie shouldn't be missed.

From the park boundary at Tioga Pass, Hwy-120 East plunges fourteen miles down the Lee Vining Grade (see p.89) past numerous good campgrounds to the small town of Lee Vining. The scenery changes rapidly from Yosemite's granite domes and alpine lakes to a land that feels a million miles away. Here in the rain shadow of the mountains you're on the fringes of the Great Basin, semi-arid uplands that stretch away across Nevada to Utah. Snowmelt streams coursing down the Eastern Sierra each spring have created the alkaline **Mono Lake**, an almost otherworldly disc shining amid miles of scrubby sagebrush. Around its shore, tufa towers make a photogenic, if unnatural, sight. On the lake's western flank, tiny **Lee Vining** is the district's service town and the only place on the eastern side of the Sierra that's close enough to be used as a base for visiting Yosemite National Park. You wouldn't want to drive daily into

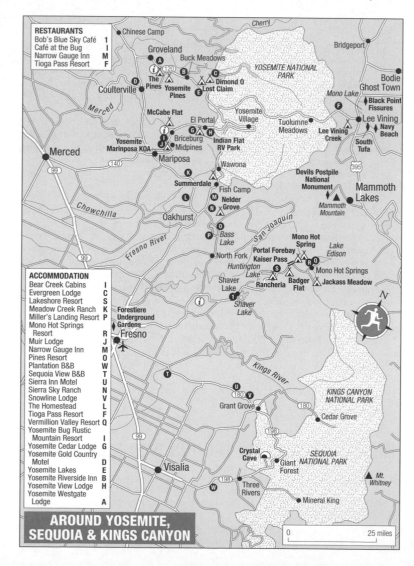

RESTAURANTS
Bob's Blue Sky Café — 1
Café at the Bug — I
Narrow Gauge Inn — M
Tioga Pass Resort — F

ACCOMMODATION
Bear Creek Cabins — I
Evergreen Lodge — C
Lakeshore Resort — S
Meadow Creek Ranch — K
Miller's Landing Resort — P
Mono Hot Springs
  Resort — R
Muir Lodge — J
Narrow Gauge Inn — M
Pines Resort — O
Plantation B&B — W
Sequoia View B&B — T
Sierra Inn Motel — U
Sierra Sky Ranch — N
Snowline Lodge — V
The Homestead — L
Tioga Pass Resort — F
Vermillion Valley Resort — Q
Yosemite Bug Rustic
  Mountain Resort — I
Yosemite Cedar Lodge — G
Yosemite Gold Country
  Motel — D
Yosemite Lakes — E
Yosemite Riverside Inn — B
Yosemite View Lodge — H
Yosemite Westgate
  Lodge — A

AROUND YOSEMITE, SEQUOIA & KINGS CANYON

0   25 miles

Yosemite Valley, sixty miles distant, but Tuolumne Meadows is within easy striking distance.

The barren hill country thirty miles north of Lee Vining appears to be an inhospitable place to live, and the twenty thousand people who once called **Bodie** home wouldn't contest that. As soon as the gold ran out, so did the people, leaving behind what many consider the most atmospheric **ghost town** in the West. It's a great spot for anyone needing a break from hiking, or looking for more boom-time history than Yosemite can supply.

Mono Lake and Lee Vining

The blue expanse of **MONO LAKE** sits in the middle of a volcanic desert tableland, its sixty square miles reflecting the statuesque, snowcapped mass of the eastern Sierra Nevada. At over a million years old, it's an ancient lake with two large volcanic islands – the light-coloured **Paoha** and the black **Negit** – surrounded by salty, alkaline water. It resembles nothing more than a science-fiction landscape, with great towers and spires formed by mineral deposits ringing the shores; hot springs surround the lake, and all around the basin are signs of lava flows and volcanic activity, especially in the cones of the Mono Craters, just to the south.

The lake's most distinctive features, the strange, sandcastle-like **tufa** formations, were increasingly exposed from the early 1940s to the mid-1990s as the City of Los Angeles drained away the waters that flow into the lake (see box, p.154). The towers of tufa were formed underwater, where calcium-bearing freshwater springs well up through the carbonate-rich lake water; the calcium and carbonate combine as limestone, slowly growing into the weird formations you can see today.

LEE VINING, overlooking Mono Lake, is the only settlement anywhere nearby. It offers the usual range of visitor services, including **accommodation** (see p.175 for listings) and **restaurants** (see p.190) – but not a great deal more.

Owens Valley hot springs

One of the pleasures of any extended foray east of Yosemite is soaking your bones in one of the numerous **hot springs** dotted through the Owens Valley, east of the Sierra Nevada. None is well signposted, and most are primarily used by locals, who are welcoming enough if you are respectful. Springs tend to be tucked miles away down some rutted dirt road, and often comprise little more than a ring of rocks or a hollowed-out tub into which people have diverted the waters to create pools of differing temperatures. Most are **clothing-optional**, but you'll stand out as a tourist if you don't strip off. The following are a few of the better-known spots, but the best idea is to gain the confidence of some local and ask directions to their favourite.

Buckeye Hot Springs Streamside hot springs reached by following US-395 25 miles north of Lee Vining to Bridgeport, then four miles further north, turning left for *Buckeye* campground and continuing 4.6 miles to where a rough track leads from a dirt parking area to three small pools beside the river.

Pulky's Pool Concrete tub with room for eight located 25 miles south of Lee Vining and four miles south of Mammoth Lakes. Heading south on US-395, turn left just after Mammoth airport by an old church. Follow Benton Crossing Road for 2.5 miles. Take the first road on the left going down the hill, then fork right after 0.2 miles. Park and walk a hundred yards north.

Travertine Hot Springs Shallow pools in an open setting near Bridgeport, 25 miles north of Lee Vining. Follow US-395 half a mile south of Bridgeport, turn left into Jack Sawyer Road, then fork left at the first junction and keep right for a mile.

A thirsty city and the battle for Mono Lake

Mono Lake is one of the oldest on the continent and has survived several ice ages and all the volcanic activity that the area can throw at it. The lake's biggest threat, however, has been the City of Los Angeles, which owns the riparian rights to Mono Lake's catchment.

From 1892 to 1904, the fledgling city of Los Angeles experienced a twelve-year drought and started looking to the Owens River as a reliable source of water that could be easily channelled to the city. Under the auspices of the Los Angeles Department of Water and Power, the city bought up almost the entire Owens Valley, then diverted the river and its tributaries into a 223-mile, gravity-fed **aqueduct** to take this water to LA. Farms and orchards in the once-productive Owens Valley were rendered useless without water, and Owens Lake near Lone Pine was left to dry up entirely.

The aqueduct was completed in 1913, but the growing city demanded ever more water. Consequently, in 1941, LA diverted four of the five streams that fed Mono Lake through an eleven-mile tunnel into its Los Angeles Aqueduct, sparking a legal battle surrounding the depletion of the lake itself – long one of the biggest **environmental controversies** in California.

Over the next fifty years, the **water level** in Mono Lake dropped over 40ft, a disaster not only because of the lake's great beauty, but also because Mono Lake is the primary nesting ground for **California gulls** and a critical resting point for hundreds of thousands of migratory **eared grebes** and **phalaropes**. The lake was down to roughly half its natural size, and as the levels dropped, the islands in the middle of the lake where the gulls laid their eggs became peninsulas, and the colonies fell prey to coyotes and other mainland predators. As less fresh water reached the lake it became increasingly saline, threatening the unique local ecosystem. About all that will thrive in the harsh conditions are brine shrimp and alkali flies, both essential food sources for the birdlife. Humans, too, are affected by the changes the lake is experiencing: winds blowing across the saltpans left behind by the receding water create alkaline clouds containing selenium and arsenic, both contributors to lung disease.

Seemingly oblivious to the plight of the lake, the City of Los Angeles built a second aqueduct in 1970 and the water level dropped even faster, sometimes falling eighteen inches in a single year. Prompted by scientific reports of an impending ecological disaster, a small group of activists set up the **Mono Lake Committee** (Ⓦ www .monolake.org) in 1978, fighting for the preservation of this irreplaceable ecosystem partly through the courts and partly through publicity campaigns – "Save Mono Lake" bumper stickers were once *de rigueur* for concerned citizens. Though the California Supreme Court declared in 1983 that Mono Lake must be saved, it wasn't until 1994 that emergency action was taken. A target water height of 6377ft above sea level (later raised to 6392ft) was grudgingly agreed upon to make **Negit Island** safe for nesting birds. Streams dry for decades are now flowing again, and warm springs formerly located by lakeside interpretive trails are submerged. The target level – 18ft higher than its recorded minimum, but still 25ft below its pre-diversion level – won't be reached by the time the agreement is up for re-negotiation in 2014, something that concentrates the ongoing efforts of the Mono Lake Committee.

Arrival and information

The most useful public transport calling at Lee Vining is the summer-only YARTS **bus** service (see p.23) between Mammoth Lakes and Yosemite Valley. The shuttles stop in the centre of town, visit the Mono Basin Scenic Area Visitor Center (see p.155) and call at the Tioga Gas Mart at the start of Hwy-120 East.

Before striking out for the lake and its tufa, call in at both of the excellent visitor centres. In the heart of Lee Vining, the town's **Mono Lake Committee Information Center** (daily: July & Aug 8am–9pm; rest of year 9am–5pm;

8

760/647-6595, www.leevining.com and www.monolake.org) is partly the showcase for the committee's battle for Mono Lake, featuring an excellent twenty-minute movie and a good bookstore concentrating on the environment and the Eastern Sierra. There's even a tasteful gift shop and **internet access**.

A mile north along US-395, the **Mono Basin Scenic Area Visitor Center** (May–Oct daily 9am–4.30pm; Nov & April daily 9am–4.30pm; Dec–March closed; 760/873-2408, www.r5.fs.fed.us/inyo) features lake-related exhibits, a good short geology film and ecology lectures by rangers.

Exploring Mono Lake

Everyone's first stop is **South Tufa**, five miles east of US-395 via Hwy-120 (unrestricted access; $3), the single best place to admire the tufa spires. Boardwalks and trails lead you among these 20ft-high limestone cathedrals and along the lakeshore, where photo ops turn up around every corner. About a mile to the east lies **Navy Beach** (free), where there are a few more (less spectacular) spires, and you can float in water at least twice as buoyant as (and a thousand times more alkaline than) sea water. Even towards the end of summer the water is chilly, however, and some find that the salt stings. Look out, too, for the small but wonderfully intricate **sand tufas** nearby.

To add an educational component to your explorations, join one of the free **guided walks** (July to early Sept daily 10am, 1pm & 6pm) around the tufa formations, run by the Mono Basin Scenic Area Visitor Center. You can also sign up for one of the Mono Lake Committee's regular hour-long **canoe trips** (mid-June to early Sept Sat & Sun 8am, 9.30am & 11am; $24; reservations recommended 760/647-6595), on which you'll paddle around the tufa towers, learning about their formation, and hear details of migrating birdlife and the brine shrimp they feed off. Alternatively go by **kayak** with Mammoth Lakes-based Caldera Kayaks (reservations on 760/934-1691, www.calderakayak.com), which runs natural history tours on Mono Lake (3hr; $110 each for two, $75 each for groups of 3 or more).

Adjacent to the south shore of the lake stands **Panum Crater**, a 700-year-old volcano riddled with deep fissures and 50ft towers of lava, accessed by the short and fairly easy **Plug Trail** and **Rim Trail**. This is the most recent of the **Mono Craters**, a series of volcanic cones stretching twelve miles south from here towards Crowley Lake. It constitutes the youngest mountain range in North America, formed entirely over the last forty thousand years.

On the north shore of the lake, three miles along US-395, a side road leads to **Mono County Park**, where a guided boardwalk trail heads down to the lakefront and the best examples of mushroom-shaped tufa towers. A further five miles along this (mostly washboard gravel) side road is the trailhead for the **Black Point Fissures**, the result of a massive underwater eruption of molten lava some thirteen thousand years ago. As the lava cooled and contracted, cracks and fissures formed on the top, some only a few feet wide but as deep as 50ft. You can explore their depths, but pick up a directions sheet from the visitor centre, be prepared for hot, dry and sandy conditions and give yourself at least a couple of hours.

Bodie ghost town

In the 1880s, the gold-mining town of **BODIE**, tucked into a fold in the bleak high country, boasted three breweries, sixty saloons and dance halls and a population of nearly ten thousand. It also had a well-earned reputation as the raunchiest and most lawless mining camp in the West. Contemporary accounts describe a town that ended each day with a shootout on Main Street, while the firehouse bell, rung once for every year of a murdered man's life, seemed never to stop sounding. The town hit the headlines in 1877, when a rather unproductive mine collapsed and exposed an enormously rich vein. Within four years this was the second-largest town in the state after San Francisco, even supporting its own Chinatown. By 1885, **gold and silver** currently valued at around $1.5 billion had been extracted, but a drop in the price of gold made mining largely unprofitable. The town dwindled and then was virtually destroyed by two disastrous fires, the second in 1932. The school finally closed in 1942, but a few hardy souls stuck it out until the early 1960s, when the site was taken over by the State of California.

What remains has been turned into **Bodie State Historic Park**, eighteen miles north of Lee Vining and then thirteen miles east of US-395 (daily: June to early Sept 9am–6pm; early Sept to May 10am–3pm; $7; ℡760/647-6445, ⓦwww .parks.ca.gov), where the lack of theme-park tampering gives the place an authentically eerie atmosphere absent from other US ghost towns. Bodie is almost 8400ft above sea level and, although the park is open throughout the year, snow often prevents vehicular access between December and April; call for road conditions. If you can get in during that time, bundle up: Bodie is often cited on the national weather report as having the lowest temperature in the US. Whenever you go, remember to bring all you need, as there are no services at the site.

Bodie highlights

A self-guided tour booklet leads you around many of the 150-odd wooden buildings surviving in a state of arrested decay around the intact town centre. Some buildings have been re-roofed and others supported in some way, but it is by and large a faithful preservation: even the dirty dishes are much as they were in the 1940s, little damaged by seventy years of weathering.

The **Miner's Union Building** on Main Street was the centre of the town's social life; founded in 1877, the union was the first in California, organized by workers at the Standard and Midnight mines. The building now houses a small **museum** (daily: June–Aug 9am–6pm; May & Sept 9am–5pm; free), which paints a graphic picture of the mining life. Various **tours** depart from here in the summer, though schedules are flexible and you should call ahead if you have specific interests. One visits the **Standard Consolidated Stamp Mill** (generally June–Aug daily, call for times; 50min duration; free) which is otherwise off limits, while another follows a ridge (weekends only at 10am; free) which offers some of the best views of Bodie. Other highlights include the **Methodist church**, with its pipe organ intact; the **general store**, where you can admire the beautiful pressed-steel ceiling; the **saloon**, still in possession of its dust-caked roulette wheel; and the **cemetery** on the hill, where lie the remains of Bill Bodey, the dirtbag prospector and discoverer of gold in these parts after whom the town was (sort of) named.

Northwest of Yosemite: Hwy-120 West

On the immediate outskirts of Yosemite National Park, almost every building along **Hwy-120 West** seems to have geared itself to park visitors. There are several decent places to stay along here, but the nearest towns that make realistic bases for exploring the park are the tiny but characterful **Groveland** and the slightly less convenient, but equally atmospheric, former gold town of **Coulterville**: for **accommodation** and **restaurant** listings in this area, see p.175 and p.190 respectively.

Leaving the Yosemite boundary at Big Oak Flat, it's a 24-mile run to Groveland, a pretty enough drive but with little reason to stop for long unless you fancy the convenience of one of the highwayside lodgings. Apart from an overpriced gas station, a couple of general stores and one restaurant, there isn't much in the way of facilities.

Pause for views down to the Tuolumne River from the **Rim of the World Viewpoint**, twelve miles west of Big Oak Flat, then continue four miles to the **Groveland Ranger Station** (Mon–Sat 8am–4.30pm, Sun 8am–3.30pm, winter closed Sat & Sun; T 209/962-7825, W www.fs.fed.us/r5/stanislaus), home to all sorts of information on the surrounding Stanislaus National Forest, including a handy "Hiking Trails" leaflet with weeks' worth of suggested trails. On the other side of Hwy-120 West, the La Casa Loma River Store is the meeting place for most companies running **whitewater rafting** trips on the Tuolumne River (see box, p.158). From here it's a further eight miles into Groveland.

Groveland

Probably the single most appealing town in the vicinity of Yosemite is diminutive **GROVELAND**, almost fifty miles west of Yosemite Valley. With its old-time tenor, some great places to **stay** and **eat** (see p.175 & p.190 respectively), and a cracking old bar called the *Iron Door Saloon* (see p.190), you can hardly go wrong. Groveland came into being in 1849 when gold was discovered nearby on the delightfully named "Garrote Creek", and the town has bumbled along ever since. Even today the town has only 1500 residents scattered across the Sierra foothills at a mild 2800ft.

Groveland runs for half a mile on either side of Hwy-120 West, its short central section retaining the verandas and wooden sidewalks of its early days. A couple of old hotels and the saloon add to the character, but, charming as it is, there's not a great deal to actually do here. Spare a few minutes, though, for **Mountain Sage**, 18653 Hwy-120 West (T 209/962-4686, W www.mtnsage.com), an eclectic shop, gallery and garden centre shoehorned into an 1867 house set back from the road. Along with a small supply of camping gear they maintain an excellent photo gallery, sell fair-trade ethnic crafts from around the world, have a small but well-chosen stock of natural history books and maps and keep a nursery garden where you can relax in a hammock. There's also a small **café** (see p.191) and a room given over to the town's **visitor centre** (Mon, Wed & Fri 9am–3pm; T 1-800/449-9120 or 209/962-0429, W www.groveland.org). Even when unattended you can pick up leaflets such as the "Groveland Historic Building Tour" map highlighting existing mid-nineteenth-century structures, and the simple neoclassical **Groveland Jail**, which you can still peer into.

Consider also heading to the eastern end of town to pop into the tiny **Groveland Museum**, 18990 Hwy-120 West (Mon, Fri & Sat 10am–4.30pm; Tues–Thurs & Sun 1–4.30pm; free; T 209/962-0300, W www.grovelandmuseum.org), which has changing exhibitions on local history, often with contributions from the area's artists. The adjacent **library** (Tues–Thurs 1–6pm, Fri & Sat 10am–2pm; T 209/962-6144) has free **wi-fi**.

If you're driving into the park, **gas** up with fairly cheap fuel a couple of miles west along Hwy-120.

Coulterville

The tiny, ancient gold town of **COULTERVILLE** was once an important waystation on the main route between the Bay Area and Yosemite. John Muir

Rafting the Tuolumne River

The **Tuolumne River** rises on the slopes of Mount Dana and Mount Lyell – the highest mountain in Yosemite National Park – then wends its way through Tuolumne Meadows and the Grand Canyon of the Tuolumne before being stilled in the waters of the Hetch Hetchy reservoir. Regaining its vigour below the O'Shaughnessy Dam, the river then tumbles through some of North America's most exalted **whitewater rafting** runs, mostly in wilderness areas away from roads and habitation. Being a dam-release river, the Tuolumne isn't quite as subject to the vagaries of snowmelt as some of its nearby kin, but there is still only sufficient capacity for a **rafting season** from April to August. Typically water is released for three hours a day (less on Saturday and often not at all on Sunday), so rafters are effectively riding a bubble of water as it makes its way downstream.

The standard **Tuolumne Run** is eighteen miles of **Class IV** whitewater, making it a thrilling trip for anyone (and possibly too exciting for timid or novice rafters). The rapids can be done as a one-day trip ($240) or spread over two ($440) or even three days ($550), camping on the bank and spending time fishing and mucking about in the river (which usually has low flows in the evening and morning). Slightly cheaper rates are offered in April and May. Those interested in scaring themselves witless should opt for the eight-mile **Cherry Creek** section of the Tuolumne (mid-March to late Sept), which is solid **Class V** and widely regarded as some of the hardest commercially run whitewater in the US. With long, fast rapids, big drops and only short pools in between, it's not for the faint-hearted: most companies test your paddling skills before letting you on the river. Day-trips cost around $290. Paddle and oar rafts are used on all trips.

As a designated **National Wild and Scenic River**, only two companies are allowed to run the river on any particular day, so contact La Casa Loma River Store, 24000 Casa Loma Rd, eight miles east of Groveland (☏209/962-5435), for information on which of the half-dozen **rafting companies** is running. Alternatively, get in touch with one of the companies specializing in running the Tuolumne: Sierra Mac River Trips (☏1-800/457-2580 or 209/962-0367, ⊕www.sierramac.com) or Zephyr Whitewater Expeditions (☏1-800/431-3636 or 209/532-6249, ⊕www.zrafting.com).

brought Theodore Roosevelt this way in 1903 when they were heading up to the park for a little camping, but as other routes into Yosemite were developed and later paved, the old stage road through Coulterville declined. The town hasn't fared much better and is a shadow of its former self, though that's the very reason you should make the brief detour here. The entirety of the town's diminutive heart, with its sagging wooden buildings and covered boardwalks, has been listed as a State Historical Site.

Some of those early travellers stayed at *The Coulterville Hotel*, now transformed into the small **Northern Mariposa County History Center** (Wed–Sun 10am–4pm; donations welcome; ☏209/878-3015), which tells the history of the founding of Coulterville and the early Gold Rush years of the 1850s. Others – Theodore Roosevelt among them – stayed across the road at the 1851 *Hotel Jeffery*, which remains the centrepiece of the town, despite closing in 2010. The building is up for sale and hopefully its wonderful Magnolia Saloon will once again be the focal point of the town's social life. Coulterville also has several low-key antique-cum-knick-knack stores, a post office, a diner and a good motel (see p.176). You'll find tourist information at the small **Coulterville Visitor Center**, 5007 Main St (mid-May to mid-Sept Wed–Mon 8am–5pm, mid-Sept to mid-May Thurs–Sun 9am–4.30pm; ☏209/878-3074).

Chinese Camp

It's easy to drive straight past **CHINESE CAMP**, another former Gold Rush town tucked off Hwy-120 West some fourteen miles west of Groveland. In 1856 the town became the centre of the Tong Wars, essentially gang wars between rival factions of Chinese miners after they had been excluded from other mining camps in the area by white miners. Racism was rampant in the southern Gold Rush camps, something that accounts for its most enduring legend, the story of the so-called Robin Hood of the Mother Lode, **Joaquin Murieta**. Murieta was an archetype representing the dispossessed Mexican miners driven to banditry by violent racist abuse at the hands of newly arrived white Americans, and likely never existed. These days there's little evidence of the violent past amid the run-down shacks and trailers other than a historic marker on the main road. Explore a little further and you'll find the still-standing remains of the 1854 **stone-and-brick post office**, as well as **St Xavier's church** (built in 1855 and restored in 1949) and several other buildings ripe for restoration.

Southwest of Yosemite: Hwy-140

The most convenient selection of accommodation outside the boundaries of Yosemite (see p.177 for recommendations) is along **Hwy-140**, the fastest road into Yosemite and the one least likely to be closed by snowfall. At **El Portal** (on the park boundary), a couple of large hotels supply several hundred rooms, while a few miles further out, **Midpines** has the *Yosemite Bug*, an excellent lodge with the only backpacker **hostel** facilities in the region. Beyond that, the former gold town of **Mariposa** makes an attractive and convenient base, though the transport nexus of **Merced** is considerably less well situated.

The road from Mariposa into Yosemite was only completed in 1926 by convict labour. It was the last of the current access roads to be built, but the first to be kept open year-round. Most people blast quickly through, or stop only to secure accommodation at one of the motels, campgrounds or lodges that line the highway. Come in March and you'll find the **redbud** trees in vibrant bloom, a herald for the snowmelt season from April to June, when the river becomes a foaming torrent – this is the best time to come **whitewater rafting** on the Merced. By July the river is typically fairly placid and can be little more than a trickle by late summer.

Heading in the other direction, leaving Yosemite Valley, Hwy-140 descends gradually to a parking lot where it's worth making a brief stop to admire **The Cascades**, which fall 500ft in a fairly untidy flight, best seen in spring. After these, the descent gets steeper for seven miles, dropping from the 4000ft valley floor to less than 2000ft at the park boundary at El Portal. Along the way you pass through the **Arch Rock** entrance station where Yosemite-bound vehicles pass between overhanging rocks that just touch at the top to form a rough arch. The Merced River cascades beside the road here, at its most vigorous in spring.

El Portal and around

The region's largest concentration of rooms (see p.177) with quick access to Yosemite Valley is at **EL PORTAL**, just fourteen miles from Yosemite Village. There's barely a town to speak of, just the El Portal Market grocery store beside the highway, a pricey gas station and the massive *Yosemite View Lodge* complex. Tucked away behind the trees is the former eastern terminus of the **Yosemite Valley Railroad**, where early twentieth-century tourists were decanted into charabancs for the relatively brief but bone-shaking ride into Yosemite Valley. The railhead is now marked by a short section of track supporting a black locomotive originally used on the Hetch Hetchy Railroad during the building of the O'Shaughnessy Dam, and later employed for hauling lumber near here. Close by is a signal box which houses the offices of the Yosemite Conservancy (no public access), a post office and a fair bit of housing for park workers who are increasingly being relocated outside Yosemite Valley.

Continuing west, Hwy-140 heads into the **Merced River Canyon** and after eight miles reaches the confluence of the main branch of the Merced and the South Fork, which drains the hills around Wawona. In the early days this was an important meeting point for the Miwok people, and once the Gold Rush hit it was deemed a propitious spot for **Savage's Trading Post**, where gold miners flocked to swap their gold dust for clothing, supplies and hooch. It was established in 1849 by James Savage, who two years later became one of the first to enter Yosemite Valley as part of the Mariposa Battalion, though he was far less a hero than the sign here would have you believe. The trading tradition continued into the twenty-first century, but the gift store has now closed. In spring it's still worth stopping here, if only to hike the **Hite Cove Trail** (Y34, see p.124).

Casting your eyes over to the north bank of the Merced you can see the level grade used by the **Yosemite Valley Railroad** to carry passengers between Merced and El Portal from 1907 until its abandonment in 1945. Recently the trackbed has had to be put into service as a major **rockfall** in 2006 blocked the main highway. Temporary bridges now divert you across the river for a few hundred yards to circumvent the slip: expect **delays** of up to fifteen minutes.

Briceburg and around

Nine miles on from El Portal you get to **BRICEBURG**, where a suspension bridge over the Merced River announces a **visitor centre** (May–Aug Fri 1–5pm, Sat & Sun 9am–5pm; ☎209/379-9414) that contains some limited natural history

---

Rafting the Merced River

Yosemite Valley offers **rafting** on the **Merced River**, but it is a far cry from the whitewater frolics on offer just outside the park. The frenetic cascade between the valley and the park boundary abates to a raftable level at **El Portal**, the beginning of the most commonly run section. Rafted during the spring snowmelt **season** (late April to early July), the **Cranberry Gulch to Briceburg** section of the Merced is graded **Class III–IV**, quite manageable for first-timers but still fun for those who've rafted before. It's usually at its rollicking best in May and early June, and the river runs right beside the road, so, for better or worse, you never feel too isolated. Day-trips here cost $140–150 midweek, $150–170 at weekends.

When the water levels drop (say mid-June to July) companies operate on the 25-mile, two-day **Cranberry Gulch to Bagby** run, which extends the standard trip with several miles of exciting whitewater. You'll camp beside the river and can expect to pay $325.

For details, contact **rafting companies** such as the non-profit ARTA River Trips (☎1-800/323-2782, ⓦwww.arta.org), Whitewater Voyages (☎1-800/400-7238, ⓦwww.whitewatervoyages.com) or Zephyr Whitewater Expeditions (☎1-800/431-3636, ⓦwww.zrafting.com).

displays along with material on the area's Gold Rush history and notes on local **mountain biking**. The 1920s suspension bridge behind the centre provides vehicular access to the river's right bank where the old trackbed has been turned into a rough road heading downstream past three $10-a-night **campgrounds** – *McCabe Flat*, *Willow Placer* and *Railroad Flat* (see p.185) – all prettily sited beside the river. Continuing west on Hwy-140, the road soon passes through the scattered community of Midpines, then on to Mariposa ten miles beyond.

Mountain biking around Briceburg

National Park restrictions severely limit **mountain biking** within Yosemite, forcing keen riders to explore elsewhere. One of the best areas is just across the Merced River from the Briceburg Visitor Center, where there's a range of rides for different abilities. Unfortunately there is no **bike rental** nearby.

The **easiest trail** simply follows the dirt road downstream from the bridge, an almost completely flat five-mile ride past the aforementioned campgrounds to a metal bridge where there's a locked gate. In summer, once the high spring flows have abated and the river has warmed up (July–Sept), you'll find plenty of inviting swimming holes. For something tougher, go for the **Briceburg Bike Loop** (15-mile loop; 2–3hr; 500ft ascent), using a map available from the visitor centre; the loop follows a fire road around the hills above the Merced River Canyon. There are great views and it's all quite manageable, though in summer it's best done in the early morning or around dusk to avoid the midday heat. The loop is accessed by the Burma Grade (Bull Creek Road), classed for 4x4s though high clearance two-wheelers can make it in good conditions. Of course, you can cycle up to the loop as well (5 miles; 1500ft ascent), though it's a real slog only partially compensated by the excellent downhill ride back to your rig.

Mariposa

The nearest town of any size on Yosemite's western flanks, 15 miles from Yosemite Valley, is **Mariposa**, a former gold town that has turned its hand to mining the rich vein of tourists passing through. Modern developments have mostly swamped the old town centre, but Hwy-140 still rattles through a short stretch of covered walkways and two-storey gold-era buildings, the best being the 1859 adobe-built former **Schlageter Hotel** on the corner of 5th Street. Though the retail core increasingly consists of wayside restaurants and knick-knack-cum-antique shops, Mariposa remains an attractive enough place.

The most historic structure is the **Mariposa County Courthouse**, corner of Jones and 10th streets, the oldest law enforcement building west of the Mississippi still in continuous use. Built without nails, the lumber was rough-cut from a nearby stand of white pine, and you can still see the saw marks on the hand-planed spectator benches. During business hours (Mon–Fri 8am–5pm) you can sit in during proceedings. The convicted were often sent down the street to the **Historic 1858 Jail**, on the corner of Bullion and 5th streets, which may be open for informal tours of the austere interior: ask around.

The town's heritage is further celebrated at the **Mariposa Museum & History Center**, corner of Jesse and 12th streets (daily 10am–4pm; $4; ☏209/966-2924, ⊛www.mariposamuseum.com), which wedges in a mildly diverting mock-up of a gold-era street (drug store, saloon, dress shop and so forth) and has a corner devoted to the local Miwok people with some fine examples of basketwork. Scattered around the outside you'll find some large-scale mining paraphernalia, including a stamp mill that is occasionally fired up for group tours. It all means a lot more if you can engage one of the docents to show you around; they might even show you the 1901 stagecoach that is still used a couple of times a year.

In truth, you're better off at the **California State Mining and Mineral Museum**, two miles south on Hwy-49 (Thurs–Sun: May–Sept 10am–5pm; Oct–April 10am–4pm; $4; Ⓦwww.parks.ca.gov), which revels in the glory days of the mid-nineteenth century with realistic reconstructions of a mine, assay office and stamp mill, plus the **Fricot Nugget**, the largest surviving specimen of crystallized gold from the Gold Rush era, a thirteen-pound chunk valued at over $1 million. An impressive geology section brings together samples from all over the state, including a beautiful piece of malachite looking like three melting candles, and a case of fluorescent rocks glowing green, yellow and blue. The use of minerals in daily life is also explored, along with suitably unearthly-looking meteorites.

Practicalities

The helpful **Mariposa County Visitor Center**, 5158 Hwy-140 (daily: mid-May to mid-Oct 7am–8pm; mid-Oct to mid-May 8am–5pm; Ⓣ209/966-2456, Ⓦwww.mariposa.org), concentrates on those Yosemite-bound but also has the handy "Historic Walking Tour" map of the key heritage buildings. Perhaps more important to those heading on to Yosemite is the extensive Pioneer Market **supermarket** (daily 8am–10pm) at the eastern end of town, complete with in-store bakery. The **library**, 4978 10th St (Mon & Sat 8.30am–4pm, Tues–Fri 8.30am–6pm), has free **internet access**. If you plan to **stay** over in Mariposa, see our accommodation and restaurant listings on p.177 and p.191 respectively.

Merced

Some eighty miles southwest of Yosemite Valley, **MERCED** is too far from the park to be considered a good base for exploring, but is very handy for its **transport connections** and has a few minor sights.

The best thing about this sleepy town is its courthouse, a gem of a building in the main square that's maintained as the **County Courthouse Museum**, corner of N Street and W 20th Street (Wed–Sun 1–4pm; free; Ⓦwww.mercedmuseum .org). This striking Italian Renaissance-style structure, complete with columns, elaborately sculptured window frames and a cupola topped by a statue of the Goddess of Justice (minus her customary blindfold), was raised in 1875 when it completely dominated the few dozen shacks that comprised the town. Impressively restored in period style, the courtroom retained a legal function until 1951, while the equally sumptuous offices were vacated in the 1970s and now display local memorabilia – most exotic among which is an 1870s Taoist shrine, found by chance in a makeshift temple above a Chinese restaurant. You might also pass a pleasant half-hour in the mostly contemporary galleries in the **Merced Multicultural Arts Museum**, 645 W Main St (Mon–Fri 9am–5pm, Sat 10am–2pm; free; Ⓦwww.artsmerced.org).

Six miles northwest of Merced, close to the dormitory community of **Atwater** – and signposted off Hwy-99 – lies the **Castle Air Museum** (daily: May–Oct 9am–5pm; Nov–April 10am–4pm; $10; Ⓦwww.castleairmuseum.org). Fifty-odd military aircraft from World War II to Vietnam – mostly bulky bombers with a few fighters thrown in, including the world's fastest plane, the SR-71 – are scattered outdoors, while inside there's a static B52 simulator, assorted military paraphernalia and a collection of some 120 model planes crafted by one enthusiast from redwood. Route #8 of Merced's transit system, "The Bus" (Mon–Sat only; Ⓣ1-800/345-3111, Ⓦwww.mercedthebus.com), runs out here about every ninety minutes for $2 each way.

None of these sights is much of a reason to visit Merced, though the convenient **bus links to Yosemite** are. Greyhounds from Bakersfield, Sacramento and San Francisco stop downtown at the **Transpo Center** on W 16th Street at N Street, where you'll find **Merced California Welcome Center**, 710 W 16th Street (daily 8.30am–5pm; ☎1-866/295-3757, ⓦwww.yosemite-gateway.org), which offers some local (and region-wide) tourist information. The **Amtrak station** is somewhat isolated at 24th and K streets, about ten blocks away on the opposite side of the town centre: follow K Street off W 16th Street.

YARTS buses (see p.23) pick up at the Transpo Center and train station on their way to Yosemite, and there are several **car rental** agencies in town (see p.22). Most people pass straight through Merced, but in case you need to stop over, we've detailed some **lodging** and **eating** options in the appropriate chapters of the guide (see p.178 & p.192 respectively).

South of Yosemite: Hwy-41 and around

After exploring southern Yosemite's Wawona and the big trees in Mariposa Grove, it's worth spending a little time in the country just south of the park, served by **Hwy-41**. Should you have trouble securing accommodation in the park, you may also find yourself staying out this way either in the roadside cluster known as **Fish Camp**, a couple of miles south of the park entrance, or the growing town of **Oakhurst**, not a pretty place, but with all the necessary facilities. We list a selection of **accommodation** and **eating** options in the relevant Listings chapters of the guide, from p.178 and p.192 respectively.

Leaving Yosemite's South Entrance you soon pass the Forest Service's convenient *Summerdale* campground, and tiny Fish Camp, followed by the entrance to *Tenaya Lodge*. Onwards it's downhill all the way to Oakhurst, a fast, winding road leading initially through pines then coming out into the oak-studded grasslands of the Sierra foothills. To the east, roads fan out to **Bass Lake** and the secluded **Sierra Vista Scenic Byway**.

If you're heading further south to visit Sequoia and Kings Canyon national parks, consider using the city of **Fresno** as a base, also paying a visit to the wonderful **Forestiere Underground Gardens**. The engagingly sleepy town of **Visalia** also makes a good base for the twin parks, and if you have more time, consider spending a couple of days in the **John Muir Wilderness**, especially around **Mono Hot Springs**.

Fish Camp

The tiny huddle of houses and lodging making up **FISH CAMP** lies just two miles from the park's South Entrance and fourteen miles north of Oakhurst, making it a convenient base for exploring Wawona and around. Most visitors spend their days in the park, but Fish Camp has something to keep the kids quiet in the form of **Yosemite Mountain Sugar Pine Railroad**, 56001 Hwy-41 (mid-March to Oct 9.30am–3pm or 4pm; ☎559/683-7273, ⓦwww.ymsprr.com). Two miles of narrow-gauge track wend their way into the forest along a line used by the Madera Sugar Pine Lumber Company which, from 1899 to 1931, hauled out almost one and a half billion board feet of timber. For a real sense of what it must have been like, ride "The Logger" (April–Oct Mon–Fri 1–3 daily, Sat & Sun 2–4 daily; adults

$18, kids 3–12 $9), a train of open cars hauled by a vintage oil-burning Shay steam locomotive; extra services are hauled by "Jenny" cars (adults $14.50, kids $7.25) powered by ancient Model A Ford engines. *The Logger* is also fired up for the family-oriented Moonlight Specials (May & Sept to mid-Oct Sat, June–Aug Wed & Sat; adults $48, kids $24; reservations essential), which includes a steak barbecue dinner, live music by the Sugar Pine Singers then a night ride on the train.

Fish Camp also has **horseriding** at Yosemite Trails Pack Station (see p.144), with rides into Mariposa Grove, and there's a range of activities at *Tenaya Lodge* (see p.178), though these are mostly aimed at guests of the hotel.

Oakhurst

OAKHURST, sixteen miles south of the park's South Entrance and fifty miles south of Yosemite Valley proper, is a booming huddle of malls, chain hotels and fast-food joints clustered around the junction of Hwy-41 and Hwy-49. It makes little of its pleasant setting in the Sierra foothills, but the abundance of lodging and restaurants does make it a handy base for both Yosemite and nearby Bass Lake. Other than a fledgling winter bus service to Badger Pass Ski Area (see p.148) there is no useful public transportation to or from Oakhurst. But with your own wheels you can easily explore the southern section of the park, and day-trips into Yosemite Valley, 45 miles away, are by no means out of the question.

Be sure to call at the **Yosemite Sierra Visitors' Bureau**, two miles north of the town centre at 41969 Hwy-41 (Mon–Sat 8.30am–5pm, Sun 9am–1pm; ☎559/683-4636, ⓦwww.yosemitethisyear.com), which has armloads of information on Yosemite. Look out for the misleadingly titled *Yosemite Sierra Visitors' Guide*, which concentrates on the area immediately south of Yosemite National Park – useful if you're planning to explore Bass Lake and the Sierra Vista Scenic Byway.

Between the highway junction and the visitors' bureau, Road 426 leads half a mile east to Road 427 (aka School Road) and the **Fresno Flats Historical Park** (daily dawn–dusk; free), where a cluster of relocated vernacular buildings recalls the original 1850s settlement of Fresno Flats where Oakhurst now stands. A self-guided tour leads around the exteriors, but it all makes more sense when you visit the **museum** (March–Dec daily 10am–4pm, Jan & Feb closed; free; ⓦwww .fresnoflatsmuseum.org), fashioned from two 1870s homes, or tack onto one of the guided tours.

Apart from the wide selection of places to **stay** (see p.178) and **eat** (see p.192), Oakhurst has the region's most functional array of shops and services, including the **Oakhurst Branch Library**, 49044 Civic Circle (Mon–Wed 10am–5pm, Thurs 1–7pm, Fri 11am–2pm; ☎559/683-4838), which has free **internet access**. Keen cyclists should visit Yosemite Bicycle & Sport (☎559/641-2453, ⓦwww .yosemitebicycle.com) behind the *McDonald's* at 40120 Hwy-41, where you can **rent bikes** ($25–100 a day depending on the model) and pick up great advice on all manner of local rides.

For **entertainment**, new-release movies play at the Met Cinemas (☎559/683-1234), corner of Hwy-49 and Hwy-41, and family-oriented, nineteenth-century melodramas are staged at the volunteer-run Golden Chain Theatre on Hwy-41, two miles north of Oakhurst (☎559/683-7112, ⓦwww.goldenchaintheatre.org; $12): come to cheer the hero and boo the villain.

Bass Lake

Just seven miles west of Oakhurst lies the biggest tourist attraction in the area, **BASS LAKE**, a pine-fringed man-made lake at 3400ft. A stomping ground of the

Hell's Angels in the 1960s – the leather and licentiousness memorably described in Hunter S. Thompson's *Hell's Angels* – Bass Lake is nowadays a family resort, crowded with boaters and anglers in summer, though the best fishing is in winter and spring. It makes a good spot to rest up for a day or two, perhaps staying in one of the lakeside campgrounds.

Road 222 runs right around the lake. At the main settlement, **Pines Village**, you can buy groceries, eat well and spend the night at the swanky *Pines Resort* (see p.179), or head to the southwestern tip of the lake to *Miller's Landing Resort* (see p.179) with more modest cabins, aquatic equipment rentals – including **fishing boats** ($70 for 6hrs) and **jet skis** ($100 an hour) – and public showers and laundry.

The western side of Bass Lake is slung with $25-a-night family **campgrounds**, most oriented towards long stays beside your camper: for tent campers, the best site is *Lupine* ($25), just north of *Miller's Landing*.

Sierra Vista Scenic Byway

If Bass Lake is too commercial and overcrowded for you, there's an antidote close at hand with the **SIERRA VISTA SCENIC BYWAY**: a ninety-mile circuit east of Hwy-41, topping out at the Clover Meadow Ranger Station (7000ft), which is the trailhead for much of the magnificent **Ansel Adams Wilderness**. Apart from trailheads and campgrounds, there's not a great deal to the road, though the **views** are fantastic and people are scarce. A straight circuit (snow-free July–Oct at best) takes five hours, and is especially slow going on the rough dirt roads of the north side. Stock up on supplies before you start: there are a couple of stores and gas stations dotted along its length but they're not cheap and the range is limited. Accommodation on the circuit is largely limited to campgrounds, all (except two free sites) costing $16.

The best source of information on the byway is the **Bass Lake Ranger District** office (Mon–Fri 8am–4.30pm; ☏559/877-2218) in the hamlet of **North Fork**, at the southern end of Bass Lake, where you can pick up a **map** – important, as there are numerous confusing forestry roads and few signposts. Before you head off, check out North Fork's **Sierra Mono Indian Museum** (Tues–Sat 10am–3pm; $5), with some good examples of local Native American basketry and beadwork, as well as a lot of stuffed animals in glass cases. You could also fill up with a Mexican meal at *La Cabaña* (see p.192), your last chance for tasty restaurant food – everything from hereon is pretty basic.

The south side

Setting out from North Fork, you initially head east along Rd 225, and then pick up Italian Bar Road a short way into the journey. The first point of interest, fifteen miles from North Fork, is the **Jesse Ross Cabin**, an 1860s hewn-log original that has been restored and brought to the site. It's left open so you can poke around inside. Ten miles on, **Mile High Vista** reveals endless views of muscle-bound mountain ranges and bursting granite domes stretching almost forever. A little further on, an eight-mile side road cuts south to the dammed **Mammoth Pool**, where anglers boat on the lake and smoke their catch at one of the four **campgrounds**, the best being *Sweetwater*.

Back on the Scenic Byway, you'll pass the rather disappointing **Arch Rock**, where the earth under a slab of granite has been undermined to leave a kind of bridge, and continue climbing to the Minarets Pack Station (mid-June to Sept; ☏559/868-3405, ⓦwww.highsierrapackers.org/min.htm). Apart from a general store and reasonable meals, the station offers simple lodging (see p.179) and **horseback trips** from $60. It's a great base for wilderness trips, many of which start by the **Clover Meadow Wilderness Station**, a couple of miles up a spur road (late June to mid-Sept daily 8am–5pm; permits available). Nearby is *Clover Meadow* (see p.186), the best of two free campgrounds.

The north side

The Minarets Pack Station marks the start of the descent from the backcountry and the end of the asphalt; for the next few miles you're on rough dirt, generally passable in ordinary passenger vehicles when clear of snow. The hulking form of **Globe Rock** heralds the return to asphalt, which runs down to **Beasore Meadow**, where **Jones Store** (open mid-June to mid-Oct) has supplied limited groceries, gas and basic meals (8am–8pm) for the best part of a century, and offers showers to hikers. A short distance further on you reach Cold Springs Meadow, the junction with Sky Ranch Road (follow it left to continue the loop) and a spur to the wonderful *Fresno Dome* campground (see p.186).

The Scenic Byway then passes several $16 campgrounds, most without running water, en route to the **Nelder Grove Historical Area** (unrestricted entry), a couple of miles north along a dirt road. Over a hundred **giant sequoias** are scattered through the forest here, though the overall impression is of devastation evidenced by the number of enormous stumps among the second-growth sugar pine, white fir and cedar. The mile-long "Shadow of the Giants" interpretive walk explains the logging activities that took place here in the 1880s and early 1890s and, with its low visitor count, offers a more serene communion with these majestic trees than in the national parks. A second interpretive trail leads from the nearby, wooded *Nelder Grove* campground (see p.186) to **Bull Buck Tree**, which with its base circumference of 99ft was once a serious contender for the world's largest tree. Though slimmer in the base, Sequoia National Park's General Sherman Tree is taller and broader at the top, so taking the prize. From here it's seven twisting miles back to Hwy-41, reached at a point around four miles north of Oakhurst.

John Muir Wilderness and Mono Hot Springs

South of Bass Lake, though more easily reached from Fresno along Hwy-168, a parched and knobbly landscape dotted with blue, live and scrub oak brings you to the Pineridge District, an excellent place for adventurous hiking. Around **Kaiser Pass**, which scrapes 9200ft, you'll find isolated alpine landscapes served by decent campgrounds, a couple of minor resorts and even some relaxing **hot springs**.

Hwy-168 penetrates seventy miles into the forest among the snowcapped peaks of the **JOHN MUIR WILDERNESS**. It's a drive of at least four hours, even in good weather – and this is an area prone to bad weather and road closure. The best source of information is the **High Sierra Ranger District** office (April–Nov daily 8am–4.30pm; Dec–March Mon–Fri same hours; ☎559/855-5355), located along Hwy-168 at Prather, five miles west of the forest entrance. There are also ranger stations near Rancheria Falls and Mono Hot Springs (see both below).

From the ranger station, the good and fast Hwy-168 climbs rapidly over eighteen miles to **Shaver Lake**, a mile-high, pine-girt community, where half of Fresno comes to fish and jet-ski. Grab a snack at *Bob's Blue Sky Café* (see p.192), stock up with supplies and keep going twenty miles east to **Huntington Lake**, which feels more isolated. Just before the lake, the *Rancheria* campground (see p.186) marks the turn-off to **Rancheria Falls**. A side road, east off Hwy-168, leads a mile to the head of the mile-long **Rancheria Falls Trail** (350ft ascent), which winds through broadleaf woods to the 150ft falls. Continuing west around Huntington Lake, you soon hit *Lakeshore Resort* (see p.179), with its cabins, great, woodsy restaurant, a lively log-built saloon, a gas station, post office and general store all a few yards from the lake. From here on, the lakeshore is almost entirely taken up by $20-a-night campgrounds.

Beyond Kaiser Pass: Mono Hot Springs and around

Just after Rancheria Falls, Hwy-162 veers off over Kaiser Pass (open June–Oct only) on a rapidly deteriorating road up to 9200ft, passing the *Badger Flat* campground (see p.186) along the way. Over the pass is a vast basin, draining the south fork of the San Joaquin River. The lumpy single-lane road drops past the beautiful *Portal Forebay* campground (see p.186) to a fork in the road: north to Lake Edison, its approach marred by a huge earth dam, and west to Florence Lake.

MONO HOT SPRINGS, two miles north of the junction on the road to Lake Edison, is the best thing about the region and a great place to relax and clean up after hikes. For the full hot springs experience, head for the *Mono Hot Springs Resort* (mid-May to Oct; see p.180) where all cabin prices include free use of the therapeutic mineral pools and spa. Right on the banks of the San Joaquin River, the resort is a modest affair with individual mineral baths ($6 for nonguests; $10 for an all-day pass), showers ($5) and massages ($40 per half-hour). Outside, there's a chlorinated spa filled with spring water, costing $6 for an all-day pass.

The resort also has a small lunch and dinner restaurant, a limited general store, the *Mono Hot Springs* campground (see p.186), and a post office used for mail and food pickups by hikers on the nearby John Muir and Pacific Crest trails (see p.135). Across the river, follow a track two hundred yards downstream to a pair of 5ft-deep concrete **bathing tanks** (unrestricted access) that are perfect for soaking your bones while stargazing. This is just one of many pools on this side of the river; ask around.

Beyond Mono Hot Springs the wonderfully scenic road continues to **Lake Edison** and the *Vermillion Valley Resort* (see p.180), often used by hikers accessing the John Muir Wilderness, by means of a small **ferry** across the lake (June–Sept twice daily; $10 each way).

Florence Lake, eight miles south of Lake Edison, is more immediately appealing than Lake Edison: there's a greater sense of being hemmed in by mountains, and it's reached through an unearthly landscape of wrinkled granite shattered over the centuries by contorted junipers. There's a small store, the *Jackass Meadow* campground (see p.186) and another **ferry** across the lake (late May to late Sept; 5 daily; $11 each way; www.florence-lake.com) which opens up multi-day hikes along the John Muir and Pacific Crest trails.

Fresno

With around 400,000 inhabitants, **FRESNO** is the largest city between LA and San Francisco, yet feels like little more than an overgrown farming town. Still, it is very much the hub of business in the San Joaquin Valley, and with its regional airport it works as a launch pad for both Yosemite and Sequoia and Kings Canyon national parks.

There are a few small sights and museums, but the one outstanding attraction is the fascinating **Forestiere Underground Gardens**, 5021 W Shaw Avenue

Campground reservations

Many campgrounds in the Sierra National Forest can be booked between Memorial Day and Labor Day through www.recreation.gov or on ☎1-877/444-6777.

(one-hour tours on the hour, inclusive: March & Nov Sat & Sun 11am–2pm; April, May, Sept & Oct Wed–Fri 11am–2pm, Sat & Sun 10am–2pm; June–Aug Wed–Sun 10am–4pm; $12; ℡559/271-0734, ⓦwww.undergroundgardens .com), seven miles northwest of the centre, a block east of the Shaw Avenue exit off Hwy-99. A subterranean labyrinth of over fifty rooms, the gardens were constructed by Sicilian émigré and former Boston and New York subway tunneller Baldassare Forestiere, who came to Fresno in 1905. In a fanatical attempt to stay cool and protect his crops, Forestiere put his digging know-how to work, building underground living quarters and skylit orchards with just a shovel and wheelbarrow, using chunks of hardpan to create supporting arches. He gradually improved techniques for maximizing his yield but wasn't above playful twists, including a glass-bottomed underground aquarium and a subterranean bathtub fed by water heated in the midday sun. He died in 1946, his forty years of work producing a vast earth honeycomb, part of which was destroyed by the construction of Hwy-99 next door, while another section awaits restoration. Wandering around the remainder of what he achieved is a fascinating way to pass an hour out of the heat of the day, enlivened by the tour guide's anecdotes.

Practicalities

The **visitor centre** is downtown on the corner of Fresno and O streets (Mon–Fri 10am–3pm, Sat 11am–2pm; ℡559/237-0988, ⓦwww.playfresno.org), housed in a distinctive, 1894 water tower. The **bus** and **train** terminals are nearby – Greyhound at 1033 H Street (℡559/268-1829) and Amtrak at 2650 Tulare Street. There is no public transport to any of the national parks, and the widest range of car rental is at the **airport** (see p.22).

Non-drivers can walk around downtown or catch the Fresno Area Express **buses** ($1, exact change; ℡559/621-7433), if only to reach Forestiere Underground Gardens. Route #20, picked up downtown on Van Ness (every 30–60min), comes within a mile of the gardens, and you can transfer to the #9 for the last stretch. Routes #22, #26 and #28 travel between Van Ness and the Tower District.

There is little accommodation beyond **motels**, many clustered near the junction of Olive Avenue (the Tower District's main drag) and Hwy-99: avoid the marginal places charging rock-bottom rates in favour of our recommendations (see p.180). The best hunting ground for **eating** is the Tower District: for our picks see p.192.

Visalia

The agricultural town of **VISALIA** makes a comfortable base for exploring Sequoia and Kings Canyon national parks, an hour's drive east along Hwy-198. It also has the only **bus service** into the parks (see p.19).

The oak forests that initially lured San Joaquin's first settlers have long gone, but Visalia remains a pretty place with a compact and leafy town centre that invites strolls in the relative cool of the evening. The visitor centre (see below) has a leaflet detailing a self-guided **walking tour** of the grand houses in its older parts.

Greyhound buses and the shuttle to Sequoia and Kings Canyon national parks use the downtown **transit centre**, 425 E Oak Street (℡559/734-3507). The shuttle also stops outside the town's **visitor centre**, 303 N Acequia Avenue (Mon–Fri 9am–5pm; ℡559/334-0141, ⓦwww.visitvisalia.org). **Accommodation** here (see p.180) is a bargain; if you're on a budget, this is a good place to splash out on a B&B. Visalia also has some of the best places to **eat** for miles around (see p.193).

Listings

Listings

9

Accommodation

O n most trips to Yosemite, **accommodation** will be your biggest expense, and procuring it could easily become a huge headache unless you reserve well in advance, especially for summer weekends and holidays. Even in spring and fall visitors find themselves paying more than they had hoped or accepting accommodation below their usual standards. The monopoly held by the park concessionaire keeps prices high for what you get, and even simple canvas tent cabins cost what you would pay for a reasonable motel elsewhere. Service isn't always efficient either, but at their best these places can be comfortable and welcoming. The best advice is to plan as early as possible, or resign yourself to being flexible.

Most people prefer to stay **in Yosemite National Park**, with the scenic splendour and hiking trailheads close at hand. All of the accommodation options within the park are listed in this chapter, with most concentrated in Yosemite Valley – the choice ranging from comfortable lodges and hotels to cabins and campgrounds.

While there's an obvious benefit to staying right in Yosemite, heavy demand for accommodation inside the park drives many visitors to consider staying **outside Yosemite** in one of the small towns along the main access roads. A couple of these towns are interesting in their own right (see Chapter 8), but most should be regarded simply as jumping-off points for the park. The best accommodation in all these towns is listed in the following pages as well. Note that accommodation in **Sequoia and Kings Canyon national parks** is covered in Chapter 13.

We've divided the accommodation into two main sections, with **hotels**, **motels**, **lodges** and **B&Bs** grouped together, and **campgrounds** and **RV parks** in a subsequent section. Visitors looking for low-cost "indoor" accommodation should also check under "Campgrounds and RV Parks" as several of the places listed rent out budget cabins.

Price codes

All the accommodation listed in this book has been categorized into one of nine price codes, as set out below. The prices quoted are for the **cheapest available room for two people in the high season**, and do not include **taxes**. These are generally 8–12 percent, though there is no tax at park campgrounds. For campgrounds, and hostels that offer individual beds or bunks, we have given the per person price (excluding tax) along with a price code for any private rooms.

In the **off season**, particularly the quiet months from December to March, prices drop by up to forty percent, though weekend rates remain high.

❶ $60 and under	❹ $101–130	❼ $201–250
❷ $61–80	❺ $131–160	❽ $251–300
❸ $81–100	❻ $161–200	❾ $301 and over

Hotels, motels, lodges and B&Bs

Virtually all noncamping accommodation **in Yosemite National Park** is managed by the park concessionaire, Delaware North Companies (**DNC**, see below). The most basic and cheapest lodging is at Curry Village, *Housekeeping Camp*, *White Wolf Lodge* and *Tuolumne Meadows Lodge*, where most guests are housed in either canvas-walled tent cabins, or three-sided concrete "cabins". Standard hotel- and motel-style rooms predominate at the *Wawona Hotel* and *Yosemite Lodge*, and for those who want to splurge, there are gorgeous rooms and suites at *The Ahwahnee*.

Near Wawona, *The Redwoods in Yosemite* is the only non-DNC accommodation in the park, but a few B&Bs can be found at **Yosemite West**, a small enclave just outside the park boundary accessible only from inside the park off Wawona Road. This is also the closest accommodation to Badger Pass Ski Area. There are more vacation homes at the private village of **Foresta**, right on the western park boundary, eight miles from Yosemite Valley, and again, only accessible from within the park.

Outside the park the choice becomes wider, with numerous motels and B&Bs lining all three highways from the west, while many more pack the surrounding towns of Groveland, Coulterville, Mariposa and Oakhurst. In the east, only Lee Vining has much in the way of accommodation, with a few motels. The budget-conscious should also be aware of **hostel** accommodation at the excellent *Yosemite Bug*, ten miles east of Mariposa and the only such place easily accessible from Yosemite Valley. See the **map** on p.152 for the locations of accommodation outside the park.

Yosemite is popular year-round, but most places offer slightly reduced prices during the **winter season** (mid-Nov to mid-March, excluding holidays). In the park, Curry Village and *Yosemite Lodge* both drop their midweek rates considerably. Outside the park, savings tend to be greater, with most places dropping at least one price code on weekdays, though at weekends prices can remain close to high-season levels.

It's also worth looking out for discount **lodging packages** through the DNC website (see below), which frequently offers off-season deals. Unless noted otherwise, assume the following places are **open all year**.

In Yosemite Valley

The Ahwahnee Shuttle stop 3; reserve with DNC, front desk ☎209/372-1407. Undoubtedly the finest place to stay in Yosemite, *The Ahwahnee* (described in detail on p.66) lies just a short distance from Yosemite Village, set among the trees and meadows below the Royal Arches. Despite rates that start around $450, you'll have to book months in advance to obtain one of the spacious rooms, each decorated with the hotel's running Native American and Oriental motifs. They come equipped with top-quality furnishings and bedding along with TV, phone, wi-fi and in many cases a wondrous view. For much the same price you might prefer one of the two-dozen guest cottages out amid the pines and cedars and with a rustic tenor, but with all the expected facilities plus, in some, a fireplace. The top floor of the hotel has been converted into four gorgeous suites in English Country style, all with antique furniture, old photos of Yosemite Valley life, real log fires and fresh flowers. It feels like you're staying in someone's very luxurious home, and so it should for $900–1000 a night.

DNC reservations

Almost all accommodation in Yosemite National Park is operated by the **park concessionaire** Delaware North Companies (**DNC**). Reservations can be made up to a year and a day in advance (though a few weeks is adequate at most times), either **online** (🌐 www.yosemitepark.com), or by phoning ☎801/559-4884.

Though grand, *The Ahwahnee* avoids stuffiness, exuding a surprisingly low-key lived-in quality that more modern places find difficult (or impossible) to achieve. During the day guests wander through in hiking gear, though to eat in the superb restaurant (p.187) you'll need to dress up. There's also a separate bar (see p.187), and a welter of other facilities including an outdoor pool (heated year-round), free coffee and pastries in the morning and free tea and cookies with piano accompaniment at 4pm daily in the Great Lounge. Special weekend deals are listed on the DNC website. ❾

Curry Village Shuttle stops 13, 13a, 13b, 14, 20 & 21; reserve with DNC. Largest of all the accommodation areas in the park, Curry Village can accommodate well over a thousand people. It dates back to 1899 when it was opened as the budget Camp Curry (see p.69), and continues its tradition of catering largely to families. Consequently it is seldom peaceful, though it's well placed for local amenities, including shops, a swimming pool (free to guests; otherwise $5), an ice rink, bike and raft rental and more. Unlike *Housekeeping Camp* (see below), there are no self-catering facilities, so you'll appreciate the proximity of restaurants and cafés (see p.189). And being on the shady side of the valley, this is the coolest accommodation on hot summer days.

Most people stay in one of the three-hundred-plus canvas-walled tent cabins (mid-March to Nov nightly, Dec to mid-March Fri, Sat & hols only) that sleep two, three or five. Though comfortable enough, they're closely packed and you'll need to use the communal bathrooms. All come with wooden floors and an electric light. Beds are made up at the beginning of your stay but you do your own housekeeping thereafter. From late Sept to mid-May there are heated tent cabins with insulation, propane heater and a small rug, but no private bathrooms.

Other options (available year-round) include over fifty larger and vastly more appealing rustic cabins with private bath and a small deck in a quiet area, and fourteen standard rooms fashioned from what was originally the 1904 dance hall. None of the accommodation options here has a phone or TV. Prices vary wildly with demand. Children 12 and under stay free in

the motel rooms and hard-walled cabins, but are charged $8 each in tent cabins. Third and fourth adults in a tent or room cost $13. Rooms ❻, cabins with bath ❹, heated cabins ❸-❹, tent cabins ❶-❸

Housekeeping Camp Shuttle stop 12; reserve with DNC. Loved by many, *Housekeeping Camp* is the only park lodging that gives you the option of doing your own cooking. It comprises a cluster of around 260 strangely primitive concrete and canvas "cabins" located among the pines by a sandy beach on the south bank of the Merced River with good views of Half Dome and Yosemite Falls. Sort of like camping without a tent, you get three concrete walls, a concrete floor, a white plastic roof and one side which opens through canvas curtains onto a cook-out area with outdoor seating made marginally private by the surrounding fence. Each cabin has a table, a light and electricity supply, an outdoor grill pit for barbecues, a double bed and two fold-down bunks: bring your own bedding or rent for $2.50 per bed, per night. There's access to toilets, showers (8am–10pm), pay laundry and an on-site grocery store; gas stoves can be rented for cooking, and all food must be stored in the bear-proof boxes dotted around. With the addition of a couple of camp beds, each cabin can sleep six, but rates are for up to four. Closed mid-Oct to March. ❸

Yosemite Lodge Shuttle stop 8; reserve with DNC. Often filled with tour groups, this sprawling site with more than 240 rooms occupies Yosemite Valley's middle ground. Accommodation is motel style; comfortable without being anything special, though its proximity to decent restaurants, a bar, swimming pool (free to guests; otherwise $5), bike rental, grocery shop and evening entertainment makes it perhaps the most convenient all-round accommodation in the valley. Rooms fall into three categories; all have private bathroom, phone and TV but no a/c. The cheapest are the Standard Rooms, some of them fairly spacious with two double or king-size beds. The Lodge Rooms are generally larger; most have ceiling fans and come with a separate dressing area, and all have a small patio or balcony with a couple of chairs for taking in the sun and scenery. Family rooms are larger still and come with a DVD player. *Yosemite Lodge* is beginning to renovate with a mind to sustainability, so you may find yourself in one of their Green Rooms, though these can't be requested at this stage. Children 12 and under stay free in the same room. Standard ❼, lodge ❽

Northern Yosemite

Tuolumne Meadows Lodge Tuolumne Meadows; reserve with DNC. Though in Tuolumne Meadows – 8775ft up and a perfect base for high-country hikes – this isn't really a lodge at all but a large cluster of seventy wooden-framed tent cabins, each with four beds and a wood-burning stove but no electricity and only candles for light. Bedding is supplied but you do your own housekeeping after arrival. This was one of the original High Sierra Camps (see box, p.182), and though much expanded it maintains the same spirit, with hikers still using it as an overnight stop on the full High Sierra Camp Loop.

The lodge is over a mile from the main Tuolumne Meadows facilities, but it has a restaurant (see p.189), showers (free for guests), and newspapers for sale. Rates are for two adults; additional adults cost $13, kids $8. Closed mid-Sept to June. ❹

White Wolf Lodge Reserve with DNC. This is the only park lodging that's away from the main human honeypots of Yosemite Valley, Tuolumne Meadows and Wawona. It's only a mile down a side road off Tioga Road, but White Wolf still feels quite isolated, surrounded by lodgepole pines, and perfectly sited for easy hikes to Harden Lake (Hike Y13), Lukens Lake (Hike Y14) and longer forays down into the Grand Canyon of the Tuolumne River (hike Y49). It has a homey feel, though with a campground nearby it can still get busy. The 24 spacious canvas tent cabins are clustered together; each sleep four and come with a wood-burning stove and candle for light, but no electricity. Bedding is supplied though there is no daily maid service. The four hard-walled cabins are like regular motel rooms with double beds, chairs on the small porch, propane heating, electricity when the generator is running, bed linen and a daily maid service. Communal showers are free to guests and there's a restaurant on site (see p.190). Closed mid-Sept to June. Tent cabins ❸, cabins ❹

Southern Yosemite

The Redwoods in Yosemite 8038 Chilnualna Falls Rd, Wawona ☎1-888/225-6666 or 209/375-6666, ⓦwww.redwoodsinyosemite .com. The only privately owned accommodation in the park, the *Redwoods* brings together some 125 fully furnished vacation rentals around Wawona, each let for a minimum of two nights (three in summer). Some are rustic log cabins, others plush modern homes, but almost all have a spacious deck with barbecue, TV and firewood for your stove or open fire. Bedding, towels and kitchen utensils are all provided but you'll need to supply all your own food. Rates for a one- or two-bedroom cottage are in the $170–260 range per night; well-appointed full-size homes go from $350 to $420. ❻–❾

Wawona Hotel Wawona; reserve with DNC, front desk ☎209/375-6556. Second in elegance only to *The Ahwahnee* in the Yosemite hierarchy, the New England-style *Wawona Hotel* (see p.97 for historic detail and other services) dates in part back to 1879, a heritage drawn upon for recent renovations. Its various buildings are all painted white, with wide wraparound verandas scattered with cane loungers, perfect for spotting the deer that occasionally graze on the lawns. Altogether there are over a hundred rooms, over half with private bath, some with clawfoot tubs. The cheapest rooms – located upstairs in the main building – are smallish and with sloping floors, and come supplied with robes for late-night dashes along the corridor to the shared bathrooms. It's a significant step up to the majority of the rooms, which are scattered in various buildings around the grounds. These more expensive en-suite rooms have been restored gracefully and have been fitted with old-style furniture, Victorian patterned wallpaper and ceiling fans. In keeping with the overall tenor, none of the rooms has phone, TV or a/c. Ask to look at a few rooms as they differ greatly: some are well suited to families, with the adults being able to watch the kids in the pool from their balcony; others link together, making them ideal for small groups; and some are perfect for a private escape – *Moore's Cabin* and *Clark Cottage* (once lived in by Galen Clark) are particularly romantic.

Meals are served in the *Wawona Dining Room* (see p.189), and you can bookend your meal with aperitifs and after-dinner drinks in the lounge listening to Tom Bopp at the piano (see p.98). It always pays to check web specials and deals. A buffet breakfast is included in the room rate and children 12 and under stay free in the same room. Closed Dec; Jan–March closed Mon–Thurs. Room with bath ❻, room with shared bath ❺

Yosemite West and Foresta

Yosemite Peregrine 7509 Henness Circle, Yosemite West ☏ 1-800/396-3639 or 209/372-8517, ⓦ www.yosemiteperegrine.com. A well-appointed B&B tastefully decorated in both Southwestern and woodsy themes, with a cooked breakfast included in the rates. They also book a vacation home and several fully self-contained condos in the area, some sleeping up to six. B&B ❻, condos ❻

Yosemite Scenic Wonders 7403 Yosemite Park Way, Yosemite West ☏ 1-888/967-3648, ⓦ www.scenicwonders.com. This vacation rental homes company manages over two dozen quality homes sleeping from two to eight, making them especially good value for families or two couples travelling together. All are comfortable, though some are more luxurious than others with hot tubs, open fireplaces and sundecks; check the website for full details. Most charge $250–350 a night for two in summer, though *Studio Condominiums* starts at $150. ❺–❾

Yosemite Vacation Homes Foresta ⓦ www.4yosemite.com. Almost a dozen independently owned vacation homes in the private enclave of Foresta, some with great views. All are well appointed and come fully equipped: just bring food and drink. Choose from: *El Capitan View* (☏ 1-888/438-3522; ❽) or *Clouds Rest* (☏ 1-866/320-1588; ❽), which sleeps four but is perfect for two. Rates are quoted for two people (extras typically pay $30 a head) and there's often a two- or three-night minimum.

Northeast of Yosemite: Lee Vining

The following are listed in order headed east from Tioga Pass (see map, p.152).

Tioga Pass Resort 2 miles east of Tioga Pass; no phone, ⓔ reservations@tiogapassresort.com, ⓦ www.tiogapassresort.com. Streamside

mini-resort at 9600ft originally built in 1914 and comprising rustic, self-contained, shingle-roofed cabins with full bathrooms, and motel units without cooking facilities. There's an excellent little diner on site. Minimum three nights for advance bookings; single nights are first come first served. Closed mid-Oct to late May. Cabins ❼, rooms ❻

El Mono Motel US-395 at 3rd St ☏ 760/647-6310, ⓦ www.elmonomotel.com. This cute motel is the cheapest in town, lacks phones and TVs and has rooms that are small but well kept and cheerfully decorated. Closed Nov to late April. Shared bathroom ❷, en-suite ❸

Hess House B&B 50 Lee Vining Ave ☏ 760/647-6416, ⓦ www.hesshousebandb.com. Tucked behind *El Mono Motel*, this welcoming homestay has a cosy feel with just two guest rooms sharing a bathroom and guest lounge. The part-Paiute owner puts on a good breakfast and knows a few local stories. ❹

Murphey's Motel 51493 US-395 ☏ 1-800/334-6316 or 760/647-6316, ⓦ www.murpheysyosemite.com. Very clean and well-presented motel in the centre of town, with cable TV and a/c. Some units have a kitchen at no extra cost, and there are bathrooms with both shower and tub. Good single rates. ❹

Northwest of Yosemite: Hwy-120 West, Groveland and Coulterville

The following places are listed in order of distance from Yosemite Valley (see map, p.152).

Yosemite Lakes 31191 Hardin Flat Rd, off Hwy-120 West, 5 miles from Big Oak Flat Entrance ☏ 1-800/533-1001 or 209/962-0121, ⓦ www.stayatyosemite.com. Mainly included here for its proximity to the entrance to Yosemite, this scattered, family-oriented place, 18 miles east of Groveland, has pricey tent and RV sites (all $48), cabins with a double bed and a set of bunks, and conical-roofed canvas-walled yurts with polished wood floors, a pleasant deck, cooking facilities, shower and toilet. The latter sleep four in considerable comfort. A two-night stay is required in the cabins and yurts. Cabins ❹, yurts ❻

Evergreen Lodge 33160 Evergreen Road, Mather, a mile west of Big Oak Flat Entrance ☏ 209/379-2606 or 1-800/935-6343,

@www.evergreenlodge.com. More than just a place to rest your head, this resort amid the pines on the road to Hetch Hetchy (7 miles north of Hwy-120 West) comprises 88 cabins scattered around the main lodge and recreation building. Traditional cabins are modernized and very comfortable, and there are even more spacious deluxe models with shower/tub. So-called "Custom campers" are provided with tent, mattress and sleeping bag. There's a general store with espresso bar, good restaurant, bar (the only places you'll find TV), and every night in summer the lodge puts on entertainment in the form of a slide show, movie or live music. You can even rent bikes and join a number of tours and activities. Custom camping ❷, cabins ❻, deluxe ❼

Yosemite Riverside Inn 11399 Cherry Lake Rd, 11 miles from Big Oak Flat Entrance ☏1-800/626-7408 or 209/926-7408, @www .yosemiteriversideinn.com. A woodsy set of motel units and riverside cabins located half a mile off the highway (14 miles east of Groveland), with good fishing and river swimming nearby. Decent doubles come with TV, a/c, slightly dated decor and a continental breakfast, though you're probably better opting for the cabins with two doubles, a small kitchen and barbecue pit. Rooms ❺, riverview cabins ❻

Yosemite Westgate Lodge 7633 Hwy-120 West, 13 miles from Big Oak Flat Entrance ☏1-888/315-2378 or 209/962-5281, @www .yosemitewestgate.com. The closest standard motel to the park on Hwy-120 West, the *Lodge* is comfortable and comes with all the expected amenities including satellite TV, phone, pool and hot tub. Some deluxe rooms have limited cooking facilities, though there's decent eating next door at the *Buck Meadow's Restaurant*. Two kids under 12 stay free with two adults, and rates drop dramatically in winter. Midweek ❺, weekend ❻

Groveland Motel & Indian Village 18933 Hwy-120, Groveland ☏1-888/849-3529 or 209/962-7865, @www.grovelandmotel.net. A wide range of accommodation dotted about pleasantly wooded grounds. Options include fairly basic air-conditioned cabins with cable TV (❸), a couple of mobile homes with small kitchens (❹), and some *in situ* tents with airbeds (❶) clustered around a campfire. You can pitch your own tent for $25.

Hotel Charlotte 18736 Hwy-120, Groveland ☏209/962-6455, @www.hotelcharlotte .com. Situated 25 miles from the Big Oak Flat Entrance, this charming ten-room hotel, dating back to 1921, has been lovingly updated. Rooms are mostly small but all have beautiful old-fashioned bathrooms, individually controlled a/c, satellite TV and phones with free calls throughout the US. Rates include a good buffet breakfast, and there's free wi-fi throughout. ❹

Groveland Hotel 18767 Hwy-120 West, Groveland ☏1-800/273-3314 & 209/962-4000, @www.groveland.com. Though originally founded in an adobe house in 1849, this historic hotel now occupies a wooden two-storey structure built in 1914 for VIP guests during the damming of Hetch Hetchy. The hotel is now run as a B&B with luxurious, antique-filled, air-conditioned rooms, most containing high, quilted beds and deep baths. Some rooms are quite small so step up to the three suites, complete with fireplace and spa tub. Wicker chairs on the veranda are perfect for catching the early evening sun before dining in the *Victorian Room* (see p.191). The owners also manage *Sugar Pine Ranch*, 3 miles east off Hwy-120, a peaceful cluster of cottages in the woods, where you can expect considerable comfort but no internet access. In all cases an excellent breakfast is included and served at the *Groveland Hotel*. Cottages ❺, deluxe cottages with TV ❻, hotel rooms ❺, hotel suites ❼

All Seasons Groveland Inn 18656 Main St, Groveland ☏1-800/595-9993 or 209/962-0232, @www.allseasonsgrovelandinn.com. Very comfortable lodging in an 1897 house uncharacteristically decorated in primary colours and bold designs, each room with a "dramatic feature", be it a small waterfall, extravagant hand-painted mural, steam room, or a private deck with a telescope. All have fridge and coffeemaker and most have a fireplace and jacuzzi. A self-serve continental breakfast is included and guests have access to a small kitchen. ❺

Yosemite Gold Country Motel 10407 Hwy-49, Coulterville ☏1-800/247-9884 or 209/878 3400, @www.yosemitegoldcountry motel.com. This excellent-value and welcoming motel, half a mile north of Coulterville, offers aged but well-kept and nicely appointed motel rooms each with a/c, VCR/TV, fridge, microwave and free wi-fi. ❷

West of Yosemite: Hwy-140, El Portal and Midpines

The following places are listed in order of distance from Yosemite Valley (see map, p.152).

Yosemite View Lodge 11136 Hwy-140, El Portal, 2 miles west of Arch Rock Entrance ☎1-888/742-4371 or 209/742-7106, ⊛www .yosemiteresorts.us. Vast and luxurious – though slightly soulless – complex with rooms, suites, moderately priced restaurant, convenience store and several swimming pools and hot tubs located on the park boundary beside the tumbling Merced River. The modern rooms all have a/c, phone, cable TV and either one king or two queen beds (and most have a balcony of some sort), but you pay a premium to get river view, fireplace, in-room spa tub and kitchenette. The entire place is often booked well in advance, but it may be worth trying for no-shows; winter prices start around $100. Premium rooms ❼, standard rooms ❻

Yosemite Cedar Lodge 9966 Hwy-140, El Portal, 8 miles west of Arch Rock Entrance ☎1-888/742-4371 or 209/742-7106, ⊛www .yosemiteresorts.us. Older and smaller cousin of the *Yosemite View Lodge* (see above), with indoor and outdoor pools, on-site restaurant, a slightly narrower variety of rooms (none of them riverside), and lower prices to match. With over two hundred rooms there's a fair chance of getting something when everywhere else is full. Suites with kitchenettes ❻, rooms ❺

Bear Creek Cabins 6993 Hwy-140, Midpines, 23 miles west of Arch Rock Entrance ☎1-888/303-6993 or 209/966-5253, ⊛www.yosemitecabins .com. Large, well-maintained log cabin accommodation, comprised of a large cabin divided into four comfortable units. Two sleep four and come with kitchenette, while the two spacious suites come with a separate living room, gas fireplace and a full kitchen. All have satellite TV, and access to a deck and barbecue area. ❹–❺

🏃 **Yosemite Bug Rustic Mountain Resort** 6979 Hwy-140, Midpines, 23 miles west of Arch Rock Entrance ☎1-866/826-7108 & 209/966-6666, ⊛www.YosemiteBug.com; office open 7am–11pm. With a couple of dozen buildings scattered through twenty acres of woodland, this low-cost to mid-range lodge is the handiest budget lodgings near Yosemite. It includes a self-catering HI-USA hostel (adhering to their conservation ethics, but generally running along looser, less institutional lines) and has an international atmosphere, though there are separate rooms away from the bustle if you'd prefer. There's also the excellent *Café at the Bug* (see p.191) on site. Mixed and single-sex dorms ($22; non-members $25) are clean and comfortable, though those wanting a little privacy might prefer the tent cabins (❶) or shared-bath private rooms (❸). For extra comfort, go for the en-suite rooms with decks but no phone or TV (❹), all distinctively decorated – including Russian, Zulu, Country French and Austin Powers themes. Other facilities include laundry, free internet and wi-fi, trails to a good summer swimming hole, gear rental (snowshoes $18 a day; tyre chains $20 a day), and access to a hot tub, sauna, massage and yoga classes. YARTS buses run into the park in just over an hour from the stop right outside. Reservations essential May–Sept. ❶–❹

Muir Lodge 6833 Hwy-140, Midpines, 23.2 miles west of Arch Rock Entrance ☎209/966-2468, ⊛www.yosemitemuirlodge.com. Old and basic motel units that haven't been upgraded for many years but are at least clean and cheap. Also one three-bed dorm ($29 per person). ❷

West of Yosemite: Mariposa

Best Western Yosemite Way Station 4999 Hwy-140 ☎209/966-7545 or 1-800/937-8376, ⊛www.yosemitebestwestern.com. Comfortable chain motel where the fairly large, modern rooms come with shower/tub, cable TV and Ansel Adams Yosemite prints on the wall. Continental breakfast is included and there's access to an outdoor pool overlooking a small stream. Rates down to $60 in winter. ❺

Comfort Inn 4994 Bullion St ☎209/966-4344 or 1-800/221-2222, ⊛www.comfortinn.com. Modern mid-range motel with wi-fi and a/c in all rooms, an outdoor pool and hot tub, and a continental breakfast included. Some suites with cooking facilities. ❹

🏃 **Highland House B&B Inn** 3125 Wild Dove Lane ☎209/966-3737, ⊛www.highland houseinn.com. You'll almost certainly see deer and hummingbirds at this tranquil B&B, tucked away amid ponderosa pines and incense cedars around 12 miles northeast of Mariposa. The three attractively furnished rooms all have private bathroom with tub and shower, and the suite (**5**) has a four-poster bed, fireplace and DVD player. Breakfasts are delicious, there's a full kitchen for guests' use and the common area even has a pool table. Located off Jerseydale Road, but call Michael for detailed directions. Reserve well ahead in summer. **4**

River Rock Inn 4993 Seventh St ☎209/966-5793, ⓦwww.riverrockncafe.com. Personal touches and stylish decor raise this peaceful and welcoming seven-room motel from above the pack. Located just off Mariposa's main drag, it has smallish rooms (and a couple of larger suites) all equipped with a/c, fridge and coffee pot. Continental breakfast (included) is served in the adjacent *River Rock Deli*. Suites **5**, rooms **3**

Yosemite Inn 5180 Jones St ☎1-866/470-7130 or 209/742-6800, ⓦwww.yosemiteinnca.com. Good-value, recently renovated motel with some new and large a/c rooms, most with two beds; all rooms have shower/tub combos and cable TV. There's a pool and hot tub, and a good continental breakfast is served. Rates may drop to as little as $60 a night in winter. **4**

West of Yosemite: Merced

Comfort Inn 730 Motel Drive ☎1-877-424-6423 or 209/383-0333, ⓦwww.comfortinn.com. Mid-range motel with all the expected facilities including pool, sauna and free wi-fi. **3**

HI-Merced Home Hostel Call for pick-up or directions once in Merced ☎209/725-0407, ⓔmerced@hiusa.com. The best place to stay in Merced if you're relying on public transportation, this reservations-only establishment is a hospitable private home with just six beds either in a single-sex dorm ($18; non-members $21) or private room ($42/48). Check-in hours and access hours are limited (7–9am & 5–10pm), but this is a small inconvenience for the benefits of a free ride to and from the train and bus stations, an enthusiastic welcome, as much Yosemite information as you can handle and a free dessert every evening. It's a great place to hook up with Yosemite-bound travellers, maybe teaming up to rent a car for a couple of days' exploration. The hostel also rents sleeping bags ($5 a night) and two-person tents ($5).

The Hooper House – Bear Creek Inn 575 W N Bear Creek Drive ☎209/723-3991, ⓦwww.hooperhouse.com. B&B in a lovely

Colonial-style house tastefully furnished with polished floors, plain painted walls and an understated smattering of antique furnishings. Breakfast is served in a grand dining room. **6**

Slumber Motel 1315 W 16th St ☎209/722-5783, ⓦwww.slumbermotel.com. The pick of a string of basic, budget motels half a mile west of the Transpo Center (left as you step out of the door), with a small pool, cable TV and free wi-fi. **1**

South of Yosemite: Hwy-41, Fish Camp and Oakhurst

The following places are listed in order of distance from the park's South Entrance (see map, p.152).

Owl's Nest Lodging 1235 Hwy-41, Fish Camp ☎559/683-3484, ⓦwww.owlsnestlodging.com; closed Oct–April. Just two self-contained chalets: one a cosy, wood-panelled loft sleeping two (**5**); the other a large cabin sleeping seven (**6**), making it an excellent deal for small groups or large families.

Yosemite Big Creek Inn 1221 Hwy-41, Fish Camp ☎559/641-2828, ⓦwww.yosemiteinn.com. Just three classy and spacious guest rooms, all with superb bathrooms and access to a massive DVD collection. There's a hot tub on the back deck where deer can often be seen, and a superb breakfast is included. **7**

White Chief Mountain Lodge 7776 White Chief Mountain Rd, Fish Camp ☎559/683-5444, ⓦwww.whitechiefmountainlodge.com; closed Nov–March. Choose from one of the ageing but well-equipped and clean motel rooms or one of the four-berth cottages, all in a peaceful setting. Good value, and there's a diner-style restaurant on site. Rooms **4**, cottages **6**

Tenaya Lodge 1122 Hwy-41, Fish Camp ☎1-888/514-2167 or 801-559-4919, ⓦwww.tenayalodge.com. This modern and attractive four-star complex, located 2.5 miles from the South Entrance, makes a fairly successful attempt to replicate the grand tradition of Western Lodges that's best exemplified by *The Ahwahnee*. It caters to conferences and Yosemite tourists with over two hundred modern, comfortable rooms, three on-site restaurants open to all-comers, indoor and outdoor pools, sauna, hot tubs and gym, and all sorts of outdoor activities such as mountain biking, horseriding, guided hiking and even a kids' entertainment programme. In summer (when you should always reserve in advance) rates start around $320, though midweek in winter rates can drop to $180. ❽

Narrow Gauge Inn 48571 Hwy-41, Fish Camp ☎1-888/644-9050 & 559/683-7720, ⓦwww.narrowgaugeinn.com. There's an alpine feel to this 26-room lodge, 4.5 miles from the South Entrance, with a wide selection of accommodation, including many rooms with a balcony and views over the forest. All rooms come with phone, TV and include continental breakfast. There's also a pool and spa, and a fine on-site restaurant (see p.192). Two-night minimum stay on summer weekends. ❺

Sierra Sky Ranch 50552 Road 632, Oakhurst ☎559/683-8040, ⓦwww.sierraskyranch.com. This woodsy lodge, sitting 12 miles from the South Entrance, dates from 1875 on what was the largest cattle ranch in the state. It still has a spacious feel with a veranda-girt main lodge, large cosy lounge with heavy wood furniture, and sunny library plus a pool, creek swimming and fishing on-site. Ageing, rustic rooms come without a phone but do have cable TV and free wi-fi. *Sara's Room* boasts a clawfoot tub. ❺

Hounds Tooth Inn 42071 Hwy-41, almost 3 miles north of Oakhurst ☎1-888/642-6610 or 559/642-6600, ⓦwww.houndstoothinn.com. Modern, luxurious B&B with a dozen individually decorated rooms, most with either a fireplace or a spa bath (or both) and all air-conditioned. The friendly hosts provide complimentary wine each evening and delicious buffet breakfasts; there's also an extensive DVD library. Rooms ❹, deluxe ❻

Days Inn 40662 Hwy-41, Oakhurst ☎1-800/329-7644 or 559/642-2525, ⓦwww.daysinn.com. The cheapest of Oakhurst's franchise motels, but still done to a high standard with comfortable rooms, HBO, free wi-fi, a pool and continental breakfast. Rates as low as ❷ in winter. ❺

America's Best Value Inn 48800 Royal Oaks Drive, Oakhurst ☎1-888/315-2378 or 559/658 5500, ⓦwww.americasbestvalueinn.com. Slightly soulless but recently refurbished chain hotel offering large, airy rooms, cable TV and access to an outdoor pool and spa. Continental breakfast is included and some rooms have a microwave and fridge. ❸

The Homestead 41110 Road 600, Ahwahnee, 4 miles northwest of Oakhurst along Hwy-49 then 2.5 miles south

☎1-800/483-0495 or 559/683-0495, ⓦwww.homesteadcottages.com. Just a handful of very attractive and beautifully outfitted adobe cottages – including a/c, TV and gas barbecue – set amid oak-filled foothills, each with full self-catering facilities, a comfortable lounge area and a deck that's perfect for those relaxing sundowners. Breakfast ingredients are supplied, and there's a two-night minimum stay at weekends. Small "Star Gazing" loft ❺, one-bedroom cottages ❼, two-bedroom cottages ❾

Meadow Creek Ranch Corner Hwy-49 and Triangle Rd ☎1-800/853-2037 or 209/966-3843, ⓦwww.meadowcreekranchinn.com. Comfortable B&B inn roughly equidistant from the park's southern and Arch Rock entrances based around a stagecoach stop dating back to 1858. The two cottages on the grounds are decorated with old-fashioned furnishings, and each has its own entrance, but the excellent breakfast is served in the main house. ❺

South of Yosemite: Bass Lake

The following are too distant from Yosemite to be used as a convenient base for exploring the park.

Miller's Landing Resort 37976 Rd 222 ☎559/642-3633 or 1-866/657-4386, ⓦwww.millerslanding.com. Family resort offering deluxe cabins fully equipped with kitchen, barbecue and satellite TV. Many are booked by the week throughout summer, but nightly stays are possible. ❻

Minarets Pack Station Sierra Vista Scenic Byway ☎559/868-3405, ⓦwww.highsierrapackers.org /min.htm. This horse packing station high in the sierra has very simple lodging for $13 a night. Closed Oct to mid-June. ❶

Pines Resort 54432 Road 432, Bass Lake ☎559/642-3121 or 1-800/350-7463, ⓦwww.basslake.com. Luxurious two-storey chalets with kitchens, or even more palatial lakeside suites. ❽

South of Yosemite: Mono Hot Spring and the John Muir Wilderness

The following are too distant from Yosemite to be used as a convenient base for exploring the park.

Lakeshore Resort 61953 Huntington Lake Rd ☎559/893-3193, ⓦwww.lakeshoreresort.com.

Resort built in the 1920s with rustic, knotty pine cabins, most sleeping four or five. There's also a great, country restaurant and bar on site. RV parking $30, rooms ❸, suites ❺

🏃 **Mono Hot Springs Resort** 12 miles east of Huntington Lake ☎559/325-1710, ⓦwww .monohotsprings.com. Excellent mountain resort where all cabin prices include free use of the therapeutic mineral pools and spa. Accommodation ranges from simple cabins with communal bathrooms and no linen to more commodious affairs with toilets and kitchen. Typically there's a three-night minimum but you may be able to slot into a shorter gap, especially at either end of the season, which runs mid-May to Oct. Tent cabins sleeping up to five ❷, rustic cabins for up to four ❸, modern cabins ❹

Vermillion Valley Resort Lake Edison ☎559/259-4000, ⓦwww.edisonlake.com. Simple resort mainly geared towards boaters and anglers but also useful for entry into the John Muir Wilderness, easily accessed by small ferry. Closed mid-Oct to May. Tent cabins ❶, motel units ❸

South of Yosemite: Fresno

The following places can be used as a base for exploring Sequoia and Kings Canyon national parks, but are too distant for commutes into Yosemite.

Days Inn 1101 N Parkway Drive ☎1-800/329-7466, ⓦwww.daysinn.com. Tower District motel that's marginally nicer than the nearby *Motel 6* for not much more money. Free wi-fi and a pool. ❶

La Quinta Inn 330 E Fir Ave ☎559/449-0928, ⓦwww.lq.com. Quality motel with comfy, well appointed rooms, a gym and staff that really care about the place. It's just off Hwy-41, 6 miles north of downtown on the way to Yosemite. ❹

Super 8 2127 Inyo St at L St ☎1-800/800-8000, ⓦwww.super8.com. Downtown motel with a pool and free continental breakfast. ❷

South of Yosemite: Visalia

The following places can be used as a base for exploring Sequoia and Kings Canyon national parks, but are too distant for commutes into Yosemite.

Ben Maddox House B&B 601 N Encina St ☎1-800/401-9800, ⓦwww.benmaddoxhouse .com. Chatty, Irish-American Lucy is an attentive host in this large, pool-equipped redwood house built in 1876 for Ben Maddox, the man who brought hydroelectricity to the San Joaquin Valley. A few rough edges need attention but it can be good value, particularly with discounts for multi-night and midweek stays. Weekdays ❺, weekends ❻

Comfort Suites 210 E Acequia Ave ☎1-800/ 4CHOICE or 559/738-1700, ⓦwww.visalia lodging.com. Modern and central hotel with little character but good facilities, including fitness centre and outdoor hot tub. ❸

Econo Lodge 1400 S Mooney Boulevard ☎1-877-424-6423 or 559/732-6641, ⓦwww .econolodge.com. The best of the town's budget motels, recently renovated, with pool, flatscreen TVs, free wi-fi and a light breakfast included in the room rate. ❶

Lamp Liter Inn 3300 W Mineral King Ave ☎1-800/662-6692, ⓦwww.lampliter.net. Pleasant 100-room hotel surrounded by lawns and featuring a very nice pool, sports bar and grill. ❹

🏃 **The Spalding House** 631 N Encina ☎559/739-7877, ⓦwww.thespalding house.com. Local lumberman W.R. Spalding built this fine Colonial Revival home, now a beautifully appointed B&B. Suites all have separate bathroom and sitting room and come with a gourmet breakfast. ❸

Campgrounds and RV parks

As with any national park, **camping** is the best way to really feel part of your surroundings, though this is perhaps less true in Yosemite Valley where the drive-in campgrounds are large and crowded, especially from May to September. Around 700,000 people camp in the valley annually, so rules are rigidly imposed and camping outside recognized sites is strictly forbidden. Beyond Yosemite Valley, things improve dramatically with a number of delightful road-accessible campgrounds.

Park campgrounds – all set amid pines – vary in altitude from 4000ft in Yosemite Valley to 8600ft at Tuolumne Meadows. Take note of the altitude listed under each campground: a balmy summer evening in Yosemite Valley could easily be decidedly chilly in Tuolumne. They typically offer plumbed toilets and potable water and cost $20 per site, though several offer more limited facilities but charge less.

In addition to the drive-in campgrounds, there's the *Camp 4* **walk-in site** in Yosemite Valley, and a couple of tent-only sites outside. **RV campers** can use all the main campgrounds but there are no hookups in Yosemite.

Outside the park there's more variety with a number of commercial campgrounds along the access roads. Most have some tent sites, but generally cater to RVs, offer all manner of facilities and diversions and charge accordingly. The entire park is surrounded by **national forests**, all offering simple campgrounds that often act as an overspill for the national park. We've mentioned those most convenient for forays into the park.

Reservations

Bookings are required year-round for campgrounds in Yosemite Valley, which remain busy for most of the year, even winter weekends. If you're headed for one of the first-come-first-served campgrounds you'll usually get a place if you arrive before noon, though your chances are better midweek. At bookable campgrounds, you can **reserve online** at Ⓦ www .recreation.gov, or **by phone** (daily: March–Oct 7am–9pm Pacific time, Nov–Feb 7am–7pm), as follows: within the US and Canada call ☏1-877/444-6777, otherwise use ☏518/885-3639, and TDD 1-877/833-6777.

Reservations open in one-month chunks, **four to five months in advance**, so to book for the month July 15–August 14 you should make contact starting March 15. Popular days between May and September often book out within minutes of becoming available. You'll be required to supply personal contact details, the park and campground you wish to stay at, dates, number of people and pets, indication of tent or RV (including length of vehicle), and any discounts you're eligible for, such as Senior Pass or Access Pass (see p.36). After booking, any changes or **cancellations** incur a cost of $10 per reservation.

Those **without reservations** will need to show up very early in the morning and hope for cancellations at one of the reservations offices, which all deal with reservations for their own area: either the Curry Village Reservations Office (May to mid-Oct daily 8am–5pm, mid-Oct to April daily 8.30am–4.30pm) or its equivalent in Tuolumne Meadows (July to early Sept daily 8am–5pm), Wawona (May–Sept daily 8am–5pm), and by the Big Oak Flat entrance station (May–Sept daily 8am–5pm).

The same reservation system can be used for groups of up to thirty, who can book special **group campgrounds** at Tuolumne Meadows, Hodgdon Meadow, Bridalveil Creek and Wawona.

Campground practicalities

Camping in Yosemite is restricted to one month in any calendar year, but between May and mid-September fourteen days is the **maximum stay**, of which seven can be spent in Yosemite Valley and seven more at Wawona. **Check-out time** is noon.

All campgrounds in Yosemite have **tent sites**, often well away from the **RV sites**. *Camp 4*, *Tamarack* and *Yosemite Creek* are tent-only campgrounds. **RVs** over 40ft are not permitted in Yosemite Valley campgrounds and 35ft is the maximum in campgrounds outside the valley. Sparing **generator use** is only permitted during daylight hours: **quiet hours** are from 10pm to 6am. Each site accommodates up to six people

Hikers who fancy carrying a light load and ending the day with a hot shower, a comfortable bed and a hearty meal might consider staying at one (or all) of the five **High Sierra Camps**, spectacularly sited complexes of tent cabins about a day's walk apart (6–10 miles) in the Tuolumne backcountry. Located at Glen Aulin (map, p.84; 7800ft), May Lake (map, p.84; 9270ft), Sunrise (map, p.84; 9400ft), Merced Lake (map, p.92; 7150ft) and Vogelsang (map, p.84; 10,300ft), each camp sleeps thirty to sixty people in four- to six-bed dormitory-style tents. They come with steel-framed beds, mattresses, pillows and blankets, so all you need to bring is sheets or a sleep sack, towel and personal items. Don't forget that hip flask for a relaxing sundowner: none of the HSCs sells alcohol. **Merced Lake** is the largest and often has openings when others are full: there's fishing and swimming nearby.

Unfortunately, the season is short (late June until after the second weekend in Sept) and the demand is high, so aspirants have to enter a **lottery** to stay in the HSCs. Applications are made online (Ⓦwww.yosemitepark.com website under "Accommodations") between September 1 and November 1, and applicants are notified by the end of January. Any spare spaces become available during the first week in February; check the website for availability then phone ☏801/559-4909 or call the front desk at *Tuolumne Meadows Lodge* which also keeps a list of vacancies for the current week.

Successful applicants pay $153 a night (excluding tax; kids 7–12 $99, children under 7 not allowed) for bed, three-course dinner, an energy-giving breakfast served family style, and hot **showers** (except at Glen Aulin and Vogelsang, where showers are not available). Tents are usually single-sex, though members of a party can be accommodated in the same tent. **Dinner** and **breakfast** may also be available to non-guest hikers who reserve in advance ($40 for both meals; ☏801/559-4909). A sack lunch is also available ($13.25): order at the camp.

The camps are mostly frequented by older, moderately well-heeled hikers who often stay here while hiking the High Sierra Camp Loop (Y50, see p.138).

(including children) and two vehicles. For more on camping rules consult Ⓦ www.nps.gov/yose/planyourvisit /campregs.htm.

Free **dump stations** exist in Yosemite Valley by the entrance to the *Upper Pines* campground (open all year), Wawona (open all year) and Tuolumne Meadows (June to early Sept). **Pets** are not encouraged in Yosemite campgrounds but are allowed in most (see Basics, p.40).

For details of **showers** and **laundry** facilities see "Travel essentials" on p.43.

Though no limitations apply in winter, summertime air quality restrictions in Yosemite Valley only allow **campground fires** between 5 and 10pm from May to September. For ecological reasons, neither firewood nor kindling (including pine cones and needles) can be gathered in the valley, so you'll need to either bring wood with you from outside the valley or buy supplies (around $8 a box) from the stores in Yosemite Village and Curry Village. Fires can be started with newspaper, which produces less smoke than pine needles. Campfires are permitted at all times in other parts of the park, but only dead and down wood may be collected, and not in the giant sequoia groves nor above 9600ft. Outside Yosemite Valley you can buy firewood at the Wawona and Tuolumne Meadows stores.

Unless noted otherwise, assume the following campgrounds are **open all year**.

In Yosemite Valley

Camp 4 Walk-In Shuttle stop 7; 4000ft; space for 210 people. First-come-first-served site west of (and away from) the other Yosemite Valley sites, and very popular with rock climbers. It's a sociable and fairly bohemian (some would say squalid) place with sites just a few yards from the dusty parking lot and shared by six people. The campground is non-reservable and often full by 9am, especially in spring and fall when climbers are here in numbers. A ranger staffs a small kiosk at the site to register campers at around 8.30am each morning, but such is the demand you may have to join the line at 7.30am and still may not get a place. There's piped water and flush toilets, but there are no showers and the already inadequate washing facilities are rendered more so by climbers not looking after them. As in the rest of Yosemite Valley, camping here is limited to seven days in the summer season (May to mid-Sept). No pets. $5 per person.

Lower Pines Shuttle stop 19; 4000ft; 60 tent and RV sites. One of three almost identical Yosemite Valley campgrounds (along with *North Pines* and *Upper Pines*), surrounded by evergreens and with the Merced River running along one side, and Stoneman Meadow on the other. This is the only valley campground specifically designed with wheelchair-accessible sites (with electric wheelchair charging outlets), and also has an RV and tent site with tap water, flush toilets, picnic tables and fire pits. The Curry Village showers are close at hand, and there's an amphitheatre for camp ranger programmes. Closed Nov to late March; $20.

North Pines Shuttle stop 18; 4000ft; 81 tent and RV sites. Similar to *Lower Pines* (see above) but slightly more isolated from Curry Village, closer to the stables and a touch quieter. Closed mid-Oct to March. $20.

Upper Pines Shuttle stops 15 & 19; 4000ft; 238 tent and RV sites. Easily the biggest of the valley campgrounds, with pine-shrouded sites, toilets, water and fire rings; especially popular with RVers. It has Yosemite Valley's only RV dump station, which can be used by guests at the other campgrounds. $20.

Yosemite Valley backpacker campground Shuttle stop 18; 4000ft; 20 sites. Small, peaceful campground only available to hikers setting off on, or returning from, backcountry trips. There's a one-night maximum stay, and campers must have a valid wilderness permit for the next or previous night. The

main access is through the *North Pines* campground. $5 per person.

Northern Yosemite

Crane Flat 6200ft; 166 tent and RV sites. Northwest of Yosemite Valley, at the beginning of the Tioga Road, this large but appealing reservable campground is handy for the Tuolumne and Merced groves of giant sequoias. There's piped water, flush toilets, fireplaces and picnic tables. Closed early Oct to June. $20.

Hetch Hetchy backpacker campground 3800ft. Small campground available only to hikers setting off on, or returning from, backcountry trips. There's a one-night maximum stay, and campers must have a valid wilderness permit for the next or previous night. $5 per person.

Hodgdon Meadow 4900ft; 105 tent and RV sites. Relatively quiet creekside campground with flush toilets right on the park's western boundary beside Hwy-120 West. Reservations are required from mid-April to mid-Oct when it costs $20, but for the rest of the year, when piped water is turned off, it becomes a $14 first-come-first-served campground. $14–20.

Porcupine Flat 8100ft; 52 tent and RV sites. Beautifully sited primitive campground along the Tioga Road, nearly forty miles from Yosemite Valley but close to Tuolumne Meadows and some important trailheads. Though small, it's often one of the last to fill at busy times, partly because facilities are limited to pit toilets, and stream water that should be treated. No pets. Closed mid-Oct to June. $10.

Tamarack Flat 6300ft; 52 tent sites. Small first-come-first-served site 2 miles down a rough road off the Tioga Road, 23 miles from Yosemite Valley and with only limited RV access. As with *Porcupine Flat*, there are pit toilets and stream water that should be treated. No pets. Closed Oct to late June. $10.

Tuolumne Meadows 8600ft; 304 tent and RV sites. Yosemite's largest campground by far, but still an attractive affair beside a subalpine meadow right by the Tuolumne River, where there's reasonable trout fishing. Popular with both car campers and backpackers, half the sites are available by advance reservation, half available by same-day reservation at the office near the entrance. Flush toilets, piped water and a dump station are all on site, but there are no showers anywhere near *Tuolumne Meadows*. Sites along Loop A are closest to the river but are generally smaller than on other loops. Closed late Sept to June. $20.

Tuolumne Meadows backpacker campground 8600ft. One section of the main *Tuolumne Meadows* campground is restricted to hikers setting off on, or returning from, backcountry trips. There's a one-night maximum stay, and campers must have a valid wilderness permit for the next or previous night. $5 per person.

White Wolf 8000ft; 74 tent and RV sites. Forest-shrouded first-come-first-served tent and RV campground a mile north of the Tioga Road, midway between Yosemite Valley and Tuolumne Meadows. It's a particularly pleasant site with good hiking all around (see hikes Y13 & Y14), but can be plagued by mosquitoes in July. Proximity to *White Wolf Lodge* (see p.174), where you can buy meals and limited groceries, adds to its attraction. There are also several one-night sites ($5) for backcountry hikers with wilderness permits. Maximum RV length 27ft. Closed mid-Sept to June. $14.

🚶 **Yosemite Creek 7700ft; 40 tent sites.** First-come-first-served tent-only site that's 5 miles down a rough road and consequently enough off the beaten track to discourage all except those keen on a bit of solitude. It's often one of the last places to fill up but can still be packed on summer weekends. Pit toilets, and stream water that must be treated, are available. Closed early Sept to June. $10.

Southern Yosemite

Bridalveil Creek Glacier Point Road; 7200ft; 110 tent and RV sites. A high-country, first-come-first-served site just off Glacier Point Road that makes a cooler midsummer alternative to Yosemite Valley. Set beside Bridalveil Creek, there are meadows all around that are gradually being invaded by lodgepole pines, and access to wilderness trails is excellent. Closed early Sept to June.

🚶 **Wawona 4000ft; 93 tent and RV sites.** The only site in the southern sector of the park, approximately a mile north of the *Wawona Hotel*, this campground is located right by the South Fork of the Merced River on a site occupied by the US cavalry for sixteen summers from 1890. Less secluded and shaded than many park campgrounds,

it is nonetheless very handy for the Merced Grove of giant sequoias and the Pioneer Yosemite History Center. The nearest public showers are in Yosemite Valley. Reservations are required from May to Sept when it costs $20, but for the rest of the year, when piped water is turned off, it becomes a $14 first-come-first-served campground. The campground reservation office is beside the stables. $14–20.

Northeast of Yosemite: Hwy-120 East and Lee Vining

The following are listed in order of distance from Yosemite's South Entrance (see map, p.152). With the exception of *Mono Vista RV Park*, all these campgrounds share the same **contact details**: ☎ 760/873-2400, Ⓦ www.fs.usda.gov/inyo.

🚶 **Tioga Lake Inyo National Forest, a mile east of Tioga Pass Entrance; 9700ft; 13 sites.** Located beside Tioga Lake with a real alpine feel, this is the best of the highway-side Inyo National Forest campgrounds. It's a first-come-first-served, RV-dominated site that's always popular and is usually the first to fill when *Tuolumne Meadows* is full. There are flush toilets, pump water, fire rings and picnic tables. Closed mid-Oct to May. $19.

Junction Inyo National Forest, 2.2 miles east of Tioga Pass Entrance; 9600ft; 13 sites. First-come-first-served tent and RV site, ranged around a meadow and popular with fishers. Less appealing than *Tioga Lake* but cheaper and with the pleasant Nunatak Nature Trail just nearby. Pit toilets and treatable stream water available. Closed mid-Oct to May. $14.

🚶 **Sawmill Walk-in Mile 1.5 Saddlebag Lake Rd; 9800ft; 12 sites.** Primitive walk-in campground around four hundred yards from its parking lot, superbly sited amid jagged peaks that feel a world away from the glaciated domes around Tuolumne. Arrive early for the most convenient sites with the best views. No reservations. Closed mid-Oct to May. $14.

Saddlebag Lake Mile 2 Saddlebag Lake Rd; 10,000ft; 20 sites. The highest road-accessible campground in California; a beautiful place to stay and with good hiking nearby. First-come-first-served. Closed mid-Oct to May. $19.

Ellery Lake Inyo National Forest, 2.5 miles east of Tioga Pass Entrance; 9500ft; 21 sites. Small first-come-first-served campground among pines and rocks with a high mountain tenor, but contrary to the name it is not right next to a lake. Piped water. Closed mid-Oct to May. $19.

Lee Vining Creek Poole Power Plant Rd, roughly 3.5 miles east of Lee Vining and 9 miles west of Tioga Pass Entrance; 7800ft; 150 sites in total. A collection of near-identical streamside campgrounds, all surrounded by trees and each with a campground host in summer. Choose from *Aspen*, *Big Bend*, *Moraine* and *Lower Lee Vining*. Closed late Oct to late April. $14–19.

Mono Vista RV Park US-395 in Lee Vining ☎760/647-6401; 6400ft; 50 sites. Pleasant RV park and campground close to Mono Lake and an easy walk from a couple of decent restaurants. There are RV hookups ($28–35), space for tents ($20), and showers which are available to non-guests ($2.50 for 5min; daily 9am–6pm). Closed Nov–April. $20–35.

Northwest of Yosemite: Hwy-120 West, Stanislaus National Forest, Groveland and Coulterville

The following are listed in order of distance from Yosemite's Big Oak Flat Entrance.

Dimond O Stanislaus National Forest, a mile west of Big Oak Flat Entrance then 6 miles north of Hwy-120 West ☎1-877/444-6777, ⊛www.Recreation.gov; 4400ft; 38 sites. Gorgeous forest campground on the fringes of Yosemite National Park with tent sites (all with table and fire ring) plus paved RV sites. There are pit toilets, piped water and fishing on the Middle Fork of the Tuolumne River. Some sites first-come-first-served, while others can be reserved in advance. Closed early Oct to late April. $21.

Lost Claim Stanislaus National Forest, Hwy-120 West, 12 miles east of Groveland and 14 miles west of Big Oak Flat Entrance ☎209/962-7825, ⊛www.fs.usda.gov/stanislaus; 3100ft; 10 sites. Small first-come-first-served tent and RV site with pit toilets and hand-pumped water. The restaurants at Buck Meadows are less than a mile away. $16.

The Pines Stanislaus National Forest, Hwy-120 West, 9 miles east of Groveland and 17 miles west of Big Oak Flat Entrance ☎209/962-7825, ⊛www.fs.usda.gov/stanislaus; 3200ft; 11 sites. Standard first-come-first-served forest

service campground near the Groveland Ranger Station with RV and tent sites amid the pines, with toilets and piped water. For kids there's the short Little Golden Trail running through the so-called Children's Forest. $16.

Yosemite Pines RV Resort Half a mile off Hwy-120, a mile east of Groveland and 25 miles west of Big Oak Flat Entrance ☎1-877/962-7690 or 209/962-7690, ⊛www.yosemitepinesrv .com; 3000ft; 160 sites. Major RV park with heaps of activities including pony rides, gold panning and bike rentals. Tent sites ($26), and full hookups ($36) are available, and there's also an array of cabins and yurts (from $89), bedding included.

West of Yosemite: Hwy-140, El Portal, Midpines and Mariposa

The following are listed in order of distance from Yosemite's Arch Rock Entrance (see map, p.152).

Indian Flat RV Park 9988 Hwy-140, 8 miles west of Arch Rock Entrance ☎209/379-2339, ⊛www.indianflatrvpark.com; 1400ft; 50 sites. The nearest hookups to Yosemite Valley are at this simple RV park with a separate and reasonably shady tent area, fire rings, picnic tables and a clean shower block ($3 for non-guests). Rates start at $25 for two tenters, going up to $37 for power and water, and $42 for waste hookup.

McCabe Flat Turn off Hwy-140 near the Briceburg Information Center, 20 miles west of Arch Rock Entrance ☎916/941-3101; 1200ft, 14 sites. The handiest of three first-come-first-served campgrounds situated at around 1000ft along the Merced River, each with pit toilets and river water that must be treated. They're all accessed by a fairly rough road along a former trackbed of the Yosemite Valley Railroad (1906–45): *McCabe Flat* is 2.3 miles along, *Willow Placer* (10 sites) 3.6 miles and *Railroad Flat* (9 sites) 4.5 miles. $10.

Yosemite-Mariposa KOA 6323 Hwy-140, Midpines, 6 miles east of Mariposa, 25.7 miles west of Arch Rock Entrance ☎1-800/562-9391 or 209/966-2201, ⊛www.yosemitekoa.com; 2600ft; 80 sites. Full facility RV-oriented site with a separate woodland tent area, laundry, outdoor swimming pool, on-site catch-and-release lake fishing and convenience store. Basic tent sites are $40, full hookup costs $50, there are log cabins (②), some with decks overlooking the lake, and some relatively luxurious lodge rooms (⑤) sleeping up to six. Closed mid-Oct to Feb.

South of Yosemite: Hwy-41, Oakhurst and Fish Camp

The following are listed in order of distance from Yosemite's South Entrance (see map, p.152).

Summerdale Sierra National Forest, 1.5 miles south of South Entrance and half a mile north of Fish Camp ℡1-877/444-6777, ⓦwww .Recreation.gov; 5000ft; 29 sites. Typically wooded site that takes the overflow when Wawona is full, and is consequently packed most summer weekends. Closed Nov–May. $20.

Nelder Grove Sierra National Forest, off Sky Ranch Rd, 9 miles east of Hwy-41, follow Road 632 which turns off Hwy-41 4 miles north of Oakhurst ℡559/877-2218; 5500ft; 7 sites. Primitive campground (no bookings) with stream water and vault toilet inconveniently sited along winding roads some distance from the park and close to a grove of sequoias threaded by a nature trail. Closed Nov–April. .

High Sierra RV Park 40389 Hwy-41, Oakhurst ℡559/683-7662, ⓦwww.highsierrarv.com; 2000ft; 126 sites. Compact RV park in the heart of Oakhurst with clean facilities, tent sites ($22, weekends $24) and electricity and water RV hookups ($34, weekends $36).

South of Yosemite: Bass Lake and the Sierra Vista Scenic Byway

The following are too distant to be useful bases for conveniently exploring Yosemite.

Clover Meadow Sierra Vista Scenic Byway ℡559/877-2218; 7000ft; 7 sites. Large and wonderfully sited campground (no reservations) with potable water and vault toilets. Nearby *Granite Creek* is also good and free. Closed Nov–May. Free.

Fresno Dome Sierra Vista Scenic Byway ℡559/877-2218; 6400ft; 15 sites. This simple campground makes a great base for a

moderately strenuous walk to the top of the exfoliated granite namesake. No water. Closed Nov–April. $17.

Lupine Road 222, Bass Lake ℡559/642-3212 or 1-877/444-6777, ⓦwww.Recreation.gov; 3400ft; 113 sites. Of the many campgrounds on the shores of Lake Bass, this one is best suited to campers. In summer, book well in advance, though no-shows are sometimes available at the Bass Lake Recreation Area office, 39900 Rd 222, on the lake's southwest side. Closed early Sept to late May. $25.

Sweetwater Mammoth Pool Road ℡1-877/444-6777, ⓦwww.Recreation.gov; 3800ft; 10 sites. Lovely, reservable, family-oriented campground away from the lake but beside a creek that has great swimming. There's potable running water, and vault toilets, but yellowjacket wasps can be a problem in midsummer. Nearby *Placer* is equally nice. Closed Oct–May. $17.

South of Yosemite: Mono Hot Spring and the John Muir Wilderness

The following are too distant to be useful bases for conveniently exploring Yosemite

Badger Flat Kaiser Pass ℡559/855-5355; 8000ft; 15 sites. First-come-first-served site with a suitably remote feel. Vault toilets but no water. Closed Nov–May. $18.

Jackass Meadow Florence Lake ℡1-877/444-6777, ⓦwww.Recreation.gov; 7200ft; 44 sites. Relaxed campground located unnervingly below the Florence Lake dam. Reservable. Closed Nov–May. $18.

Mono Hot Spring 12 miles east of Huntington Lake ℡1-877/444-6777, ⓦwww.Recreation .gov; 6600ft; 26 sites. Forest campground beside the San Joaquin River and next to *Mono Hot Spring Resort*. Closed late Sept to early June. $18.

Portal Forebay Kaiser Pass ℡559/855-5355; 7200ft; 11 sites. Beautiful first-come-first-served site with vault toilets and access to lake water. Closed Nov–May. $16.

Rancheria Hwy-168 near Huntington Lake ℡1-877/444-6777, ⓦwww.Recreation.gov; 7000ft. Large and popular campground; some sites have lake views. $20.

Eating and drinking

W ith the notable exception of the *Ahwahnee Dining Room* and the *Mountain Room Restaurant*, **eating** in Yosemite is more a function than a pleasure. Dishes at the better places can be tasty, but food, whether in restaurants or in the grocery stores, is around twenty percent more expensive inside the park than out.

By judicious selection, even those on a tight budget can get by. The cheapest option is to make your own meals, buying food outside the park – Mariposa (see p.161) has the closest large supermarket – or in some of Yosemite's **grocery stores**. The largest and most varied is at Yosemite Village, and there are narrower selections at Curry Village, Wawona, Crane Flat and Tuolumne Meadows (summer only). You can also order **box lunches** from some of the park hotels by calling the front desk the night before.

There are enough restaurants and snack bars in Yosemite Valley to satisfy most needs, and many of the more upscale restaurants serve alcohol. Most of the valley's real **drinking** action, though, takes place in the *Mountain Room Lounge* at Yosemite Lodge, with outdoor possibilities at the *Pizza Deck and Curry Village Bar* in Curry Village, and more refined imbibing at the *Ahwahnee Bar*.

We've listed all eating options within the park and a selection of the best places in the surrounding **gateway towns** of Groveland, Mariposa, Oakhurst and Lee Vining, which all have plenty of good restaurants charging reasonable prices, as well as a smattering of bars. Note that most places reduce their **opening hours** in shoulder seasons, and sometimes close altogether in winter. Even in summer few places serve much later than 9pm.

Inside the park

Yosemite Village and The Ahwahnee

🏃 **Ahwahnee Bar** *The Ahwahnee*; shuttle stop 3. Intimate piano bar where you can sit at the bar, at tables out on the terrace, or in the cosy recess at one end and try one of their draught beers and microbrews, or indulge in something more sophisticated. Attentive bar staff will rustle up one of their classic Martinis ($15), a classy Manhattan ($10), or perhaps something from their selection of single malts (mostly $13–26), Cognacs, Armagnacs and ports. Light meals such as

Caesar salads ($10), antipasto plates for two ($23) and wild boar chilli con carne ($10) are served, to a backdrop of live music most Friday and Saturday nights, usually something subdued. Daily 11am–11pm; in the morning (7–11am) it operates as an espresso bar.

🏃 **Ahwahnee Dining Room** *The Ahwahnee* ☎209/372-1489; shuttle stop 3. Quite simply one of the most beautiful restaurants in the US, designed in baronial style with 34ft-high ceilings of exposed sugar pine beams, rustic iron chandeliers, and floor-to-ceiling leaded windows that look out into

Supermarkets near Yosemite

If you're planning to **self-cater** while in Yosemite, or even just need picnic supplies and snacks, you can save money (and ensure more choice) by doing your grocery shopping outside the park. The best bets nearby are the Pioneer Market in Mariposa (see p.161) and one of the large supermarkets in Oakhurst. For details of stores inside the park, see Chapter 12.

the forest. Tables graced with starched white tablecloths and tall candles provide the setting for what is by far the best food in Yosemite (appetizers $14–17, main courses $27–48). Dinner might consist of an Atlantic salmon terrine with dill and crème fraîche, or an endive and watercress salad followed by hot seared Ahi tuna with shoyu butter and wasabi, all washed down with something striking from the extensive and not-too-pricey California-heavy wine list.

Earlier in the day, expect simpler dishes such as a breakfast wrap ($16) or eggs Benedict ($18) for breakfast, then a Portobello mushroom and sun-dried tomato roll ($12) or a smoked duck Caesar salad ($15) for lunch. The Sunday brunch ($44) is particularly stupendous.

Dress casual during the day. At dinner men need long pants, a collared shirt and closed shoes, and women should be similarly smartly attired.

A number of annual events are also hosted here, usually booked out way in advance: see pp.196–197 for details of the Chefs' Holidays (Jan & Feb), Vintners' Holidays (Nov & Dec), and the Bracebridge Dinner (Dec). Regular opening hours are daily: breakfast 7–10.30am, lunch 11.30am–3pm, dinner 5.30–9pm (reservations essential), Sun brunch 7am–3pm.

Degnan's Café Yosemite Village; shuttle stop 4. Fair selection of ready-made sandwiches plus smoothies and filter coffee. There are newspaper boxes outside and internet kiosks within. June to mid-Sept daily 11am–6pm.

🏃 **Degnan's Deli Yosemite Village; shuttle stop 4.** Some of the best take-out food in Yosemite Valley with bowls of soup ($3–4) and chilli ($4–5), and massive made-on-the-spot sandwiches, burritos and salads for around $7, all big enough for two small appetites – try the pastrami served with onion, Swiss cheese, lettuce, tomato and mustard. There's also a good selection of snacks and drinks, along with

a more limited supply of groceries. Daily 7am–5pm.

Degnan's Loft Yosemite Village; shuttle stop 4. When it's too cold or wet for the Curry Village Pizza Patio, head for this cosy spot for build-your-own pizzas (medium $14–18; large $17–22), and a selection of soups and salads, plus draught beers and bottled wines. Mid-April to June, Sept & Oct Mon–Fri 5–9pm, Sat & Sun noon–9pm; July & Aug daily noon–9pm.

Village Grill Yosemite Village; shuttle stop 2. Fast food Yosemite-style, with the likes of bacon cheeseburgers ($7), garden burgers ($7), and burger-fries-and-drink combos ($9–10) to eat out on the deck. April–Oct daily 11am–5pm.

Yosemite Lodge

Mountain Room Lounge Shuttle stop 8. Yosemite Valley's only straightforward drinking bar that's good anytime for a few beers, but especially convivial in cooler or inclement weather when everyone huddles around the huge circular central fireplace heated by a big brazier. Seats outside in warmer weather are perfect for escaping the continual sports TV inside. There's full bar service along with light snacks (until 9pm). Mon–Fri 4.30–11pm, Sat & Sun noon–11pm.

🏃 **Mountain Room Restaurant ☎209/372-1281; shuttle stop 8.** Second only to the *Ahwahnee Dining Room* in Yosemite's culinary hierarchy, the *Mountain Room* offers semi-formal dining in a more modern setting with huge picture windows that afford an outstanding view of Yosemite Falls from nearly every seat: dine early outside midsummer or you'll miss the view. A short menu is offered which includes soup ($4.95–7.25), then perhaps an appetizer of smoked trout with apple horseradish ($10), then prime rib ($30), followed by a flour-free chocolate almond torte ($7). There's also a three-course fixed menu ($35), a kids' menu and a decent wine and cocktail list. Daily 5.30–9pm.

Yosemite Lodge Food Court Shuttle stop 8.
Bright and cheerful self-serve café/
restaurant that sees the bulk of the dining
action around *Yosemite Lodge*. It serves a
full range of cold and cooked breakfasts
($4–8), muffins, Danish pastries and
espresso, plus lunches and dinners that
range from a grilled chicken sandwich, pizza
or gyro platter (all $7) to pasta and
meatballs ($9) or chicken, vegetables and
rice ($9). There is some outdoor seating
where assorted small forest creatures will try
to steal your meal. Open daily: breakfast
6.30–11am, lunch and dinner 11.30am–
9pm, coffee and snacks served all day.

Curry Village

Coffee Corner Shuttle stops 14 & 20. Simple
coffee bar serving light breakfasts, bagels,
Danish pastries, muffins, moderately
palatable espresso coffees and ice cream
starting from $2. April–Nov & winter
weekends daily 6am–10pm.

Pavilion Buffet Shuttle stops 14 & 20.
Attractive wood-panelled cafeteria
decorated with old photos and aquatints of
Camp Curry and serving all-you-can-eat
breakfast and dinner. Breakfast ($11.50) is
particularly good value with plenty of fresh
fruit, juices, eggs, bacon, hash browns,
breakfast burritos, waffles, pancakes,
French toast, yoghurt, muffins and coffee.
Dinner ($15.25) suffers a little from over-
cooked vegetables and sloppy preparation
but you can still fill up on salads, build-your-
own tacos, chicken, fried steak, corn, chow
mien, simple pasta dishes, cake, fruit
cobbler and sodas. Buy a beer or wine at
the adjacent bar and carry it through. April–
Oct daily: breakfast 7–10am, dinner
5.30–8pm.

**Pizza Deck and Curry Village Bar Shuttle
stops 14 & 20.** Very much the place to
repair on a balmy evening after a hard day's
hiking with everyone sharing stories and
comparing experiences. Fight for an outdoor
table while you wait for a pretty decent
build-your-own pizza ($22 for 12 slices with
2 toppings), and maybe an elegant 23oz
schooner of quality draught beer ($8) or a
daiquiri, margarita or two ($7.60). Mid-April
to Nov daily noon–10pm; rest of year Fri
5–9pm & Sat noon–9pm.

Taqueria Shuttle stops 14 & 20. Hole-in-the-
wall take-out joint with deck seating and
simple menu of basic Tex-Mex concoctions.
Choose from a taco ($4), beef and bean
burritos ($5–6), or taco salad ($8.75) and a
selection of sodas. April–Sept daily
11am–5pm.

The rest of the park

Tuolumne Meadows Grill Tuolumne Meadows.
Basically a canvas-roofed shed containing
a take-out fast-food counter with outside
seating; reasonably good value, and
always popular with hungry hikers. Eggs,
bacon, hash browns and biscuits ($8.25)
are served until 11.30am, then it's
cheeseburgers ($5.50), grilled chicken
sandwiches ($7) and hot dogs ($5) until
closing. Filter coffee, soda and soft-freeze
ice cream are on offer all day, and the
Tuolumne Store, next door, sells a decent
range of groceries plus firewood, ice and
beer. Mid-June to late Sept daily
8am–6pm.

**Tuolumne Meadows Lodge Dining Room
Tuolumne Meadows ☎209/372-8413.** Family-
style tent dining room that mainly caters to
lodge guests but also serves non-guests
with hearty breakfasts, either continental
($6.25) or full ($10.25) with bacon, eggs and
pancakes. There's a choice of equally filling
dinners, from a cheeseburger ($10) to the
likes of pistachio-crusted trout ($19) and
New York steak ($31). Beer and wine are
served, and they'll also prepare box lunches
($10) if requested before 8pm the night
before. Mid-June to mid-Sept daily:
breakfast 7–9am, dinner (reservations
essential) 5.50pm & 8pm.

**Wawona Dining Room Wawona Hotel
☎209/375-1425.** White linen
tablecloths, candles, chunky silverware and
uniformed waitresses in a grand century-
old room lend the *Dining Room* a
semi-formal atmosphere, though neither
the food nor service is particularly special.
Still, the decor and views across the lawns
are appealing and you can dine reasonably
well during the day on the likes of soup
($4), chicken alfredo, ratatouille, or a club
sandwich ($10). In the evening they request
smart attire and collared shirts while you
tuck into dishes such as pan-fried trout
($26) or baked halibut ($29) followed by
apple blueberry crisp ($8). In summer you
can eat on the broad veranda. Look out
too for the Lawn Barbecue on summer

Saturdays (late May to early Sept 5–7pm; no reservations; adults $20.25) where you eat from gingham tablecloths. April–Nov daily: breakfast 7.30–10am, lunch 11.30am–1.30pm, dinner 5.30–9pm (reservations advised), cocktails 5–9.30pm; Jan–March Fri, Sat & hols same hours.

White Wolf Lodge White Wolf, just off Hwy-120 East on the way to Tuolumne Meadows ✆ 209/372-8416. This simple lodge serves large portions of good-value American food in rustic surroundings: at wooden tables on a broad veranda or, on those cool Sierra evenings, inside beside a roaring fire.

Standard breakfasts are available ($10) and the fixed-menu dinner ($23), which changes nightly, always comes with soup, salad, vegetables, rice or pasta and a roll. Expect the likes of grilled chicken lasagne or steak with sautéed mushrooms, though there's always a vegetarian dish, a short children's menu ($8), and the place is licensed for beer and wine sales. Guests can order box lunches ($6.50) and the adjacent store has ready-made sandwiches. Mid-June to mid-Sept daily: breakfast 7.30–9.30am, dinner (reservations essential) 6–8pm.

Outside the park

Northeast of Yosemite: Hwy-120 East and Lee Vining

Latte Da US-395 ✆ 760/647-6581. Organic espresso and tea, free wi-fi and a stack of local books to peruse. Late April–Oct daily 8am–5pm or later.

Nicely's US-395 in Lee Vining ✆ 760/647-6477. Great Fifties vinyl palace serving up reliable diner food to tourists and dedicated locals. All your favourites are there including a three-egg omelette ($9), jumbo burger and fries ($8), breaded steak ($13) and the obligatory slice of one of their many fruit pies ($4). Daily 6am–9pm (closed Tues & Wed in winter).

Tioga Pass Resort 2 miles east of Tioga Pass. Cosy wood-panelled diner with the usual range of egg and pancake breakfasts ($7–10), burgers and sandwiches ($8–12), and a superb line in fruit pies and cobblers made on the premises ($6). Late May to mid-Oct daily 7am–9pm.

Whoa Nellie Deli Tioga Gas Mart, corner of Hwy-120 East & US-395 ✆ 760/647 1088. The best quick food for miles around is served in this less than inspiring location, though in summer you can sit at tables outside. There's always a lively atmosphere and they dish up great tortilla soup, jambalaya ($13), fish tacos ($12), burgers and steaks, along with espresso coffees, microbrews and margaritas. There's also pizza by the slice, free wi-fi, and on Thursday and Sunday evenings in July and August there's usually live music outside. April–Oct daily 8am–9pm.

Northwest of Yosemite: Hwy-120 West and Groveland

Café Charlotte 18959 Hwy-120 West, Groveland ✆ 209/962-6455. Excellent little restaurant where the casual atmosphere belies a serious approach to the quality of the food. There's everything from pasta (including vegan and kids' dishes) to chicken Jerusalem (with artichokes and mushrooms) and succulent steaks (all $16–25) plus lip-smacking desserts. Licensed and BYO. Summer daily 11.30am–3pm and 6–10pm; winter Thurs–Sun 6–10pm.

Cocina Michoacana 18370 Hwy-120 West, Groveland ✆ 209/962-6651. Authentic and low-priced Mexican food, specializing in dishes from immediately west of Mexico City. Ten bucks will get you a great breakfast of perhaps scrambled eggs with strips of steak or one of the daily lunch specials, and later in the day they serve a full range of Mexican favourites including great fajitas ($21–25 for two) and melt-in-your-mouth breaded shrimps ($13). Daily 10am–9pm.

Iron Door 18761 Main St, Groveland ✆ 209/962-6244. Head into the dim world of what is reliably claimed as one of the oldest saloons in California, dating back to 1852. It was originally a general mercantile store and later served as a post office, but has been a dedicated bar since 1937 and comes festooned with paraphernalia on the walls, baseball caps and dollar bills pinned to the ceiling, and a pool table in the corner. Most weekends, as you sit at the bar or in booths enjoying one of the microbrews, there's some kind of live music. The saloon may be the star, but this is also a good place to eat, with the *Iron Door Grill* serving the likes of chicken Portabello ravioli ($19), ribeye steak ($24) or salmon teriyaki ($21), all nicely prepared and presented. Daily 11am–9pm (bar to 1am or later).

Mountain Sage Café 18653 Hwy-120 West, Groveland Occupying a corner of the Mountain Sage store, this great café is devoted to great espresso, bagels and fine breakfast quiche. Free wi-fi. Mon–Sat 7am–5pm, Sun 8am–4pm.

Stan's "Que" Outdoor Grill 18745 Back St, Groveland ☎209/962-0806. Convivial outdoor barbecue with meats pit-grilled over almond wood. Sink your teeth into a tri tip dinner ($19), half a chicken ($15) or an equally juicy burger or sandwich ($8). Fill up on salads and corn-on-the-cob, and wash it all down with bottled beer or sodas. May–Oct Sat 11am–4pm, Sun 11am–6pm.

Two Guys Pizza Pies 18955 Ferretti Rd, Groveland ☎209/962-4897. Basic sit-in or take-out pizzeria with tasty gourmet and traditional pizzas ($18 for one feeding 2–3), plus microbrews. Daily 11am–10pm (closes 9pm in winter).

Victorian Room *Groveland Hotel*, **18767 Hwy-120 West, Groveland** ☎209/962-4000. The best restaurant in town (and for miles around), decorated in keeping with the rest of the *Groveland Hotel*, and featuring a seasonally changing menu plus nightly chef's specials. Dishes might include crab cakes with cilantro and caper sauce, and honey-glazed baby back pork ribs. Expect to pay $45–50 for three courses plus something from their massive wine list – try the red or white wine flight of four samples ($16). Reservations suggested in summer. May–Oct daily 5.30–9pm; Nov–April generally Thurs–Sun same hours.

West of Yosemite: Hwy-140, El Portal and Midpines

Café at the Bug *Yosemite Bug Rustic Mountain Resort*, **Midpines**. Superb-value licensed café with the emphasis on quality food at a good price. Wholesome breakfasts ($4.50–8), packed lunches ($6.50) and dinners ($8–18) are served to all-comers, so if you're staying anywhere

around Mariposa and don't mind the slightly frenetic hostel atmosphere, it's definitely worth the drive. Expect the likes of slow-roasted Cajun pork or baked trout fillet with butter pecan sauce, each with salad roll, rice and vegetables. Good microbrews on tap and a deck to sit out and knock it back. Also free wi-fi and internet access. Daily: breakfast 7–10am, lunch 7am–3pm, dinner 6–9pm, bar until around 10.30pm.

Yosemite View Lodge 11136 Hwy-140, El Portal, 2 miles west of Arch Rock Entrance ☎209/379-2681. One lodge with two restaurants: the family-oriented pizza parlour with traditional and speciality combinations at reasonable prices, plus the more upscale *Woody's*, with a New Orleans slant that extends to jambalaya, blackened chicken pasta and red beans, rice and Andouille sausage. Lunch dishes around $13; dinner $15–23. Daily: lunch 11.30am–2pm, dinner 5–10pm or later.

West of Yosemite: Mariposa

49er Club 5026 Hwy-140 ☎209/742-4000. A dark bar with table football, pool and a line of bar stools. Daily noon–midnight or later.

Happy Burger 5120 Hwy-140 at 12th St ☎209/966-2719. An enormous array of good, cheap diner food – breakfast burrito ($5), tuna melt ($6), teriyaki chicken salad ($7) – to take out or eat in at formica booths. There's a fine jukebox and the entire place is decorated with tragic Seventies album covers. Free wi-fi. Daily 5.30am–8pm.

High Country Café Corner Hwy-140 & Hwy-49. Health-food café with sandwiches for vegetarians and omnivores ($6–7) along with salads, burritos, fruit smoothies and filter coffee. There's also a health-food store next door (Mon–Fri 9am–6pm, Sat 9am–5pm) offering good bread, organic fruit and goodies in bulk bins that are great for making up trail mix. Mon–Sat 9am–3pm.

Mariposa Pizza Factory 5005 Hwy-140 ☎209/966-3112. Basic eat-in and take-out pizza joint with traditional toppings as well as gourmet combos in five different sizes. Filling and fairly cheap, with something around $15 usually sufficient for two. Daily 11am–10pm.

Savoury's 5034 Hwy-140 ☎209/966-7677. The pick of Mariposa's restaurants, offering a relaxed atmosphere with a touch of class. Modern decor of bare concrete floors and painted block walls hung with striking Yosemite prints sets the tone for a delectable menu of dishes such as chipotle chicken ($17), roasted garlic cream scallops ($22), and spinach and pine nut pasta ($16), perhaps followed by chocolate bread pudding ($5). Wine is available by the bottle or glass. Daily except Wed 5–10pm.

Sugar Pine Café 5038 Hwy-140 ☎209/742 7793. Red leatherette booths and diamond-tiled floors give a retro feel to this quality diner where everything is made from scratch, including great baked goods – apple turnovers, scones, blackberry pie and German chocolate cake. There's a short menu of breakfasts, burgers and a handful of dinner mains. Tues–Sat 7am–8.30pm, Sun 7am–3pm.

West of Yosemite: Merced

Café Cinema 661 W Main St ☎209/722-2811. Retro salt and pepper shakers behind the open kitchen match the lime green counter stools in this quality breakfast and lunch diner offering the usual range of burgers and sandwiches, plus Mexican specials. Daily 7am–3pm.

La Nita's 1327 18th St at T ☎209/723-2291. Authentic Mexican dining about ten blocks from the bus station offering all the expected south-of-the-border staples along with *menudo* (tripe and hominy soup) and *albondigas* (meatballs), both $8. Lunch specials change daily and there are hearty combination plates for under $10. Mon 9am–3pm, Tues–Sat 9am–9.30pm, Sun 8am–9.30pm.

Wired 450 W 18th St at Canal ☎209/386-0206. Downtown internet café handy for the Transpo Center, with good coffee, muffins, bagels and fast internet access ($5/hr). Mon–Fri 6.30am–2pm.

South of Yosemite: Fish Camp, Oakhurst and around

The Grind 40879 Hwy-41, a mile north of Oakhurst ☎559/683-8815. This local java joint with mismatched chairs, old tables and free wi-fi makes a relaxed setting for digging into breakfast burritos, toothsome muffins, sandwiches, cakes and good espresso at modest prices. Also operates as a bar, often with live music at weekends. Mon–Sat 6.30am–midnight, Sun 6.30am–10pm.

Jackalope's Bar & Grill *Tenaya Lodge*, **1122 Hwy-41, Fish Camp** ☎559/683-6555. Probably the pick of the restaurants at *Tenaya Lodge* (see p.178) where you can sit outside (around the brazier if there's a chill in the air) and order from a menu laden with soups, salads, sandwiches, burgers, pizza and pasta dishes (mostly around $12). Next door, the *Sierra Restaurant* is a little more formal and pricier, and the classy Embers satisfies the more refined palate. Daily 7am–11pm.

La Cabaña 32762 Road 222 in North Fork, 8 miles southeast of Oakhurst ☎559/877-3311. A nondescript shack serving excellent and authentic Mexican meals and burgers, most for under $8. Tues–Sat 10.30am–3pm & 4.30–7.30pm, plus longer hours for takeaways.

The Narrow Gauge Inn 48571 Hwy-41, Fish Camp ☎559/683-6446. Fine dining in a candlelit setting warmed by a log fire makes this one of the picks on the south side of the park. Start by dipping sourdough into a rich fondue and continue with charbroiled swordfish or filet mignon. Main courses are around $30–35 and, though it's licensed, you can bring your own wine (corkage $15). Mid-April to mid-Oct Wed–Sun 5.30–9pm.

South of Yosemite: Mono Hot Spring and the John Muir Wilderness

Bob's Blue Sky Café 41781 Hwy-168. Good espresso and wi-fi café also serving breakfast. Daily 7am–5pm.

South of Yosemite: Fresno

Chicken Pie Shop 861 E Olive Ave ☎559/237-5042. This busy diner is locally famed for its chicken (and excellent fruit) pies at bargain prices. Mon–Fri 7am–8pm, Sat & Sun 7am–3pm.

Java City 2134 Kern St Downtown spot for good java, soups and bagels. Daily 7am–4pm.

Roger Rocka's Dinner Theater 1226 N Wishon, Fresno ☎559/266-9494, ⓦwww.rogerrockas .com. Broadway-style shows in this 250-seat theatre are preceded either by a sumptuous buffet (Wed, Thurs & Sun matinee; $45 all up) or a table-service meal (Fri & Sat; $48). Closed Mon & Tues.

Sequoia Brewing Company 777 E Olive Ave
℡ 559/264-5521. There's always plenty
happening at this brewpub (with eleven
excellent tap beers), including free live
music (Wed, Fri & Sat). Good-value lunches
and dinners extend to brick-oven pizzas,
pasta dishes and salads. Mon–Thurs
11.30am–10pm, Fri & Sat 11.30am–
midnight, Sun 9am–9pm.

Veni Vidi Vici 1116 N Fulton St ℡ 559/266-5510.
For something special visit this dim and
moody restaurant (with a patio for outdoor
dining) for dishes like Vietnamese baby
spinach salad ($8) and juniper berry pork
chop ($28). After 10pm it becomes a lively
bar. Tues–Sun 5.30pm–midnight.

South of Yosemite: Visalia

Brewbakers 219 E Main St ℡ 559/627-2739.
Dine among the polished steel and brass
tanks of this lively brewpub, which serves
tempting burgers, salads and thick, chewy
pizza, all for under $10. There's often live

music to encourage you to sample their half-
dozen brews. Daily 11.30am–10pm or later.

Café 225 225 W Main St ℡ 559/733-2967. A
modern bistro and tapas bar with an
eclectic menu that features artichoke fritters
($5.50), steak frites ($17) and prosciutto and
roasted garlic pizza ($12). Mon–Sat
11am–10pm.

Tazzaria 208 W Main St ℡ 559/732-5282. Lively
daytime spot for great lunches, cakes,
espresso and free wi-fi. Mon–Wed
7am–3pm, Thurs–Sat 7am–9pm.

The Vintage Press 216 N Willis St
℡ 559/733-3033. Serving California
continental cuisine, this fine restaurant has
ranked as one of the best in the San Joaquin
Valley for over four decades. Succumb to
wild mushrooms in puff pastry with cognac,
followed by red snapper with toasted
almonds and capers and finally a dessert
and coffee, all for around $55 a head – or
much more if you explore the vast and
wonderful wine list. Mon–Sat 10am–2pm &
5.30–10pm, Sun 10am–2pm & 5–9pm.

EATING AND DRINKING | Outside the park

⑪

Organized events and entertainment

With boundless opportunities for sightseeing, hiking and other outdoor pursuits, you'll have little trouble keeping busy, but your experience can be greatly enhanced by taking advantage of some of the park's organized activities and entertainment, the majority of which are in the form of **ranger programmes** and include walks, talks and campfires. Put on by the Park Service (often in conjunction with the park concessionaire, the DNC or the Yosemite Conservancy), most are informative, fun and free. The bulk of what's available takes place in Yosemite Valley, but the rest of the park isn't ignored, with events in Wawona, Tuolumne Meadows, at Glacier Point, and even at a couple of the popular campgrounds.

Activities vary with the seasons, with most happening from June until the end of September. There are also **films**, **slide presentations** and **musical performances**, which generally take place at night.

Yosemite can be a great place for **kids**, what with all the adventuring, camping and swimming to be done – just don't expect them to thank you for dragging them on long treks. Most of the standard ranger programmes are suitable for children – star gazing, or learning about bears, for example – but there are also programmes designed especially for young families such as campfire sing-alongs, storytelling and even kids' art classes. Children might also enjoy the hands-on and basket-weaving sections of the Yosemite Museum (see p.63) and can become either a Junior Ranger or Little Cub (see box, p.198). **In winter**, the Badger Pass Ski Area is a great place for families, with an extensive kids' programme (see box, p.148).

The best source of current **information** for all these programmes is the *Yosemite Guide* newspaper, though you might also go direct to the *Yosemite Lodge* and Curry Village tour desks, and keep your eye open for bulletin boards as well. The park concessionaire's website (ⓦwww.yosemitepark.com) also has full details of events.

Daytime programmes

From early in the morning until the sun goes down there's an unending array of organized activities to keep visitors entertained, particularly in Yosemite Valley. The core of the daytime ranger programmes is the general **ranger walks**, though variations include specific **photography walks**, a **Historic Ahwahnee Tour** and some free art classes out in the meadows.

Children are equally well catered for in the valley, though in the rest of the park you'll be best served in Wawona where the popular horse-drawn stage rides are run (see p.98).

Mostly for adults

Art Classes Mid-April to Oct Tues–Sat 10am–2pm; free. Yosemite can be so overwhelming that the sheer grandeur obliterates the small beauties. One way to re-focus on particular elements is to spend time painting – waterfalls and dogwood blooms in spring; the lazy serenity of the Merced River in summer; and the colours of the oaks and maples in fall. The Yosemite Art and Education Center (Yosemite Village, shuttle stop 2; ☏ 209/372-1442) runs informal outdoor art classes for adults in a range of media – watercolour, acrylic, pen and ink, etc – with each class led by a visiting artist. For the current schedule go to Ⓦ www .yosemiteconservancy.org/ and also check out Ⓦ www.yosemiteart.blogspot .com. Bring your own art supplies, or buy at the Yosemite Art and Education Center. Genuinely interested children aged 10 and over are welcome at the adult classes.

Historic Ahwahnee Tour All year Mon, Wed & Fri at 11am; free. A chance to spend an hour wandering around Yosemite's grandest building learning something of its history and admiring its fine furnishings.

Mariposa Grove Nature Walk June–Aug generally daily 10am & 2pm; free. An hour-long stroll through the big trees with a ranger.

Parsons Memorial Lodge Summer Series Mid-July to late Aug Sat & Sun 2pm; free. This series of one-hour seminars in a historic lodge in Tuolumne Meadows encompasses a broad sweep, from storytelling walks to slide presentations on the cycles of stream flow along the Tuolumne River. Allow time for the walk (30min) from the Lembert Dome parking lot or the Tuolumne Meadows Visitor Center.

Photography Walks All year; prices vary. The Ansel Adams Gallery offers a wide-ranging slate of photography walks and courses. See "Photography" (p.41) for full details.

Ranger Walks All year; check Yosemite Guide for times; free. Spend an hour and a half with a ranger, perhaps learning about Yosemite's first people, wandering to Mirror Lake or exploring Yosemite Valley's geology. Every walk is different and depends largely on where you are. Look out too for the twilight strolls making the best of the golden hour, usually passing some great photo ops. Most walks take place in Yosemite Valley but there are less frequent walks in Tuolumne Meadows and at Glacier Point.

Yosemite Conservancy field seminars April–Dec; prices vary. The nonprofit Yosemite Conservancy (see p.45) runs a series of small-group outdoor education "field seminars", predominantly in summer. Mostly two to four days long, they cover a wide range of topics from alpine botany and Miwok basketry to photographing moonbows and backpacking trips. Prices are typically $200–300, and some seminars have reserved campgrounds and/or hotel rooms at an additional cost. You'll find full seminar listings on Ⓦ www.yosemite conservancy.org.

Mostly for kids

Arts & Crafts see Yosemite Guide for times; free. The Yosemite Art and Education Center (Yosemite Village, shuttle stop 2; ☏ 209/372-1442) runs dedicated outdoor classes aimed at introducing budding artists aged 8 and up to sketching, watercolour and charcoal drawing. Under 12s must bring an adult.

Ranger Ned's Big Adventure May to early Sept; see Yosemite Guide for times; free. An entertaining and fast-paced hour-long interactive play following the tribulations of the novice ranger. There are typically morning and afternoon shows Thursday to Sunday at the amphitheatres at either Curry Village or the Lower River (opposite *Housekeeping Camp*).

Wee Wild Ones All year 3–7 weekly, check Yosemite Guide for times; free. Though aimed specifically at those six and under, parents are encouraged to participate in these 45-minute sessions using games and stories to learn about Yosemite wildlife and geology. Held at the outdoor amphitheatres in *Yosemite Lodge* and Curry Village when warm enough, otherwise by the huge fireplace in the Great Lounge at *The Ahwahnee*.

In the off season, Yosemite's concessionaire pulls out all the stops to fill the hotels. The well-heeled are lured to high-end dinners and wine tastings, with many staying in great comfort at *The Ahwahnee*, where the bulk of events are held. In addition, there are end-of-winter celebrations at the Badger Pass Ski Area, and a couple of music festivals just outside the park.

January
Chefs' Holidays Early Jan to early Feb; reservations ☏801/559-4884, ⓦwww .yosemitepark.com. Put off that post-Christmas diet and visit gastronomic heaven for a couple of days. Some of America's top chefs lead cooking demonstrations, conduct behind-the-scenes kitchen tours and finish off with a fabulous five-course gala dinner ($249 by itself) in the *Ahwahnee Dining Room*. Two-person packages range from $766 including two nights at *Yosemite Lodge* and the gala dinner, up to $1275 with three nights at *The Ahwahnee*.

February
Nordic Holiday Race ☏209/372-1000. California's oldest cross-country ski race takes place at Badger Pass on the last weekend of February or the first in March. The Saturday Nordic race is followed by a Telemark race in the afternoon, followed by a big party and a Sunday freestyle race to Glacier Point and back.

March
Spring Fest ☏209/372-1000. A traditional winter carnival at Badger Pass on one of the last Saturdays of the ski season (usually late March or early April). Dual slalom racing, costume contests, cross-country skiing, obstacle course races and more.

May
Strawberry Music Festival ☏209/984-8630, ⓦwww.strawberrymusic.com. Camp Mather, just outside the park near Hetch Hetchy, plays host to this three-day, start-of-summer festival of bluegrass, swing, rock, blues and gospel. Pretty much everyone camps on site, making for a celebratory atmosphere. It takes place over Memorial Day weekend (the last in May) and is important enough to lure relatively big names: Michael Franti, Lucinda Williams and Lyle Lovett in recent years. Call to book

Evening programmes

Few come to Yosemite expecting more from their **evening entertainment** than a few stories and a beer or two around the campfire, but there's actually plenty more to do when night falls. Much of the action in Yosemite Valley is concentrated around the amphitheatres at Curry Village and *Yosemite Lodge*, where a full **evening programme** of talks, slide shows and films takes place. At Yosemite Village the Valley Visitor Center Theater is put to good use for a series of **live performances**, mostly for a small fee.

Outside the valley, the eternal mainstay is the **Old Fashioned Campfire**, an hour-long talk around a raging campfire that takes place most nights in summer (and weekends in spring and fall), while the *Wawona Hotel* lounge plays host to pianist Tom Bopp and his "**Vintage Songs of Yosemite**" (which you can also catch in Yosemite Valley during the summer months).

as far in advance as you can and expect to pay $190 for three days including camping. There's a repeat performance in fall.

August
Tuolumne Meadows Poetry Festival Usually third weekend; free. Local poets and musicians get together at Parsons Memorial Lodge in Tuolumne Meadows for entertaining morning (Sat & Sun 10–11.30am), afternoon (Sat & Sun 2–3.30pm) and evening (Sat 7.30–10pm) sessions. Allow half an hour to walk from Lembert Dome parking lot or Tuolumne Meadows' visitor centre.

September
Strawberry Music Festival ☎209/984-8630, ⓦwww.strawberrymusic.com. The end-of-summer equivalent of the May festival (see opposite) takes place over Labor Day weekend (the first in Sept).

November
Vintners' Holidays Early Nov to early Dec; reservations ☎801/559-4884, ⓦwww .yosemitepark.com. As fall turns into winter *The Ahwahnee* puts on these two- and three-day wine appreciation seminars with panel discussions and tastings led by industry experts. Several top wineries are represented and there's a last-night, five-course, candlelit dinner where you can dine with the winemakers in the *Ahwahnee Dining Room*. Two-person packages at *Yosemite Lodge* (two nights $766, three nights $900) and *The Ahwahnee* (two nights $1106, three nights $1275) include tastings and the dinner. Gala dinner-only tickets cost $249.

December
Bracebridge Dinners Dec 13–26; reservations ☎801/559-4884, ⓦwww .yosemitepark.com. Christmas at *The Ahwahnee* centres on these four-hour, seven-course feasts held in the *Dining Room*, which is decked out to look like a seventeenth-century English manor as described in Washington Irving's novel *Squire Bracebridge*. There's much song and revelry with staff dressed in period costume and guests in tuxedos and ball gowns. Two-night accommodation packages for two, including the dinner and a gift, go for around $1000 at *Yosemite Lodge*, over $1700 at *The Ahwahnee*. Dinner-only tickets go for $425.

Theatre shows

All the following shows take place in the **Valley Visitor Center Theater**: reserve through any tour desk in the park (☎209/372-1240) or buy a ticket at the auditorium half an hour in advance. Check *Yosemite Guide* for current schedules.

John Muir stories Mid-May to Sept 2–3 weekly 8pm; adults $8, kids 5–12 $4. A collection of fun one-man shows featuring the well-honed talents of actor Lee Stetson, who's been impersonating John Muir since 1982 Muir's entertaining and inspiring adventures are explored through three different performances. In summer, "Conversations with a Tramp" explores Muir's conservationist philosophy and his lifelong battle to defend his beloved Yosemite; "Among the Animals" follows his encounters with wild animals in the Sierra and Alaska; and "The Spirit of John Muir" relates Muir's wild adventures. These shows last around ninety minutes and are recommended for ages 8 and older.

Return to Balance: A Climber's Journey Check *Yosemite Guide* for details; adults $8, kids 5–12 $4. Stunning shots of Yosemite and brilliant rock climbing photography are the highlights of this video, presented by rock climbing superstar Ron Kauk, who views rock climbing as a way of life and a means to discover the beauty and mystery of nature. Suitable for ages 8 and older.

Junior Ranger Programme

The free *Yosemite Guide* usually contains a page of activities to keep the little ones entertained, but for something more structured, enrol them in the summertime **Junior Ranger Programme** (geared towards ages 7–13), designed to bring the sheer scale of Yosemite down to something tangible to the young mind. To become a Yosemite Junior Ranger (and earn the Junior Ranger patch) you'll need to attend a guided programme with a ranger, pick up a bag of litter, and complete an educational booklet ($3.50). Younger kids (aged 3–6) can earn the **Little Cubs** button by completing their own self-guided booklet ($3).

Both booklets are available from visitor centre bookstores around the park and from the **Nature Center at Happy Isles** (see p.70), which is specifically set up to introduce children and their parents to what's out there alongside the trails. Alternatively, undertake some amateur botanising with the Junior Ranger page in the *Yosemite Guide* paper.

Vintage Songs of Yosemite weekly in summer; free. Tom Bopp brings his Wawona show (see below) to Yosemite Valley one night a week and throws in a re-creation of the Firefall (see box, p.70).

Other evening activities

Evening Programmes All year, mostly 8pm; free. During the warmer months the amphitheatres at *Yosemite Lodge*, Curry Village and the *Lower Pines* campground are usually packed for these hour-long talks and slide shows which might cover topics as varied as early twentieth-century Yosemite through the eyes of a Buffalo Soldier, the secret life of bats, or the Firefall (see box, p.70). In winter they take place at *Yosemite Lodge* and start around 7pm.

LeConte Memorial Lodge Late May to Sept Fri–Sun; free. Yosemite Valley-based evening programmes that are a little more academic than those elsewhere in the park and might include a presentation or talk by some luminary: check *Yosemite Guide* for details.

Starry Skies Over Yosemite June–Sept 8pm or 9pm; adults & kids $5, families $20. Yosemite's policy of using minimal lighting makes for brilliant starry skies even in relatively populated Yosemite Valley. Wander out into the meadow, lie down and listen to the tales, which mostly depend on the interests of the ranger involved – celestial navigation, native folklore, constellations, distant galaxies, and so forth. Starry Skies typically takes place three times a week in Yosemite and once a week in Wawona: check *Yosemite Guide* for details. Stargazing walks also take place in Tuolumne Meadows (usually free).

Vintage Songs of Yosemite Typically April–Oct Tues–Sat; Nov–March some weekends; free. Tom Bopp plays the piano and sings old songs in the lounge at the *Wawona Hotel*, occasionally accompanied by a Yosemite-oriented slide show. For more details see p.98.

Shopping

W hen you're looking for that perfect Yosemite souvenir, you'll find numerous places where you can avail yourself of a "Go Climb a Rock!" T-shirt or Half Dome paperweight. Though no **shopping** paradise, Yosemite is far better supplied than most national parks, and you can satisfy most practical needs, including groceries, books and clothing, as well as hiking and camping essentials.

The majority of shops are in Yosemite Valley, with few found elsewhere. General **grocery stores** (open daily roughly 8am–8pm in summer and 8am–5pm in winter) can be found in Yosemite Valley at *Yosemite Lodge*, Curry Village and *Housekeeping Camp*, and outside the valley at Crane Flat, Tuolumne Meadows and Wawona. These generally stock ice, beer and wine, firewood and postcards along with snacks, drinks, ice cream and ready-made food, though they are usually poorly supplied with ingredients for genuine cooking. Yosemite Village has the only **supermarket** in the park. Many shops also stock branded clothing and modest souvenirs.

General stores stock Yosemite-related **books**, though there's a far better selection at the Yosemite Bookstore (see p.200) and the Ansel Adams Gallery (see below). **Newspapers** – the *New York Times*, *LA Times*, *San Francisco Chronicle*, *USA Today* and others – are available from boxes outside *Degnan's* in Yosemite Village, Yosemite Village Store, in front of the Curry Village Store, near the front desk at *Yosemite Lodge*, from the Ahwahnee Sweet Shop and from *Housekeeping Camp*.

While cost-conscious hikers and campers should bring their **gear** with them, almost all the **backpacking supplies** you're likely to need can be bought within the park at higher but not unreasonable prices.

Prices for groceries and incidentals are around twenty percent higher than you might expect outside the park. Throughout this chapter we've quoted normal summer **opening hours**: expect shorter hours in May, June, September and October, and occasional winter closures.

Outside the park, gateway towns offer a much wider selection of supplies. The best bets are Mariposa (on Hwy-140 to the west) and Oakhurst (on Hwy-41 to the south). Both have large **supermarkets** and a range of specialist stores (though none dedicated to the needs of hikers, campers and climbers).

Yosemite Valley

Ansel Adams Gallery Yosemite Village ⓦwww .anseladams.com; shuttle stops 4, 5 & 9. The excellent selection of Ansel Adams books, calendars, postcards and posters is supplemented by other quality photography books, and top-quality photographic prints, as well as a superior selection of novels and non-fiction books. Daily 9am–6pm.

Ahwahnee Gift Shop *The Ahwahnee*; shuttle stop 3. Quality and prices are a notch or two higher than the Yosemite norm in this flagship store, which comes artfully arrayed with authentic Native American jewellery, along with handicrafts, rugs, leather goods, works by local artists, prints, books, CDs and a good deal more. Daily 8am–10pm.

Ahwahnee Sweet Shop *The Ahwahnee*; shuttle stop 3. A little nook selling newspapers, stamps, handmade chocolates, sodas, local wine and drinks. Daily 7am–10pm.

Curry Village Mountain Shop Curry Village; shuttle stops 14 & 20. *The* place for serious outdoor gear with tents, sleeping bags, thermal and waterproof clothing, camp cooking gear and fuel, dried meals, and bear canisters, plus aid and free-climbing equipment at competitive prices. Also keeps the best stock of hiking and climbing guidebooks. Daily 8am–8pm.

Village Sport Shop Yosemite Village; shuttle stops 2 & 10. A modest range of fishing gear plus a fair selection of non-specialist outdoor gear such as freeze-dried meals, day packs, hiking shoes, Coleman fuel and camping gas canisters. Daily 9am–6pm.

Yosemite Art & Education Center Yosemite Village; shuttle stops 2 & 10. Sells a good range of art supplies and a modest stock of fine art books and original artworks. Mid-April to Oct daily 9.30am–5pm.

Yosemite Bookstore Yosemite Village; shuttle stops 4, 5 & 9. Vies with the Ansel Adams Gallery as the park's best bookstore, with everything from social history and kids' books to maps, climbing guides and lovely coffee-table glossies. Daily 9am–5pm.

Yosemite Museum Shop Yosemite Village; shuttle stops 5 & 9. Gorgeous little shop specializing in Native American handicrafts such as beadwork, chokers and necklaces, silver and bead jewellery, soaproot baskets, Miwok charmstones and books. Some items are pricey, but much is quite affordable, and all is bought directly from Native Americans with its provenance fully documented. Some of the basketware dates back decades, while some is new, made by park ranger and basket-maker Julia Parker, whose work is held by the Smithsonian Institution. Daily 9am–5pm.

Yosemite Village Store Yosemite Village; shuttle stops 2 & 10. Easily the biggest shop in Yosemite Valley, with gifts, a book corner, and a small supermarket stocking the best selection of groceries, beer and wine and even fresh fruit and vegetables (something virtually unheard of elsewhere in the park). Daily 8am–10pm.

Tuolumne Meadows and Crane Flat

Crane Flat Store Gas station (24hr with credit card) and general store stocked with postcards, books, film, snacks and a modest grocery selection, including ice, beer and wine, plus firewood. Also an ATM. Daily 8am–8pm.

Tuolumne Meadows Store Much used by campers and hikers, this seasonal tent store (with ATM) stocks a decent selection of supplies (even a limited range of fresh fruit and vegetables) plus s'mores packs, postcards, Yosemite books, simple camping equipment, Coleman fuel, gas canisters and

denatured alcohol firewood. Mid-June to late Sept daily 8am–8pm.

Tuolumne Sport Shop Housed in the gas station close to *Tuolumne Meadows Grill*, this smaller cousin of the Curry Village Mountain Shop primarily caters to the needs of Tuolumne hikers and climbers, stocking quality brands of tents, packs, climbing gear and outdoor clothing. Early June to late Sept daily 9am–5pm or 6pm.

White Wolf Store A basic hole-in-the-wall store with a skimpy supply of essentials. Mid-June to mid-Sept daily 7am–9pm.

Wawona, Glacier Point and Badger Pass

Badger Pass Sport Shop Sells ski clothing, sunglasses, waxes and other incidentals. Mid-Dec to late March daily 9am–5pm.

Glacier Point Gift Shop A few snacks and ice creams but mostly a gift store specializing in clothes and gifts relating to geology and astronomy. Bizarrely, it's closed when large numbers of people hit Glacier Point at sunset. June–Sept daily 9am–6pm.

Wawona Golf Shop A limited supply of golfing essentials and tennis requisites for use on the nearby courts and the golf course across the road. May–Sept daily 9am–5pm.

Wawona Store A modest supply of groceries, beer, wine, ice, firewood and camping supplies, but mostly snacks, clothing, gifts and books. Daily: June–Aug 8am–8pm; Sept–May 8am–7pm.

Sequoia and Kings Canyon

Sequoia and Kings Canyon

13

Sequoia and Kings Canyon national parks

Nominally separate parks but jointly run, and with a long common border, **SEQUOIA AND KINGS CANYON NATIONAL PARKS** effectively form a single protected area. That said, the parks are far from uniform, and contain an immense variety of geology, flora and fauna. **Sequoia National Park**, as you might expect from its name, boasts the thickest concentration – and the biggest individual specimens – of giant **sequoia trees** to be found anywhere. These ancient trees tend to outshine (and certainly outgrow) the other features of the park – an assortment of meadows, peaks, canyons and caves swathed in pine and fir. **Kings Canyon National Park** doesn't have as many big trees but compensates with a gaping canyon gored out of the rock by the Kings River, which cascades in torrents down from the High Sierra during the spring snowmelt period. There's less of a packaged tourism feel here than in Yosemite: the few established sights (principally the big trees) are near the main roads and concentrate the crowds, leaving the vast majority of the landscape untrammelled and unspoiled, but well within reach of willing hikers. Indeed, **hiking** is one of the parks' great pleasures, with an abundance of superb trails, from loops around sequoia groves to multi-night backcountry epics – we've detailed twenty of the best in our hiking section, later in this chapter.

Most trailheads and many of the major sights are on, or close to, the **Generals Highway**, actually a fairly slow and winding paved road which links the world's two biggest sequoias, the **General Sherman Tree** and the **General Grant Tree**. Approaching from the south you twist your way up from Three Rivers to **Giant Forest**, site of the parks' best museum, right in the heart of a huge grove of enormous trees. From here, Crescent Meadow Road spurs off southeast past the dramatic **Moro Rock** and under the **Tunnel Log** to **Crescent Meadow** and **Tharp's Cabin**, fashioned from a fallen sequoia. The Generals Highway continues to **Lodgepole**, base for some excellent hiking trails through deep forests, the longer treks rising above the tree line to reveal the barren peaks and magnificent sights of the High Sierra. Further north, **Grant Grove** offers accommodation and dining, making a good base for visiting sights such as the General Grant Tree and

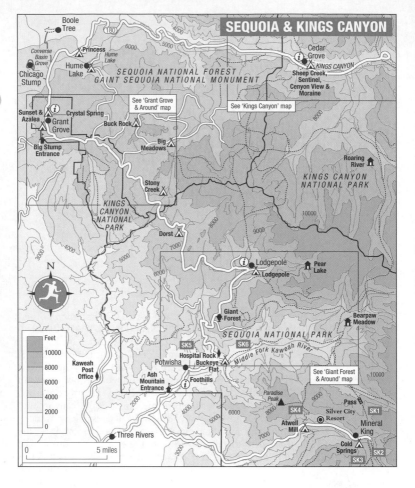

assorted **sequoia graveyards** – fields of massive severed stumps. Some 25 miles to the east, **Cedar Grove** huddles in the bottom of **Kings Canyon** at the start of most of the marked hikes. Access is along Hwy-180, which spectacularly skirts the colossal canyon.

The **best time to come** to the parks is in late summer and fall, when the days are still warm, the nights are getting chilly at altitude, the roads remain free of snow, and most visitors have left. Bear in mind that although most roads are kept open through the winter, Hwy-180 into Kings Canyon is **closed** (usually mid-Nov to mid-April) and snow blocks the road into Mineral King (see "Winter in the parks" box, p.217). May and June can also be good, especially in Kings Canyon, where snowmelt swells the Kings River dramatically and the canyon-side yuccas are in bloom.

Some history

The land now encompassed by the Sequoia and Kings Canyon national parks was once the domain of **Yokuts sub-tribes** – the Monache, Potwisha and Kaweah peoples – who made summer forays into the high country from their

Park, monument or forest?

With two national parks and the Giant Sequoia National Monument, all surrounded by the Sierra National Forest and the Sequoia National Forest, the Sequoia and Kings Canyon region has become a confusing patchwork of federally administered areas. For the most part, it won't matter which section you're in, though rules (particularly for hunting and camping) are more relaxed in the national forests. Our maps clearly show the park and forest boundaries.

permanent settlements in the lowlands, especially along the Middle Fork of the Kaweah River.

It was Spanish Army lieutenant **Gabriel Moraga** who named the Kings River after coming across it at Epiphany (January 6, 1806), though he christened it El Río de los Santos Reyes – the River of the Holy Kings. He later went on to name Yosemite's Merced River. The first real European contact came with the 1849 California **Gold Rush**, when prospectors penetrated the area in search of pasture and a direct route through the mountains. Word of abundant lumber soon got out and loggers came to stake their claims in the lowlands. The high country was widely ignored until, in 1858, local natives led **Hale Tharp**, a cattleman from Three Rivers, up to the sequoias around Moro Rock. Tharp spent the next thirty summers up there in his log home; John Muir visited him and wrote about the area, bringing it to the attention of the general public and the loggers. Before long, narrow-gauge railways and log flumes arrived on the scene, mainly for clearing fir and pine rather than the sequoias, which tended to shatter when felled.

As the Kaweah Colony (see box, p.211) established itself, Visalia conservationist George Stewart campaigned in Washington for the introduction of **preservation** measures to protect the big trees. Yosemite Valley and the Mariposa Grove of Giant Sequoias had already been protected since 1864, and Yellowstone had been designated the country's first national park in 1872. It wasn't until September 25, 1890 that **Sequoia National Park** got the nod. A week later Yosemite officially became a national park, and four square miles around Grant Grove became **Grant Grove National Park**. Finally, in 1940, Grant Grove National Park was incorporated into the newly formed **Kings Canyon National Park**.

Arrival and information

The national parks are accessible by public transportation on the **Sequoia Shuttle** ($7.50 each way, including park entrance fee; ☎ 1-877/287-4453, ⓦ www.sequoia shuttle.com), a two-and-a-half-hour run between Visalia and Giant Forest. Once in the parks, make use of **three free shuttles** (late May to early Sept daily 9am–6pm every 15min): the **Gray Route** links Giant Forest with Crescent Meadow via Moro Rock; the **Green Route** plies the Generals Highway between Giant Forest, the Sherman Tree, Lodgepole and Wuksachi; and the Purple Route continues north from Lodgepole and Wuksachi to the *Dorst* campground.

The twin parks are also easy to reach by **car**. The fastest approach is along Hwy-180 from Fresno, though it's slightly shorter following Hwy-198 from Visalia, a 55-mile drive including a tortuous fifteen-mile ascent. Consider looping in one entrance and out the other, and make sure you stock up in advance with **cash** and **gas**, though some of both is available (see p.40 & p.37 respectively).

While visiting Sequoia and Kings Canyon you'll most likely choose to **eat** close to wherever you happen to be, so we've listed restaurants throughout the chapter. There are **grocery stores** and fairly basic summer-only **cafeterias** at Lodgepole (the most extensive), Stony Creek and Cedar Grove, though none of them is spectacular and prices are higher than places outside the park, such as Three Rivers. Much the same applies to **restaurants**, with Three Rivers offering the best local selection at reasonable prices. In the restaurants inside the parks, diner fare prevails, with the exception of the restaurant at Wuksachi.

For details of **banks**, **gas**, **internet access**, **laundry**, **mail**, **phones**, **showers** and much more see the Travel essentials section of Basics. For California **road conditions** check ⓦ www.dot.co.gov or call ⓣ 1-800/427-7623. There's also a park-specific recorded message at ⓣ 559/565-3341.

The parks are always open: **park entry** costs $20 per car, or $10 per hiker or biker, and is valid for seven days. Fees are collected at the entrance stations, where you'll be given an excellent map and a copy of the free quarterly newspaper with the latest listings of **ranger programmes** and general information on the parks.

For **information** visit the parks' **website** (ⓦ www.nps.gov/seki) or call at one of the five **visitor centres**: the park headquarters at Foothills (see p.212), a mile north of the southern (Hwy-198) entrance; and others at Lodgepole, Giant Forest Museum, Grant Grove and Cedar Grove. There's also a useful **ranger station** at Mineral King; see the relevant accounts for opening hours.

For details of hikes and campgrounds in the surrounding Sequoia National Forest, visit the **Hume Lake Ranger District Office**, 35860 Hwy-180 at Clingan's Junction, seventeen miles west of the Big Stump Entrance (Mon–Fri 8am–4.30pm; ⓣ 559/338-2251, ⓦ www.r5.fs.fed.us/sequoia). You could also check the comprehensive, 24-hour recorded **information line** (ⓣ 559/565-3341), with details on camping, lodging and road conditions, and the facility to order information by mail.

Accommodation

Upgrading in recent years has raised the standard of **accommodation** in the parks, shifting away from rustic towards greater luxury, though simple cabins are still available at Grant Grove and there are masses of **camping** opportunities. You can occasionally pick up cancellations upon arrival, but space is at a premium during the summer, when booking a couple of months in advance is advisable. **Rates** quoted are for the summer season, but huge savings can be had outside peak times, especially at the pricier places.

Heavy demand and the relatively high price of accommodation forces many to stay **outside the parks**, in the motels and B&Bs lining the approach roads a few miles from the entrances. There is limited choice along **Hwy-180**, but **Three Rivers**, on Hwy-198, has a good selection: booking is advised at weekends through the summer and holidays. Rates can also be up to one price code higher on Friday and Saturday nights, though this varies with demand. Finally, you might consider basing yourself in **Fresno** or **Visalia**, both close enough to the parks to be used as a launch pad for day-trips there. Both towns are covered in Chapter 8, with accommodation listings in Chapter 9.

Below, we list all roofed accommodation available within the parks, as well as a selection of the best places to stay outside the parks.

Hotels, motels, lodges and B&Bs

Inside the parks, accommodation is managed by two **concessionaires**: Sequoia-Kings Canyon Park Services (**SKC**; ☎559/335-5500 or 1-866/522-6986, ⓦwww.sequoia-kingscanyon.com) operates in Cedar Grove, Grant Grove and Stony Creek; while Delaware North (**DN**; ☎1-888/252-5757, ⓦwww.visitsequoia.com) covers Lodgepole and Wuksachi, plus the Bearpaw High Sierra Camp. Unless noted otherwise, assume the following places are **open all year**.

In the parks and national forest

Bearpaw High Sierra Camp Reserve with DN. Soft beds, fluffy towels, hot showers and hearty meals served up in magnificent wilderness are the trump cards for this cluster of six wooden-floored permanent tents (each with two single beds and floor space for one additional person). At 7800ft on the High Sierra Trail, it's an 11-mile walk east of Giant Forest: just follow the High Sierra Trail from Crescent Meadow. There's no electricity, everything is helicoptered in for the season, and breakfast and dinner are included in the price. Most weekends and holidays are taken immediately after booking opens on January 2, though you've a reasonable chance of an on-spec place on weeknights in June and September. Closed mid-Sept to mid-June. $350 for two (full board) plus $75 for an additional adult in the same tent.

Cedar Grove Reserve with SKC. Cosy lodge with private bathroom and a/c, right by the Kings River and in the same block as the fast-food restaurant and shop. Closed mid-Oct to mid-May. Standard rooms ❹, patio rooms ❺

Grant Grove Cabins Reserve with SKC. The parks' widest selection of beds under a roof, with most options accommodating up to four people. The most basic are the summer-only canvas-roofed cabins (early June to early Sept; ❷), with linen service but no electricity. More solid rustic cabins (late May to late Nov; ❸) were mostly built in the 1920s, and many have been nicely restored and modernized and come with cooking stove and propane heater. For a private bath step up to the bath cabins (❹), the only option open all year.

John Muir Lodge Grant Grove; reserve with SKC. Modern hotel in a two-storey wooden lodge offering very comfortable, if unspectacular, hotel rooms and wi-fi. Shares check-in and eating facilities with *Grant Grove Cabins*. ❻

Kings Canyon Lodge Hwy-180 ☎559/335-2405, ⓦwww.thekingscanyonlodge.com. Guarding the entrance to Kings Canyon, with views of Spanish Mountain, this quaint and rustic 1930s former hunting lodge has simple rooms and cabins, a two-bedroom cabin sleeping eight with full kitchen (❺) and a straightforward café/bar with bear and mountain lion skins on the ceiling. Closed Dec to late April. ❹

Montecito Lake Resort Generals Hwy (Hwy-198), between Grant Grove and Giant Forest ☎1-800/227-9900 (reservations) or ☎1-800/843 8677 (lodge), ⓦwww.mslodge.com. This large but low-key family resort is tastefully set next to an artificial lake with all manner of activities: canoeing, swimming, horseriding, wakeboarding and volleyball in summer; snowshoeing, skating and cross-country skiing in winter. The rustic cabins ($99 per person, weekends $139) or lodge rooms with private bath ($129 per person, weekends $159) are booked in six-night blocks from mid-June to early September (though you can book Saturday night separately). Rates include all meals (which are pretty good) and many of the activities.

Stony Creek Generals Hwy (Hwy-198), between Grant Grove and Giant Forest; reserve with SKC. Plain, comfortable motel-style rooms with satellite TV and showers in a block, with a good restaurant and a grocery store. A generous continental breakfast is included. Discounts in May, Sept & Oct. Closed early Oct to early May. Weekends ❻, weeknights ❺

Activities in Sequoia and Kings Canyon

Hiking is easily the most popular activity in these parts, with everything from gentle meadow strolls to multi-day backpacking trips into the hundreds of square miles of backcountry – see our Hiking section, from p.221, for a guide to the twenty best hikes in Sequoia and Kings Canyon, as well as information on wilderness permits and backcountry camping.

Bikes are not permitted on trails within the parks, limiting you to cycling on park roads, many of which are very steep and have limited space for passing. A better bet is the network of trails in the surrounding national forest, where there are no restrictions on cycling. Better still, opt for a larger saddle and go horseriding from the stables and pack stations. These exist in three locations throughout the national parks and surrounding forest, mostly open from mid- or late May to early September: the Horse Corral between Lodgepole and Grant Grove (℡559/565-3404; ⓦwww .horsecorralpackers.com), Grant Grove (℡559/335-9292) and Cedar Grove (℡559/565-3464). All offer anything from an hour in the saddle ($40) to multi-day backcountry excursions.

There are no boating activities within the parks, but the Kaweah River to the south at Three Rivers offers some excellent, fun whitewater rafting. From mid-April to the end of June, Kaweah Whitewater Adventures (℡1-800/229-8658, ⓦwww.kaweah -whitewater.com) runs a series of rafting trips on the Kaweah River between Three Rivers and Lake Kaweah. Trips range from a relatively gentle two hours ($50) to serious Class IV full-day trips ($140).

Wuksachi Lodge 1 mile northwest of Lodgepole on the Generals Highway (Hwy-198). Reserve with DN. Directly competing with the *John Muir Lodge* for the best rooms in the park, the *Wuksachi* consists of several blocks of rooms (ask for mountain views) widely scattered in the woods around an elegant central lounge and restaurant area. Rooms ❻, suites ❽

South of the parks: Lemon Cove, Three Rivers and Mineral King

Buckeye Tree Lodge 46000 Hwy-198, Three Rivers, just south of the park entrance ℡559/561-5900, ⓦwww.buckeyetree.com. Small and ageing but comfortable rooms with TV, private bathrooms and verandas overlooking the foaming river. Comes equipped with a nice pool and free wi-fi. They also run *Sequoia Village Inn* (same phone number) across the road with some appealing, woodsy, self-contained cabins, each with a barbecue area and some sleeping twelve. Rooms midweek ❹, weekend ❺, cabins ❺

The Gateway 45978 Hwy-198, Three Rivers, just south of the park entrance ℡559/561-4133, ⓦwww.gateway-sequoia.com. Old but clean and perfectly functional motel-style rooms with satellite TV, plus a honeymoon cabin with dry sauna and patio (❻) and a two-bedroom house sleeping eight with self-catering facilities ($265–325). It's located right beside the Kaweah River, and the better rooms have a deck overlooking the water. Midweek ❹, weekends ❺

Lazy J Ranch Motel 39625 Hwy-198, Three Rivers, 8 miles south of the park entrance ℡1-888/315-2378, ⓦwww.bvilazyj.com. Trade park proximity for a peaceful setting in this well-cared-for motel with well-spaced, air-conditioned units and cottages set back from the road. Cottages have a full kitchen, while suites sleep up to eight. Everyone has access to the pool and volleyball court, and kids have a play area and farm animals to pet. Rooms ❸, cottage ❺, suite ❼

Plantation B&B 33038 Hwy-198, Lemon Cove, 17 miles south of the park entrance ℡1-800/240-1466, ⓦwww.theplantation .net. Luxurious seven-room B&B with comfortable en-suite rooms (some with balconies) and truly delicious breakfasts, located on a citrus orchard twenty minutes' drive from the park entrance. Rooms follow a *Gone with the Wind* theme to the extent that the Belle Watling room comes bordello-hued with a clawfoot tub. Outside there's a heated pool, hot tub, and lawns dotted with palm trees, ideal for relaxing. Rooms ❺, suites ❼

Sierra Lodge 43175 Hwy-198, Three Rivers, 4 miles south of the park entrance ☎1-888/575-2555, Ⓦ www.sierra-lodge.com. Usually the cheapest motel in the district, this old but spacious and clean lodge offers a pool and modernized en-suite rooms, many with decks and some featuring wood-burning fireplaces. Also has suites, some of which have cooking facilities. Free internet and wi-fi. Rooms ❸, suites ❻

🏃 **Silver City Mountain Resort** Mineral King, 20 miles east of Three Rivers ☎559/561-3223, Ⓦ www.silvercityresort.com. A bucolic bolt hole in the woods that's been catering to committed regulars and casual visitors since the 1930s. The rustic cabins are gorgeous, with potbelly stoves, kitchen and propane lighting, and some come with a toilet. The more modern chalets have full bathroom and electric lighting whenever the generator is running. Sheets and towels are provided for out-of-state guests (otherwise bring your own) and there's a two-night minimum stay. Bring food for self-catering, though there's a store with limited supplies, and the resort has a restaurant attached (see p.212). There's limited wi-fi for guests. Closed early Oct to late May. Rustic cabins sleeping four ❹, comfy cabins sleeping six ❻, deluxe chalets mostly ❾, with one at ❽

Three Rivers Hideaway 43365 Hwy-198, 3.7 miles south of the park entrance ☎559/561-4413, Ⓦ www.threerivershideaway.com. This small RV and tent site (see p.210) also has ageing but renovated cabins (some with kitchens ❷) at the lowest prices in the district. Cabins ❷, kitchen cabin ❹

Along Hwy-180

Sequoia View B&B 1384 S Frankwood Ave, Sanger, just off Hwy-180 ☎1-866/738 6420, Ⓦ www.svbnb.com. A small winery, 20 miles east of Fresno and 35 miles west of the park entrance, with three large and tastefully furnished luxury suites, two with king-sized sleigh beds and one with a balcony above the tasting room. A full country breakfast is served. ❺

Sierra Inn Motel 37692 Hwy-180, Dunlap ☎559/338-0678. Basic, old and barely functional motel rooms with TV and a/c, located 14 miles west of the Big Stump entrance and next to a sandwiches-and-steaks restaurant and bar. ❷

Snowline Lodge 44138 Hwy-180, 8 miles west of the park entrance ☎59/336 2300, Ⓦ www.cindis snowlinelodge.com. After years of decay this place finally has a committed owner. Cindi is rapidly doing the place up and already has the simple en-suite rooms (some with a/c) smartened up and is serving breakfast on the deck. A honeymoon suite and family room with kitchen are in the pipeline, and a woodsy restaurant and bar should be up and running by the time you read this. There's also a rustic two-room cabin up behind. Everyone can use the hot tub, there's internet access and you'll probably find your national flag flying from one of the flagpoles. Rooms ❸, cabin ❺

Campgrounds and RV parks

Except during public holidays, there's always plenty of **camping space** in Sequoia and Kings Canyon parks and the surrounding national forest. All sites operate on a first-come-first-served basis, with **no reservations** taken, except for *Dorst, Hume Lake, Lodgepole, Princess* and *Stony Creek* (for all these reserve up to six months ahead on ☎1-877/444-6777, Ⓦ www.recreation.gov). RV drivers won't find any hookups inside the parks, but they're available nearby in Three Rivers, and there are summer-only dump stations at *Dorst, Lodgepole, Potwisha* and *Princess*. Collecting "dead and down" firewood is permitted in both the national park and the national forest, but for cooking you really want to bring along a portable stove. There are public **showers** at several locations (see p.43). For **backcountry** camping, see p.221. The following campgrounds are listed south to north, and the night-time temperatures you can expect are indicated by the site's altitude. **Fees** are sometimes reduced or waived outside the main summer season and when piped water is disconnected, especially in winter.

South Fork South Fork Drive, 10 miles southeast of Three Rivers; 3600ft; 10 sites. Trailer-free site a twisting 13 miles east of Lake Kaweah on the very southwestern tip of the park. Non-potable piped water available. $12 fee charged May–Sept.

Three Rivers Hideaway 43365 Hwy-198, 3.7 miles south of the park entrance ☏ 559/561-4413, Ⓦ www.threerivershideaway.com; 800ft; 40 sites. Small and somewhat cramped commercial RV and tent site with flush toilets and showers, and close to a selection of restaurants. Tents $30, RV hookups $29–34.

🏃 **Cold Springs** Mineral King; 7500ft; 40 sites. Excellent shaded riverside campground 25 miles west of Hwy-198, with some very quiet walk-in sites. Drinking water available. Closed Nov to late May. $12.

Atwell Mill Mineral King; 6650ft; 21 sites. Quiet and pleasant campground on the site of a former Potwisha summer camp. Slightly less appealing than *Cold Springs*, but 5 miles closer to the highway. Some tent-only sites. Water available. Closed Nov to late May. $12.

Potwisha Hwy-198; 2100ft; 40 sites. Smallish, RV-dominated site close to Hwy-198, 3 miles northeast of the park's southern entrance and beside the Marble Fork of the Kaweah River. Water and flush toilets. $18.

Buckeye Flat Hwy-198; 2800ft; 28 sites. Peaceful, trailer-free site 6 miles east of Hwy-198, close to the park's southern entrance and beside the Middle Fork of the Kaweah River. Water and flush toilets. Closed mid-Oct to late May. $18.

🏃 **Lodgepole** Hwy-198, 4 miles north of Giant Forest; 6700ft; 205 sites. Largest and busiest of the sites, with a store, snack stand, laundry and showers close by. Reservations essential (contact info given above) late May to late September, when pay showers, a camp store, water and

flush toilets are all made available. $18, or $20 if reserved.

Dorst Hwy-198, 8 miles northwest of Lodgepole; 6700ft; 210 sites. Another large site, with flush toilets and water during the season. Can reserve sites (see p.209). Closed early Sept to late June. $20.

Stony Creek Hwy-198; 6400ft; 49 sites. Peaceful forest site with flush toilets half a mile from Stony Creek with its gas, food, showers and small store. Can reserve sites (see p.209). Closed Oct to mid-May. $20.

Buck Rock 7600ft; 5 sites. Excellent and underutilized national forest site 3 miles east of the highway, midway between Lodgepole and Grant Grove. No water. Closed Nov to late May. Free.

🏃 **Big Meadow** 7600ft; 25 sites. Similar site to *Buck Rock*, a mile further east among exfoliated granite domes. Mosquitoes in summer. Stream water. Closed Nov to late May. Free.

Sunset, **Azalea** and **Crystal Springs** Grant Grove; 6500ft; total of 300 sites. Comparable large sites all within a few hundred yards of the Grant Grove visitor centre. *Azalea* open year-round, others as needed. $18 (*Azalea* only $10 in winter)

Princess Hwy-180, 6 miles north of Grant Grove; 5900ft; 88 sites. National forest campground with water and toilets, handily sited on the way into Kings Canyon. Reserve through the Forest Service (see contact details above). Closed Oct to mid-May. $18.

Hume Lake Hume Road; 5200ft; 74 sites. Reservable national forest site (contact details above) with water, toilets and lake swimming for the brave. Closed Nov to late May. $20.

Sheep Creek Sentinel, **Canyon View** and **Moraine** Cedar Grove; 4600ft; total of 330 sites. A series of all-but-contiguous forest sites around the Cedar Grove visitor centre. *Canyon View* is tents-only. All have flush toilets. Closed mid-Oct to early May. $18.

Three Rivers and Kaweah

Heading towards the parks from the south, you pass through **THREE RIVERS**, a lowland community strung out for seven miles along Hwy-198, and providing the greatest concentration of accommodation and places to eat anywhere near Sequoia and Kings Canyon. As you approach the centre of town, six miles south of the park entrance, a sign directs you three miles west to what remains of the Kaweah Colony (see box above), essentially just the **Kaweah Post Office**, the smallest still operating in California, with its original brass-and-glass private boxes.

Beyond this, there's little to detain you in town, though it does have several good **places to eat**: *Serrano's*, 40869 Hwy-198, six miles south of the park entrance (℡559/561-7283), looks spartan but dishes up authentic, low-cost Mexican, best eaten outside on a balmy summer's evening with a Mexican beer; friendly *We Three Bakery*, 43368 Hwy-198, 3.7 miles south of the park entrance (℡559/561-4761), makes a great stop for breakfast or lunch either inside or out, or for their freshly baked cakes and free wi-fi; and the *Gateway Restaurant*, 45978 Hwy-198, just south of the park entrance (℡559/561-4133), superbly set by the Kaweah River, is great for a lunch of chicken tostadas ($14) or salmon burgers ($14), the Sunday Champagne brunch ($26), or very good dinners (mains $25–39). For **accommodation** in Three Rivers, see the listings on p.208.

Mineral King

A couple of miles north of Three Rivers, the twisting, early-1880s Mineral King Road (open late May to Oct) branches 25 miles east into the southern section of the parks to **MINERAL KING**, a collection of private cabins and a couple of campgrounds sitting in a scalloped bowl at 7800ft, surrounded by snowy peaks and glacial lakes. This is the only part of the high country accessible by car (but not RVs, buses or trailers) and makes a superb hiking base. Eager prospectors built the thoroughfare hoping the area would yield silver. It didn't, the mines were abandoned and the region was left largely in peace until the mid-1960s, when Disney threatened to build a huge ski resort here. Thankfully the plan was defeated and the region was finally included in Sequoia National Park in 1978. Today there are just a few small stands of sequoias, one quaint resort and near-complete tranquillity. Having negotiated the six-hundred-odd twists and turns from the highway, you may barely notice the batten-built **Grace Alice cabin** (June–Oct Sun 11am–3pm; free), an old homesteader's house once owned by local character Grace Alice. Located by the *Atwell Mill* campground, it is preserved much as it was when she died in 1981, aged 94, and comes alive when you get talking to interpreters about her life and the early days of Mineral King.

Apart from a little relaxing beside the river, the main reason to be here is to go **hiking**, perhaps up over steep Sawtooth Pass and into the alpine bowls of the glaciated basins beyond – see p.222 for more on hiking routes and trails. There's also a gentler introduction to the flora and fauna of Mineral King by way of a short **nature trail** from the *Cold Springs* campground. The **ranger station** (June to early Sept daily 8am–4pm; ☏559/565-3768), opposite the campground, dispenses practical information and wilderness permits (see p.221).

Signs all around Mineral King warn of the threat of **marmots**, which seem to like to hide in the engine compartment of vehicles parked at trailheads, sometimes amusing themselves by chewing radiator hoses and the like: vehicles have to be towed every year. The problem is most acute from late May to mid-July when you should protect your vehicle while you're hiking by creating a skirt around it with chicken wire. Wire can be rented ($10 plus $10 deposit) from *Silver City Mountain Resort* (see p.209), five miles before the end of the road; unless you're committed to camping, this is the place to **stay** around here. It also has a small, low-cost **restaurant**, which is fully open Thursday to Monday but only open for coffee and their excellent home-made fruit pies on Tuesday and Wednesday. The *Atwell* campground is nearby.

The Generals Highway

Entering the park on **Hwy-180 from Visalia**, you wind through Three Rivers, pass the turn-off for Mineral King (see p.211) and cross the East Fork of the Kaweah River before entering the twin parks at the **Ash Mountain entrance**. Continue a mile to the **Foothills Visitor Center** (daily: June–Aug 8am–6pm; Sept–May 8am–4.30pm; ☏559/565-3341) where there's a bookshop and a ranger station for backcountry permits.

Suitably informed, press on along the Generals Highway past *Potwisha* campground (see p.210) to **Hospital Rock**, five miles north of the Foothills Visitor Center. For several hundred years this transition zone between the dry foothills and the wetter forest above was home to native Potwisha who lived in brush and bark houses, weaving baskets and living off hunting and gathering. Stone knives and arrow points have been found, and a flat rock, signposted beside the road, is pocked with almost fifty **mortar holes** – the smaller ones for grinding acorns, the larger for pounding buckeye nuts, which lend their name to the nearby *Buckeye Flat* campground (see p.210).

Opposite the mortar rock is **Hospital Rock** itself, the overhung southern side of which provides a canvas for dozens of **petroglyphs**, many of them birds with varying degrees of stylization. It was the Potwisha from here who helped Hale Tharp (see p.215) become one of the first white men to visit Giant Forest in 1858. He was back two years later when his friend, John Swanson, was injured while exploring the area. The Indians rapidly cured him with jimsonweed leaves and

---

Driving restrictions on the Generals Highway

The maximum vehicle length on the Generals Highway between Potwisha campground and Giant Forest Museum is 22ft, effectively ruling out medium- and large-sized RVs.

bear fat, but the Hospital Rock moniker actually comes from an event in 1873 when one Albert Everton was treated by a doctor here after being shot in the leg while setting up a bear trap. By this stage the Potwisha, diseased and dispirited, had left the area.

Giant Forest and around

North of Hospital Rock, the **Generals Highway** really starts to zigzag, twisting rapidly uphill into **GIANT FOREST**, the world's greatest accessible concentration of giant sequoias. A major tourist draw, Giant Forest contained a small village until 1998, but concerns over the health of the sequoias prompted the Park Service to raze the settlement. Almost three hundred hotel and restaurant structures built virtually on top of the sequoias' root systems were removed, intrusive paths have been re-routed, and the whole area has been restored and re-seeded. These days, you'd hardly know anything had been there but for the former shop, restaurant and gas station now operating as the **Giant Forest Museum** (daily: July & Aug 8am–6pm; June & Sept 8am–5pm; Oct–May 9am–4.30pm; free), which admirably illustrates the life and times of the giant sequoias and shows some great footage of sequoia-felling and early tourism. Outside, the fire-damaged Sentinel Tree is barricaded to allow seedlings a chance to get established.

Various short paths fan out from here through the trees, including the **Big Trees Trail** (0.6-mile loop; 30min–1hr), which follows a well-formed boardwalk along the perimeter of Round Meadow, and the **Beetle Rock Trail** (5min round-trip),

The life of the giant sequoia

Call it what you will – the sierra redwood, *Sequoiadendron giganteum*, or just "big tree" – the **giant sequoia** is the earth's most massive living thing. Some of these arboreal monsters weigh in at a whopping one thousand tons, courtesy of a thick trunk that barely tapers from base to crown. They're also among the oldest trees found anywhere, many reaching 2000 or even 3000 years of age.

Sequoias are only found in around 75 isolated groves on the western slopes of California's **Sierra Nevada** and grow naturally between elevations of 5000ft and 8500ft from just south of Sequoia National Park to just north of Yosemite National Park. They only occur in some 38,000 acres of forest, and only a thousand trees exceed 20ft in diameter – the real "Big Trees". Specimens planted all over the world during the nineteenth century seem to thrive but haven't yet reached the enormous dimensions seen here.

The cinnamon-coloured bark of young sequoias is easily confused with that of the incense cedar, but as they age, there's no mistaking the thick spongy outer layer that protects the sapwood from the fires that periodically sweep through the forests. **Fire** is, in fact, a critical element in the propagation of sequoias; the hen-egg-sized female cones pack hundreds of seeds but require intense heat to open them. Few seeds ever sprout as they need perfect conditions, usually where an old tree has fallen and left a hole in the canopy, allowing plenty of light to fall on rich mineral soil.

Young trees are conical, but as they mature the lower branches drop off to leave a top-heavy crown. A shallow **wide root system** keeps them upright, but eventually heavy snowfall or high winds topple ageing trees. With its tannin-rich timber, a giant sequoia may lie where it fell for hundreds of years. John Muir discovered one still largely intact with a 380-year-old silver fir growing out of the depression it had created.

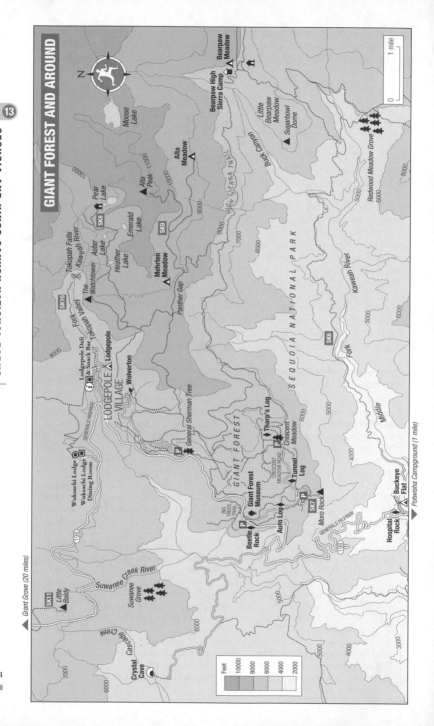

GIANT FOREST AND AROUND

N

0 _____ 1 mile

Grant Grove (20 miles)

Cascade Creek

Suwanee Creek River

Crystal Cave

Little Baldy

SK11

Suwanee Grove

Big Trees Trail

Beetle Rock

Auto Log

Giant Forest Museum

Moro Rock

SK7

Tunnel Log

General Sherman Tree

Crescent Meadow

Tharp's Log

Wolverton

Waksachi Lodge
Waksachi Lodge Dining Room

Generals Highway

LODGEPOLE VILLAGE

Lodgepole Deli & Snack Bar

Lodgepole

The Watchtower

Tokopah Falls

Marble Fork Kaweah River

Lodgepole & Tokopah Valley

SK10

Aster Lake

Heather Lake

Emerald Lake

Pear Lake

SK8

Moose Lake

Alta Meadow

Alta Peak: 11000

Mehrten Meadow

SK9

Panther Gap

HIGH SIERRA TRAIL

Bearpaw High Sierra Camp

Bearpaw Meadow

Little Bearpaw Meadow

Sugarbowl Dome

Buck Canyon

Redwood Meadow Grove

SEQUOIA NATIONAL PARK

Middle Fork Kaweah River

GIANT FOREST

Hospital Rock

Generals Highway

Buckeye Flat

Potwisha Campground (1 mile)

SK6

Feet
10000
8000
6000
4000
2000

which affords a view down to the San Joaquin Valley. The latter passes the **Beetle Rock Family Nature Center** (late June to mid-Aug daily 1–4pm; free) with a kids' bookstore and a range of family-oriented ranger programmes, some of which take place on the smooth rock outside. For information on **longer hikes** from Giant Forest, see p.224

Crescent Meadow Road

The densest concentration of sights (a couple specifically engineered for that purpose) is along **Crescent Meadow Road**, which spurs off the main highway just before the Giant Forest Museum. The first photo op is the **Auto Log**, a fallen trunk originally chiselled flat enough for motorists to nose up onto it, though rot has now put an end to this practice. Beyond here, a side loop leads to the dramatic **Moro Rock**, a granite monolith streaking wildly upward from the green hillside. Views from its remarkably level top can stretch 150 miles across the San Joaquin Valley and, in the other direction, to the towering Sierra. Thanks to a concrete staircase, it's a comparatively easy climb to the summit (see p.224), although at an altitude of nearly 7000ft the nearly four hundred steps can be a strain.

Back on the road, you pass under the **Tunnel Log**: a tree that fell across the road in 1937 and has since had a vehicle-sized hole cut through its lower half. Further on, **Crescent Meadow** is, like other grassy fields in the area, more accurately a marsh, and too wet for the sequoias that form an impressive boundary around it. Looking across the meadow gives the best opportunity to appreciate the changing shape of the ageing sequoia. The trail circling its perimeter (1.5 miles; 1hr; mainly flat) leads to **Log Meadow**, to which a farmer, Hale Tharp, searching for a summer grazing ground for his sheep, was led by local Native Americans in 1858. He became one of the first white men to see the giant sequoias, and the first to actually live in one. He spent his summers living in a fallen, hollowed-out specimen known as **Tharp's Log** from 1861 until 1890, even hosting John Muir who dubbed it a "noble den". Admire the stone chimney then peer into the gloom, where a table, bench seat and bed frame have all been fashioned from local timber. From here the loop presses on to the still-living **Chimney Tree**, its centre completely burnt out so that the sky is visible from its hollow base. Hardy backpackers can pick up the High Sierra Trail here and hike the 62 miles to Mount Whitney, the tallest mountain in the continental US.

The General Sherman Tree

North of Crescent Meadow Road, the Generals Highway enters the thickest section of Giant Forest and the biggest sequoia of them all (reachable on foot by various connecting trails). The 2100-year-old **General Sherman Tree** is 275ft tall and has a base diameter of 36ft. While it's certainly a thrill to be face-to-bark with what is widely held to be the largest living thing on earth, its extraordinary dimensions are hard to grasp in the midst of all the almost equally monstrous sequoias around – not to mention the other tremendous batch that can be seen on the **Congress Trail** (2 miles; 1–2hr; negligible ascent), which starts from the General Sherman Tree itself. Parking is several hundred yards from the General Sherman Tree; if you want to be dropped closer, catch the **free shuttle bus** from Giant Forest.

Crystal Cave

When you've had your fill of the magnificent trees, consider a trip nine miles from Giant Forest along a minor road to **Crystal Cave** (45min guided tours mid-May to Oct daily 11am–4pm; $13), which has a fairly diverting batch of stalagmites and stalactites. The early morning tours are not usually full, and whatever time you go, remember to take a jacket as the cave is at a constant 50°F. Those with a deeper interest in the cave's origins and features should join the ninety-minute **Discovery Tour** (mid-June to Aug Mon–Fri 4.15pm; $20), or even the **Historic Candle-light Tour** (mid-June to late Sept Thurs–Sun at 5.30pm; $20), which dwells on the cave's discovery with candles adding atmosphere.

Tickets for cave trips cannot be bought at the caves themselves, but must be purchased at the Lodgepole or Foothills visitor centres at least a couple of hours beforehand.

Wolverton, Lodgepole, Wuksachi and Stony Creek

Access to the General Sherman Tree parking area is off a side road which leads to **Wolverton**, once the site of a small, downhill ski area and now home to some riding stables and a major trailhead. The area's name recalls early cattleman, James Wolverton, who served under General Sherman in the Civil War and honoured his leader by naming the world's largest tree after him. If you're staying around these parts, don't miss the **Wolverton BBQ Dinner** (mid-June to early Sept daily at 6pm; adults $22, kids $10; tickets on the day from *Wuksachi Lodge* and the Lodgepole grocery store – see both below), an all-you-can-eat affair with pork ribs, chicken, burgers, hot dogs, corn bread, salads and dessert, which takes place at Wolverton meadow. You can buy beer and wine on site, and the event is usually accompanied by a free ranger show; bring bug spray.

Whatever your plans, make sure you stop at **LODGEPOLE**, three miles north of the General Sherman Tree, where the **visitor centre** (July & Aug daily 8am–6pm; May, June & Sept daily 8am–5pm; ☎559/565-4436) shows the eight-minute *Saving Sequoias* movie on the restoration of the Giant Forest area in the late 1990s. With its grocery store, burger bar, showers, laundry and campground, Lodgepole is very much at the centre of Sequoia's visitor activities, and its situation at one end of the Tokopah Valley, a glacially formed canyon (not unlike the much larger Yosemite Valley), makes it an ideal starting point to explore a number of **hiking trails** – see p.224 for our favourites.

Eating is done at the *Lodgepole Deli and Snack Bar* (closed Nov–March), the best of the parks' budget eating places with respectable readymade sandwiches, salads and ice cream at the deli (daily 11am–6pm) and a selection of burgers, fries and drinks at the snack bar (daily 8am–7.45pm).

Beyond Lodgepole the Generals Highway turns west and runs just over a mile to Wuksachi, just a fancy modern lodge (p.208) and the *Wuksachi Lodge Dining Room* (☎559/565-4070), the **finest restaurant** in the twin parks, with Reuben sandwiches and the like ($10) at lunch and more formal dinners such as seared trout ($20) and steaks ($25) all served in a modern baronial-style room. There's also a buffet breakfast (continental $8; full $13) and the bar is open daily until 11pm.

The road soon swings north again and passes into the **Giant Sequoia National Monument** – where *Stony Creek* offers accommodation (see p.207) and a fairly mainstream **diner/restaurant** (late May to Oct daily 11am–2pm & 4–7.30pm) serving decent pizza and calzone. Accommodation can also be found at *Montecito Lake Resort*, whose restaurant serves hearty buffet breakfasts (7.30–9am; $9), lunches (noon–1.30pm; $10) and dinners (5.30–7pm; $20) communally at large tables. There's a bar open until 10pm.

Grant Grove and around

A good base for exploring the northern sections of the parks, **GRANT GROVE** is set amid concentrated stands of sequoias, sugar pines, incense cedars, black oaks and mountain dogwoods. Along with accommodation (see p.207), a post office and a small supermarket, you'll find a **restaurant** with diner fare – burgers, sandwiches and breakfasts – plus fish, chicken and steak dinners for $15–20 and pizza to stay or go (from $14 for a 14-inch; summer only). There's also an espresso kiosk with seating out on the umbrella-shaded terrace. The useful **visitor centre** (daily: June–Aug 8am–7pm; May & Sept 8am–5pm; Oct–April 9am–4.30pm; ☎559/565-4307) can supply all the background information you'll need, and contains a small **museum** (free entry) with old-time photos, a cross section of a tree and a kids' Discovery Room where you can examine tree seeds under a microscope.

Those tiny seeds grow into the massive trees found hereabouts, a couple of which rival the General Sherman for bulk: the **Robert E. Lee Tree** and the **General Grant Tree**, after which the area is named. The General Grant is the world's second-largest tree and was proclaimed as "The Nation's Christmas Tree" by President Coolidge in 1926. Every year, on the second Sunday in December, the people of the nearby town of Sanger hold a yuletide celebration with carols sung under its snow-weighted boughs. It's also the nation's only living shrine, dedicated to all those who have died in war. A half-mile path wends its way among these and other giants, calling in at the **Fallen Monarch**, which you can walk through, and the **Gamlin Cabin**, where Israel and Thomas Gamlin lived while exploiting their timber claim until 1878. The massive stump of one of the trees' scalps remains after

---

Winter in the parks

The high country of Sequoia and Kings Canyon is covered in a blanket of **snow** each winter, usually from November until April or May, and while this limits a great deal of sightseeing and walking it also opens up opportunities for some superb cross-country skiing. With chains, **access** is seldom much of a problem. Both main roads into the parks are kept open all year. The Generals Highway is also ploughed after snowfall, but sometimes takes a few days to clear: it's best, then, to choose one section of the parks as a base. Kings Canyon's Cedar Grove is off limits to cars from mid-November to mid-April, but **Grant Grove** stays open all year. Facilities are restricted and camping is only available at snow-free lowland sites.

The big winter activities up here are **cross-country skiing** and **snowshoeing**. Hwy-180 gives access to two places at the hub of miles of marked trails: the Grant Grove Ski Touring Center (Nov–April; call park concessionaire on ☎559/335-5500), where there's ski and snowshoe rental, guided naturalist snowshoe walks at weekends, restaurants and accommodation; and the *Montecito Lake Resort* (see p.207), with its own groomed trails, also open to day visitors for $25. Nearby, the mile-long Big Meadows Nordic Ski Trail is perfect beginner's terrain. To the south, *Wuksachi Lodge* (see p.208) has groomed trails and plenty of scope in the backcountry: skis ($24 a day) and snowshoes ($15) can both be rented. Unless you're staying at *Wuksachi Lodge* or are a super-hardy camper, you'll need to return to Three Rivers for somewhere to stay.

Experienced skiers and snowshoers should spend the night 9200ft up at the ten-bunk **Pear Lake Ski Hut** (mid-Dec to April; Mon–Thurs $30 per person, Fri–Sun $38), beautifully sited at the end of a steep six-mile trail from Wolverton Meadow: contact the Sequoia Natural History Association (☎559/565-3759, ⍟www.sequoia history.org) for reservations (initially allocated by lottery).

Snowmobiles are banned in the national parks, but can be used on designated routes in the national forest, such as Big Meadows, Quail Flat and Cherry Gap.

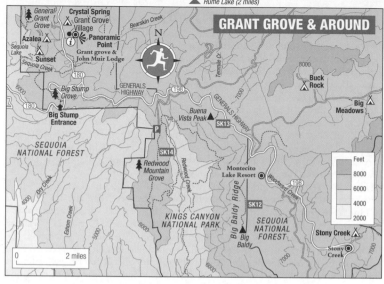

a slice was shipped to the 1876 Centennial Exhibition in Philadelphia – an attempt to convince cynical easterners that such enormous trees really existed.

Back at the visitor centre, a twisting, two-mile drive heads east past the *John Muir Lodge* up to **Panoramic Point**, where you can admire distant views over Kings Canyon. Further magnificent views can be enjoyed from a number of fairly easy **hikes** in the area – for details, see p.225.

Big Stump area

Two miles south of Grant Grove, the **Big Stump Area** unsurprisingly gets its name from the gargantuan stumps that litter the place – remnants from early logging of sequoias carried out during the 1880s. An easy trail (one to two miles depending on how many sad stumps you can bear to see) leads through this scene of devastation to the **Mark Twain Stump**, the headstone of another monster killed to impress: a sliver of this one resides in New York's American Museum of Natural History and another was sent to the British Museum in London. Look too for hollows in the ground (known as feather beds), where pine boughs were laid on the ground to break the fall of huge trees, and check out the meagre foundations of the sawmill which once processed all the lumber.

Hume Lake

About eight miles north of Grant Grove, a minor road spurs off three miles to **Hume Lake**, actually a reservoir built in 1908 to provide water for logging flumes, and now forming the heart of an underpopulated area of the Sequoia National Forest. Handily placed for local hiking trails (see p.225), it's also a delightful spot to swim or launch your canoe, and makes a good place to spend a night beside the lake at the comparatively large *Hume Lake* **campground** (see p.210). At the head of the lake, the facilities of the *Hume Lake Christian Camp* provide expensive gas, groceries, an ATM and a coffee shop.

Kings Canyon

Let our law-givers then make haste before it is too late to set apart this surpass-
ingly glorious region for the recreation and well-being of humanity, and all the
world will rise up and call them blessed.

John Muir wrote these lines in a heartfelt article for *Century* magazine in 1891. It
wasn't until almost fifty years later, in 1940, that Kings Canyon National Park was
created, and even then commercial interests eyeing the wonderful water-storage
opportunities of the region kept the canyon itself out of the park. The main body
of Kings Canyon was finally protected and included in its namesake park in 1965.

From Grant Grove, Hwy-180 – here known as Kings Canyon Highway (and
usually closed mid-Nov to mid-April) – heads into **KINGS CANYON** itself,
which at 7900ft is claimed as the deepest canyon in the US. This is measured from
the summit of Spanish Mountain down to the river, so although the literature
rightly claims it is deeper than the Grand Canyon, it doesn't have quite the same
impact. Whatever the facts, its walls of granite and gleaming blue marble, and the
white pockmarks of spectacularly blooming yucca plants (particularly in May and
early June), are visually stunning. A vast area of the wilderness beyond is drained
by the South Fork of the Kings River, a raging torrent during the springtime
snowmelt spate, and perilous for wading at any time: people have been swept away
even when paddling close to the bank in a seemingly placid section.

Chicago Stump and Converse Basin

The approach to Kings Canyon leads through a section of the Giant Sequoia
National Monument with two rewarding excursions a short drive off the highway.
The first spurs a mile and a half west to the **Chicago Stump**, yet another epitaph
to a felled giant, this one carted in numbered sections to Chicago in 1893 where it
was reassembled for the World's Columbian Exposition. So huge was the slice of
sequoia that fair-goers thought it was a hoax.

A more alluring diversion leads two miles north into **Converse Basin**, once the
world's largest sequoia grove but now a sad testament to the skill and determination
of the loggers. In the late nineteenth and early twentieth centuries, almost every
last mature sequoia was felled, mostly for low-value products such as pencils and
grape stakes. A complex network of cableways carried the logs to the five sawmills,
and when John Muir visited Hyde's Sawmill in 1877 he found it "booming and
moaning like a bad ghost". Drive past the sequoia graveyard, **Stump Meadow**, to
a trailhead for the **Boole Tree**, the world's fattest sequoia (the eighth-largest
overall) and one that towers above the forest where all other sequoias were felled.
The loggers apparently appreciated its girth and spared it, naming it after their
boss, Frank Boole. Despite this and some fine examples of fire scarring, it's seldom
visited, perhaps on account of its position on a two-mile loop trail: take the
gentler left-hand trail and you'll be there in around half an hour.

Kings Canyon Lodge, Boyden Cavern and
Grizzly Falls

Around eight miles further along Kings Canyon Highway, **Kings Canyon Lodge**
offers simple accommodation (see p.207), diner meals and sells gas from what is
claimed as the oldest pair of working gravity-fed pumps in the country. They date
back to the 1920s and very photogenic they are, too.

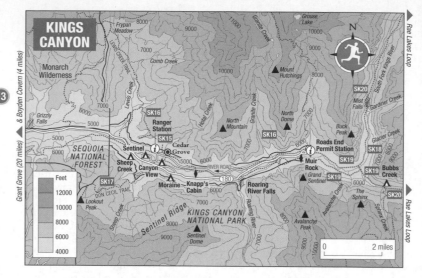

Near the foot of the canyon, the road passes the less compelling of the region's two show caves, the **Boyden Cavern** (45min tours on the hour daily: June–Aug 10am–5pm; late April to May & Sept to early Nov 11am–4pm; $13; ☎559/338-0959, ⓦwww.boydencavern.com), whose interior has a number of bizarre formations growing out of the 40,000-year-old rock, their impact intensified by the cave's cool, still interior. Follow the link on their website to learn more about (and reserve) a range of guided adventure tours including exploring cave passages, rappelling in nearby canyons and even full-on canyoning.

The next section of highway sticks close to the South Fork of the **Kings River**, a surging maelstrom in spring with foaming cataracts interspersed with somewhat calmer sections backed by pines and cedars. Several pull-outs give you a chance to stop and marvel at the power of the water. Stop briefly at **Grizzly Falls**, where a pretty waterfall cascades down a side canyon.

Cedar Grove

Once properly into the national park, the canyon sheds its V-shape and gains a floor, where **CEDAR GROVE** sprawls among incense cedars at 4600ft. It is the area's only settlement, with a lodge (see p.207), several campgrounds, a **visitor centre** (mid-June to early Sept daily 9am–5pm; ☎559/565-3793), a food store and a **snack bar** that sells barely adequate self-serve meals on paper plates. It is open for standard egg and pancake breakfasts (7–10.30am), burger and sandwich lunches (11am–2pm), plus a handful of steak and chicken dinners for around $15–20 (5–8pm).

Knapp's Cabin, Roaring River Falls and Zumwalt Meadow

Wealthy California businessman, George Knapp, chose a spot two miles east of Cedar Grove to build **Knapp's Cabin**, used as a storage shed for a number of elaborate summer camping trips to the region during the "Roaring Twenties". It's nothing special to look at but it is the oldest building in Cedar Grove and is only a few steps from the road. Another mile on, **Roaring River Falls** merit their name, particularly when in spate. Apart from the obvious appeal of the scenery, the main things to see around here are the **wildflowers** – leopard lilies, shooting stars, violets, Indian paintbrush, lupins and others – and a variety of birdlife. The longer hikes (see p.206) are fairly stiff challenges, but an easy alternative is to potter along the **nature trail** (1.5 miles; 1–2hr; flat) around the edge of **Zumwalt Meadow**, which is wheelchair-accessible. The meadow – named after a Southern Pacific Railway Company attorney who in the 1880s worked to have this land protected from settlement as a forest reserve – boasts a collection of big-leaf maple, cat's-tails, and creek dogwood, and there's often a chance for an eyeful of animal life. The forbidding grey walls of Grand Sentinel and North Dome rise up on either side.

Road's End, Muir Rock and River Road

Just a mile further, Kings Canyon Highway comes to an end at **Road's End**, from where a network of **hiking trails** penetrates the multitude of canyons and peaks that constitute the Kings River Sierra – for trail descriptions, see p.226. Almost all are best enjoyed with a tent and some provisions. To obtain wilderness permits in this area, call at the Road's End Wilderness Permit Station (June to mid-Sept daily 7am–3pm) at the end of Hwy-180. The less ambitious only need to venture a hundred yards riverward to **Muir Rock** to see where John Muir (see box, p.60) conducted early meetings of the Sierra Club. One member claimed Muir would never "speak of his love for the mountains in a more fitting auditorium". It is indeed a fine spot, often occupied by families on sunny days, the kids launching themselves off into the refreshing river.

On the way back down the valley, cut right just before the road crosses the Kings River and follow the unmarked **River Road** (westbound only) along the north side of the river back to Cedar Grove.

Hiking in Sequoia and Kings Canyon

The **trails** in Kings Canyon and Sequoia see far less traffic than those in Yosemite, but can still get busy in high summer. Almost all those leaving from Mineral King and Kings Canyon climb very steeply, so if you're looking for easy and moderate hikes, jump to those around Giant Forest, Lodgepole and Grant Grove.

There are **no restrictions on day walks**, but a quota system (operational late May to late Sept) applies if you're planning to camp in the backcountry. A third of the places are offered on a first-come-first-served basis and, provided you're fairly flexible, you should be able to land something by turning up at the ranger station nearest your proposed trailhead from 1pm on the day before you wish to start. Details for advance **wilderness permits** are given at ⓦ www.nps.gov/seki /planyourvisit/wilderness_permits.htm, where you can download an application form. There's a one-off $15 **wilderness camping fee** per person which entitles you to camp more or less anywhere in the backcountry, though the authorities prefer you to use already impacted sites. Reservations are accepted after March 1 and at least two weeks before your start date, and outside the quota period permits can be self-issued at trailheads. Park visitor centres stock the free *Backcountry Basics* newspaper and sell the excellent 1:80,000-scale Trails Illustrated **topographical map** of the parks (#205; $12).

Remember that this is **bear country**: read the box on p.10. Bear canisters can be rented ($5 per trip) at Mineral King, Foothills, Lodgepole, Grant Grove and Cedar Grove, and bought ($66) at the Lodgepole store and most visitor centres.

Hikes from Mineral King

The following hikes are ordered by increasing difficulty.

SK1 Timber Gap

Difficulty Moderate
Distance 4 miles round trip
Estimated time 4–5hr
Elevation gain 1700ft ascent
Season mid-June to Oct, though there is likely to be snow under foot early in the season

When the Eagle and Mosquito Lake trails are a little too busy for your liking (not that they ever get very busy) head for this fairly steep hike up to **Timber Gap**, a col at 9450ft with views north into the drainage of the Middle Fork of Kaweah River. The wildflowers are abundant from late June into July, and you'll often see marmots sunning themselves on rocks, particularly on a large boulder two-thirds of the way up to Timber Gap. If you don't see any marmots, look for their piles of droppings then sit quiet and wait a while: their inquisitive heads will soon pop out.

SK2 Eagle Lake

Difficulty Strenuous
Distance 7 miles round trip
Estimated time 4–6hr
Elevation gain 2200ft ascent
Season June–Oct, though there is likely to be snow under foot early in the season

Starting from the parking area a mile beyond the ranger station, this there-and-back hike begins gently but gets tougher towards the lovely **Eagle Lake**. This is actually a reservoir, formed by a small dam built by the Mt Whitney Power and Electric Company in the early 1900s. Dropping lake levels throughout summer make the lake less attractive by early fall. Highlights include the **Eagle Sink Hole** (where the river vanishes) and some fantastic views.

SK3 Mosquito Lakes No. 1

Difficulty Strenuous
Distance 7 miles round trip
Estimated time 4–5hr
Elevation gain 1150ft ascent
Season June–Oct, though there is likely to be snow under foot early in the season

This trail follows the first two miles of the Eagle Lake trail then branches left to the lowest of the **Mosquito Lakes**, at 9000ft. Before retracing your steps, you can extend the hike by pressing on into the upper mosquito basin and more lakes, often frequented by fishers.

SK4 Paradise Peak via Paradise Ridge

Difficulty Strenuous
Distance 10 miles round trip
Estimated time 5–6hr
Elevation gain 2800ft ascent
Season Mid-June to Oct, though there is likely to be snow under foot early in the season

This superb walk starts opposite the *Atwell Mill* campground and initially switch-backs steeply through **Atwell Grove** which, at around 8000ft, is the highest of all sequoia groves. The largest trees are towards the top of the grove. The trail then climbs more gently up **Paradise Ridge**, which affords views of Moro Rock. From here it's a fairly flat stroll to **Paradise Peak** (9362ft) with vistas of the high sierra peaks, air quality permitting. Return the way you came.

Hikes from Potwisha and Hospital Rock

When hiking in the foothills, be alert for poison oak, ticks and rattlesnakes.

SK5 Marble Falls

Difficulty Strenuous
Distance 7 miles round trip
Estimated time 4hr
Elevation gain 2000ft ascent
Season All year, but best March to May

Lovely hike that's particularly good in spring, when the river is in spate, and in early summer when the wildflowers are at their best. Ideal when most other trails are still under snow. Start by site #14 at the *Potwisha* campground, follow a dirt road across a concrete ditch with the Marble Fork of the Kaweah River visible (and probably audible) off to your left. Soon you're on a narrow path winding your way up the canyon, with **wildflowers** all about. Chaparral gradually gives way to more alpine scenery as the vegetation opens out, affording a view of **Marble Falls** ahead in **Deep Canyon**. The 70ft falls themselves aren't especially spectacular, but it's a wonderfully pretty spot. Explore the canyon, where several shorter cascades course over marble slabs. Any keen hikers in the party can push further up to Admiration Point and Ash Peaks Ridge while the others rest in the shade by the falls. Return the way you came.

SK6 Middle Fork

Difficulty Strenuous
Distance 18 miles round trip
Estimated time 6–8hr
Elevation gain 2300ft ascent
Season All year

Though this hike through chaparral might sound dauntingly long, it really isn't. There is no essential destination, so you can walk as far as you fancy then turn back. A top-down view of the vertiginous **Panther Creek Falls** (6 miles round trip; 3hr) makes a worthy shorter destination. Being in the lowlands, Middle Fork is a good off-season hike that comes with some great views courtesy of a track that mostly stays high above the Middle Fork of the Kaweah River. That also means there are relatively few chances to get down to the river for a refreshing summer dip, but the route does cross several side streams. Along the way there are great views of Moro Rock to the north, and Castle Rocks to the south, and if you're after an overnight adventure, there are a couple of backcountry campgrounds along the way: obtain a wilderness permit from the Foothills Visitor Center. It's also possible to use this trail as part of a multi-day hiking route, either emerging at Mineral King or heading north towards Bearpaw Meadow and the High Sierra Trail. The trailhead is along the dirt road that extends 1.3 miles east of the *Buckeye Flat* campground.

Hikes around Giant Forest and Lodgepole

The area around Giant Forest and Lodgepole offers perhaps the widest selection of excellent trails in the twin parks, and there's sustenance not far away at both Lodgepole and Wuksachi. We've listed the trails from south to north through the area.

SK7 Moro Rock

Difficulty Easy to moderate
Distance 0.5 miles round trip
Estimated time 1hr
Elevation gain 300ft ascent
Season All year, but take great care when icy (likely Nov–April)

The great, granite dome of **Moro Rock** is the most popular spot to watch the sun set within Sequoia National Park, hardly surprising with the spectacular view you get of the Great Western Divide and the western half of the park. Though a short walk, it is steep, mostly on concrete steps that wend their way to the rounded summit past a handful of viewpoints. Give yourself plenty of time to get a good position, and take some means of illuminating your way back – it gets dark surprisingly quickly. The stairs start at a parking lot two miles southeast of Giant Forest.

SK8 The Watchtower and Lakes Trail

Difficulty Strenuous
Distance 13 miles round trip
Estimated time 6–8hr
Elevation gain 2300ft ascent
Season June to mid-Oct

This fatiguing trail is one of Sequoia's most popular full-day hikes, taking in The Watchtower lookout and a quartet of wonderful alpine lakes. It starts at the Wolverton trailhead and initially follows Wolverton Creek to a trail junction where you head right and fairly steeply up to **The Watchtower** (3–5hr round-trip), an exposed tower of granite overlooking Tokopah Falls far below. From here the path leads past four lakes – Heather, Aster, Emerald and Pear – in increasingly gorgeous and stark glacial cirques. The two furthest lakes, **Emerald Lake** (9200ft) and **Pear Lake** (9500ft), have campgrounds that, for the adventurous and experienced, make good starting points for self-guided trekking into the mountains. Head back the way you came, though you can avoid re-ascending The Watchtower by taking a lower and easier route to the south.

SK9 Alta Peak and Alta Meadows

Difficulty Strenuous
Distance 14 miles round trip
Estimated time 8–10hr
Elevation gain 4000ft ascent
Season June to mid-Oct

Vying with The Watchtower trail for the attention of serious day-hikers, this trail also starts at Wolverton and follows the Lakes trail for the first couple of miles. At a trail junction head right through Panther Meadow to **Panther Gap** where you can enjoy the fabulous views. There's lovely camping ahead at Mehrten Meadow, followed by fairly gentle terrain until the final climb up to **Alta Peak**, the high point on the ridge overlooking the Tokopah Valley and Peak Lake. Overnighters wanting to stay at **Alta Meadow** need to retreat down the hill a couple of miles then turn east for another mile and a half.

SK10 Tokopah Falls

Difficulty Moderate
Distance 3 miles round trip
Estimated time 2–3hr
Elevation gain 500ft ascent
Season April–Nov

Fairly easy valley walk beside the Marble Fork of the Kaweah River, which is superb in early summer, cascading over rocks and forming chutes and huge eddies. The valley walls gradually close in until you're among impressive granite cliffs. The river tumbles down one such cliff forming the 1200ft **Tokopah Falls** (more a tumbling cascade than a fall), which ends in a cool pool – raging during the snowmelt but perfect for a bracing dip in late summer. The trail starts by the Marble Fork Bridge at the eastern end of the *Lodgepole* campground.

SK11 Little Baldy

Difficulty Moderate
Distance 3.5 miles round trip
Estimated time 2–3hr
Elevation gain 700ft ascent
Season May–Nov

This fairly short and accessible there-and-back hike up to a good viewpoint starts from Little Baldy Saddle, six miles north of Lodgepole. The initial short climb is followed by several switchbacks, so you gain height quickly before the trail levels off towards the granite summit of **Little Baldy** at 8044ft. There are spectacular views all around, though sadly those down to the San Joaquin Valley are often marred by a thick blanket of smog. Take plenty of water as you most likely won't find any along the way.

Hikes around Grant Grove

Many people drive along the central section of the Generals Highway without stopping, eager to get to the big trees at Giant Forest or Grant Grove. This is a mistake, particularly if you like the idea of relatively easy walks to panoramic viewpoints and a little-visited sequoia grove. The following hikes are listed from south to north.

SK12 Big Baldy

Difficulty Moderate
Distance 4.5 miles round trip
Estimated time 2–3hr
Elevation gain 650ft ascent
Season Year-round but best April–Nov

It's surprising how few people hike to the dramatically exfoliated granite dome of **Big Baldy** (8209ft) as it offers superb views for relatively little effort. The trail starts from the Generals Highway, a mile or so north of *Montecito Lake Resort*, then takes you up a number of short climbs before levelling off considerably as you traverse **Big Baldy Ridge**. Gaps in the trees give glimpses of the Redwood Mountain Grove of sequoias on the other side of the 2000ft-deep Redwood Canyon to the west. Forested patches of trail are mostly fairly open, so you soon get a view of your destination; once there, you're rewarded with a wide panorama to the west. Enjoy the view then return the way you came.

SK13 Buena Vista Peak

Difficulty Easy
Distance 2 miles round trip
Estimated time 1hr
Elevation gain 450ft ascent
Season Year-round but best April–Nov

Enjoy great 360-degree views for minimal effort from the glacier-polished granite of **Buena Vista Peak** (7605ft). Start at a trailhead parking lot on the west side of the highway, just south of the Kings Canyon Overlook, and head into the trees. You're soon out on a granite ridge with the summit up ahead. After taking in views of Big Baldy, Redwood Canyon and the distant Sierra Nevada sawtooth ridge, descend the way you came.

SK14 Redwood Canyon: Sugar Bowl Loop

Difficulty Moderate
Distance 6.5 miles round trip
Estimated time 3hr
Elevation gain 1000ft total ascent
Season May–Nov

Most of the sequoias in **Redwood Canyon** don't have the girth or height of the true giants of the Sierra, but what is one of the largest of all sequoia groves compensates by the sheer density of young to middle-aged trees. In recent decades, the old idea of immediately putting out all fires, natural or otherwise, has been replaced with a "prescribed burn" policy (see box, p.241) whereby period fires are encouraged. These vigorous young sequoias are the proof of this method's efficacy.

To see the best of the trees, make straight for the **Sugar Bowl Loop**, part of a network of trails starting at the **Redwood Saddle** trailhead, two miles down a rough dirt road (closed in winter) some six miles south of Grant Grove. The loop first heads gently uphill towards Redwood Mountain through mixed conifer forest. It's never very tough, but take breaks to admire the granite scalp of Big Baldy across the valley. Before you reach the highest point on the ridge the path cuts sharply back left and drops steadily into the **Sugar Bowl**, the grove's sequoia heartland. When you hit Redwood Creek, turn left and wind your way steadily back up to the parking lot.

If you turn right at Redwood Creek you can make a larger loop, also visiting the **Fallen Goliath**, a rotting sequoia, and **Hart Tree**, the largest tree in the grove. This larger loop is around ten miles and will take 4–5 hours. **Camping** is also possible in the grove: find a site at least a mile from the road and 100ft from water.

Hikes from Kings Canyon

Kings Canyon offers a wonderful array of hikes, from gentle walks to viewpoints and waterfalls up to one of the most popular multi-day hikes in the Sierra. The following are listed from west to east.

SK15 Cedar Grove Overlook

Difficulty Moderate
Distance 5 miles round trip
Estimated time 3–4hr
Elevation gain 1200ft ascent
Season May to mid-Nov; best June and mid-Sept to mid-Nov

Starting half a mile north of Cedar Grove on Pack Station Road, this trail switchbacks steeply through mixed conifer forest running roughly parallel to **Hotel Creek**. You gradually emerge in more open chaparral with canyon live oak, chinquapin and manzanita. This is an area that has burned several times in recent decades and you can see the succession of new growth as species gradually take over from each other to form a maturing forest.

The slope is south facing and exposed to the sun so start early to beat the heat, or make it a late afternoon hike. The terrain now eases as you climb into ponderosa and Jeffrey pines. At a trail junction turn left and descend a little to the **Cedar Grove overlook**, which affords great views along the length of Kings Canyon and north to the mountains of the Monarch Divide. Return the way you came.

SK16 Lewis Creek—Hotel Creek Loop

Difficulty Moderate
Distance 7-mile loop
Estimated time 3–5hr
Elevation gain 1500ft ascent
Season May to mid-Nov; best June and mid-Sept to mid-Nov

This excellent and moderately popular loop trail develops on the hike up to the Cedar Grove Overlook (see opposite). After soaking up the superlative views from the overlook, return to the trail and continue northwest as you skirt around a hillside. At a trail junction, turn left and head down the Lewis Creek trail, unsurprisingly tracing **Lewis Creek**. This spills you out beside Hwy-180, a good place for a vehicle pick-up if you have amenable friends or family. Otherwise you've got a relatively dull, though not unpleasant, undulating walk back to the trailhead.

SK17 Don Cecil Trail to Lookout Peak

Difficulty Strenuous
Distance 13 miles round trip
Estimated time 7–9hr
Elevation gain 4000ft ascent
Season June–Oct

This fairly tough trail starts four hundred yards east of Cedar Grove and heads southeast, largely following the old route into Kings Canyon used prior to the completion of Hwy-180 in 1939. It's steep going, but relatively cool since it's on the north-facing slope of the canyon. After two miles you reach the shady glen of **Sheep Creek Cascade** before pressing on up the canyon to the wonderfully panoramic **Lookout Peak** (8531ft). Return the way you came.

SK18 Mist Falls

Difficulty Moderate
Distance 9 miles round trip
Estimated time 3–5hr
Elevation gain 600ft ascent
Season June–Oct

The most popular of the day hikes from Road's End heads to Mist Falls, one of the twin parks' largest waterfalls (really just the steepest section of a wonderfully long and tumbling cataract that keeps you company as you hike parallel to the South Fork of the Kings River). From Road's End the trail is easy and sandy, through white fir and ponderosa pines that don't provide much shade in the midday heat. After a couple of miles, turn left at a trail junction and start climbing more steeply into **South Fork Canyon** through forest and chaparral, past an impressive show of rapids. These get louder and fiercer until you reach **Mist Falls** itself. If you're bounding with energy there's nothing stopping you continuing upriver toward Paradise Valley, but (unless you're doing the Rae Lakes Loop; see below) you'll have to turn round and head back the way you came.

SK19 Bubbs Creek to The Sphinx

Difficulty Strenuous
Distance 8 miles round trip
Estimated time 3–5hr
Elevation gain 1200ft ascent
Season June–Oct

The full Bubbs Creek Trail comprises around a third of the Rae Lakes Loop (see below), but here we've taken a smaller bite, turning it into a moderate to strenuous day-walk with the option of staying at the backcountry campground (permit needed). From Road's End you're on the initial flat section of the Mist Falls trail until, two miles along, signs point you across the South Fork of the Kings River and into the **Bubbs Creek** drainage. Switchbacks kick in with a vengeance, but you're quickly rewarded with great views straight back down Kings Canyon. The mountain that's initially straight ahead, then on your right as the path swings round, is **The Sphinx** (9146ft), a granite mountain named by John Muir for its apparent similarity to the Egyptian icon – it takes a bit of imagination, certainly from this angle. At a trail junction, the Sphinx Creek trail heads right towards Avalanche Pass while the Bubbs Creek trail continues straight ahead. Just beyond the junction there's a campground with river water, a handy location for a spot of backcountry camping, only four miles from the trailhead.

Turn back here and head down the switchbacks. Just before you cross back over the South Fork of the Kings River, consider an alternative finish which heads left and follows the left bank of the Kings River. You'll get views across the river of Muir Rock, then just downstream you can cross back to Road's End by means of a swing bridge.

SK20 Rae Lakes Loop

Difficulty Strenuous
Distance 46-mile loop
Estimated time 4–5 days
Elevation gain 7000ft ascent
Season June to mid-Oct

This is one of the best of the multi-day hikes in these parts – and one of the more popular – following the Kings River up past Mist Falls and beyond, through Paradise Valley and Castle Domes Meadow to Woods Creek Crossing, where the route meets the **John Muir Trail**. It follows this for eight miles (so you're bound to meet people just down from, or headed towards, Mt Whitney), passing Rae Lakes before returning to Kings Canyon along Bubbs Creek and the South Fork of the Kings River. This is also on the **Pacific Crest Trail** (see p.135): through-hikers will be coming along it in late June. Permits (best reserved well in advance; see p.221) can be picked up from the Road's End ranger station – you'll need to spell out your plan, taking into account the maximum stay of two nights at Rae Lake, Charlotte Lake and Kearsage Lakes. Bear-resistant food lockers can be found at these and several other spots around the loop. Avoid building campfires, especially above 10,000ft, where wood supplies are very scarce.

Contexts

Contexts

History of Yosemite

Yosemite's written history dates back only 160 years, when Gold Rush pioneers chased the native Ahwahneechee from their home in what is now Yosemite Valley in 1851. Since then, its scenic splendour has drawn ever more people: John Muir for its wild beauty, Ansel Adams for its picture-perfect rocks and trees, and millions more to hike, climb the magnificent granite monoliths, or stroll through the meadows. Of course, the story starts well before that: we've covered the early **geology** and mountain-forming under "Geology, flora and fauna" from p.238.

The Ahwahneechee

Native Americans have been visiting Yosemite for over seven thousand years, with the **Ahwahneechee** tribe (see box, p.65) living in and around the park for the last three thousand years, maybe longer. Until around 2500 years ago, the tribe relied on spear-hunting deer, catching trout and foraging for seeds, but as they grew more sophisticated they shifted to efficient bow and arrows, and added acorns to their diet. Grinding holes for pounding acorns have been found throughout Yosemite Valley, though their locations are not widely advertised. Clam shells found in archeological digs indicate contact with coastal tribes, and the Ahwahneechee also developed trade with the **Paiute** people on the eastern side of the Sierra, trading pinyon nuts and obsidian. Typically they would move with the seasons, spending the cooler months in the fertile valleys, following the deer up to higher (and cooler) elevations in summer.

Historical evidence shows that a couple of generations before the arrival of white folk, a devastating plague swept through the Ahwahneechee, possibly a European disease that had spread inland from the Spanish on the coast. The few survivors teamed up with neighbouring tribes, leaving Yosemite Valley vacant. Though raised among the Mono Lake Paiutes, **Chief Tenaya** had heard tell of a "deep, grassy valley", and after visiting Yosemite decided to lead the remnants of his people – perhaps only two to three hundred of them – back.

Early exploration

In the early half of the nineteenth century, what we now know as central California was still loosely under **Spanish** control, ruled from Mexico. Despite over a hundred years of exploration along the Californian coast, non-natives had yet to penetrate more than a few miles inland, and certainly not far enough to set eyes on Yosemite. Spanish Army lieutenant **Gabriel Moraga**, who was the first white man to explore the Californian interior, didn't see the Merced River meandering through Yosemite Valley, but when he stumbled on its lower reaches on September 29, 1806 (five days after the feast of Our Lady of Mercy), he dubbed it "El Río de Nuestra Señora de la Merced".

History of Sequoia and Kings Canyon

The history of Sequoia and Kings Canyon national parks is covered in Chapter 13.

Over the next few decades, European Americans started straying into Alta California, as it was known, from the east. The first to penetrate the Sierra was a Wyoming fur trapper, **Jedediah Smith**, who crossed the mountains in 1827, and whose tales of good trapping in the California sun inspired others. Among these adventurers was one Joseph Walker, leading what is now known as the **Walker Party** over the mountains from Nevada in late 1833. Deep snows claimed the lives of many horses and the party members were in a sorry state when they became the first whites to enter the Yosemite region. They recorded seeing giant sequoias (probably the Tuolumne or Merced groves) and may have been the first to sight Yosemite Valley from one of the surrounding ridges, though their accounts are too vague to be sure.

The '49ers and the Mariposa Battalion

The **discovery of gold** in central California in 1848 changed everything. Suddenly argonauts from all over the United States and beyond were flooding into the region, and the delicate balance that had existed between the Spanish and the Indians was destroyed. While the gateway towns of Groveland and Mariposa were important gold settlements, the goldseekers – known as the **'49ers**, in reference to the year they came to California – left Yosemite alone as there was little to indicate the source of gold lay in that direction. But traders and pastoralists followed the gold diggers, and whites were soon encroaching on native territory, threatening their supply of game, stealing land and using superior firepower to remove anyone who stood in their way. To protect Ahwahneechee interests, raiding parties were dispatched to nearby encampments, and by 1851 the whites in the surrounding towns were losing patience. An initial punitive foray in January 1851 was led by **James Savage**, a trading post owner at the settlement of Big Oak Flat on the Tuolumne River. It met with little success, and a month later the fledgling state of California sanctioned the formation of a vigilante group, subsequently dubbed the **Mariposa Battalion**. With Savage installed as "Major" and chief scout, they followed the South Fork of the Merced River to present-day Wawona where some Ahwahneechee were captured and others surrendered. The battalion pursued the rest to their villages and became the first non-native Americans to set foot in Yosemite Valley.

The group's surgeon, **Dr Lafayette Bunnell**, became the first of many to lyrically describe Yosemite Valley, later writing that "none but those who have

Naming Yosemite

The Ahwahneechee people had always known Yosemite Valley as **Ahwahnee**, meaning "land of the gaping mouth" – an apt description of Yosemite Valley when seen from its western end. When the Mariposa Battalion arrived in 1851, they camped in the valley and agreed to call it Yosemite, wrongly believing it to be the native name for the area. There seems to be some dispute about how this misunderstanding came about. Some claim it is a corruption of *uzumati*, which means "grizzly bear" and probably refers to the dominant subtribe within the Ahwahneechee. Others contend the battalion misheard the Ahwahneechee word *yohemite* or *yohometuk*, which translates to "some of them are killers", and may have been a reference to the battalion itself.

visited this most wonderful valley can even imagine the feelings with which I looked upon the view that was there presented. The grandeur of the scene was but softened by the haze that hung over the valley – light as gossamer – and by the clouds which partially dimmed the higher cliffs and mountains. This obscurity of vision but increased the awe with which I beheld it, and as I looked, a peculiar exalted sensation seemed to fill my whole being, and I found my eyes in tears with emotion." The party camped in Bridalveil Meadow and Bunnell proposed that the valley be known as "Yosemite", incorrectly honouring what he thought to be the Ahwahneechee name for the area (see box opposite).

A second expedition by the Mariposa Battalion, under Captain **John Boling**, tracked down the rest of the Ahwahneechee, capturing their chief, **Tenaya**, on the shores of what is now Tenaya Lake. Defeated, most of the remaining population was relocated to the baking San Joaquin Valley near Fresno, where many succumbed to European diseases before the rest were allowed back. Chief Tenaya was effectively forced into signing a treaty with the whites, but even the US Senate subsequently determined that it was invalid. The Indians still officially owned the land, but white violence and murder soon drove the remaining Ahwahneechee away, clearing the path for white settlement.

White settlement and early tourism

White foresters and farmers established themselves in Yosemite Valley by using the high-country grasslands, particularly Tuolumne Meadows, for summer grazing. Lured by tales of great waterfalls, the first 48 **tourists** arrived in the summer of 1855. Among them were San Francisco writer (and later Yosemite hotel owner) **James Mason Hutchings** and artist **Thomas Ayers**, whose publicizing works were just the first of many. The famed editor of the *New York Tribune*, Horace Greeley, added his effusive praise, and upper-class Americans began to realize that what they had at home was as good as their traditional stomping grounds in the European Alps. Despite the lack of anything more than a horse trail, numbers of visitors increased steadily, though in the first decade the number of hotel registrations was still only 653.

Another one of those 1855 tourists was mining company employee **Galen Clark**, who the following year quit his job for health reasons and homesteaded 160 acres at what is now Wawona. Clark had heard rumours of enormous trees in those parts, and in May 1857 "discovered" Mariposa Grove and cut a trail to them as an added attraction for the fledgling tourist industry. Clark subsequently guided pioneer landscape photographers Charles Weed and Carlton Watkins and the painter **Albert Bierstadt**, all critical in getting out the message of Yosemite's wonders.

As the giant sequoias became an essential tourist sight, the first stagecoach road was routed this way and visitors spent the night in Wawona before continuing towards Yosemite Valley. In the latter half of the 1850s several hotels sprang up in Yosemite Valley and a few homesteaders started to take up residence, at least during the warmer months of the year. One was **James Lamon**, who built a cabin at the eastern end of the valley, tended a garden and planted an orchard that still produces fruit near Curry Village. Meanwhile, many of the remaining Ahwahneechee had filtered back to the valley, the men adopting European dress and working as guides, wranglers and woodcutters. The women retained more traditional ways, adapting their basket-making to the demands of souvenir hunters. Towards the end of the 1860s, visitor numbers rose to over a thousand a year, and as the focus of tourism shifted progressively towards the valley new and more direct roads were pioneered, most of them being cut in the early 1870s.

Protection and administration

As academic interest in California grew, the California State Geological Survey (always known as the **Whitney Survey**) was sent, under Josiah D. Whitney, to explore the Sierra Nevada. In the early 1860s they named Mount Whitney along with numerous mountains and features in Yosemite, and developed theories on how glaciers helped shape much of the landscape. They were adamant, though, that Yosemite Valley could only have been caused by a great cataclysm or devastating earthquake. Into this framework strode **John Muir** (see box, p.60), who arrived in 1868 and spent much of the next ten years living in or frequently visiting Yosemite, soaking up everything it had to offer and expanding on his theory of the valley's glacial formation. Muir also became a vociferous advocate for the protection and preservation of the land he had come to love.

Around the same time, hoteliers were converting meadows into hay fields and cutting down trees. This didn't sit well with public-spirited men of influence, and in 1864 senator John Conness convinced congress to establish the **Yosemite Land Grant**, with Yosemite Valley and Mariposa Grove transferred from federal to state ownership under the guardianship of Galen Clark. As the first area expressly set aside to protect wilderness, it became the template for the first national park, Yellowstone, which was established eight years later. Illegal homesteaders were forced to leave or sign a lease, but most refused. Hutchings even took his claim to the US Supreme Court and lost, though the California legislature saw fit to award him the princely sum of $60,000 as compensation for the land he never had any right to in the first place.

Though the Yosemite Land Grant afforded some protection, Muir wasn't happy with the logging and sheep grazing taking place. In 1889, he met Robert Underwood Johnson, editor of the influential *Century* magazine. They camped together in Tuolumne Meadows just after some sheep had eaten their way through, and Johnson convinced Muir to write a couple of articles stating his case. These, and Underwood's machinations in Washington, helped bring about the creation of **Yosemite National Park**, which in 1890 became the nation's third (after Yellowstone in Wyoming, and Sequoia).

Here comes the cavalry

Yosemite came under the jurisdiction of the Department of the Interior, who sent in the **cavalry** to help drive out illegal homesteaders, poachers and hopeful prospectors. They stayed in Yosemite until 1914, their role gradually changing from enforcement to management. In 1903, troops of African American "**Buffalo soldiers**" became some of the first "rangers" to be assigned to protect the park. After a short unregulated period, the cavalry were replaced in 1916 by rangers from the newly formed **National Park Service**.

The park's protection was also high on the agenda for the **Sierra Club**, the environmental campaigning organization formed by Muir and others in 1892. He became its first president, and continued in that role for 22 years until his death. Muir's reputation by now was huge, so it was no surprise when President **Theodore Roosevelt** asked Muir to accompany him on his tour of Yosemite. Muir took the opportunity to bend Teddy's ear about the parlous state of Yosemite Valley, which at this stage was still part of the Yosemite Land Grant and managed by the State of California. His arguments obviously had some effect, and in 1905 the valley and Mariposa Grove were finally incorporated into the national park.

But all was not rosy at the Sierra Club headquarters. The same bill also reduced the size of Yosemite National Park by chipping away at sections to the southwest and on the eastern boundary, which were deemed strategic by mining and forestry interests. Buoyed by their success in reducing the size of Yosemite, commercial interests now set their sights on building a dam inside the park boundary at **Hetch Hetchy** (see box, p.79). After twelve years of battles, Congress finally authorized the construction of the O'Shaughnessy Dam in 1913. Though a defeat for Muir and the Sierra Club, it galvanized opposition to such projects elsewhere, helping mark a turning point in government attitudes to protection inside national parks.

Promoting the park

Yosemite had initially been visited by the relatively well-off, but with its designation as a national park, and the existence of several coach roads, numbers increased rapidly to include tourists from a broad spectrum of social classes. In 1899, David and Jennie Curry established **Camp Curry**, the forerunner of today's Curry Village (see p.67), to cater to these new arrivals in modest fashion, and their business grew quickly. With the arrival of the railroad at El Portal in 1907 and the park's legalization of automobile traffic in 1913, Yosemite became truly accessible to the public. By 1916, the Curry Company had been awarded the concession to run services in Yosemite for the annual influx of 35,000 visitors.

During his twelve-year tenure as director of the National Park Service from 1917 to 1929, **Stephen T. Mather** sought to further increase visitor numbers with an aggressive policy of **park development** that led to now unthinkable proposals. He championed the building of the Wawona golf course and the ice rink at Curry Village, made an unsuccessful bid to host the 1932 Winter Olympics at Badger Pass, and even proposed building a road beside Vernal and Nevada falls to Tuolumne Meadows. The Curry Company quickly fell in line, promoting the idea of building a dam on the stream above Yosemite Falls so the flow could be regulated and the tourist season extended. Luckily few of these proposals came to pass, though **bear feeding** was introduced for the edification of tourists. Garbage was spread out for bears each evening, arrayed on specially built platforms in front of visitors. Bears, of course, took a liking to easy meals provided by humans, and 81 people were treated for bear-related injuries in 1929 alone. The bears were the ones blamed, and many were relocated or even killed before the feeding practice was halted in 1940. At much the same time, the few Indians still left in the valley were encouraged to perform **native dances**, often involving teepees and feather headdresses that had nothing to do with the life of their forebears.

By 1930, half a million people were visiting Yosemite each year, and the Park Service was forced to impose controls. Camping in and driving through meadows was banned, and there were greater efforts to manage development. Nonetheless, numbers continued to grow steadily – though the group that initially laid claim to the lands was on its way out. By the late 1960s, the last of the Ahwahneechee residents were effectively forced out of the valley and their village razed (see box, p.65). Meanwhile, the park's image was growing exponentially thanks in part to the efforts of **Ansel Adams** (see box, p.68), who had begun photographing the park to matchless effect as far back as the late 1920s. He also campaigned to maintain Yosemite's ecological values, mainly through his role as a director of the Sierra Club, which he held through the middle of the century.

It was in the late 1960s, near the end of Adams' tenure, that climbers began arriving in droves to scale the great rocks of Yosemite; the era lives on as the Golden Age of Yosemite climbing. The counterculture ethic espoused by many climbers flowed through the next decade when **hippies** started arriving, camping in the meadows, hanging out and generally getting up the noses of uptight rangers. Matters came to a head leading up to Independence Day in 1970 with the **Stoneman Meadow Riots**, when mounted rangers fought a pitched battle with the hippies to clear them out of the meadows. A few dozen were jailed for a short time but both sides compromised and peace returned to the valley.

Modern Yosemite and the future

It has long been recognized that Yosemite is poorly set up to cope safely with almost four million visitors a year while maintaining its ecological and scenic integrity, and in recent decades this has become the park's foremost issue. Recognizing that Yosemite was unable to cope with the tourist strain, the Park Service released the **General Management Plan** in 1980, a document that engendered much talk but little action. At this point there were well over a thousand buildings in the valley so the Plan called for reducing visitor accommodation by seventeen percent and more than halving employee housing. In addition the Wawona tennis courts and golf course were to go, and the Curry Village ice rink was to be pulled up, all by 1990. Almost none of this happened.

Matters really came to a head in the mid-1990s after a couple of major **rockfalls** threatened buildings, and in January 1997, devastating **floodwaters** swept through the valley wiping out large sections of some campgrounds and sluicing away lodging. The valley was closed for ten weeks and you can still see markers around the valley showing the astonishing level the floodwaters reached. The need to site buildings away from the cliffs and out of the Merced River's floodplain presented the Park Service with a golden opportunity to make big steps towards restoring the balance (see box opposite).

These natural disasters hastened the production of the **Final Yosemite Valley Plan**, which came out in 2000 and looked set to dictate the park's development over the next couple of decades. Among other things, traffic was to be reduced in the valley by installing parking elsewhere and bussing visitors in, and electrical hookups were to be added in some campgrounds. The emphasis was on coping with increased visitor numbers, though as the plan came out it was becoming apparent that **park visitation** numbers were actually going down. After peaking in 1996 at 4.2 million, numbers dropped steadily, with 2006 recording only around 3.4 million, easing the impetus for change.

Still, improvements have been made around the base of Lower Yosemite Fall, the shuttle bus system has been extended and gone hybrid, and riparian restoration continues to improve the margins of the Merced River.

The decline in visitor numbers has variously been ascribed to the downturn in the economy, reduced travel after the September 11 terror attacks in 2001, rumours about overcrowding in Yosemite Valley and images of devastation after the 1997 flooding. One Yosemite-specific factor was the brutal murder of four women – three tourists and a worker – in 1999 by Carl Stayner, an employee at one of the

Restoring the balance

Over the last four thousand years, human activity has had a significant impact on Yosemite's environment. The most obvious ongoing impact is in Yosemite Valley, changed in numerous ways by both Miwok and white settlement. The most significant changes made by **Miwok** was with fire (see box, p.241), which changed the balance between black oaks and conifers. **European Americans** then arrived and started messing around with the Merced River. During the wetter months of the year, early valley visitors and residents had to contend with wet feet and slippery boardwalks as they made their way between hotels. The park's guardian, Galen Clark, solved the problem in 1878 by **dynamiting the moraine**, thereby lowering the water table. The trouble was, this dried out the valley too much, and ever since, trees have been invading the meadows. In other places early settlers placed boulders and barriers in the river, deepening and widening it and changing the flows for various purposes: fishing, boating, even to create a source of ice which was stored in a nearby icehouse. River users and hikers wandering along the banks had a detrimental effect on the riparian environment, accelerating **erosion** and limiting shelter for riverlife. In recent years, the Park Service has been striving to return the Merced River to something like its natural condition: barriers have been removed, rafters are encouraged to stick to designated access and egress points, and fallen trees which were previously removed are now left in place.

The adjacent **meadows** act like a sponge, soaking up water during the snowmelt period then gradually releasing it over the dry months of summer and fall. Over the years, millions of visitors have wandered across the meadows, compacting the soil and increasing run-off. Until the 1930s, horses and cows were allowed to graze the meadows, further exacerbating the situation.

Heavy-footed hikers also crush plants, damage nests and kill small animals. Less obviously, the survivors find it difficult to rebuild in the compressed soil. Visitors are now encouraged to stick to boardwalks and the meadow margins, while restoration projects have removed old drainage ditches, dug up former roadbeds, and sensitive areas have been protected by fences so that native plants have a chance to regain their toehold.

Elsewhere, **non-native plants** have been removed, black oak saplings have been protected from grazing deer, buildings have been moved out of flood zones and swimmers have been directed to less vulnerable beaches.

As yet there are no moves to return grizzly bears to Yosemite, but the long absent **peregrine falcons** have returned, though still in very small numbers. Access to rock climbs in falcon nesting areas is restricted in spring.

motels in El Portal, just outside the park. These so-called **Yosemite Murders** hit headlines across the nation and undoubtedly dented Yosemite's appeal.

Since 2006, visitor numbers have gradually climbed (almost 3.9 million in 2009), putting increased pressure on Yosemite Valley accommodation. **Rockfalls** in and around Curry Village in 2008 did little immediate damage but further highlighted the need to site facilities in less vulnerable locations. Around a third of all lodging (over 230 cabins and tent cabins) has been permanently closed along with the main shower house. Meanwhile, the increasing popularity of the hike up Half Dome means that a permit system is now in place limiting numbers of hikers at weekends.

Under the 2009 settlement of legal challenges to the Final Yosemite Valley Plan, the Park Service has essentially agreed to maintain the status quo, though riparian restoration will continue and it is still hoped that a new Indian Cultural Center will one day be constructed on the site of the last occupied Indian village in Yosemite. For more information, consult the park's frequently updated planning website @www.nps.gov/yose/parkmgmt/planning.htm.

Geology, flora and fauna

Yosemite sits astride the Sierra Nevada, a four-hundred-mile-long range that rises steadily from the San Joaquin Valley in the west then drops away steeply almost 10,000ft into the Owens Valley. The park's landscapes stretch from semi-arid foothills in the west to the alpine summits of the Sierra Nevada in the east, with much of the intervening country covered by mature evergreen forests that John Muir felt were the "grandest and most beautiful in the world". Along with the meadows, streams and lakes, the forests provide habitats for eighty-odd species of mammals, hundreds of varieties of plants and wildflowers, a hundred and fifty bird species, and dozens of types of reptiles and amphibians.

Geology

Yosemite National Park is defined by its distinctive granite architecture of domes, spires and waterfall-strung cliffs, much of which was shaped by deep rivers of ice over the last million years. But the formation of the rock itself dates back 500 million years to a time when what is now central California was under a primordial sea. Over the eons, marine sediments were deposited on the sea floor to form **sedimentary rocks**.

Around 200 million years ago, plate tectonics came into play as the Pacific plate started to slide under the North American plate. As the Pacific plate was subducted, the rock melted, welled up, then cooled some six miles underground into dome-shaped blocks of granite known as **batholiths**. Granite is part of the **plutonic igneous** family of rocks characterized by large crystals formed as the molten rock cooled extremely slowly. There are seven types of granite in Yosemite Valley alone, all with slightly different colours and chemistry, the hardest and most weather-resistant forming the steepest cliffs. Half Dome is actually made from one of the youngest types of rock, just 87 million years old.

By 50 million years ago, the sea had receded, leaving a gentle landscape of rolling hills with the Merced River winding through hardwood forests on a bed of sedimentary rock with no granite in sight. Over the next forty million years or so, rivers and streams gradually eroded away the overlying sedimentary and metamorphic rock, while the Merced River cut a V-shaped valley 3000ft deep. The removal of this overburden of rock allowed the granite to expand, forming cracks parallel to the surface, a process still evident today at road cuttings in the high country where distinctive onion-layers are evident. As the rock peeled away, the classic granite domes were formed.

The redwood forests and much of the vegetation familiar today was already established when the Ice Ages began around a million years ago. The first wave of glaciation lasted until 250,000 years ago and covered the entire Yosemite area with glaciers forging down the V-shaped river valleys, scouring away the weaker rock to form the classic glacial **U-shaped valley**. Most of the overlying sedimentary rock was ground away, leaving the awe-inspiring granite features we now know as Half Dome and El Capitan. Thirty thousand yeas ago, the most recent Ice Age brought the **Yosemite Glacier** into Yosemite Valley to add the finishing touches. As the last glacier receded, it left a terminal moraine just west of El Capitan. Behind this moraine the waters of the Merced River created the prehistoric Lake Yosemite, a shallow, five-mile-long lake that over the

Yosemite's glacial wonderland

A few permanent ice fields tucked away high on remote mountains is all that remains of the huge **glaciers** that once carved Yosemite's granite into the wonderful forms we see today. Some 250,000 years ago, the entire park was covered by a thick sheet of ice which chiselled out **U-shaped valleys** such as Yosemite Valley, a classic example which contrasts with the unglaciated V-shape of the Merced River Canyon further downstream.

As the ancient glaciers melted, rock carried along with the ice was deposited to form a **terminal moraine**, which typically held back a lake. Over the millennia these lakes filled with sediment to form the characteristic **flat floor** of glaciated valleys. Tributary glaciers fed into the large glaciers but carved shallower channels which, when the ice melted, left **hanging valleys** and fabulous waterfalls such as Upper Yosemite Fall, Bridalveil Fall and Ribbon Fall.

Even in the depths of the Ice Ages when glaciation was at its maximum extent, the very highest peaks stood above the ice sheet as unglaciated **nunataks**, forming spiky mountaintops such as Tuolumne's Cathedral and Unicorn peaks. As the ice ground its way across the land, rocks embedded in its base scraped across the bedrock leaving telltale parallel scarring known as **striations**. In places the effect is so pronounced that large patches of rock were rubbed smooth to form **glacial polish** that gleams in the sunlight. Pothole Dome in Tuolumne is a prime example.

As the world warmed and the glaciers melted, rocks carried along with the ice were randomly deposited as **erratics**, and large hunks of ice left behind by retreating glaciers melted to form **kettle lakes** in the deep impression they created. Dana Meadows, east of Tuolumne, contains numerous classic examples.

None of this was even suspected until the middle of the nineteenth century, but when **John Muir** arrived in Yosemite in 1868 he began to apply the emerging theories of glaciation to his new home. He came against stubborn resistance from learned geologists who had long believed Yosemite Valley was created in a gargantuan earthquake, but by relentlessly publishing treatises on the matter he eventually won over academia.

millennia filled with sediment carried down by the river. Eventually it formed the flat valley floor we see today, with the Merced River gently winding its way through.

Ecosystems and flora

Because of the huge range of elevations – 2000ft to over 14,000ft – Yosemite, Sequoia and Kings Canyon contain a vast diversity of flora that can be loosely divided into forest **ecosystems** or zones. As elevation increases, moisture levels broadly increase while average temperatures drop, creating zones where different tree species tend to dominate. Smaller flora also change along with the fauna they support, but it is the large trees by which the zones are characterized. Generally porous soils and uneven precipitation make the parks more suited to relatively drought-resistant evergreens, but deciduous trees can be found wherever there's an abundant water supply, generally close to lakes and streams and in moist meadows. The area where meadow meets the oak and coniferous forest is known as an **ecotone**, and it is here that you'll find the greatest wildlife diversity.

The foothills

Yosemite is approached from the west through the Sierra **foothills**, which range between 500ft and 4000ft in altitude. This encompasses the countryside around all the western gateway towns, the western fringes of the park (which start at around 2000ft), and extends up into Yosemite Valley (covered in more detail on p.49). The foothills of Sequoia and Kings Canyon around Three Rivers encompass similar territory. This is a region characterized by wet, cool winters that give way to a moist spring when most of the new growth takes place. Summers are relatively hot and dry, so most species are adapted to cope with fairly frequent **fires** (see box opposite)

Outside the parks you'll travel through open **grasslands** mostly comprising exotic grasses such as wild oat and foxtail fescue. Green in spring, they brown off through summer, and, when fires strike, the perennial grasses can re-sprout from the root crowns. Here you might expect to see wildflowers such as the bright orange **California poppies**, distinctive patches of **baby blue-eyes**, and **lupins**, a species found throughout the Sierra.

In riparian woodlands like those along the Merced River Canyon and into Yosemite Valley, deciduous species predominate. The shrubby **Western redbud** provides a riot of magenta blooms from February to April, and you'll also come across black cottonwood, California sycamore, big-leaf maple and Pacific dogwood (see below).

Shallow well-drained soils provide a perfect terrain for **chaparral**, Spanish for "scrub oak". Low thickets of **canyon oak** are usually interspersed with species of smooth red-barked **manzanita**, a plant with small, thick leaves that resist moisture loss. The scrubby **ceanothus** shares these characteristics along with the ability to sprout from the root crown after fire. Such fires, fuelled by oils in the plants themselves, burn very hot and tend to kill larger trees, ensuring the continued dominance of these species. Manzanita and ceanothus also exist at much higher elevations

Between 2000ft and 4000ft, you'll find **savannah** woodlands dominated by the deep-rooted **blue oak**, which thrives in dry climates.

Yosemite Valley, Wawona and Kings Canyon

The bulk of Yosemite's indoor accommodation and campgrounds are around the 4000ft mark, mostly in **Yosemite Valley** and at **Wawona**. The floor of **Kings Canyon** around Cedar Grove is at 4600ft and falls into the same ecosystem. This interzone region marks the upper reaches of the foothills where chaparral merges with the mixed coniferous forests that predominate higher up. Among these **transition forests**, the dominant features are **meadows** such as those found on the Yosemite Valley floor.

Black oak woodlands and evergreens

As the valley's post-glacial lake dried out, the valley floor was colonized by forests of **black oak**, a large deciduous tree with big, yellow-green leaves and a dark trunk. It is an important source of acorns for squirrels and mule deer, but the tree's bounty was also appreciated by the Ahwahneechee, who encouraged its growth by using fire to keep conifers at bay.

Since then, **fire suppression** (see box opposite) has caused the balance to shift towards **evergreen** species, whose saplings shaded the young oaks and quickly outgrew them. One of the most drought-resistant evergreens is the tall **ponderosa pine**, easily identified by its irregular scaly plates of reddish-yellow bark and long needles in clusters of three. Well adapted to fire, it has thick bark and high

Wild Sierra

With a combined area of 2500 square miles, and hunting prohibited, wild animals live the good life in Yosemite, Sequoia and Kings Canyon national parks. Bears, mule deer, marmots and numerous small forest creatures are common sights, though you can consider yourself lucky if you spy a mountain lion or California bighorn sheep. These animals are free to roam the parks, from the hot and dry foothills through the mid-elevation forests to the icy Sierra peaks. Wherever you go you'll see an abundance of wildflowers: wonderful en masse but especially fascinating when you get down on your knees for closer inspection.

Dogwood ▲

Sequoia grove ▼

Wildflowers

The parks boast a huge array of **wildflowers**. In the foothills, at an altitude of around 2000ft, they start blooming with the arrival of spring in early March, but up at around 9000ft, in the beautiful high meadows, the short growing season forces them into a burst of colour from July to early September. In the high alpine regions around 13,000ft, the last of the wildflowers won't seed until October, just before the first snows.

Purple **lupin** have adapted wonderfully to just about every ecological niche. Other species are much more picky. The bright orange **California poppy** – the official state flower – is found in open areas and along roadsides up to 4000ft, while the vibrant lilac **wild iris** favours marshy meadows from 4000 to 8000ft, and the creamy **dogwood** blooms are at their best down in Yosemite Valley. Other favourites include **shooting stars**, whose heads have yellow and black tips with purple petals that appear like the trailing tail of a meteorite, and **Indian paintbrush**, whose low-growing clusters of red flowers look like they were dipped into a paint pot.

Sequoias

The **giant sequoia** (a cousin of the coastal redwood) is the earth's most massive living thing. Up to 300ft high and 30ft in diameter, some of these arboreal monsters weigh in at a whopping 1000 tons, courtesy of a broad trunk that barely tapers from base to crown. Some live for three thousand years, partly due to the thick, cinnamon-coloured **bark** that protects the sapwood from the periodic forest fires, and gives the tree its redwood tag. Once common throughout the western Sierra Nevada, sequoias are now only found in around 75 isolated groups, at altitudes between 5000 and 8500ft. The biggest individual specimens are in Sequoia and Kings Canyon national parks, where there are over two dozen **groves**. Yosemite has just three main groves: Mariposa, Tuolumne and Merced. Early residents also planted several in Yosemite Valley – some by the chapel and others in the cemetery – though none is yet above 6ft in diameter.

Marmots

In the Sierra high country above 10,000ft, the evergreens are getting thinner and more stunted, and wildlife seems scarce... except for the **yellow-bellied marmot**. These shy and shaggy ten-pound rodents waddle about the talus slopes searching for grass, flowers, bugs and even bird eggs, their favourite food.

At the slightest danger, they whistle to their mates, which has earned them the nickname of "whistle pig". Quickly they dive for cover into one of several burrows fashioned among the loose rocks. Coyotes and golden eagles are what they're really worried about, but a swift movement on your part and they'll be gone – though you'll soon see their inquisitive noses poking out to test if the coast's clear. After all, they've got a lot of fattening up to do before they hibernate through the worst of the winter snows.

Mule deer

Around dawn and dusk **mule deer** browse the meadows around Yosemite Village, seemingly oblivious to all the tourist traffic. They seem pretty tame and will often let you get quite close, but they are wild animals. Deer cause more injuries than bears in the park.

▲ Marmot

▼ Mule deer

Easily identified by their mule-like ears, white rump and black-tipped tail, they weigh in at 100 to 200 pounds and a full-grown buck is tall enough to look you in the eye when standing on all fours.

Mule deer are typically content to browse on berries and herbaceous plants; when disturbed they bound away landing on all four feet at each leap. Fences are no obstacle.

Bears

Despite its prominence on the state flag, the grizzly bear has been extinct in California since 1922 when the last specimen was shot close to Sequoia National Park. In Yosemite, Sequoia and Kings Canyon you'll only come across the smaller **black bear**, whose fur might range from anything between blond or cinnamon to black or brown. Females weigh around 250 pounds, with males generally a hundred pounds heavier, though the largest recorded was a mighty 700 pounds.

With several hundred resident bears in each park, they are relatively common, but can be hard to spot. They generally rest in the shade or go about their business quietly during the day, so you're more likely to spot them around dawn or dusk when they are feeding. Backcountry sightings are relatively rare but, perhaps counter-intuitively, you'll often see them where people congregate, particularly around campgrounds or prowling around the parking lots after dark in search of human food. The Park Service goes to great lengths to discourage this behaviour: see box, p.10. In winter, bears den for short periods to conserve energy, but don't truly hibernate, and hikers should never assume there are no bears around.

ideal for **Douglas fir**, with its soft, inch-long needles and numerous, distinctive three-pronged bracts which protrude from the brown, egg-shaped cones.

Scattered among these other trees you'll find **sugar pines**, the largest of the Sierra pines and with the biggest cones, some a massive eighteen inches long. With their long, straight trunks, sugar pines are a target species for loggers who have removed most trees outside protected areas such as Yosemite. During the decades of fire suppression, these majestic conifers have gained an understorey of shade-loving **white fir**, which has thin, grey bark and branches that sweep to the ground making it susceptible to fire.

Riparian areas and meadows

Along river banks, beside lakes and in shady, moist side canyons the **Pacific dogwood** thrives. Catch it in late April and May and few are unmoved by the display of large, creamy white blossoms. These trees seldom grow taller than thirty feet, but their elegant shape makes a beautiful contrast to the backdrop of pines. The dogwood often has the company of the **big-leaf maples**, which populate the talus slopes at the foot of the valley cliffs. They're distinguished by palm-shaped leaves up to a foot across, which turn golden yellow in autumn. Look too for the smaller **mountain maple**, with much smaller but equally pretty leaves.

The meadows of Yosemite Valley, Wawona and Kings Canyon are prime **wildflower** habitats. You may not get the visual impact of some of the higher meadows, but here you'll find the longest wildflower season (roughly April to August) and a more diverse selection than anywhere else. Wildflower buffs return year after year to experience the meadows at slightly different seasons, but if here from May to July look out for the **shooting stars**, which take the Latin name *Dodecatheon*, meaning "Twelve Gods". The idea is that the pattern of yellow, pink and purple is so delicate it must have taken a dozen Greek gods to complete the job. Visit El Cap Meadow from May to July for the display of the lilac and white **wild iris**, which also goes by the name of Western Blue Flag. Other favourites include the purple **elegant brodiaea** and the even deeper purple **winecup clarkia**, but there are really too many gorgeous examples to mention.

Middle elevations

Elevations between 6000ft and 8000ft support the so-called **mid-elevation forests**, which benefit from higher levels of snow and rainfall. Temperatures are cooler, though, and these two factors combine to favour a different set of dominant trees, easily seen from Tioga Road and the Generals Highway. **White pines** find their greatest expression in the middle elevations, where they can form stands that are up to eighty percent pure. These tend to be intermixed with **Jeffrey pines**, easily confused with ponderosa pines though distinguished by their larger cones (5–8 inches) with prickles that turn inwards at the ends of the scales. The two species don't overlap much, and Jeffrey pines have darker and more furrowed bark with bunches of three needles over eight inches long. At higher elevations they often appear stunted and twisted. A fairly narrow band between 6500ft and 8000ft – where there is reliable moisture year-round – is now the sole preserve of the **giant sequoias** (see box, p.213). There are only three groves of these magnificent trees in Yosemite and a couple of dozen more in Sequoia and Kings Canyon, almost all mixed with white fir and Jeffrey pine.

Many of the wildflowers mentioned above exist at these higher elevations, but also look out for the brilliant magenta **mountain pride penstemon**, which grows in roadside clusters on low bushes, and the scarlet **Indian paintbrush**.

Fire: friend or foe?

Summer visitors to Yosemite often wonder why there are several **fires** burning with no one trying to put them out. While often thought of solely in terms of the harm they do, fires don't destroy a forest, but are an important part of the forest ecosystem that keeps the ratio of species in balance and recycles nutrients to the soil.

Historically, **lightning strikes** have started fires which would burn at relatively cool temperatures and sweep slowly through the forest singeing the base of the trees and the lower branches. With the forest canopy still largely intact, the forest could then regenerate quite quickly. Some species even evolved to benefit from this process, and certainly the giant sequoias can't regenerate without periodic fires (see box, p.231). Over a period of twenty to fifty years a patchwork of fires would tidy up the whole forest.

Into this dynamic but relatively stable scene stepped the **Miwok** people, about four thousand years ago. They relied on oak trees for their acorn supply and made abundant use of meadow plants for food, medicinal and ceremonial purposes. Fire became an important tool for clearing conifers and creating open oak woodlands and meadows where milkweed, dogbane, sedge root and bunch grass would grow. When **European Americans** started living in Yosemite Valley in the 1860s, black oaks predominated, but settlers put an end to Miwok burns.

Fire suppression has since drastically reduced the number of black oaks, and over the next hundred years the meadows were colonized particularly by white fir which is normally kept at bay by fire. Thick-barked trees which benefit from fires – Douglas fir, incense cedar, red fir and Jeffrey pine – were progressively crowded out. The once open groves where Muir liked to walk "along sunny colonnades and through openings that have a smooth park-like surface" have become much harder to find. For an idea of what the valley once looked like you'll need to search out the oak woodland close to Pohono Bridge, though the Park Service is giving the black oaks a chance to re-establish themselves by fencing off natural oak nurseries to stop people trampling the soil, and protecting the young shoots with plastic tubes to keep out the grazing deer. Look for examples around Yosemite Village.

Decades of fervent fire suppression left dangerous levels of **debris accumulation** on the forest floor, and any fire would quickly become a raging **crown fire** killing everything in its path. Forests now took many years to regenerate. It wasn't until the late 1960s, after over a century of fire suppression, that ecologists recognized fire's pivotal role in forest regeneration and started revising their approach. The current fire policy has two facets. **Lightning-strike fires** are left to burn themselves out, so it is not uncommon to find backcountry fires burning throughout summer and fall. This puts some areas (and trails) off-limits for months, and Yosemite Valley visitors can wake to find the valley full of **smoke**, which gradually lifts and blows away as the day wears on. If such fires threaten human life or property they are extinguished as quickly as possible, so you're unlikely to find wildfires close to Yosemite Valley, Tuolumne Meadows or Wawona. In such populated areas where no fires have occurred for long periods, the Park Service removes the forest floor debris by **prescribed burns**, which are intentionally set when light winds are blowing in the right direction and moisture levels are high enough to limit the risk of a raging blaze. They are closely monitored as they slowly clear out the woody debris.

first branches that make it hard for fires to "ladder" up to the crown where more damage can be done. Ponderosas range up to around 8000ft but start as low as Yosemite Valley and Wawona where they were once the dominant evergreen. That mantle has now passed to the more shade-tolerant **incense cedar**, which with its feathery cinnamon-red bark can sometimes be confused with a young sequoia. The name comes from its soft, lacy foliage that is fragrant when crushed. Wetter locales, such as side canyons off Yosemite Valley and against north-facing cliffs, ar

The high country

Between 8000ft and 10,000ft you're in the **high country**, commonly experienced around Tuolumne Meadows and on hikes in Sequoia and Kings Canyon. This **subalpine** zone receives the heaviest snowfall, meaning dominant species are moisture-loving. **Red fir**, also evident in the middle elevations, become ever more prevalent above 8000ft. They often grow in pure stands, their cinnamon-coloured trunks rising to a dense canopy that shades the ground allowing snow to remain well into summer. Like all firs, their cones grow upright on the branches, in this case rising six to eight inches.

Shallower, drier soils (often in glacially scoured basins) support near-pure stands of **lodgepole pines**, the pines within the Sierra with two needles per cluster. Paradoxically these trees also favour boggy ground and can range right up to the tree line. The lodgepole takes its name from close cousins that were used for teepee poles by Plains Indians, though the Sierran lodgepole is usually too stout. Fire is often required to open the cones, but once achieved, lodgepoles are quick to root in burned or disturbed areas. Little else grows in the lodgepole forest except the shrubby **Labrador tea**, which bears white flowers from June to August, and **red mountain heather** with its pink, bell-shaped flowers.

Lodgepole forests are frequently intermixed with **mountain hemlock**, which prefers cool, shaded habitats where winter snowdrifts pile deep. Identifiable by their drooping tip, they can be best spotted between Tenaya Lake and Tuolumne Meadows. Other relatively common species at these elevations include the five-needled **western white pine**, which is similar to the sugar pine but with cones half as long, and the squat and stunted **whitebark pine**, common around the 10,000ft mark. Perhaps even more gnarled, the **western juniper** also occupies some of the highest ground, clinging to whatever crevices it can get its roots into. According to John Muir it seemed to live on just "sunshine and snow", but some manage to hang on for over a thousand years, becoming beautifully weathered in the process. Among all these evergreens it might seem strange to find groves of deciduous trees, but in the upper regions close to the tree line you'll see groves of **aspen**, with its smooth, white bark and heart-shaped leaves that seem to flutter, earning it its usual moniker of "quaking aspen".

Along with some of its most beautiful forests, the Sierra high country boasts the most abundant lakes, typically either in bedrock hollows scoured by ancient glaciers or in kettle lakes. The surrounding **meadows** are usually too wet for substantial trees to grow, but they make wonderful areas for **wildflowers**. Many favourites from lower elevations crop up (albeit in slightly different forms), but are supplemented by the **camas lily**, with its gold anthers, the bell-shaped **leopard lily**, and many more.

Above 10,500ft is the **alpine zone**, which contains few trees but does have plants adapted to a very short growing season. They mostly grow low to the ground in cushions or mats, such as **moss campion**.

Fauna

The rich diversity of Sierra **wildlife** is largely the result of its wide-ranging ecosystems, which support a variety of animals. Most visitors to Yosemite, Sequoia and Kings Canyon don't make any special effort to look for wildlife, but almost everyone sees plenty. Spend a few hours in Yosemite Valley, around Wawona, in Mariposa Grove, along Sequoia's Crescent Meadow Road or in Kings Canyon, for example, and you'll more than likely spot mule deer grazing.

Large mammals

On any visit to the parks you'll almost certainly see a few campground critters, but other mammals are often hard to see. The most common sightings are **mule deer**, which are found everywhere, though they migrate throughout the year, favouring the lower valleys in cooler seasons and the high country in summer. That said, even in July you'll see their distinctive mule-like ears and black-tipped tail around Yosemite Valley and Wawona as they graze the meadows virtually oblivious to human activity. For the best viewing head towards shaded areas in the morning and evening.

Also common throughout the parks are **black bears** (see *Wild Sierra* colour section, and "Smarter than the average bear" box on p.10). At 250–350 pounds they're the largest mammals in the Sierra, and are most commonly seen foraging around campgrounds at dusk.

Wolves have been wiped out locally, but **mountain lions** (cougars) survive, always keeping a very low profile, usually alone in the high country. Five feet long (plus a 3ft black-tipped tail) and weighing up to two hundred pounds, they are very rarely seen, though you may come across their four-toed clawless footprints or scratch marks on trees. Mountain lions mainly hunt for deer and smaller animals, but when they get the chance they're happy to chow on **bighorn sheep**. Before white settlers came to the Yosemite region, these High Sierra grazers were relatively common, but loss of habitat, disease and hunting eradicated them from the park by 1914. Attitudes changed, and in 1986, 27 bighorns were reintroduced to Lee Vining Canyon, east of Tioga Pass. After a couple of harsh winters and continued mountain lion and coyote predation, the sheep were finally listed as an endangered species in 2000 and with greater preservation efforts their future seems far more assured. Your best chance of seeing one is in Lee Vining Canyon, where the light brown fur is a suitable camouflage, though the male's massive curved horns give the game away.

Other largish mammals include: stumpy-tailed **bobcats**, which hunt small game in scrub and chaparral; the voracious small-bear-like **wolverine**, which hunts and scavenges mostly in alpine and subalpine regions; the silver-grey **coyote**, which eats just about anything it can find as it ranges from the foothills to the tree line; and a couple of species of **fox** (the grey and the rare red) only found in oak woodlands, chaparral and lowland forests.

Smaller critters

Smaller mammals are almost too numerous to mention, and wherever you go in the Sierra you'll be visited by scavenging creatures of some description. **Chipmunks** show up everywhere in Yosemite Valley, especially around campgrounds, where you might also see tree squirrels such as the white-chested **Douglas squirrel** and the **Western Gray squirrel**, with its impressive bushy tail. During the spring mating season, look out for the Western Grays chasing each other and fighting.

There's an abundance of **mice**, **shrews**, burrow-digging **moles**, **bats**, **wood rats**, **weasels**, **martens** and **voles** but only a few are of much interest to the non-specialist. **Raccoons** inhabit riparian areas at lower elevations, **badgers** range through the open forests over a wide elevation range, and **skunks** ferret around the foothills.

Up in the high country you may spot the **Belding's ground squirrel**, which is usually known as the "picket pin" for its habit of sitting bolt upright and whistling sharply when disturbed. They inhabit the red fir forests and high-country meadows and hibernate through winter. Another high-country resident is the guinea-pig-sized **pika**, which lives among rocks gathering hay so that it can survive through the winter snow without hibernating. You'll probably hear its distinctive "enk" whistle before you see it. The highest-living of the mammals is the ten-pound **yellow-bellied marmot**, a large rodent at home in extensive rock piles where it can often be seen sunning itself, though not when any coyotes or golden eagles are around. Tioga Pass and Sequoia's Mineral King are prime marmot territory.

Birds

A quarter of all North American **bird species** have been recorded in Yosemite, though only around 150 species are regular visitors. Of all campground foragers, the boldest and most raucous is the **Stellar's jay**, a western cousin of the blue jay, with its bright blue sides and black topknot. Its distinctive caw-like screech and year-round presence means it seldom goes unnoticed. **Woodpeckers** can be heard among the trees, especially the pilated, acorn, downey and white-headed varieties, and soaring high on the cliffs you might even spot acrobatic **peregrine falcons** which have recently returned to Yosemite in small numbers. They can sometimes be seen near El Capitan and around Glacier Point, where around a dozen birds are regularly tending a handful of nests built on narrow rock ledges high above the valley floor. With keen eyesight it can dive at almost 200mph, capturing its prey in midair. Removed from the federally endangered list in 1999, the peregrines is just one of four species of falcon in the park (along with the prairie falcon, kestrel and merlin), and can be identified by its hood of dark feathers and light underside.

Other raptors found in Yosemite are **golden eagles**, occasionally seen in the valley but more commonly at higher elevations. Look for a very large dark brown bird that holds its broad wings flat when soaring, though juveniles have white areas on the wings and tail. One bird you probably won't see is the endangered **great gray owl**, though you've a better chance of seeing it in Yosemite than just about anywhere else, most likely on forest margins near meadows.

Fish, amphibians and reptiles

Historically Yosemite (like much of the Sierra) had virtually no **fish** in the rivers and streams above 4000ft, but early promoters saw the opportunity to attract anglers to the park. Hatcheries were built in Wawona (1895) and Happy Isles (1927), and streams and lakes were stocked with introduced trout – brown, brook, cutthroat and golden – which supplemented the native **rainbow trout**. All species grow to ten pounds under favourable conditions. Over the same period, migratory salmon and steelhead have been prevented from spawning in Yosemite streams as their passage has been halted by dams downstream. High-country lakes are no longer stocked for sport, but self-sustaining populations keep the occasional fishermen interested.

The presence of introduced trout has had a detrimental impact on **amphibians** as small frogs form a major part of the trout diet. Still, Yosemite has more than a dozen species of frogs, toads and salamanders. Found in or near water, the two most interesting are the **Mount Lyell salamander** and the **limestone salamander**, both largely endemic to Yosemite, the latter very rare and only discovered in 1952. The half-dozen species of **lizard** between them inhabit virtually the whole park, with the northern alligator lizard favouring forested areas up to the alpine zone.

Snakes are also well represented with over a dozen species. The only venomous representative is the **Western rattlesnake**, most common below 5000ft, though the occasional rattler has been seen at double that elevation. Well camouflaged in forest, they often sun themselves on rocks. Though they may look dangerous, there's nothing to fear from other snakes. A case in point is the attractive California **mountain kingsnake** with its black, white and red banding. It is occasionally seen crossing the road. Another pretty example is the **ringneck snake**, which has an orange-yellow ring around its neck and a red, yellow and orange belly.

Rock climbing in Yosemite

Yosemite Valley and Tuolumne Meadows are renowned for their excellent granite walls and domes, and fine weather – a combination that has made Yosemite National Park the Mecca for **rock climbers** from all over the world. For many, the pinnacle of climbing achievement is the 3000ft face of **El Capitan**. The routes are highly convoluted, but what is probably the world's most famous climb, **The Nose**, lies straight ahead, tracing a line up the prow of El Capitan past the relative luxury of El Cap Towers. This 20ft-by-6ft patio, over 1500ft above the valley floor, is used as a bivouac spot by climbers who typically spend three to five nights on the route. Dozens of other routes follow barely imaginable sequences of cracks and ledges up the cliffs to the left and right. To the right lies the **North American Wall**, where a route of the same name passes directly through a large mark on the rock looking remarkably like a map of North America. Left of The Nose is the **Salathé Wall**, named after one of the valley's pioneer climbers.

The early years

John Muir was Yosemite's first climber; some would say he was also Yosemite's first climbing bum as he effectively dropped out of society in the early 1870s to be among the mountains. While he never bothered with ropes, his explorations took him to places many people can barely reach today, even with a full rack of climbing gear. Perhaps his finest ascent was **Cathedral Peak**, south of Tuolumne Meadows, which when he left it was as natural and pristine as before.

At much the same time, Scottish trail builder and blacksmith **George Anderson** became the first person to stand on the top of **Half Dome** after he had drilled holes, five to six feet apart, all the way up its northeast shoulder. This was Yosemite's first **aid climb** (see box opposite), and the divergent climbing ethics of these two Scotsmen set a pattern for the future.

Yosemite has long captured the imagination of climbers, but technical rock climbing didn't kick off here until the early 1930s. In 1933, four Bay Area climbers reached what is now known as the Lunch Ledge, 1000ft up Washington Column – the tower opposite Half Dome. That same year, Yosemite climbing pioneers Dick Leonard, Jules Eichorn and Bestor Robinson made two abortive attempts on **Higher Cathedral Spire** having used Ansel Adams' photographs of the spire to plan a likely route up. A third, successful, attempt in April 1934 is considered Yosemite's first landmark climb.

In these primitive times, heavy steel pitons were driven into cracks and weighty karabiners attached the pitons to ropes that were so weak the protection they provided was mostly psychological. Still, climbers continued to knock off new climbs, including the fifteen-pitch **Royal Arches** route, which weaves its way up the ledges and slabs behind *The Ahwahnee*. On this ascent, Morgan Harris became Yosemite Valley's first recorded practitioner of the pendulum traverse.

During World War II, many climbers enlisted in the army helping form its 10th mountain division, enabling them to keep climbing. After being demobbed, climbers employed newly developed, tough nylon ropes and lightweight safety equipment to push standards to new levels, and pipe dreams

For practical details of rock climbing – including courses and guided climbs – see Chapter 6, "Summer activities".

Bathooks and bugaboos

Many of the most celebrated routes in Yosemite are what's known as "Big Wall" routes, tackled by **aid climbing**, where bits of metal are hammered into cracks and hauled on to achieve upward movement. The demands of ever harder climbs have pushed the development of an extensive armoury that's totally baffling to the uninitiated: bathooks, birdbeaks, bongs, bugaboos, circleheads, fifi hooks, a funkness device, lost arrows and RURPs are all employed either to grapple a ledge or wedge into cracks of different sizes. The scale of Yosemite's walls is such that few cracks can be followed from bottom to top, and to get from one crack to another, climbers employ death-defying **pendulums**, and repeatedly sweep across the face, gaining momentum until they can lunge out at a tiny flake or fingertip hold. All this "nailing" and swinging takes time, and most Big Wallers are forced to spend nights slung in a kind of lightweight camp bed known as a **portaledge**. Food, gallons of water, sleeping bags, warm clothing and wet-weather gear must all be lugged up in haul sacks, along with a well-loaded iPod – after all, it can get a bit tedious hammering away up there for hours on end. As Yosemite veteran John Long writes: "Climbing a wall can be a monumental pain in the ass. No one could pay you enough to do it. A thousand dollars would be too little by far. But you wouldn't sell the least of the memories for ten times that sum."

became realistic propositions. An early conquest, in 1947, was **Lost Arrow Spire**, rising to the right of Yosemite Falls and easy to spot in the early morning and late afternoon light when the spire casts a shadow on a nearby wall. This was the first route intentionally approached as a multi-day ascent, much of the groundwork being laid by Swiss-born blacksmith **John Salathé**. He was at the cutting edge of climbing, putting up technically demanding aid routes through the late 1940s and early 1950s, and even fashioning his own tougher carbon-steel pitons from the axles of a Model A Ford. These were put to good use in 1950 when Salathé and another Valley leading light, **Allen Steck**, made the first ascent of the face of Sentinel Rock. This was Salathé's last major route and was done in typically pure style, only drilling a protection bolt into the rock when it was absolutely necessary.

Scaling the big cliffs

For the next twenty years, two talented climbers with widely divergent styles assumed Salathé's mantle. Classical purist **Royal Robbins** followed Salathé's ethical approach, whereas hard-living **Warren Harding** was prepared to drill a bolt just about anywhere if it would help him get up something new. Little love was lost between them, though they did team up for the first, unsuccessful, attempt on the Northwest Face of **Half Dome**. Months later, in 1957, when Robbins led a different team up the route, Harding got wind of their ascent and was on the summit to congratulate them. It was a magnificent effort and ranked as the hardest climb in North America at the time. Yosemite became an international forcing ground for aid climbing, and Americans were suddenly matching, and even surpassing, the achievements of previously dominant Europeans.

Now even the mighty El Cap seemed possible, and Harding, having been robbed of the prize of Half Dome, had the strongest incentive. **The Nose** was the most obvious line but refused to submit for seventeen months, even after Harding used four massive pitons fashioned from stove legs scavenged from the Berkeley city dump and drove them into what are still known as the Stoveleg Cracks. Harding and two colleagues finally topped out in 1958 after a single thirteen-day push, the culmination of 47 days' work on the route.

These siege tactics didn't sit well with Robbins who, in 1960, pulled together a team that climbed The Nose in a self-contained seven-day effort. This team included up-and-coming youngsters, **Chuck Pratt** and **Tom Frost**, who joined Robbins the following year to put up a route on the **Salathé Wall** to the left of The Nose. It wasn't until 1965 that a two-man team completed an El Capitan route, the **Muir Wall**, which was then climbed a year later by Robbins, solo.

The Golden Age

With these critical ascents completed, climbers' aspirations broadened and the 1960s became the **Golden Age** of climbing in Yosemite Valley, when it drew a motley collection of dropouts and misfits, many ranking among the world's finest climbers. For some, climbing had now become a lifestyle, and park residency rules were ignored as people learnt to get by on next to nothing if it meant they could stay in *Camp 4* for months and climb. With this level of commitment, climbing standards shot up. Almost all the major walls and hundreds of minor routes were completed at this time, but the old guard was still at work. In 1967 **Liz Robbins** became the first woman to climb Half Dome when she climbed it with her future husband, Royal. Women climbers were still a rarity in the valley at this time, but by 1973 El Capitan had been topped by the first all-women team.

The final chapter in the Robbins/Harding saga took place in 1970 when Warren Harding and Dean Caldwell climbed a new El Capitan route called the **Dawn Wall**. It became controversial after they'd been on the wall about three weeks and worried friends called for a rescue. The climbers were fine and refused the rescue, finally topping out a week later to a full media welcome. Their faces were plastered all over the national newspapers. Harding had placed over three hundred bolts on the climb, something Robbins felt was totally unjustified and would set a bad precedent as new climbs could basically be constructed from a long series of bolts. To make his point he started climbing the route cutting out most of the bolts as he went. He soon had to acknowledge that the quality and difficulty of the climbing on the route justified the bolting, and he climbed the rest without cutting any more bolts.

The Stone Masters and their disciples

By the mid-1970s, all the obvious lines and the major cliffs had been climbed, and some of the originality had seeped out of the climbing. The new breed were searching for something new and as the Golden Age came to an end, the so-called **Stone Masters** began demolishing old standards. According to one of the original Stone Masters, **John Long**, the requirements were "one, you had to climb Valhalla which is 5.11, one of the hardest routes in the country; two, you had

---

Naming rights

Generally the first people to climb a route get **naming rights**. Traditionally names were straightforward descriptions such as Northwest Face and East Buttress, but very soon a little more imagination was required. Good climbing guidebooks often explain the sources of names like *Left Rabbit Ear Route* and *Ephemeral Clogdance*, but many more get lost in time. One story from 1967 tells of Royal Robbins eschewing the traditional use of pitons and adopting the new European practice of climbing using non-intrusive metal wedges known as "nuts" for protection. He put up a brilliant five-pitch route and called it *Nutcracker Sweet* (now known simply as *The Nutcracker*). Robbins' long-time rival, Warren Harding, found the whole Tchaikovsky reference preposterous and immediately set about climbing a new route nearby, which he then named *Cocksucker Concerto*. It now goes by the abbreviated moniker of *CS Concerto*.

to be a young, arrogant punk; and three, you had to have the capacity to smoke enormous amounts, prodigious amounts, of really, really bad marijuana; and we all had those talents, and so that was the glue that held the whole thing together." Somehow, Long, head Stone Master **Jim Bridwell**, and Billy Westbay kept their heads together long enough to complete the first **one-day ascent of The Nose** on midsummer's day 1975. Meanwhile languid afternoons and "rest" days back in *Camp 4* were spent trying to climb the boulder problem known as "Midnight Lightning" on the Columbia Boulder in the middle of the campground. Finally, in 1978, **Ron Kauk** sent the final move and set the standard for the thousands who have tried to follow his example.

As the 1980s dawned, the creation of new, sticky rubber climbing shoes helped make climbing even more athletic. Purists became disenchanted with the artificiality of aid ascents and began to concentrate on **free climbing**, only using their body to climb the rock, but still using ropes and climbing hardware to provide protection in case of a fall. Jim Bridwell, John Long, Ron Kauk and others had "freed" about half of Salathé Wall back in 1975, but it wasn't until 1988 (27 years after Robbins' first ascent) that Todd Skinner and Paul Piana completed the first free ascent of the whole route.

The culmination of years of cutting-edge climbing, and months of route-specific training, was **Lynn Hill**'s ground-breaking free ascent of The Nose in 1993, praised and admired by all, if ruefully by some in Yosemite's traditionally macho climbing community. Hill repeated the climb in a day the following year, something not matched until **Tommy Caldwell**'s 2005 ascent in under twelve hours.

A totally different approach was taken by **Mark Wellman** who in 1989 became the first paraplegic to climb El Capitan. Together with climbing partner Mike Corbett, who's climbed El Cap over fifty times, Wellman was able to ascend The Nose by doing over seven thousand pull-ups over seven days.

Speed climbing, enchainment and free soloing

There is always scope for new routes, and variations are being put up all the time, but much of the cutting-edge action in Yosemite in recent years has been in **speed climbing** (usually a combination of free and aid climbing). It is not something to be undertaken lightly. To shave time off a climb, practitioners both climb together with a length of rope between them, the leader placing gear for protection that is later taken out by the second. Eventually the leader will run out of appropriate gear and they'll regroup before continuing. When **simul-climbing** in this way there may only be one or two pieces of protection between the climbers, and a mistake could result in a fall of a hundred feet or more, with the obvious risk of serious injury or death.

Speed climbing goes hand in hand with **enchainment**, linking together two or more big climbs in a day. In 1986, Yosemite hardmen **Peter Croft** and **John Bachar** set a landmark by climbing both El Capitan and Half Dome in a day. Then in 1993 Croft hooked up with **Hans Florine** for an ascent of The Nose in an impressive 4 hours 22 minutes. Since then, the time has been progressively knocked down to a superhuman 2 hours 36 minutes and 45 seconds, done in November 2010 by **Dean Potter** and **Sean Leary**.

Throughout the 1990s younger climbers were increasingly attracted to **bouldering**, effectively free solo climbing with no ropes or equipment. Typically boulder problems don't get more than a few feet off the ground, but there is a venerable tradition of **free soloing** far longer routes. Peter Croft, John Bachar and Dean Potter are all renowned for their bold solo climbs where one false move would mean certain death. The sport's fans rave about the Zen calmness that descends as a way of overcoming the fear, while its detractors regard this sub-branch of rock climbing as something of a dead end.

Books

M ost of the following **books** are widely available in stores in either Yosemite National Park or Sequoia and Kings Canyon National Parks (or both) and the surrounding towns. They may be harder to find further afield and are virtually unseen outside North America. All are available through the major internet booksellers, but first try the Yosemite Conservancy's online shop (®www.yosemiteconservancystore.com), which has all worthwhile Yosemite-related books. For books on the southern twin parks visit the Sequoia Natural History Association's site ®www.sequoiahistory.org. Particularly recommended books are marked with the ⚑ symbol.

Travel and impressions

Elizabeth Carmel *The Changing Range of Light: Portraits of the Sierra Nevada* Gorgeous photos taken throughout the range, accompanied by inspirational quotes and an up-to-date take on how the area is likely to be affected by global warming.

⚑ **Claude Fiddler, Steve Roper** et al *Yosemite Once Removed – Portraits of the Backcountry*. Claude Fiddler's photos, and accompanying essays by renowned Yosemite mountaineers and hikers, make this picture book come alive. The emphasis is on the vast majority of the park that is outside Yosemite Valley, and you can hardly flick through without wanting to go just about everywhere.

⚑ **John Muir** *The Yosemite*. There are various paperback versions of this Muir classic, but it's worth splurging on the North Books large-format version ($25), which includes a hundred excellent colour photos by Galen Rowell. It contains the full text, a wonderful introduction to Yosemite, its history, flora, fauna and plenty of full-blooded tales of Muir's adventures.

⚑ **John Muir** *The Wild Muir: 22 of John Muir's Greatest Adventures*. Some readers find Muir's more wordy moments a little heavy going, but this volume boils it all down to 22 thrilling and often death-defying adventure stories: riding an avalanche from the Yosemite Valley rim, scaling Mount Ritter, experiencing a windstorm from atop a tree, and playing chicken with the wind-swayed Upper Yosemite Fall.

John Muir *The Eight Wilderness Discovery Books*. The Muir completist's Bible, containing over a thousand pages, including the full text of *The Story of my Boyhood and Youth*, *A Thousand Mile Walk to the Gulf*, *My First Summer in the Sierra*, *The Mountains of California*, *Our National Parks*, *The Yosemite*, *Travels in Alaska* and *Steep Trails*.

⚑ **Steve Roper** *Camp 4: Recollections of a Yosemite Rockclimber*. The Yosemite veteran tells an entertaining and engaging tale about Yosemite's Golden Age of rock climbing during the 1960s and 1970s. Catches the spirit of the times wonderfully.

History, people and society

⚑ **Ansel Adams** *An Autobiography*. Written in his final years, this is a fascinating insight into the man and his work (both photographic and environmental); liberally illustrated with Adams' own photographs.

Hank Johnston *They Felled the Redwoods* A lively and entertaining trawl through the lives and times of loggers and mill workers around Hume Lake and the Converse Basin in Sequoia and Kings Canyon. Contains stacks of evocative photos.

Hank Johnson and Martha Lee *Guide to the Yosemite Cemetery*. Slim tome on who is interred in the Yosemite Cemetery near the museum. Just $3.50.

Margaret Sanborn *Yosemite*. Probably the best all-round book on Yosemite history, eschewing the sequential timeline in favour of focusing on specific events and the lives of the key players in Yosemite's development.

Shirley Sargent *Yosemite's Innkeepers*. Sargent, a prolific historian, profiles the life in Yosemite's many early

inns; an interesting if somewhat specialist read.

Douglas H Strong *From Pioneers to Preservationists*. A concise but pertinent history of Sequoia and Kings Canyon national parks.

William Tweed *Kaweah Remembered*. A slender history of this short-lived utopian community (see box, p.211) near Sequoia National Park.

Dwight Willard *A Guide to the Sequoia Groves of California*. Yosemite's three sequoia groves, a couple of dozen more in Sequoia and Kings Canyon plus around thirty others along a narrow band of the Sierra Nevada are covered. Includes colour photos, full details of each grove and the historical framework of their exploitation and preservation.

Native life and legends

S.A. Barrett and E.W. Gifford *Indian Life of the Yosemite Region: Miwok Material Culture*. An academic but readable depiction of Miwok life after European contact, researched in the early 1900s and published in 1933. Learn about herbal medicines, basket-making, food production and much more.

Frank La Pena, Craig D. Bates and Steven P. Medley *Legends of*

the Yosemite Miwok. Contains what are thought to be the most authentic versions of Miwok legends about Yosemite geology and environment. Nicely illustrated too.

Robert D. San Souci *Two Bear Cubs – A Miwok Legend from California's Yosemite Valley*. Probably the best Yosemite-related kids' book, telling the tale of the creation of El Capitan (see box, p.51) with lovely illustrations.

Landscapes: geology, flora and fauna

Gary Brown *The Bear Almanac*. Exhaustive tome, full of photos and facts, providing everything you always wanted to know about all types of bears, not just the black variety found in the Sierra Nevada.

Richard P. Ditton and Donald E. McHenry *Yosemite Road Guide*. Just about every wayside point of interest (and many of only marginal interest) along all of Yosemite's roads. The style's a bit dated but it's only $3.50.

David Gaines and Keith Hansen *Birds of Yosemite and the East Slope*. The best guide to the birds of Yosemite and the Mono Lake region, fully illustrated with location and occurrence maps, drawings and photos, plus full coverage of species found in the area.

N. King Huber *Geologic Story of Yosemite National Park*. The most authoritative description of how Yosemite was formed, with a minimum of pointy-headedness.

John Muir Laws *Sierra Birds: A Hiker's Guide*. Cheap and easy reference that's ideal for beginner birders and those new to Sierra species.

 Lynn Wilson, Jim Wilson and Jeff Nicholas *Wildflowers* *of Yosemite*. Handy and easy-to-use guide to identifying Yosemite's wildflowers, with lots of colour photos, comprehensible text and maps to illustrate the range of many species.

Outdoor activity guides

Alan Castle *The John Muir Trail: Through the Californian Sierra Nevada*. Comprehensive guide to the JMT including additional access routes, ascent profiles, numerous maps and full trip-planning details.

Michael Frye *Photographer's Guide to Yosemite*. Colour guide to photographing Yosemite, with numerous technical tips, suggestions for different seasons and times of day, and recommended locations. Almost equally relevant for Sequoia and Kings Canyon.

John Moynier *Backcountry Skiing California's High Sierra*. A collection of day and overnight backcountry skiing and snowboarding routes, including multi-day classics and most of the important descents.

Don Reid *Yosemite: Free Climbs*. The definitive guide with general route descriptions for a huge number of free climbs in Yosemite Valley and nearby. *Tuolumne Meadows* and best-of *Yosemite's Select* round out the series.

Jeffrey P. Scheffer *Yosemite National Park: A Natural History Guide to Yosemite and its Trails*. True to its subtitle, with flora, fauna and geology notes to a hundred hikes through the park, plus a supplementary topographic map.

Supertopo (ⓦwww.supertopo.com) A series of guides giving highly detailed route descriptions for selected climbs. They're mostly available in both print and downloadable eBook form (PDF), and titles include *Yosemite Valley Free Climbs*, *Tuolumne Free Climbs*, *Yosemite Big Walls*, *Yosemite Valley Bouldering*, *Tuolumne Bouldering* and *The Road to The Nose*.

Elizabeth Wenk *Guide to the John Muir Trail*. The best guide to the JMT with heaps of background for planning, great maps, ascent profiles, GPS coordinates and much more. A little too heavy for lightweight backpacking.

Michael C. White *Snowshoe Trails of Yosemite*. Meticulous details of over forty of Yosemite's most scenic trails for a range of abilities.

Glossary

Ahwahnee Native Miwok name for Yosemite Valley and now the name of its best hotel.

Ahwahneechee The local subtribe of the native Miwok people.

Ahwiyah Miwok name for Mirror Lake, meaning "quiet water".

Aid climbing Placing climbing hardware in cracks and on ledges then using them to gain upward movement.

BASE jumping Parachute jumps from Buildings, Antennae, Structures and Earth.

Big Wall Large cliffs scaled by rock climbers; El Capitan and the face of Half Dome are obvious examples.

Bivvy Short for bivouac, this usually refers to a tent-free night under the stars, or maybe hanging on one of the Big Wall climbs.

Cairn Small pile of rocks used to mark trails and trail junctions, also known as a "duck".

Cholok Miwok name for Yosemite Falls.

Cirque Amphitheatre of rock walls at the head of an ancient glacier.

Dikes Feldspar and quartz intrusions that leave four-to-eight-inch-wide straight lines scarring smooth sheets of grey granite.

DN Delaware North, the concessionaire for accommodation and restaurants in Sequoia National Park.

DNC Delaware North Company (Yosemite), the concessionaire which runs lodging, restaurants, tours and so forth in Yosemite National Park.

Duck See "Cairn".

Erratic A boulder carried by an ancient glacier then dumped far from its original home as the glacier melted.

Exfoliation Geologic process where, over millennia, bands of rock peel off like layers of an onion.

Free climbing Using your body to climb the rock, but still employing ropes and hardware to provide protection in case of a fall.

Glacial polish Shiny, almost reflective rock worn smooth by glaciers. Good examples are found on Lembert Dome (see p.84) and Pothole Dome (see p.84).

Hanging valley Side valley high on the rock walls of the larger valley where a side glacier once met the main branch. Most of Yosemite's highest waterfalls – including Bridalveil and Upper Yosemite – cascade from such hanging valleys.

HSC High Sierra Camp (see p.182).

JMT The 211-mile John Muir Trail from Yosemite Valley to Mount Whitney (see box, p.135).

Kettle Lakes Lakes formed in depressions created by large lumps of ice left behind when ancient glaciers receded.

Kosuko Miwok name for Cathedral Rock.

Moonbow Night-time rainbow created by moonlight shining on the spray from waterfalls.

Moraine Mass of glacially transported rubble.

Nailing Aid climbing (see above).

Nunatak Jagged mountain top that was never subject to glacial smoothing, always standing above ancient ice sheets.

Pohono Miwok name for Bridalveil Fall, meaning "puffing wind".

Portaledge A light kind of camp bed used by climbers which can be slung from the rock wall for overnighting on climbs.

Redwood Large trees of the sequoia family. "Redwood" is usually reserved for the tall but relatively slender coastal redwoods.

Roche moutonnée A smooth lump of rock (literally a "sheep rock") formed by glaciers grinding over their surface leaving a gentle slope on the upstream side, and a steeper face downstream. Lembert Dome is a large example and there are several smaller ones in the meadows towards Tioga Pass.

Sequoia Large trees of the sequoia family. "Sequoia" typically refers to the immense trees found in the Sierra Nevada.

SKC Sequoia-Kings Canyon Park Services, the concessionaire which runs lodging and restaurants in Kings Canyon National Park.

Soloing Rock climbing with no ropes or gear for protection.

Striations Parallel scratch marks in smooth bedrock ground by rocks embedded in the base of ancient glaciers.

Talus Piles of rocky rubble at the base of cliffs, the product of millennia of rockfall.

Terminal moraine A barrier of rock rubble left behind at the furthest extent of an ancient glacier.

Tis-sa-yak Miwok name for Half Dome (see box, p.51).

Tu-tok-a-nu-la Miwok name for El Capitan (see box, p.51).

U-shaped valley Flat-floored, vertically walled valley carved out by a glacier. In dramatic contrast to the river-formed V-shaped valley.

Wakalla Miwok name for the Merced River.

Yokuts Native people who inhabited the area now covered by Sequoia National Park.

People

Ansel Adams (1902–84) The finest photographer Yosemite has ever had. See box, p.68.

George Anderson (see p.54) Scottish blacksmith who made the first ascent up the shoulder of Half Dome in 1875.

Galen Clark (1814–1910). Yosemite's first guardian and early resident of Wawona.

James Lamon (1817–75) Early Yosemite Valley settler known for his apple orchard in what is now Curry Village.

Joseph LeConte (1823–1901). Important geologist who spent time in Yosemite with John Muir. The Le Conte Memorial is named after him.

Gabriel Moraga Spanish army lieutenant who named both the Kings River and the Merced River in 1806.

John Muir (1838–1914) Scottish naturalist and adventurer. See box, p.60.

Frederick Law Olmsted (1822–1903). The first chairman of the Yosemite Park Commission and joint architect of New York City's Central Park. Olmsted Point is named after him.

Gilbert Stanley Underwood (1890–1960) Architect of *The Ahwahnee* hotel.

Joseph Walker (1798–1876). Leader of the Walker Party, the first group of whites to travel through the Yosemite region.

Visit us online
www.roughguides.com
Information on over 25,000 destinations around the world

- **Read** Rough Guides' trusted travel info
- **Access** exclusive articles from Rough Guides authors
- **Update** yourself on new books, maps, CDs and other products
- **Enter** our competitions and win travel prizes
- **Share** ideas, journals, photos & travel advice with other users
- **Earn** points every time you contribute to the Rough Guide community and get rewards

BROADEN YOUR HORIZONS

Small print and

Index

A Rough Guide to Rough Guides

Published in 1982, the first Rough Guide – to Greece – was a student scheme that became a publishing phenomenon. Mark Ellingham, a recent graduate in English from Bristol University, had been travelling in Greece the previous summer and couldn't find the right guidebook. With a small group of friends he wrote his own guide, combining a highly contemporary, journalistic style with a thoroughly practical approach to travellers' needs.

SMALL PRINT

The immediate success of the book spawned a series that rapidly covered dozens of destinations. And, in addition to impecunious backpackers, Rough Guides soon acquired a much broader and older readership that relished the guides' wit and inquisitiveness as much as their enthusiastic, critical approach and value-for-money ethos.

These days, Rough Guides include recommendations from shoestring to luxury and cover more than 200 destinations around the globe, including almost every country in the Americas and Europe, more than half of Africa and most of Asia and Australasia. Our ever-growing team of authors and photographers is spread all over the world, particularly in Europe, the US and Australia.

In the early 1990s, Rough Guides branched out of travel, with the publication of Rough Guides to World Music, Classical Music and the Internet. All three have become benchmark titles in their fields, spearheading the publication of a wide range of books under the Rough Guide name.

Including the travel series, Rough Guides now number more than 350 titles, covering: phrasebooks, waterproof maps, music guides from Opera to Heavy Metal, reference works as diverse as Conspiracy Theories and Shakespeare, and popular culture books from iPods to Poker. Rough Guides also produce a series of more than 120 World Music CDs in partnership with World Music Network.

Visit www.roughguides.com to see our latest publications.

Rough Guide credits

Text editor: Melissa Graham
Layout: Anita Singh
Cartography: Deshpal Dabas
Picture editor: Emily Taylor
Production: Louise Daly
Proofreader: Janet McCann
Cover design: Dan May, Mark Thomas
Photographer: Paul Whitfield
Editorial: London Andy Turner, Keith Drew,
Edward Aves, Alice Park, Lucy White, Jo Kirby,
James Smart, Natasha Foges, Róisín Cameron,
James Rice, Emma Beatson, Emma Gibbs,
Kathryn Lane, Monica Woods, Mani Ramaswamy,
Harry Wilson, Lucy Cowie, Alison Roberts,
Lara Kavanagh, Eleanor Aldridge, Ian Blenkinsop,
Joe Staines, Matthew Milton, Tracy Hopkins;
Delhi Madhavi Singh, Jalpreen Kaur Chhatwal,
Jubbi Francis
Design & Pictures: London Scott Stickland, Dan
May, Diana Jarvis, Mark Thomas, Nicole Newman,

Sarah Cummins; **Delhi** Umesh Aggarwal, Ajay
Verma, Jessica Subramanian, Ankur Guha,
Pradeep Thapliyal, Sachin Tanwar, Nikhil Agarwal,
Sachin Gupta
Production: Rebecca Short, Liz Cherry,
Erika Pepe
Cartography: London Ed Wright, Katie Lloyd-
Jones; **Delhi** Rajesh Chhibber, Ashutosh Bharti,
Rajesh Mishra, Animesh Pathak, Jasbir Sandhu,
Swati Handoo, Lokamata Sahu
Marketing, Publicity & roughguides.com:
Liz Statham
Digital Travel Publisher: Peter Buckley
Reference Director: Andrew Lockett
Operations Coordinator: Becky Doyle
Publishing Director (Travel): Clare Currie
Commercial Manager: Gino Magnotta
Managing Director: John Duhigg

Publishing information

This fourth edition published May 2011 by
Rough Guides Ltd,
80 Strand, London WC2R 0RL
11, Community Centre, Panchsheel Park,
New Delhi 110017, India

Distributed by the Penguin Group

Penguin Books Ltd,
80 Strand, London WC2R 0RL

Penguin Group (USA)
375 Hudson Street, NY 10014, USA

Penguin Group (Australia)
250 Camberwell Road, Camberwell,
Victoria 3124, Australia

Penguin Group (NZ)
67 Apollo Drive, Mairangi Bay, Auckland 1310,
New Zealand

Rough Guides is represented in Canada by
Tourmaline Editions Inc. 662 King Street West,
Suite 304, Toronto, Ontario M5V 1M7

Cover concept by Peter Dyer.

Typeset in Bembo and Helvetica to an original
design by Henry Iles.

MIX
Paper from
responsible sources
FSC™ C018179
www.fsc.org

Help us update

We've gone to a lot of effort to ensure that the
fourth edition of **The Rough Guide to Yosemite,
Sequoia and Kings Canyon** is accurate and
up-to-date. However, things change – places
get "discovered", opening hours are notoriously
fickle, restaurants and rooms raise prices or lower
standards. If you feel we've got it wrong or left
something out, we'd like to know, and if you can
remember the address, the price, the hours, the
phone number, so much the better.

Please send your comments with the subject
line "**Rough Guide Yosemite, Sequoia and
Kings Canyon Update**" to ©mail
@uk.roughguides.com. We'll credit all
contributions and send a copy of the next edition
(or any other Rough Guide if you prefer) for the
very best emails.

Find more travel information, connect with
fellow travellers and book your trip on ®www
.roughguides.com

Acknowledgements

Thanks go out to all those who contributed to this book in any way, sharing hikes and bar room tales, voicing opinions, and helping out with logistics. Assistance from park rangers and visitor centre staff is particularly appreciated: you know who you are.

Special thanks go out to Chris Kapka for a home from home in San Fran and to those at the Rough Guides office in London, particularly to Melissa Graham who helped make this edition what it is.

And lastly to Marion for fortitude through long absences, support back home when the writing days got long and indexing became mind-numbingly boring. Thanks.

Photo credits

All photos © Rough Guides except the following:

Introduction
Hang-gliding in Yosemite © Bill Ross/Corbis
High-country backpacking in Kings Canyon National Park © Stephen Matera/Aurora Photos/Corbis
Grizzly Falls, Kings Canyon © Paul Whitfield

Things not to miss
01 Climbing Half Dome © Ron Koeberer/Getty Images
06 Mineral King, Sequoia National Park © Galen Rowell/Corbis
10 Muirs Rock, Kings River © Paul Whitfield
14 Moro Rock © Paul Whitfield

Active Yosemite colour section
Rock climber on the Nose of El Capitan © Galen Rowell/Corbis

Wild Sierra colour section
Mule Deer, Lembert Dome © Paul Whitfield
Redwood Mountain Grove © Paul Whitfield
Marmot, Mineral King © Paul Whitfield
Brown bear in tree © Richard Nowitz/Getty Images

SMALL PRINT

Index

Map entries are in colour.

S

T

INDEX

Map symbols

maps are listed in the full index using coloured text

State boundary		Point of interest
National park boundary		Information office
US highway		Internet access
State highway		International airport
Limited-access road		Accommodation
Other road		Restaurant
Yosemite hiking trail		Road-accessible campground
Sequoia & Kings Canyon hiking trail		Backcountary campground
Other trail		Post office
River		Toilets
Tram route & stop		Parking
Park entrance		Gas station
Ranger station		Golf course
Peak		Sequoia grove
Viewpoint		Mine
Waterfall		Chapel
Spring		Shuttle bus stop
Ski area		Building
Ski hut/high sierra camp		Christian cemetery
		Park

So now we've told you about the things not to miss, the best places to stay, the top restaurants, the liveliest bars and the most spectacular sights, it only seems fair to tell you about the best travel in

es

www.roughguides.com
MAKE THE MOST OF YOUR TIME ON EARTH

ROUGH GUIDES